Retardation in Young Children

A DEVELOPMENTAL STUDY OF COGNITIVE DEFICIT

Retardation in Young Children

A DEVELOPMENTAL STUDY OF COGNITIVE DEFICIT

Sarah Broman
Paul L. Nichols
Peter Shaughnessy
Wallace Kennedy

NATIONAL INSTITUTES OF HEALTH

LAWRENCE ERLBAUM ASSOCIATES, PUBLISHERS
1987   Hillsdale, New Jersey   London

Lawrence Erlbaum Associates, Inc., Publishers
365 Broadway
Hillsdale, New Jersey 07642

Library of Congress Cataloging in Publication Data

Retardation in young children.

  Bibliography: p.
  Includes index.
  1. Mentally handicapped children—
United States.   I. Broman, Sarah H.
HV894.R48   1987   618.92′858807   86-32947
ISBN 0-89859-989-X

Printed in the United States of America
10 9 8 7 6 5 4 3 2 1

Contents

PREFACE   *vii*

FOREWORD   *ix*

1
INTRODUCTION   *1*

2
METHODS   *13*

3
CHARACTERISTICS OF THE
MENTALLY RETARDED CHILDREN   *24*

4
PRENATAL AND OBSTETRIC FACTORS   *38*

5
THE NEONATAL PERIOD   *75*

6
INFANCY   *96*

7
THE PRESCHOOL PERIOD
122

8
THE SCHOOL-AGE PERIOD
144

9
SUBGROUPS OF THE MENTALLY RETARDED
195

10
FAMILIAL PATTERNS OF MENTAL RETARDATION
268

11
SUMMARY AND CONCLUSIONS
275

APPENDIX 1:
VARIABLES ASSOCIATED WITH RETARDATION
280

APPENDIX 2:
GLOSSARY
297

APPENDIX 3:
CORRELATIONS AMONG INDEPENDENT VARIABLES
304

APPENDIX 4:
PRENATAL DRUG EXPOSURE
310

APPENDIX 5:
DISTRIBUTIONS AND UNIVARIATE STATISTICS
FOR DISCRIMINATING CHARACTERISTICS
OF THE MILDLY RETARDED SUBGROUP
322

REFERENCES
346

AUTHOR INDEX
352

SUBJECT INDEX
355

Preface

This study focuses on the antecedents and correlates of mental retardation in a population of 36,800 children followed from gestation to age 7 in the Collaborative Perinatal Project. The large data base, derived from sequentially administered examinations and interviews, was analyzed to identify the biological and social risk factors for severe and mild cognitive deficit at age 7. Comparisons made between the retarded and nonretarded groups in the samples of white and black children revealed factors related to normal cognitive development as well.

An investigation of this size and complexity required the efforts of many people. We wish to acknowledge the basic contributions of the multi-disciplinary data collection teams and the mothers and children enrolled in the 12 collaborating study centers. We want to thank Dr. Joseph S. Drage of the National Institute of Neurological and Communicative Disorders and Stroke for his support and encouragement, Mr. James D. Pomeroy for his skillful computer programming, and Ms. Kristan E. Lucas for her help in preparing the final manuscript. For their valuable comments on an earlier version of the manuscript, we are grateful to Dr. Jerome Kagan, Dr. Arthur H. Parmelee, and Dr. Zena A. Stein.

Sarah Broman
Paul L. Nichols
Peter Shaughnessy
Wallace Kennedy

Foreword

In this monumental and fascinating study, Broman, Nichols, Shaugnessey, and Kennedy address current major questions in the field of mental retardation, namely the genesis of mild and profound retardation and the validity of the two-group approach. Without an understanding of the etiology of retardation, efforts to understand its nature and to improve the lives of retarded people must be seriously compromised.

In the past, workers in mental retardation have generally failed to acknowledge the importance of etiological differences among the retarded in understanding the nature, course, and outcome of mental retardation. In fact, many have argued against the utility of differentiating retarded individuals by etiology. Norman Ellis (1969) asserted that: "In spite of all the possible criticisms of ignoring etiology in behavioral research, it should be strongly emphasized that rarely have behavioral differences characterized different etiological groups" (p. 561). In summarizing the prevailing views of the field, MacMillan (1982) noted that "there is now considerable skepticism as to the usefulness of classifying mental retardation by form, due primarily to our current inability to separate sociological and psychological forces" (p. 60). Similar statements have been made by Baumeister and MacLean (1979), Leland (1969), Luria (1963), Spitz (1963), and others.

In contrast, Zigler and others (Dingman & Tarjan, 1960; Penrose, 1963) have championed the two-group approach. They assert that there are two basic types of retarded individuals: cultural-familial and organic. The familial group is seen as representing the lower end of a normal distribution of intelligence. Their cognitive growth follows the same course of development as that of nonretarded persons, but progresses at a slower rate and reaches a lower end. Concerning organic retardation, Zigler (1969) stated, "If the etiology of the phenotypic intelligence (as measured by an IQ) of the two groups differs, it is far from logical to assert that the course of development is the same, or that even similar contents in their behaviors are mediated by exactly the same cognitive processes" (p. 563). Zigler's formulation thus emphasized that etiological differences have clear consequences for psychological functioning.

Broman, Nichols, Shaugnessey, and Kennedy have developed an impressive data base to assess the probable cause of mild and severe retardation, and to evaluate the ramifications of contrasting etiologies. In so doing, the authors provide extensive evidence to support the value of the two-group framework particularly in the White population. Using an IQ of approximately 50 as a cut-off, the authors found numerous differences in the origin of mild and severe retardation. Mildly retarded children tended to come from low socioeconomic status backgrounds, and generally had retarded relatives. In contrast, most severely retarded children had suffered some organic insult, came from relatively privileged backgrounds, and had no relatives suffering from retardation.

In further support of the two-group approach, Broman and colleagues, found that severely retarded children (below 50 IQ) without organic damage came from backgrounds resembling those of the mildly retarded children without organic insult, while the mildly retarded children who had suffered some organic damage were more similar to the severely retarded group on demographic variables. This finding provides further evidence in support of the value of differentiating mental retardation by etiology, rather than simply by IQ.

The data derived from the Black population in this study provides further support for the two group approach, with an important difference; that is, the range of IQ is shifted down approximately 15 points. This discrepancy between populations points to the need for further differentiation of etiology in the study of mental retardation. Zigler and Hodapp (1986) have discussed the value of fine-grained examinations of etiologically defined groups. Further refinement of the research question could be achieved differentiating by such demographic variables as gender, mental health history, degree and type of institutional background, and drug dosage, if relevant.

As the work of these researchers makes clear, intelligence is a function of environmental and genetic interaction, although the precise proportions are unclear, and may vary in different populations. The authors point to the need for further research to illuminate the precise nature of these interactions. The work of Broman, Nichols, Shaugnessy, and Kennedy highlights the importance for investigators of considering the role of both genes and environment in etiology. More research must still be done in order to assess the relative importance of genetic and environmental variables. This study provides an important link in further attempts to gain a better understanding of mental retardation, and future research should build on this important effort. This study is a seminal contribution that provides workers with a sound empirical base for future investigations of the continuing mysteries of mental retardation. The field of mental retardation owes these authors a debt of gratitude.

Edward Zigler
Yale University

REFERENCES

Baumeister, A., & MacLean, W. (1979). Brain damage and mental retardation. In N. Ellis (Ed.), *Handbook of mental deficiency: Psychological theory and research* (2nd ed.). Hillsdale, NJ: Lawrence Erlbaum Associates.

Dingman, H., & Tarjan, G. (1960). Mental retardation and the normal distribution curve. *American Journal of Mental Deficiency, 64,* 991–994.

Ellis, N. (1969). A behavioral research strategy in mental retardation: Defense and critique. *American Journal of Mental Deficiency, 73,* 557–566.

Leland, H. (1969). The relationship between intelligence and mental retardation. *American Journal of Mental Deficiency, 73,* 533–535.

Luria, A. (1963). *The mental retarded child.* New York: Pergamon.

MacMillan, D. (1982). *Mental retardation in school and society,* (2nd ed.). Boston: Little, Brown & Co.

Penrose, L. (1963). *The biology of mental defect.* London: Sidgwick & Jackson.

Spitz, H. (1963). Field theory and mental deficiency. In N. Ellis (Ed.), *Handbook of mental deficiency.* New York: McGraw-Hill.

Zigler, E., & Hodapp, R. (1986). *Understanding mental retardation.* New York: Cambridge University Press.

Zigler, E. (1969). Developmental versus difference theories of mental retardation and the problem of motivation. *American Journal of Mental Deficiency, 73,* 536–556.

1
Introduction

Societies have long been concerned about the problem of mental retardation. In the United States, this concern led to a serious government-funded effort to identify preventable causes of mental subnormality in the Collaborative Perinatal Project. Only in recent history has etiology been a major focus of investigations or theories of mental retardation. Attitudes toward the mentally subnormal have changed from avoidance to acceptance, from institutions for isolation to schools for teaching, and finally, from considering the affliction inexplicable and unchangeable to changeable, at least trainable, and perhaps even preventable. Historically, intelligence has been widely recognized as a dimension with a presumed continuity between high and low, or more and less, some mystical pecking order in which we all place ourselves—smarter than some, duller than others.

This chapter presents a brief history of research in mental retardation and the evolution of etiological theories. For detailed reviews and discussions of other aspects such as educational and treatment programs, refer to Clarke and Clarke (1975), Ingalls (1978), or Robinson and Robinson (1976).

EARLY THEORIES OF MENTAL RETARDATION

The physically deformed, emotionally maladjusted, and mentally defective were lumped together in early theories of mental subnormality (Penrose, 1963). But in the reign of Edward I (1272–1307), a legal distinction was made between the mentally retarded, or "born fool," and the mentally ill, or "lunatic" (Clarke & Clarke, 1975, p. 14). Woolfson (1984) recently discovered a text written in 1614 by the Portuguese physician Filipe Montalto who discussed the diagnosis, prognosis, and cure of mental retardation. Montalto's *Archipathologica* predates

1

by nearly two centuries the generally accepted beginning of scholarly writing on the subject (Kanner, 1964).

The first scientific study of retardation is credited to the French physician Jean-Marc Itard (1801, 1807/1932), whose efforts to socialize and educate the so-called "Wild Boy of Aveyron" in the early 19th century influenced not only the attitude of the general public toward the retarded, but that of educators as well. Great efforts were expended to educate the retarded who were at last separated from the insane. Esquirol (1838) not only distinguished between insanity and mental retardation, but suggested that language facility was the key to a classification of the retarded.

After immigrating to the United States, Itard's student, Edouard Seguin (1866/1971), stimulated interest in the problem of mental retardation. Seguin was a supporter of two distinct levels of retardation, with perhaps two separate causes: a profound type, caused by a defective central nervous system; and a superficial type, caused by a damaged or weakened peripheral nervous system. The terms "idiot" and "feebleminded" were commonly used to label the severely and mildly retarded.

In 1876, Seguin and five of his colleages formed the Association of Medical Officers of American Institutions of Idiotic and Feebleminded Persons, the forerunner of today's American Association on Mental Deficiency and its *American Journal of Mental Deficiency* (Crissey, 1975; Sloan & Stevens, 1976). The major function of the Association was the care and training of the retarded. Yet, etiology was given little consideration by the professional community. Familial patterns or birth injury were presumed the major causes. High fevers and head injuries were also recognized as causal factors.

Around the beginning of the 20th century, the public, parallelling the belief of scientists such as Francis Galton (1870) and James Cattell (1890) that high intelligence was equated with faster perceptions, faster reactions, and general superiority, began to view the mentally retarded as inferior in all ways. They became the target of "social Darwinists" who considered feeblemindedness not only hereditary, but also strongly associated with delinquency, pauperism, sexual immorality, alcoholism, and other social disorders. In the United States, sterilization laws were passed in many states to prevent the incidence of new cases based on the oft-cited study by Henry Goddard (1912) that traced the ancestry of an institutional inmate to a Revolutionary soldier and a retarded girl. Their descendants, called the Kallikaks by Goddard, included several generations of criminals, alcoholics, and other degenerates. This same soldier also married a refined Quaker girl, and they became the ancestors of several generations of fine, upstanding citizens.

In 1924, Fernald pointed out that although some studies indicated that lawbreakers were often feebleminded, the assumption that all defectives had criminal tendencies was illogical. The harsh treatment suffered by retarded individuals as a result of this stereotype, which he called "the myth of the feebleminded," was obviously unjustified. "Defective delinquent" remained a classification category, however, until the 1950s.

As public interest gradually was aroused, publication of research on mental retardation increased at a rapid pace. A comprehensive bibliography covering January 1940 to March 1963 (Heber, Simpson, Gibson, & Milligan, 1963) listed more than 15,000 references, but included no evaluation of the quality of the work (Zigler, 1978). In 1962, President Kennedy appointed the President's Panel on Mental Retardation. One of its 99 recommendations was the establishment of federally funded, multidisciplinary, mental retardation research centers, 12 of which are currently in operation. Their research has been summarized by Robinson and Begab (1984).

EARLY EFFORTS AT MEASURING INTELLIGENCE

As techniques for training and educating the mentally defective became more highly developed, attention was turned to ways of defining or measuring mental ability. For example, Chaille (1887), a Louisiana pediatrician, in an effort to improve communication with parents, developed a questionnaire which focused on their children's social, emotional, and mental abilities. The questionnaire, arranged by age level, resulted in a score that could be converted to a mental-age equivalent, a relatively precise way of reporting developmental level that was needed particularly for the in-between child who was neither obviously normal nor seriously retarded.

Concurrent with the work of Seguin and Chaille, Galton (1870, 1874, 1888) studied intelligence through measurements of sensory acuity and judgment. He used correlation and regression as mathematical tools to describe intelligence, which he presumed to be largely inherited. High and low intelligence were viewed as genetically determined variations best described in terms of deviations from the mean of a normal distribution. Galton's analyses of measurements of the motor and sensory capabilities of some 9000 subjects did little, however, to further the understanding of mental subnormality.

In America, G. Stanley Hall (1883, 1891) was defining intelligence in terms of concept mastery with a greater emphasis on cognitive processes than on preceptual–motor acuity. Hall developed an objective measure of intelligence in a questionnaire designed to demonstrate what children know when they enter the first grade. He did not take into account the effect of chronological age differences, but did recognize those accounted for by environment, such as differences in the knowledge of rural and urban children. Of importance was the fact that although Hall's questionnaire was an adequate measure of the knowledge of first graders, it did not predict success in school.

This task was achieved by Alfred Binet in France (Binet & Simon, 1905a, 1905b, 1908, 1916) with the help of Stern's (1912/1914) concept of the intelligence quotient that allowed comparisons across age ranges. Binet defined intelligence as aptitude for academic achievement. By including in his intelligence test samples of skills that affected academic success, Binet developed an instrument that could predict school performance.

Following the work of Binet in the Paris school system at the beginning of the 20th century, retardation was defined primarily in terms of deficits in specific skills related to academic success without reference to probable etiology. The prerequisite skills, which became associated under the general concept of intelligence, were those in vocabulary and in quantitative and perceptual–motor tasks. Hall, Binet, and others assumed that mastery of the essential skills and concepts was accomplished during the critical preschool years. The level of intellectual functioning established in childhood was thought to be permanent.

LATER MEASUREMENTS OF INTELLIGENCE

G. Stanley Hall was not only an important contributor to the field of mental measurement but the catalyst who produced others such as Lewis Terman, who developed the Stanford–Binet Intelligence Scale, and Henry Goddard, who founded the Vineland Training School, one of the early educational institutions for the retarded in the United States.

The Stanford–Binet was carefully standardized on a sample of school children and their siblings and provided an intelligence quotient, or IQ, calculated by dividing the mental age derived from the test by chronological age and multiplying by 100. It became the yardstick by which all future tests of intelligence were measured, representing a compromise between the theoretical position of Galton and the applied orientation of Binet. Believing in the theoretical concept of a genetically predetermined dimension of pure intelligence, Terman defined intelligence operationally as educability. The mentally retarded, then, were those uneducable except via special schools.

As was reflected in both the content and standardization of the test, Terman (1916), like Binet, focused upon the task of predicting academic success. The standardization sample had few severely retarded children and a disproportionate number of the intellectually superior. Nevertheless, three levels of mental retardation were defined: the educable, the trainable, and the profound. His system was a nonetiological classification based on the child's ability to deal effectively with classroom instruction. Terman's efforts resulted in intelligence becoming synonymous with IQ, which in turn referred to educability.

Goddard (1914) was concerned with developing a classification of the mentally retarded that would be useful in rehabilitation. Although convinced on the basis of familial patterns found at Vineland that mental retardation was genetically determined and basically unalterable, he believed that a higher level of performance could be obtained through improvements in training techniques. Verbal ability, the major factor evaluated in the Stanford–Binet and later intelligence tests, was of less concern to Goddard whose goal was to establish independence for his students, who were often found working outside the institution in neighboring farms and industries. Goddard defined intelligence in terms of ability to perform a wide variety of developmental tasks, equating it with life-adjustment potential rather than educational potential. In spite of his strong belief in the heritability of intelligence and its biological basis, Goddard opened the 20th century on a positive note concerning the potential for rehabilitation among persons categorized by society as subnormal.

Introducing a change in methodology, Wechsler (1939, 1949) discarded the conept of mental age and derived IQ scores by comparing each subject's performance with that of individuals in the same age group. Although IQ testing has become controversial, tests such as the Stanford–Binet and those developed by Wechsler predict academic achievement with considerable success. The debate over the utility, validity, and biases of intelligence testing has been reviewed by Jensen (1980).

LATER THEORIES OF MENTAL RETARDATION

At the beginning of the 20th century, the field of mental retardation was subject to several diverse influences. First, the work of Esquirol, Hall, Binet, and Terman gave language development and academic potential cardinal roles in the classification of the mentally retarded. The idiot-imbecile-moron stratification was based largely on levels of language usage: the idiot, mostly mute; the imbecile, limited to a few words for common objects; and the moron, capable of short, focused sentences to express his needs. The idiot–savant, however, remained a mystery. The alternate approach of Chaille (1887), Goddard (1914), and Doll (1953) was based on ability to perform appropriate developmental tasks. Although useful in enlightened state institutions, this concept of intelligence lacked influence at the time, perhaps because the national educational explosion made academic potential more important than self-help skills.

Galton's hope of defining the neurological basis of intelligence was kept alive by the work of Arnold Gesell (1928, 1934, 1945, 1954; Gesell & Amatruda, 1962; Gesell et al., 1940). As a graduate student with Lewis Terman under G. Stanley Hall at Clark University, Gesell began his work of observing and recording the development of neurological, perceptual, and motor components of intelligence in infancy and early childhood. He had great influence in perpetuating the search for the biological roots of intelligence.

As these influences emerged from the fields of education, rehabilitation, and child development, considerable progress was being made in medicine in identifying physical abnormalities associated with mental retardation. These physical conditions, regarded as part of a complex of symptoms of which mental retardation was one (Gellis & Feingold, 1968), included hydrocephaly and microcephaly, Down's syndrome (Down, 1866), cretinism, and cerebral palsy (Little, 1862). Other etiological factors recognized around the turn of the century were head injury, high fevers, encephalitis, and reactions to toxic substances. Birth injury, a broad term with poorly defined criteria, became a favored explanation for mental retardation not considered to be hereditary nor part of a known syndrome. Presumed causes were prolonged or difficult labor, forceps delivery, or slowness in breathing at birth.

Parents of children with idiopathic or unexplained mental retardation were frequently asked if the delivery was difficult and if the child had sustained any head injuries or experienced any high fevers perhaps accompanied by seizures. These inquiries were usually answered affirmatively—few children have not had a high fever or sharp fall on the head and most labors are considered difficult—resulting in a dramatic increase in the number of retarded children thought to have suffered insults to the brain. Evidently, there were few efforts to ask the same questions of mothers of normal children or to determine the frequency of these events in the medical records of the non-retarded. Many psychologists, educators, and physicians were strong advocates of the "organic" and hereditary causes of mental retardation; environmental influences were considered to be negligible.

In the United States, experience with immigrants and the massive testing of young men reporting for service during the First World War made the concept of general intelligence as a neurological unfolding of academic potential an inadequate one. Nonverbal tests of critical reasoning and tests of motor and perceptual–motor skills were developed by Arthur Otis (1922), Robert Yerkes (1921; Yerkes, Bridges, & Hardwick, 1915; Yerkes & Foster, 1923), and Lewis Terman (1916). These instruments were built upon the nonverbal tasks developed earlier by Edouard Seguin (1866/1971), William Healy, and George Fernald (Healy & Fernald, 1911). Although restricted to adult males of military age, this large-scale testing revealed cultural, ethnic, and geographical differences in functional intelligence as defined by both traditional IQ tests and by performance tests not dependent upon literacy. The results indicated that perhaps as many as 5% of the population of young men in the United States were mentally retarded; previous estimates had been below 1%. Those examined who fell into this category were considered incapable of responding to training and permanently unfit for military duty (Yerkes, 1921).

On both the Stanford–Binet and the Wechsler intelligence scales, retardation was defined as an IQ score below 70. In the United States, this criterion turned out to include an over-representation of blacks and other minority group children compared to their representation in the population (Mercer, 1973). With the focus in the late 20th century on problems of inequalities in education, teachers began to note that many disadvantaged children classified as retarded seemed brighter in nonscholastic ways than their IQ scores suggested (Jensen, 1969). This observation, plus evidence that many of these individuals functioned adequately in society after their school years, led to a redefinition of retardation to include social as well as academic incompetence (Grossman, 1973). For example, the President's Panel on Mental Retardation defined the mentally retarded as children and adults who, as a result of inadequately developed intelligence, are significantly impaired in their ability to learn and to adapt to the demands of society (1962, p. 1). More recently, however, Zigler, Balla, and Hodapp (1984) argued that because social adaptation is a vague concept difficult to measure, it should not be included in a definition of mental retardation.

A two-group classification of mental retardation had been proposed by Lewis in 1933. The pathological group included cases attributed to trauma, central nervous system malformation, or mongolism and other congenital syndromes. The subcultural group, which included cases with no identifiable cause, was thought to represent the lower end of a genetically determined normal distribution. In 1963, Penrose revised etiological theory by emphasizing the importance of genetic disorders as a cause of pathological retardation and de-emphasizing the role of trauma. He also proposed that mild retardation could be caused by social deprivation as well as genetic variation. Other investigators at the time (e.g., Stein & Susser, 1960) reported that environmental factors were major determinants of mild retardation.

Later research began to point to the important effects of environmental influences within the family on early cognitive development as opposed to those from extrinsic sources such as quality of schools or neighborhood amenities (e.g., Firkowska, Ostrowska, Sokolowska, Stein, Susser, & Wald, 1978). Zigler (1978) described mild retardation as resulting from a complex interaction between genetic and environmental factors with little known about exact etiological mechanisms, a view that probably represents a consensus of current opinion. Two recent reports, however, suggest that birth injury may also be a causal factor. Hagberg, Hagberg, Lewerth, and Lindberg (1981) found high frequencies of both perinatal complications and central nervous system abnormalities among mildly retarded children born between 1966 and 1970 in Bothenberg, Sweden. Costeff, Cohen, and Weller (1983) also found a high rate of perinatal complications among mildly retarded children examined in Israel from 1964 to 1968.

Currently, severe retardation is considered to be the result of a major disorder of the central nervous system. The disorder may be caused by a chromosomal abnormality (as in Down's syndrome), by a single gene (phenylketonuria), by prenatal infection (rubella), or by an endocrine disorder (hypothyroidism). Other cases are associated with a congenital malformation of the central nervous system such as hydrocephaly or with the motor disorder of cerebral palsy. Clearly, severe retardation is a heterogeneous classification that can have literally hundreds of causes, mostly rare. Down's syndrome, the most frequent known cause of severe retardation, accounts for only about 10% to 15% of the severely retarded.

THE ROLES OF HEREDITY AND ENVIRONMENT

A controversy begun in the mid-1930s regarding the relative contributions of environment and heredity to intellectual functioning continues today. With the widespread use of both individual and group intelligence tests in America, two important concepts became accepted: the first, that intelligence was IQ (or what intelligence tests measure) and, therefore, intelligence was scholastic aptitude; the second, that IQ was constant. It was assumed that environmental influences might have a small effect, or, given major environmental adversity, even a large effect; but for the most part, intelligence was an unchangeable trait that expressed an individual's "potential."

Given the stability of IQ, or scholastic aptitude, the categories of under-achievement and overachievement were used to describe children not performing at the academic level predicted. The upper or mild level of mental retardation (IQs of approximately 50 to 69) was viewed primarily as academic dysfunction, or a deficiency in learning ability with etiology usually unknown. The conceptualization of severe retardation (IQs below 50) as a serious biologically caused handicap remained unchanged. These children could be identified by stigmata and by physical diagnosis, and accounted for less than 1% of academically incompetent individuals.

Due to the practice of routine testing throughout the public school systems and compulsory education, which brought to the attention of the schools many children who formerly would have remained at home, mild mental retardation was recognized as being much more prevalent than severe retardation, and in addition, was recognized as being strongly associated with ethnic, cultural, and socioeconomic variables (Goodenough, 1939, 1940a, 1940b). During the late 1930s and early 1940s, experimental efforts in remedial education began to shed doubt on the concept of IQ constancy and even on the etiological factors involved for a considerable portion of the educationally mentally retarded children being identified in kindergarten and elementary school. As a result, IQ constancy gained the stipulation of environmental constancy as a necessary condition. Demonstrating the effect of environment, the Iowa Child Welfare Station, in addition to conducting nursery school and kindergarten programs that altered the IQ scores of children (Wellman, 1932, 1945), found that children removed from orphanages were able to maintain higher than expected IQ scores following early placement in relatively advantaged homes (Skodak & Skeels, 1949).

That was not to say that the concept of genetic intelligence was dead.

William MacDougal's student Cyril Burt (1947, 1958, 1968, 1972), an admirer of Francis Galton, continued to examine hereditary patterns of intelligence using both individual and group data. His conclusion that intelligence is highly heritable was strongly supported by Henry Garrett (1960, 1962) and, in a more reasoned fashion, by Arthur Jensen (1967, 1968, 1969) and Richard Herrnstein (1971). More recently, the legitimacy of Burt's data has been seriously challenged (Jensen, 1978; Kamin, 1974).

Questions were raised again about the effects of culture on IQ tests and the feasibility of developing culture-free or culture-fair instruments. It was apparent that the IQ scores of young children were difficult to change, regardless of the contributing factors. In the early 1960s, several large-scale normative studies were completed and others got underway (Baughman & Dahlstrom, 1968; Deutsch, Katz, & Jensen, 1968; Miller & Dreger, 1973) that gave a broader picture of mental retardation as a cultural–familial pattern. A normative study of southeastern black children of elementary school age (Kennedy, 1969; Kennedy, Van De Riet, & White, 1963) indicated that these children entered grade school with a mean IQ of about 80 and a standard deviation of 11, which placed about 15% of them in the retarded range according to the Stanford–Binet criterion. Occurring shortly after the first large-scale movement in integration following the U.S. Supreme Court decision in 1954, this finding had important implications for both the primary definition of mental retardation and for definitions within the legal and educational systems. The proportion of minority children with IQs in the retarded range was obviously far too high to be accounted for by previous assumptions regarding the etiology of retardation.

Several alternative explanations were offered, the most obvious being test bias. The Binet, for example, was originally standardized on white, middle-class children with items drawn from middle-class school materials. That minority children grew up in a different environment that provided different sets of stimulating conditions was apparent. The test bias, then, tended to identify children as retarded when they were simply unexposed to the material on the test. This explanation led to several suggestions, the first being to develop tests that were either culture-fair or suited to the subculture. The second was to take the deficit at face value and attempt to introduce intellectual enrichment into the lives of these children to prepare them better for school and, consequently, to raise their IQs.

The compensatory education programs developed by Gray in Tennessee (Klaus & Gray, 1968) and by Deutsch in New York (1964a, 1964b) became the Head Start Program of the 1960s, a six week summer program of traditional kindergarten activities that was expected, rather naively, to change classroom-related behaviors of disadvantaged children to a closer approximation of middle-class norms. Such optimism, typical of the decade, was doomed from the onset. Methods and procedures developed in university-affiliated nursery schools and kindergartens with mainly upper–middle-class children were used in the summer program with the basic skills of reading, spelling, arithmetic, and writing considered unimportant. Lower-class children entered the program with about a 20% deficit in school "readiness" and at the end of the first grade demonstrated that same degree of deficit, with or without the Head Start Program (Cicirelli, Evans, & Schiller, 1970; Datta, 1970; Williams & Evans, 1969). Modification of the program to include highly focused instruction in language and quantitative skills plus an extension throughout the academic year yielded better results (Van De Riet, Van De Riet, & Sprigle, 1968), but the magnitude of the academic deficits among children of the disadvantaged remained relatively constant as reported in long-term studies of those who finished high school (Jencks et al., 1972).

Neither genetic nor neurological models of mental retardation were adequate to explain this large group of educationally retarded children. Yet once this low level of intellectual functioning was established, it had great tenacity and was predictive of functional illiteracy in adulthood (Kennedy, 1973). At the same time, other studies, most notably those of Bayley (1965), were indicating that in spite of the likelihood of little prenatal care and poor maternal diet, infants of minority mothers were generally average to superior in perceptual–motor development, a fundamental precursor of later intellectual level.

By the end of the 1950s, two major causes of mental retardation were identified. The first was related to abnormalities in fetal or post-natal development caused by genetic or other, often unknown, factors that accounted for only a small proportion of retardation, primarily of a severe degree (Carter, 1965, 1975). Implicated as antecedents were the general factors of age and health of the mother; pregnancy complications that included toxemia, diabetes, and maternal infections; trauma and other complications of delivery; prematurity and/or low birthweight of the infant, and asphyxia-anoxia (Apgar, Girdany, McIntosh, & Taylor, 1955; Lilienfeld & Pasamanick, 1956; Pasamanick & Lilienfeld, 1955). The second cause seemed to be environmental, related to family living conditions as well as to cultural stimulation from outside the home. Apparently, the largest single environmental determinants were socioeconomic class and ethnic group membership. Environmental causes seemed to account for the largest proportion of children who were subnormal in intelligence, but appeared to be unrelated to the smaller, severely handicapped group.

It had become apparent that attempts to account for mental retardation on the basis of a single cause were ill-fated. It also had become evident that the retrospective study could not provide reliable data on early risk factors. A large prospective study, beginning in pregnancy, was needed to examine the rarest disorders and provide sufficient variation in socioeconomic, ethnic, and geographic factors.   These were the motives for initiation of the Collaborative Perinatal Project by the National Institute of Neurological and Communicative Disorders and Stroke.

THE COLLABORATIVE PERINATAL PROJECT

In 1950, almost a decade of planning began for the Collaborative Perinatal Project, a large-scale multidisciplinary study of relationships between prenatal and perinatal complications and developmental abnormalities including mental retardation (Broman, 1984). In the surrounding time period, associations had been reported between low IQ and asphyxia (Darke, 1944), Rh incompatibility (Chown, 1954), prematurity (Alm, 1953), socioeconomic status (Eells, Davis, Havighurst, Herrick, & Tyler, 1951), ethnicity (Klineberg, 1928), and family size (Thomson, 1950). Lilienfeld and Parkhurst (1951) expanded Ingalls and Gordon's (1947) concept of a "biological gradient of disease" into the "continuum of reproductive wastage." Later, Lilienfeld and Pasamanick (1955) used the term "continuum of reproductive casualty." In 1956, Pasamanick, Rogers, and Lilienfeld wrote: "a hypothesis of a continuum of reproductive casualty is formulated consisting of brain damage incurred during these periods leading to a gradient of injury extending from fetal and neonatal death through cerebral palsy, epilepsy, mental deficiency, and behavior disorder [p. 617]." Their retrospective studies showed an association between perinatal complications and mental retardation (Pasamanick & Lilienfeld, 1955).

In this context, data collection began in 1959 for a prospective study of associations between events surrounding pregnancy and delivery and later outcome in the child. Previous attempts to relate retardation to perinatal complications were based on retrospective data. The Collaborative Perinatal Project would include both data uniformly collected before and at delivery on a large sample of women and data from systematic psychological and pediatric-neurological examinations of their children.

Surveys on a smaller scale of retarded populations have been conducted in Scotland (Birch, Richardson, Baird, Horobin, & Illsley, 1970), Sweden (Hagberg, 1979; Hagberg, Hagberg, Lewerth, & Lindberg, 1981), Hungary (Czeizel, Lányi-Engelmayer, Klujber, Métneki, & Tusnády, 1980), and the United States (Gruenberg, 1964; Moser & Wolf, 1971). Risk factors identified in these studies and examined in the Collaborative Perinatal Project included prematurity and other perinatal complications, maternal age, maternal height, perinatal infections, and socioeconomic status.

The data base of the Collaborative Perinatal Project has many advantages for a study of mental retardation. For example, for each participant in the study, a very large amount of prospectively-collected information was gathered in socioeconomic and medical history interviews, prenatal examinations, labor and delivery observations, and follow-up examinations of the children. The sample size was extremely large—over 53,000 initial registrants. The number of white and black children was approximately equal, so comparisons between ethnic groups can easily be made. The data base also provided a unique opportunity for family studies. Many women registered for more than one pregnancy, reported relatives in the study, or had multiple births; therefore, retardation could be investigated among twins, siblings, half-siblings, and cousins. All children in the study were given individually administered IQ tests.

A disadvantage of the Collaborative Perinatal Project data base for studying mental retardation is the absence of a measure of adaptive behavior. In the current study, retardation is defined by traditional IQ score cutoffs. Readers who are unhappy with the categories used may prefer to think of this as a study of factors associated with low IQ rather than with mental retardation.

Among the questions addressed are:

To what extent are perinatal complications related to mental retardation?

What happens to these associations after socioeconomic and other possible confounding factors are controlled?

Do the data in this study agree with results reported from retrospective studies?

Do the data suggest any risk factors not previously reported?

What etiological hypotheses do the family data support?

What is the nature of the relationship between socioeconomic factors and retardation?

Do the data fit a two-group theory of retardation equally well in both ethnic groups?

PLAN OF THE BOOK

The Collaborative Perinatal Project is described in more detail in the next chapter and the statistical methods used in the study are presented. In Chapter 3, the samples of retarded children are described in terms of cognitive, medical, and demographic characteristics. The next five chapters present findings from the prenatal period through age 7 for the severely and mildly retarded children. Chapter 9 examines subgroups of the mentally retarded. The familial analyses are presented in Chapter 10. The final chapter summarizes and discusses the data. Appendices include a chart of significant variables and others that were screened, a glossary, analyses of relationships among important predictors, and analyses of prenatal drug intake among mothers of the retarded children.

2
Methods

The data base was collected as part of the Collaborative Perinatal Project, a prospective investigation of the developmental consequences of complications in pregnancy and the perinatal period. Between 1959 and 1974, offspring from 53,000 pregnancies were followed from gestation through age 8 by multidisciplinary research teams in 12 medical centers. Women in the study were representative of the patients receiving prenatal care in the participating centers. Mental retardation was an abnormal outcome of special interest as were cerebral palsy, congenital malformations, and learning disorders. Causes of prematurity and of perinatal death and factors related to physical and cognitive growth were also investigated. The concept of a continuum of reproductive casualty, referred to earlier, was a major influence in the initiation and design of the Collaborative Project. The methodology and findings from this large-scale longitudinal study are described in several comprehensive reports (Broman, 1984; Broman, Bien, & Shaughnessy, 1985; Broman, Nichols, & Kennedy, 1975; Hardy, Drage, & Jackson, 1979; Lassman, Fisch, Vetter, & LaBenz, 1980; Nichols & Chen, 1981; Niswander & Gordon, 1972).

THE SAMPLE AND THE STUDY GROUPS

A sample of at least 40,000 pregnancies was originally proposed for the Collaborative Perinatal Project in order to provide an adequate number of cases of rare catastrophic outcomes. The number of pregnancies enrolled in the study under standard selection procedures and with complete perinatal records was 53,043. This number includes repeat pregnancies from 7522 of the women registrants. Table 2-1 shows the distribution of the sample by institution or study center and ethnic group. During the 6 years of intake, cases were selected on the basis of a

13

Table 2-1
Sample Size by Institution and Ethnic Group
in the Collaborative Project Population

Institution	Ethnic Group				
	White	Black	Puerto Rican	Others	Total
Boston Lying-In Hospital	10803	1198	25	167	12193
Providence Lying-In Hospital	2096	672	5	49	2822
Children's Hospital, Buffalo	2383	59	12	15	2469
Columbia-Presbyterian Medical Center	633	876	602	27	2138
New York Medical College	269	1558	2630	17	4474
Pennsylvania Hospital	882	8580	316	14	9792
Johns Hopkins Hospital	798	2744	1	6	3549
Medical College of Virginia	831	2367	0	6	3204
Univ. of Tennessee College of Medicine	22	3501	0	0	3523
Charity Hospital, New Orleans	0	2582	0	0	2582
Univ. of Minnesota Hospital	2986	19	2	140	3147
Univ. of Oregon Medical School	2216	861	1	72	3150
Total	23919	25017	3594	513	53043

"sampling frame" defined for each study center. A common exclusion was patients with no prenatal visits prior to the day of delivery. Some centers selected all eligible women registering for prenatal care and others, a random sample (Broman, 1984).

Sample loss occurred over the 16 years of data collection. The problem of maintaining adequate follow-up is a typical one in longitudinal studies, and the large-scale Collaborative Project was no exception. The number and characteristics of children lost to the study have been discussed in detail elsewhere (Broman et al., 1975; Hardy et al., 1979; Niswander & Gordon, 1972). Follow-up rates for survivors in the total population of 53,043 pregnancies were 88% at 1 year, 75% at 4 years, and 79% at 7 years. At 3 years, speech, language, and hearing examinations were not administered in the two largest study centers and the follow-up rate was only 48%.

Subjects in the current study were the 17,432 white children and the 19,419 black children who were given a psychological examination at the age of 7.

Included in this cohort were 30 white and 23 black institutionalized children who were traced and evaluated by Central Office staff. Except for one mildly retarded case, all were found to be severely retarded. Mean age at examination was 7.1 ± .4 years in the white sample and 7.2 ± .8 years in the black sample. The sex ratios were 1.06 and .98, respectively.

Retarded and comparison groups were defined by IQ score at age 7. For all but 1% of the children in each sample, the criterion measure was the Full Scale IQ from the Wechsler Intelligence Scale for Children (Wechsler, 1949). Four verbal subtests (Information, Comprehension, Vocabulatory, and Digit Span) and three performance subtests (Picture Arrangement, Block Design, and Coding) were administered. Children for whom the WISC was inappropriate ($N = 334$) were most often evaluated with the Stanford–Binet Intelligence Scale or the Leiter International Performance Scale. Other developmental tests (the Cattell Infant Intelligence Scale, the Bayley Scale of Infant Mental Development, and the Vineland Social Maturity Scale) were confined almost entirely to the severely retarded. An estimated IQ level was assigned to 49 untestable children (20 in the white sample and 29 in the black sample). Thirty-nine of these were classified as severely retarded and 10 as mildly retarded. For computational purposes, IQ scores of 25 and 60, respectively, were assigned.

Children with an IQ under 50 were categorized as severely retarded and those with IQs between 50 and 69 as mildly retarded. Two hundred twenty severely retarded and 1096 mildly retarded children were identified in the total study sample of 36,851 children. Prevalence rates for the severe and mild degrees of mental retardation were .53% and 1.15% in the white sample and .66% and 4.61% in the black sample. The nonretarded children were divided into three comparison groups. For the purposes of this study, the groups were defined as borderline (IQ scores of 70 to 89), average (scores of 90 to 119), and above average (scores of 120 to 152). The percentage of children in each group was 14, 73, and 11% among whites and 43, 51, and 1% among blacks. Demographic and psychometric characteristics of the five IQ groups and neurological disorders among the severely and mildly retarded are presented in the following chapter.

PROCEDURES

The severely and mildly retarded groups were compared with all higher IQ groups on 389 characteristics derived from examinations and interviews conducted in the Collaborative Perinatal Project (Appendix 1). The data were recorded on standardized precoded forms that, when completed, were sent to the Perinatal Research Branch at the National Institute of Neurological and Communicative Disorders and Stroke[1] (NINCDS) for editing and then transfered to

---

[1]At that time called National Institute of Neurological Diseases and Blindness.

computer tape; copies were retained by the study centers. Instruction manuals accompanied each protocol, and workshops and training sessions were held periodically for research personnel. The major points of data collection were during prenatal visits; at delivery and in the newborn nursery; during infancy and the preschool period; and at age 7.

In visits to the prenatal clinic, the mother provided interviewers with her medical history and with socioeconomic and genetic information about herself and her family and the baby's father and his family. Obstetricians recorded the results of physical examinations, histories, and laboratory tests. Prenatal clinic visits were scheduled every month during the first 7 months of pregnancy, every 2 weeks during the 8th month, and every week thereafter. At admission for delivery, the mother's physical status was reevaluated and the events of labor and delivery were recorded by a trained observer. A summary of labor and delivery was completed by the obstetrician in charge. The placenta was examined by pathologists who also conducted postmortem examinations of stillbirths and neonatal deaths.

The neonate was observed initially in the delivery room and examined by a pediatrician at 24-hour intervals in the newborn nursery. A neurological examination was performed at 2 days. Other information from the nursery period included nurses' observations and the results of laboratory tests. A diagnostic summary of the nursery period was completed by a physician on the research team.

After the neonatal stage, the child was seen at specified intervals. At each follow-up examination, the mother was interviewed about the child's interval history (with records of medical treatment obtained if appropriate) and the child's physical measurements were taken. A pediatric examination was given at 4 months; psychological examinations at 8 months, and 4 and 7 years; pediatric-neurological examinations at 1 and 7 years; and a speech, language, and hearing examination at 3 years and following the endpoint of this study at 8 years. Interval histories were kept up to date at 18 months, and at 2, 5, and 6 years. Family and social history information was obtained from the mother at the time of the 7-year examinations. Diagnostic summaries were prepared by physicians following the 1st year and the 7th year.

Data from the maternal and child assessments were grouped into six epochs, the last, representing the 7th year, being divided into three catagories. All variables are listed in Appendix 1 with relationships to severe and mild retardation indicated. The epochs are:

1. *The Prenatal Period.* The 64 variables screened included demographic characteristics of the family reported in maternal interviews; age, reproductive history and other characteristics of the mother; and complications of pregnancy.

2. *Labor and Delivery.* Length of labor, fetal heart rate, type of delivery, and administration of anesthetics were among the 31 variables screened.

3. *The Neonatal Period.* The 52 variables from this epoch included birth-weight, gestational age, Apgar scores, malformations, genetic syndromes, and other complications in the neonate.

4. *Infancy.* Measures of physical and cognitive development in the first year of life were height, weight, head circumference, test scores and behavior ratings from the research version of the Bayley Scales of Infant Development, and findings from a pediatric-neurological examination at 1 year of age. Forty-four variables were screened.

5. *The Preschool Period.* Data from the preschool epoch consisted of summary ratings from the speech, language, and hearing examination at age 3 and results from the 4-year psychological examination that included assessments of intellectual functioning (Stanford–Binet Intelligence Scale), motor skills, concept formation ability (Graham–Ernhart Block Sort Test), and behavior in the testing situation. Physical measurements at age 4 were also screened resulting in a total of 24 preschool variables.

6. *Characteristics at Age 7.*

(a) Demographic and other family characteristics were reassessed at the time of the seven-year examinations in an interview with the mother or other caretaker. Thirty variables were screened.

(b) Medical status was evaluated in 120 variables drawn from a pediatric-neurological examination at this age and from medical histories covering the interval between 1 and 7 years.

(c) Intellectual and perceptual–motor functioning was assessed by a battery of instruments that included the criterion measure, the Wechsler Intelligence Scale for Children, the Goodenough Harris Draw-a-Person Test, the Bender–Gestalt Test, the Auditory Vocal Association Test from the Illinois Test of Psycholinguistic Abilities, and the Tactile Finger Recognition Test. Academic achievement was evaluated with the Wide Range Achievement Test and ratings were made of behaviors observed in the testing situation. Twenty-four variables were screened.

ANALYTIC TECHNIQUES

The study was planned to identify the developmental factors related to severe and mild retardation and to assess their relative importance and explanatory power. All analyses were performed within the white and black samples; sex of child was treated as a potential predictor or independent variable. Subgroups of the retarded were analyzed with the same methods as the primary study groups. The basic procedures, carried out in each sample, consisted of:

1. *Univariate Tests.* Each of 389 variables was analyzed individually to determine if the mean value differed significantly between a retarded group and the

comparison groups (four higher IQ levels for the severely retarded and three for the mildly retarded). The t and chi-square tests were used for quantitative and qualitative variables, respectively. Group differences were considered significant at $p < .05$.

2. *Two-Group Discriminant Function Analyses.* Variables passing the univariate screen in each of the seven comparisions were grouped by developmental epoch and, as noted earlier, by category in the sixth epoch, and entered in stepwise two-group discriminant function analyses. Those that were retained ($p < .05$) are presented in the following chapters.[2] In addition, four sequential summary analyses were performed for the severely and mildly retarded combining the discriminators through delivery, those through the perinatal period, and through ages 1 and 4 years. Reported in the following tables are the standardized discriminant function coefficient for each variable in a given analysis and the canonical correlation between the set of variables and the group classification.

For each of the discriminators, mean values or relative frequencies in the 5 IQ groups are presented along with F or chi-square tests for group differences and the Pearson correlation coefficient between the variable and IQ score. For some continuous measures, a standardized variate, calculated by subtracting the sample mean and dividing by the sample standard deviation, is shown graphically.

Because of the size and complexity of the study, it is unlikely that all assumptions underlying the statistical techniques used were always met or that every relationship between retardation and a potential risk factor or correlate was examined optimally. The study, then, is primarily data analytic, or exploratory, and relies on the robustness of the techniques employed (Mosteller & Tukey, 1977). These are described in some detail in the following sections and investigations of potential problems are discussed.

t and χ^2 Tests

In the chi-square procedure, which is a standard test of the equality of two proportions, the Yates correction for continuity was used, a conservative approach (Grizzle, 1967; Plackett, 1964) that was probably unnecessary because of the large sample sizes. For the dichotomous variables with one or more expected cell frequency below 5, Fisher's exact test was used (Conover, 1971). The t-test was the standard test for mean differences based on the assumption of equal variances (Mendenhall & Ott, 1980), one of the issues that was examined.

The t-test, and also the F-test reported from the one-way analysis of variance, assumes that the variable of interest has an underlying normal distribution, although it is generally regarded as robust to deviations from normality (Bradley, 1968). For variables that take on very few values, however, or whose distribu-

---

[2]Variables significant in the univariate screen only are shown in Appendix 1.

tions are highly asymmetric or skewed (conditions that were infrequent in this study), significance levels associated with this test must be considered approximate. Because the t-test was used only to compare mean differences in the initial screen, and because the distribution of the sample mean approaches normality as sample size increases, the normality assumption is not likely to be a problematic one for this study. The t-test is known to be less robust to deviations from the assumption of equal variances in the two groups of interest (Bradley, 1968). The extent to which violations of this assumption would alter results was assessed in a companion study from this data base in which 20 variables were randomly selected for further analysis (Broman et al., 1985). For the two-group comparison under consideration, 10 variables yielded significant mean differences and 10 were insignificant using the equal variance t-test. Nineteen of the 20 did not change categories (i.e., from significant to insignificant or vice versa) when the unequal variance t-test was used. The one that did change was significant ($p = .043$) using the pooled variance test and insignificant ($p = .057$) using the separate or unequal variance test. A general tendency for the pooled or equal variance test to yield lower p-values was observed. This may have resulted in a small number of variables passing the univariate screen that would not have passed if the separate variance t-test were used.

Pearson Correlation

The Pearson correlation coefficient is perhaps the most commonly used measure of bivariate association between two variables. In order to calculate significance levels exactly, however, the sample correlation coefficient must be based on two variables which are normally distributed. In fact, the accuracy of significance levels associated with the Pearson correlation coefficient is known to be sensitive to departures from this underlying assumption. Nevertheless, for the sake of uniformity in presenting a measure of association between each independent variable and IQ score, the Pearson correlation coefficient was used. Regardless of the inaccuracies of the significance levels that might exist in some cases, the interpretation of the Pearson correlation is the same whether or not the underlying distribution is normal. The squared correlation coefficient can be interpreted as the percentage of variation in IQ associated with the variation in the independent variable of interest. For the reasons of uniformity across all variables and the straightforward, useful interpretation of the Pearson correlation, it was considered appropriate not to use a variety of types of correlation coefficients depending on the distributional properties of each independent variable.

Standardized Variables

The statistical properties of a number of variables that differed significantly between the retarded and comparison groups are presented in both tabular and graphic form in the following chapters, although the number of graphic presentations was held to a minimum because of the large amount of data reported. For dichotomous variables, the graphs depict the percentage of cases in each of the five IQ groups with the attribute of interest and are readily interpretable. The variables that were either continuous or took on several values, however, yielded graphic displays that varied widely because of the scale on which each variable was measured. For this reason, these variables were standardized, as noted earlier, placing them on a uniform scale with a mean of 0 and a standard deviation of 1. The standard scores were then graphed to reflect mean values for a given variable by IQ group. This procedure permits a ready visual comparison among different continuous variables measured in standardized units. As mentioned, standardization was carried out within each sample, using the sample mean and standard deviation to standardize all white or black cases.

Discriminant Function Analysis

Because many of the antecedents and correlates of mental retardation were themselves intercorrelated, it was necessary to use a multivariate technique to identify those variables that remained significantly related to outcome in the context of all possible independent variables in a given epoch. Stepwise discriminant function analysis was used for this purpose. A modification of the Statistical Package for the Social Sciences (SPSS) discriminant function program (Hull & Nie, 1981) allowed the analyses to be conducted by using correlation matrices as input to the discriminant function approach. This permitted the calculation of individual correlation coefficients using pairwise complete data for each variable. The primary advantage of this procedure was that despite the fact that data for most variables were at least 90% complete, it would have been necessary to delete large numbers of cases from the analyses if only those with complete data on all variables were used. Relatively large numbers of variables passed the within-epoch univariate screens and were entered in the discriminant function analyses. Although few variables had missing data on a large number of cases, the likelihood that a given case would have missing data on at least one variable was substantial. In order to overcome the problem of eliminating a considerable proportion of all cases on this basis, pairwise complete correlation matrices were calculated and used as input to the discriminant function program.

As with the t-test, chi-square test, and Pearson correlation coefficient discussed earlier, it was not possible to ensure that every theoretical assumption required by the discriminant function technique was satisfied. Again, because of the magnitude of the study and the number of analyses conducted, it is unlikely that each individual relationship was examined using the optimal technique, either in a bivariate or multivariate sense. Departures from certain assumptions were investigated in the companion study (Broman et al., 1985), and will be discussed later.

Discriminant function coefficients can be standardized or unstandardized

(Timm, 1975). Standardized coefficients were used in presenting the findings of this study because they are not dependent on the original scale of the variables and often range between -1 and $+1$. The magnitude of the standardized coefficient represents a specific variable's contribution to the calculation of a discriminant score that can be used to classify individual cases. It reflects the contribution of the variable to the discriminatory strength of the function in a multivariate context. A negative sign accompanying a coefficient indicates that the mean value or frequency of the variable is lower in the study or retarded group than in the comparison group.

Except when a stepwise procedure is employed, no straightforward indicator of the statistical significance of a given coefficient is possible. An advantage of the stepwise procedure is its ability to assess whether a variable makes a statistically significant contribution to the overall discriminatory power of the linear discriminant function. However, as with any stepwise procedure, specific variables may fail to enter because of their association with variables that entered the discriminant function on preceding steps.

The fundamental intent of two-group discriminant function analysis is to construct a linear function which has mean values for group one and group two such that the difference between these two mean values is as large as possible. Several statistics are available to measure this distance or the general strength of the discriminant function (Goldstein & Dillon, 1978). One such statistic is an analog of the multiple correlation coefficient (coefficient of determination) in regression analysis (Klecka, 1980). The canonical correlation associated with the two-group discriminant function analysis has the same basic meaning as the multiple correlation in regression analysis. That is, the square of the canonical correlation can be interpreted as the percentage of variation in the dichotomous (group indicator) variable due to or associated with variation in the discriminators.

In discriminant function analysis, the vector of discriminators is assumed to follow a multivariate normal distribution. Linear discriminant function techniques are, however, also regarded as relatively robust with respect to deviations from this assumption (Goldstein & Dillon, 1978). Further, the intuitive interpretation of the canonical correlation remains intact regardless of the nature of the underlying multivariate distribution that characterizes the vector of discriminators (in much the same manner as the Pearson correlation coefficient described earlier).

Many of the discriminant function results presented in the following chapters are based on functions that involve both continuous and dichotomous variables. Discriminant analysis was selected as the fundamental multivariate technique rather than logistic regression or other classification procedures because it could be used in a stepwise manner, and because of the utility of the canonical correlation in characterizing the discriminatory power of variables within epochs and then pooled across epochs. It is to be emphasized, however, that the discriminant function approach was used as a data analytic tool and the significance levels associated with the explanatory power of the discriminant function are approximate.

Extending the concept of variance equality (discussed with respect to the *t*-test) to the multivariate case, the two-group discriminant function procedure employed assumes equality of covariance matrices for the vector of discriminators across the two groups. In general, the assumption of covariance matrix equality was not tested, but the univariate assessments involving the results of the pooled and separate variance *t*-tests suggest that violations of this assumption, while resulting in approximate *p*-values, would be unlikely to alter the major study findings.

For the most part, incomplete data was not a major issue, but some variables had a relatively high frequency of missing values. In the companion study, the ramifications of the correlation matrix input approach to treating incomplete data were assessed using two procedures. First, for selected discriminant functions, the variable with the highest proportion of incomplete values was used to divide all cases into two groups, one with incomplete values for that variable and the other with complete values. These groups were then compared using the remaining discriminators in the original discriminant function. The purpose was to determine if there was a pattern of association between complete and incomplete cases and the remaining discriminators in the original function. Secondly, for selected discriminant functions, the variable with the highest proportion of incomplete values was again selected and a second discriminant function, using the same discriminators as the first, was estimated using only cases with complete data on that variable. Discriminant function coefficients and canonical correlations in the original discriminant function and the "complete cases" discriminant function were then compared.

In the second case, in which analyses were deliberately chosen that included discriminators with more incomplete information than most, only minimal differences were found in canonical correlations and standardized coefficients, indicating that the approach taken in dealing with missing data was similar to recalculating the discriminant functions on the basis of complete data for those variables that were retained. For the first type of missing data analyses, the canonical correlations were always small, always less than the canonical correlation for the original discriminant function, and often insignificant. It did not appear that the method of handling incomplete cases had any major effects on the findings of the study.

RELIABILITY OF THE CRITERION MEASURE

In a series of "quality control" trials, the reliability of the psychological tests administered at age 7, as well as other examinations in the Collaborative Project, was assessed. Excluding children whose families were identified as uncooperative, a random sample of 400 children was selected for retesting after an interval of 3 months. The sample included 174 white children (83 boys and 91 girls) and 226 black children (111 boys and 115 girls). The retest was conducted by an examiner from a different study center and observed and scored independently by the original examiner. Retests were scheduled throughout each year over a 7-year period.

The test–retest reliability of the WISC Full Scale IQ was .85 in the white subsample and .80 in the black subsample. The interobserver reliability was .99 in both groups. Verbal and Performance IQs had test–retest reliabilities of .83 and .72 among whites and .77 and .66 among blacks. The interobserver reliabilities ranged from .97 to .99 in the two groups.

3

Characteristics of the Mentally Retarded Children

Demographic, psychometric, and biological characteristics of the severely and mildly retarded children are presented in this chapter. Three levels of socioeconomic status (SES) derived from the socioeconomic index scores of the families at the 7-year follow-up (Nichols & Chen, 1981) were defined. SES I includes scores in the lowest quartile of the distribution in the total study population; SES II, scores in the middle 50%; and SES III, scores in the upper quartile.

SOCIOECONOMIC STATUS

Retardation frequencies were inversely related to socioeconomic status (Table 3-1). In the white sample, the frequency of severe retardation decreased from .83% in the lowest socioeconomic status (SES I) to .40% in SES III (p < .05). A much greater decrease was found for mild retardation, from 3.34% in SES I to .30% in SES III (p < .00001). In SES I, mild retardation was about four times as frequent as severe, but in SES III, there were more severely than mildly retarded children. Socioeconomic effects were apparent at both ends of the IQ distribution, as shown by the following contrast: In SES I, there were approximately half as many children in the above-average group (IQ $\geq$ 120) as in the mildly retarded group. In SES III, however, there were 68 times as many above-average as mildly retarded children. In other words, the ratio of above-average to mildly retarded children differed by a factor of over 100 between the high and low socioeconomic levels.

In the black sample, severe retardation frequencies decreased from .94% in SES I, to .56% in SES II, to .44% in SES III. These percentages were very similar to those in the white sample (.83%, .61%, and .40%). Mild retarda-

Table 3-1
Percent of Children in Retarded and Nonretarded Groups
by Socioeconomic Status

Socioeconomic Status	N	Severely Retarded	Mildly Retarded	Borderline	Average	Above Average
White						
I	2276	0.83	3.34	28.47	65.64	1.71
II	7920	0.61	1.31	17.20	75.64	5.29
III	6950	0.40	0.30	5.71	73.31	20.27
Unknown	286	0.35	0.00	23.08	68.88	7.69
Total	17432	0.53	1.15	14.19	73.30	10.84
Black						
I	6683	0.94	7.75	50.58	40.42	0.31
II	9830	0.56	3.59	40.61	54.52	0.72
III	2025	0.44	1.19	25.53	69.68	3.16
Unknown	881	0.11	0.00	48.81	50.85	0.23
Total	19419	0.66	4.61	42.84	51.08	0.81

tion was about seven times as frequent in SES I (7.75%) as SES III (1.19%). Like the white sample, above average IQs were about ten times as frequent in SES III as SES I.

SEX DIFFERENCES

The proportion of children in the retarded and nonretarded groups is shown by sex and socioeconomic status in Table 3-2. Sex differences in the frequency of retardation were slight. Among whites, severe retardation was more frequent among boys than girls (.65% vs. .40%, $p < .05$), and the frequency of mild retardation did not differ significantly by sex. The ratio of mild to severe retardation was twice as great among girls as boys ($p < .01$). In the black sample, both severe and mild retardation were more frequent among boys ($p < .01$ and .05, respectively), and the mildly retarded to severely retarded ratio did not differ significantly by sex.

At the upper end of the IQ distribution, white boys more often had above-average scores than did white girls ($p < .001$). Among blacks, the low frequencies of above-average scores were nearly the same for boys and girls.

Table 3-2
Percent of Children in Retarded and Nonretarded Groups
by Sex and Socioeconomic Status

Socioeconomic Status	N	Severely Retarded	Mildly Retarded	Borderline	Average	Above Average
White Boys						
I	1159	1.12	3.02	27.09	66.52	2.24
II	4089	0.73	1.22	16.70	75.30	6.04
III	3555	0.39	0.20	5.20	72.69	21.52
Unknown	153	0.65	0.00	25.49	66.01	7.84
Total	8956	0.65	1.03	13.63	72.97	11.72
White Girls						
I	1117	0.54	3.67	29.90	64.73	1.16
II	3831	0.37	1.41	17.72	76.01	4.59
III	3395	0.41	0.41	6.24	73.96	18.97
Unknown	133	0.00	0.00	20.30	72.18	7.52
Total	8476	0.40	1.29	14.77	73.64	9.90
Black Boys						
I	3346	1.20	8.31	50.96	39.21	0.33
II	4801	0.69	3.92	41.64	53.01	0.75
III	1014	0.49	1.38	24.85	70.12	3.16
Unknown	461	0.22	0.00	47.29	52.06	0.43
Total	9622	0.82	4.99	43.38	49.97	0.84
Black Girls						
I	3337	0.69	7.19	50.19	41.62	0.30
II	5029	0.44	3.28	39.63	55.96	0.70
III	1011	0.40	0.99	26.21	69.24	3.17
Unknown	420	0.00	0.00	50.48	49.52	0.00
Total	9797	0.50	4.24	42.31	52.17	0.79

Table 3-3
Mean IQ Scores in the Retarded and Comparison Groups

Group	White			Black		
	N	Mean	SD	N	Mean	SD
Severely Retarded	92	31.68	13.09	128	32.39	11.11
Mildly Retarded	201	62.51	5.33	895	63.50	4.76
Borderline	2473	82.73	5.00	8319	81.58	5.30
Average	12777	103.80	7.87	9919	98.76	6.81
Above Average	1889	126.07	5.80	158	123.91	4.29
Total	17432	102.37	14.68	19419	89.54	13.06

Table 3-4
Verbal and Performance IQs in the Retarded and Comparison Groups

Group	White			Black		
	N	Mean	SD	N	Mean	SD
Severely Retarded						
Verbal IQ	9	54.89	3.72	23	52.39	4.44
Performance IQ	9	47.67	3.61	23	49.43	4.33
Mildly Retarded						
Verbal IQ	177	67.32	7.25	852	67.58	6.53
Performance IQ	176	65.78	8.61	853	66.22	7.96
Borderline						
Verbal IQ	2454	82.69	7.57	8310	81.86	7.24
Performance IQ	2456	85.99	8.39	8311	84.68	8.20
Average						
Verbal IQ	12758	101.22	9.50	9909	96.79	8.41
Performance IQ	12761	105.93	10.23	9910	101.11	9.44
Above Average						
Verbal IQ	1884	122.09	8.96	158	120.25	8.64
Performance IQ	1884	125.56	9.30	158	123.54	8.20
Total						
Verbal IQ	17282	100.49	13.88	19252	89.20	12.03
Performance IQ	17286	104.79	14.59	19255	92.59	13.54

IQ SCORES

Mean IQs within each group and for the total white and black samples are shown in Table 3-3. The scores were determined from the WISC or from alternate tests administered when the WISC could not be used. In the total white and black samples, more than 99% of the children were given the WISC. The few severely retarded children tested with the WISC had IQs near 50. The difference between Verbal and Performance IQ varied by IQ group (Table 3-4). Except for the retarded children, performance scores were higher than verbal scores.

MAJOR CNS DISORDERS

Children with one or more of the following conditions were classified as having major central nervous system (CNS) disorders: Down's syndrome, other syndromes, post-traumatic deficit, CNS malformations, cerebral palsy, epilepsy, blindness, or deafness. The percentage of severely and mildly retarded children with these disorders is shown by socioeconomic status in Table 3-5. Prevalence varied with degree of retardation, ethnicity, and SES. As expected, the severely

Table 3-5
Percent of Retarded Children with Major CNS Disorders

Disorder	White				Black			
	SES				SES			
	I	II	III	Total	I	II	III	Total
Severely Retarded								
Present	63.1	70.5	82.1	71.7	46.0	60.0	66.7	53.9
Absent	36.9	29.5	17.9	28.3	54.0	40.0	33.3	46.1
N	19	44	28	92[1]	63	55	9	128[1]
Mildly Retarded								
Present	7.9	12.5	42.9	13.9	6.6	5.9	4.2	6.3
Absent	92.1	87.5	57.1	86.1	93.4	94.1	95.8	93.7
N	76	104	21	201	518	353	24	895

[1]Included one case with unknown SES.

Table 3-6
Distribution of Major CNS Disorders by
Socioeconomic Status Among Severely Retarded Children

| Disorder | White | | | | | Black | | | | |
| | SES | | | | (%) | SES | | | | (%) |
	I	II	III	Total		I	II	III	Total	
Down's syndrome	3	8	4	15	(16.3)	7	10	1	18	(14.0)
Other syndromes	3	6	5	14	(15.2)	0	7	1	9[1]	(7.0)
Post traumatic deficit	0	1	0	1	(1.1)	2	1	0	3	(2.3)
CNS malformations	2	4	3	9	(9.8)	2	1	0	3	(2.3)
Cerebral palsy	3	10	6	19	(20.6)	9	8	3	20	(15.6)
Epilepsy	1	2	4	7	(7.6)	7	5	1	13	(10.2)
Sensory deficits	0	0	1	1	(1.1)	2	1	0	3	(2.3)
None	7	13	5	26[1]	(28.3)	34	22	3	59	(46.1)
Total	19	44	28	92	(100.0)	63	55	9	128	(100.0)

[1]Includes one case with unknown SES.

retarded were much more likely to have major CNS disorders than the mildly retarded. Among whites, 72% of the severely retarded but only 14% of the mildly retarded were affected. The percentages were lower in the black sample; 54% of the severely retarded and 6% of the mildly retarded were affected. In general, the proportion of children affected increased with increasing SES level. This trend was greatest among mildly retarded whites, where the percentage with CNS disorders increased from 8% in SES I to 43% in SES III. Mild retardation was rare among white children in SES III and was often accompanied by CNS disorders usually found among the severely retarded.

The specific CNS disorders found in the severely retarded children are listed in Table 3-6. In this table, children are counted only once, even if they had more than one of the conditions. The disorders are ordered hierarchically, so that, for example, if a child had both cerebral palsy and epilepsy, he or she was counted under cerebral palsy only. In both samples, cerebral palsy and Down's syndrome were the most common diagnoses. A later table tabulates the disorders so that all combinations of conditions can be seen.

Table 3-7
Other Syndromes, CNS Malformations, and Sensory Deficits
Among the Severely Retarded Children

	White	Black
Other Syndromes		
Post rubella	2	4
Post meningitic encephalitis	1	3
Pneumococcal meningitis	0	1
Herpes encephalitis	1	0
Cytomegalovirus inclusion disease	1	0
Turner's	1	0
Chromosomal translocation	1	0
Phenylketonuria	1	0
de Lange	1	0
Carnosinemia	1	0
Aminoaciduria	1	0
Hypothyroidism	0	1
von Recklinghausen's	1	0
Apert's	1	0
Cleido-cranial dysostosis	1	0
CNS Malformations		
Hydrocephaly	5	3
Craniocynostosis	1	0
Agenesis of corpus callosum	1	0
Meningocele	1	0
Encephalocele	1	0
Sensory Deficits		
Bilateral deafness	1	1
Binocular blindness	0	2

Specific syndromes, malformations, and sensory deficits are shown for the severely retarded children in Table 3-7. The most common syndromes, other than Down's, were post-rubella and post-meningitic encephalitis. None of the other 13 syndromes listed occurred in more than one child. Among the CNS malformations, eight were hydrocephaly and one each of craniosynostosis, agenesis of the corpus callosum, meningocele, and encephalocele. The primary sensory deficits were two cases each of blindness and deafness.

Table 3-8 shows 17 combinations of disorders found in the severely retarded white children. Cerebral palsy, epilepsy, and sensory deficits were often second-

Table 3-8
Neurological Conditions Among the Severely Retarded White Children

Down's Syndrome	Other Syndromes	CNS Malformations	Post Traumatic Deficit	Cerebral Palsy	Epilepsy	Sensory Deficits	N
●							14
●					○		1
	●						5
	●			○	○		2
	●			○		○	2
	●			○	○	○	2
	●			○			2
	●				○		1
		●					4
		●		○			3
		●		○	○	○	1
		●			○		1
			●	○	○		1
				●			10
				●	○		9
					●		7
						●	1
Primary condition	15	14	9	1	19	7	1	66
Secondary condition	0	0	0	0	13	18	5	
Total	15	14	9	1	32	25	6	

● Primary condition
○ Secondary condition

Table 3-9
Neurological Conditions Among the Severely Retarded Black Children

Down's Syndrome	Other Syndromes	CNS Malformations	Post Traumatic Deficit	Cerebral Palsy	Epilepsy	Sensory Deficits	N
●							17
●					○		1
	●			○			1
	●			○	○		3
	●			○	○	○	1
	●			○		○	2
	●					○	2
		●					3
			●	○			2
			●	○	○		1
				●			8
				●	○		10
				●	○	○	1
				●		○	1
					●		13
						●	3
Primary condition 18	9	3	3	20	13	3	69
Secondary condition 0	0	0	0	10	17	7	
Total 18	9	3	3	30	30	10	

● Primary condition
○ Secondary condition

Table 3-10
Distribution of Major CNS Disorders by
Socioeconomic Status Among Mildly Retarded Children

Disorder	White					Black				
	SES				(%)	SES				(%)
	I	II	III	Total		I	II	III	Total	
Down's syndrome	1	1	1	3	(1.5)	0	0	0	0	(0.0)
Other syndromes	1	0	1	2	(1.0)	5	3	0	8	(0.9)
Post traumatic deficit	0	0	0	0	(0.0)	3	0	0	3	(0.3)
CNS malformations	0	2	4	6	(3.0)	3	1	0	4	(0.5)
Cerebral palsy	3	6	2	11	(5.4)	9	6	1	16	(1.8)
Epilepsy	1	3	0	4	(2.0)	11	9	0	20	(2.2)
Sensory deficits	0	1	1	2	(1.0)	3	2	0	5	(0.6)
None	70	91	12	173	(86.1)	484	332	23	839	(93.7)
Total	76	104	21	201	(100.0)	518	353	24	895	(100.0)

ary conditions. The 19 primary cases of cerebral palsy correspond to the number shown in Table 3-6. In addition, 13 other children had cerebral palsy secondary to specific syndromes, CNS malformations, or a post-traumatic deficit. Most of the 25 children with epilepsy had another condition that was considered primary. Three of the children had 4 of the CNS disorders, and, in all, 102 were present among the 66 children.

The severely retarded black children had 16 combinations of conditions, shown in Table 3-9. As was the case in the white sample, most of the children with epilepsy or sensory deficits had other primary conditions. One child had 4 conditions, and altogether the 69 affected children had a total of 103 conditions.

Table 3-10 shows the CNS disorders diagnosed in 28 white and 56 black mildly retarded children. These children had fewer syndromes than the severely retarded; cerebral palsy and epilepsy were the most frequent disorders. As shown in Table 3-11, post-rubella and hydrocephaly were the most common syndrome and CNS malformation among the mildly retarded children. Seven other syndromes were found in only one child; three of these syndromes—post-men-

Table 3-11
Other Syndromes, CNS Malformations, and Sensory Deficits
Among the Mildly Retarded Children

	White	Black
Other Syndromes		
Post rubella	0	3
Post meningitic encephalitis	0	1
Turner's	0	1
Klinefelter's	1	0
Chromosomal deletion	0	1
Trisomy 15 mosaic	0	1
Pierre Robin	1	0
von Recklinghausen's	0	1
CNS Malformations		
Hydrocephaly	2	4
Microcephaly	3	0
Cerebellar astrocytoma	1	0
Sensory Deficits		
Bilateral deafness	1	4
Binocular blindness	1	1

ingitic encephalitis, Turner's, and von Recklinghausen's—were also diagnosed in the severely retarded. The primary sensory deficits included five children who were deaf and two who were blind.

There was little overlap among the conditions in the mildly retarded white group (Table 3-12). The 28 children had 32 conditions—3 of those with cerebral palsy also had epilepsy, and 1 child with a CNS malformation (hydrocephaly) was also blind. Table 3-13 shows the condition combinations in the mildly retarded black children, where 56 children had a total of 66 conditions. Ten children had cerebral palsy, epilepsy, or sensory deficits as secondary diagnoses.

STUDY CENTER

Differences in IQ group distribution among the participating study centers, shown in Table 3-14, reflect socioeconomic differences among the centers. For example, the study registrants in Buffalo were patients of private obstetricians rather than clinics. Their children's IQ distribution, with more scores in the

Table 3-12
Neurological Conditions Among the Mildly Retarded White Children

Down's Syndrome	Other Syndromes	CNS Malformations	Cerebral Palsy	Epilepsy	Sensory Deficits	N
•						3
	•					2
		•				5
		•			○	1
			•			8
			•	○		3
				•		4
					•	2
Primary condition						
3	2	6	11	4	2	28
Secondary condition						
0	0	0	0	3	1	
Total						
3	2	6	11	7	3	

• Primary condition
○ Secondary condition

severely than in the mildly retarded range, closely resembled the SES III distribution shown in Table 3-1. Other study centers, such as those in Providence or Philadelphia, had IQ distributions similar to that of SES I.

In general, frequencies of severe retardation did not differ greatly, except when samples were very small. There were more severely retarded than expected in the Providence black sample (1.85%), but it was found that 6 of the 10 cases had IQs between 46 and 49. The New Orleans sample had the lowest mean socioeconomic index of the study centers (Broman et al., 1975) and, by far, the largest percentage of mildly retarded children (10.25%).

Table 3-13
Neurological Conditions Among the Mildly Retarded Black Children

Other Syndromes	CNS Malformations	Post Traumatic Deficit	Cerebral Palsy	Epilepsy	Sensory Deficits	N
●						6
●			○		○	1
●					○	1
	●					2
	●		○			2
		●				3
			●			13
			●	○	○	1
			●	○		2
				●		19
				●	○	1
					●	5
Primary condition						
8	4	3	16	20	5	56
Secondary condition						
0	0	0	3	3	4	
Total						
8	4	3	19	23	9	

● Primary condition
○ Secondary condition

Table 3-14
Percent of Children in Retarded and Nonretarded Groups by Study Center

Study Center		N	Severely Retarded	Mildly Retarded	Borderline	Average	Above Average
Children's Hospital,	White	7692	0.52	0.60	9.82	76.31	12.75
Boston	Black	870	0.23	1.26	18.74	76.09	3.68
Child Study Center,	White	1579	0.51	2.22	27.36	67.38	2.53
Brown Univ.	Black	541	1.85	5.55	41.59	50.65	0.37
Children's Hospital,	White	2050	0.39	0.34	5.22	73.12	20.93
Buffalo	Black	48	0.00	0.00	14.58	79.17	6.25
Columbia-Presbyterian Medical	White	483	0.41	1.66	12.84	77.43	7.66
Center	Black	709	0.71	2.12	20.73	72.64	3.81
New York Medical	White	42	2.38	0.00	38.10	57.14	2.38
College	Black	493	0.61	5.27	40.16	53.55	0.41
Children's Hospital,	White	508	0.98	3.15	25.59	67.72	2.56
Philadelphia	Black	6739	0.64	4.07	44.50	50.16	0.64
Johns Hopkins	White	551	0.73	0.91	31.40	63.70	3.27
Hospital	Black	2332	0.60	3.00	37.99	57.46	0.95
Medical College of	White	577	0.69	3.81	30.85	62.74	1.91
Virginia	Black	2088	1.05	5.99	49.66	42.91	0.38
Univ. of Tennessee College of	White	3	0.00	0.00	33.33	66.67	0.00
Medicine	Black	2779	0.36	3.71	43.40	52.14	0.40
Charity Hospital,	White	0	0.00	0.00	0.00	0.00	0.00
New Orleans	Black	2117	0.76	10.25	55.98	32.78	0.24
Univ. of Minnesota	White	2287	0.39	1.18	12.16	73.12	13.07
Hospital	Black	11	0.00	0.00	9.09	81.82	9.09
Univ. of Oregon Medical	White	1660	0.66	2.11	20.54	73.07	3.61
School	Black	692	0.43	3.47	38.29	57.51	0.29
Total N	White	17432	0.53	1.15	14.19	73.30	10.84
	Black	19419	0.66	4.61	42.84	51.08	0.81

4
Prenatal and
Obstetric Factors

The prenatal factors examined in this study include family and maternal characteristics as well as events in pregnancy. Of the 64 variables screened, 44 had values in one or both retarded groups that differed significantly ($p < .05$) from those in a higher IQ group. They were entered in two-group discriminant function analyses to identify the independent differences between retarded and nonretarded groups in each sample. Of the 31 labor and delivery characteristics screened, 24 were retained for entry in the multivariate analyses. Discriminators from both epochs were then pooled in summary analyses of the period prior to birth.

The results are presented in tables that show standardized discriminant coefficients and canonical correlations for the four comparisons between the severely retarded and higher IQ groups in each sample and the three comparisons between the mildly retarded and higher IQ groups. The size of the coefficient indicates the relative importance of a discriminator in a given analysis, and the magnitude of the canonical correlation indicates the effectiveness of the set of variables in discriminating between the retarded and the comparison group. Descriptive data for the significant prenatal and obstetric factors are presented in tables that list means or relative frequencies by IQ group, compare the five IQ groups using F ratios or chi-squares, and show correlations with IQ score in the total white and black samples. Group comparisons significant in the discriminant function analyses are indicated in bold or italicized type, as noted. For selected quantitative variables, standard scores computed within each sample are displayed graphically.

THE SEVERELY RETARDED

Prenatal Factors

The most important prenatal discriminators between the severely retarded and higher IQ groups were socioeconomic index score of the family, seizures in

38

Table 4-1
Standardized Coefficients for Prenatal Discriminators Between the Severely Retarded and Comparison Groups

Variable	Comparison Group[a] White MR	BL	AV	AA	Black MR	BL	AV	AA
Socioeconomic index	.41	.35	−.03	−.23	.44	—	—	−.51
Seizures in pregnancy	—	—	.43	.25	.51	.48	.46	—
Maternal education	.51	.36	—	−.30	—	—	−.57	—
Maternal SRA score	—	—	−.39	−.26	—	—	−.26	−.61
Pregnancy-free interval	—	.31	—	—	—	—	—	−.20
Retarded siblings	—	.56	.68	.40	—	—	—	—
Weight gain in pregnancy	−.32	−.25	−.22	—	—	—	—	—
Number of prenatal visits	—	—	−.31	−.25	—	—	—	—
Age at menarche	−.48	—	—	—	—	—	—	—
Rubella in pregnancy	—	.44	—	—	—	—	—	—
Hospitalizations since LMP	—	—	—	.15	—	—	—	—
Parity	—	—	—	.14	—	—	—	—
Anemia in pregnancy	—	—	—	.13	—	—	—	—
Birthweight of last child	—	—	—	—	—	−.27	−.24	−.17
Urinary tract infection in pregnancy	—	—	—	—	−.47	−.32	—	—
Housing density	—	—	—	—	−.49	—	—	—
Rheumatic fever in pregnancy	—	—	—	—	—	.61	—	—
Maternal age	—	—	—	—	—	.36	—	—
Fetal or neonatal death at last delivery	—	—	—	—	—	.31	—	—
Toxemia	—	—	—	—	—	—	.33	—
Mother employed	—	—	—	—	—	—	−.30	—
Canonical correlation	*.34**	*.14**	*.08**	*.36**	*.18**	*.09**	*.09**	*.56**

Note: Coefficients with negative signs indicate that the mean value or frequency of the variable was lower in the retarded than in the comparison group.

[a]MR = mildly retarded, IQ 50-69; BL = borderline, IQ 70-89; AV = average, IQ 90-119; AA = above average, IQ 120-152.

*$p < .00001$

Table 4-2

Prenatal Socioeconomic Index Score by IQ Group

	1 Severely Retarded	2 Mildly Retarded	3 Borderline	4 Average	5 Above Average	F	r_{IQ}
	M S.D.	M S.D.	M S.D.	M S.D.	M S.D.		
White	51.0 21.6	**40.4 18.8**	**44.4 17.9**	*57.1 20.5*	*73.2 18.1*	583.38*	.39*
Black	35.1 19.3	**30.0 14.8**	*34.6 16.1*	*40.9 18.0*	***54.9 20.7***	238.50*	.24*

Differs from severely retarded in D.F.
Differs from mildly retarded in D.F.
Differs from severely and mildly retarded in D.F.s
*p <.00001

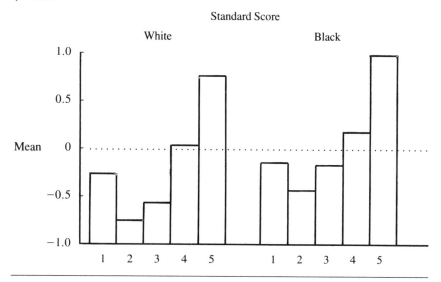

Standard Score

Note. Group Ns: White-   87   192   2383   12485   1864
              Black-   122   864   8084   9676   156

pregnancy, maternal education, and maternal score on a nonverbal intelligence test developed by Science Research Associates (Table 4-1). The three demo-graphic-maternal variables had highly similar nonlinear relationships to IQ level. Seizures in pregnancy were most frequent in the severely retarded group. The socioeconomic index, a percentile score based on occupation and education of head of household and family income (Myrianthopoulos & French, 1968), was higher in the severely retarded than in the mildly retarded, (or, among

Table 4-3

Years of Maternal Education by IQ Group

	1 Severely Retarded		2 Mildly Retarded		3 Borderline		4 Average		5 Above Average		F	r_{IQ}
	M	S.D.	M	S.D.	M	S.D.	M	S.D.	M	S.D.		
White	10.6	2.6	**9.2**	**2.6**	**9.8**	**2.3**	*11.3*	*2.3*	***13.4***	***2.4***	671.00*	.40*
Black	9.5	2.5	9.1	2.3	*9.9*	*2.1*	***10.6***	***2.0***	*11.9*	*2.2*	219.81*	.23*

Differs from severely retarded in D.F.
Differs from mildly retarded in D.F.
Differs from severely and mildly retarded in D.F.s
*$p <.00001$

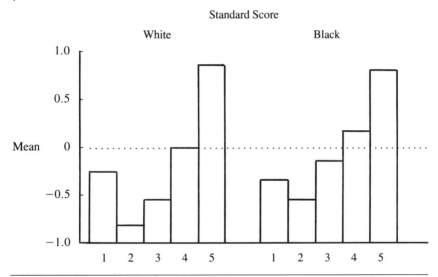

Standard Score

Note. Group Ns: White-   87   195   2407   12513   1865
            Black-   127   882   8213   9782   156

whites, the borderline group) but lower than in the average or above-average groups. Mean scores, shown in Table 4-2, were higher among whites than blacks in all IQ groups and the correlation with IQ score was higher in the white sample. Similarly, a higher level of maternal education discriminated between the severely retarded and the mildly retarded and borderline groups among whites. In both the black and white samples, the level was significantly lower than in the average or above-average group. These data are shown in Table 4-3.

Table 4-4

Maternal SRA Score by IQ Group

	1 Severely Retarded	2 Mildly Retarded	3 Borderline	4 Average	5 Above Average	F	r_{IQ}
	M S.D.	M S.D.	M S.D.	M S.D.	M S.D.		
White	37.7 10.3	34.5 8.9	*38.2 7.9*	***41.8 7.0***	***45.3 5.9***	210.63*	.29*
Black	30.7 8.1	29.9 8.8	*32.7 8.5*	***35.1 8.1***	***39.2 7.3***	94.27*	.20*

Differs from mildly retarded in D.F.
Differs from severely and mildly retarded in D.F.s
*p <.00001

Standard Score

Note. Group Ns: White-   35   97   1559   8484   1307
              Black-   51   463   4620   5620   85

Mothers of the severely retarded had lower scores on the SRA, a 10-minute oddity discrimination test, than did mothers of the average and above-average children in both samples. Among whites, SRA score was less highly correlated with IQ at age 7 than was maternal education (Table 4-4). Seizures were reported in prenatal interviews by more than 3% of the mothers of the severely retarded, discriminating between them and the average and above-average groups among whites, and the mildly retarded, borderline, and average groups among blacks (Table 4-5).

Table 4-5

Seizures in Pregnancy by IQ Group

	1 Severely Retarded	2 Mildly Retarded	3 Borderline	4 Average	5 Above Average	χ^2	r_{IQ}
			Percent				
White	3.57	0.53	1.17	**0.55**	**0.17**	30.11***	−.03**
Black	3.33	**0.71**	**0.47**	**0.39**	0.00	25.03**	−.02*

Group Ns: White-   84 189 2307 11816 1737
           Black- 120 844 7910   9338   149
Differs from severely retarded in D.F.
 *p <.01
 **p <.0001
 ***p <.00001

As shown by the canonical correlations, prenatal factors were most effective in discriminating between the severely retarded and above-average black children ($R = .56$). In the white sample, they were equally effective in discriminating between the extreme groups and the two retarded groups ($R = .36$ and $.34$). The extreme groups among whites differed on five additional variables. Retardation in older siblings, reported in a prenatal interview by mothers of more than

Table 4-6

Retarded Siblings by IQ Group

	1 Severely Retarded	2 Mildly Retarded	3 Borderline	4 Average	5 Above Average	χ^2	r_{IQ}
			Percent				
White	15.52	8.21	**6.52**	*3.26*	**2.20**	75.56**	−.09**
Black	7.14	3.32	4.06	3.41	2.00	6.50	−.02*

Group Ns: White-   58 134 1610 8183 1000
           Black-   70 542 4831 5756   100
Differs from severely retarded in D.F.
Differs from severely and mildly retarded in D.F.s
 *p <.05
 **p <.00001

Table 4-7

Maternal Parity by IQ Group

	1 Severely Retarded		2 Mildly Retarded		3 Borderline		4 Average		5 Above Average		F	r_{IQ}
	M	S.D.	M	S.D.	M	S.D.	M	S.D.	M	S.D.		
White	2.2	2.2	2.3	2.2	2.2	2.1	1.8	1.9	*1.1*	*1.4*	95.91*	−.16*
Black	2.5	2.6	2.9	2.9	*2.4*	*2.4*	2.2	2.2	*1.9*	*1.9*	27.77*	−.08*

Differs from mildly retarded in D.F.
Differs from severely and mildly retarded in D.F.s
*p <.00001

Standard Score

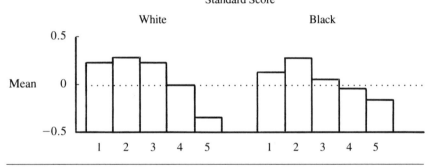

Note. Group Ns: White-   91   200 2470 12751 1886
               Black-   128   891 8307   9903   158

15% of the severely retarded, was a discriminator in comparisons with the borderline and average groups as well as the above-average (Table 4-6). Parity, or number of previous pregnancies of at least 20 weeks, was higher for mothers of the severely retarded and the number of prenatal visits was lower; a significant factor in comparison with the average group also. The modest negative correlation between parity and IQ was higher among whites than blacks (Table 4-7). The number of prenatal visits was positively correlated with IQ in both samples (Table 4-8). The frequencies of reported hospitalization early in pregnancy (prior to the first prenatal visit) and of maternal anemia were higher in the severely retarded than in the above-average group (Table 4-9). The prevalence of anemia, defined as any hemoglobin reading under 10 or hematocrit under 30%, was strikingly higher among blacks than whites. An additional discriminator between extreme groups in the black sample was a shorter pregnancy-free

Table 4-8
Number of Prenatal Visits by IQ Group

	1 Severely Retarded		2 Mildly Retarded		3 Borderline		4 Average		5 Above Average		F	r_{IQ}
	M	S.D.	M	S.D.	M	S.D.	M	S.D.	M	S.D.		
White	8.5	4.4	8.4	4.2	8.7	4.2	*10.0*	*4.1*	***11.3***	***3.6***	116.85*	.18*
Black	7.4	3.7	6.8	3.5	*7.4*	*3.5*	*8.2*	*3.6*	*9.3*	*3.7*	78.44*	.13*

Differs from mildly retarded in D.F.
Differs from severely and mildly retarded in D.F.
*p <.00001

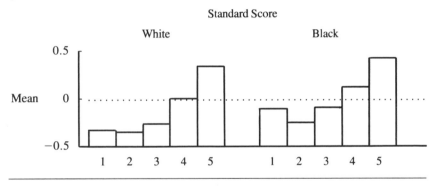

Standard Score

Note. Group Ns: White-   92   200   2467   12766   1885
Black-   128   894   8311   9911   157

interval for mothers of the severely retarded (an opposite finding was significant for whites in comparison with the borderline group). Lower reported birthweight of the previous child was a significant factor in comparisons with all nonretarded groups (Table 4-10).

The severely and mildly retarded groups in the white sample differed in the maternal factors of weight gain in pregnancy and age at menarche. The lower weight gain among mothers of the severely retarded discriminated between them and mothers of the borderline and average children as well (Table 4-11). Age at menarche, however, was similar to that in the nonretarded groups, with the oldest age reported by mothers of the mildly retarded (Table 4-12). Additional discriminators between retarded groups in the black sample were also negative risk factors for severe retardation; housing density, or persons per room, was lower among families of the severely retarded (Table 4-13), and maternal uri-

Table 4-9

Pregnancy Complications: Hospitalizations and Anemia by IQ Group

	1 Severely Retarded	2 Mildly Retarded	3 Borderline	4 Average	5 Above Average	χ^2	r_{IQ}
			Percent				
			Hospitalization in Early Pregnancy				
White	18.68	21.00	17.90	*13.72*	**9.07**	79.96***	− .07***
Black	21.09	16.82	14.57	*13.71*	16.67	13.44*	− .03**
Group Ns: White -	91	200	2452	12694	1885		
Black -	128	892	8247	9839	156		
			Anemia in Pregnancy				
White	13.04	14.00	13.41	9.65	**4.84**	94.63***	− .09***
Black	39.52	39.01	36.67	32.76	27.10	42.89***	− .06***
Group Ns: White -	92	200	2461	12721	1882		
Black -	124	887	8247	9835	155		

Differs from mildly retarded in D.F.
Differs from severely and mildly retarded in D.F.s
  *$p<.01$
 **$p<.001$
***$p<.00001$

nary tract infection in pregnancy was less frequent than in either the mildly retarded or borderline group (Table 4-14).

Other prenatal characteristics were identified in comparisons with the borderline group. Rubella in pregnancy among whites and the rare complication of rheumatic fever among blacks were more frequent among mothers of the severely retarded children (Table 4-15). In the black sample, a fetal or neonatal death was more often reported as the outcome of the last pregnancy (Table 4-16), and mothers were older at registration for prenatal care than mothers of children in the borderline group (Table 4-17). When compared with the average group, mothers of the severely retarded black children had a higher frequency of toxemia, defined by Friedman and Neff (1977) as presence of elevated blood pressure and/or proteinuria during pregnancy (Table 4-18), and were less often employed in the prenatal period (Table 4-19). The positive correlation between maternal employment and IQ, however, was higher in the white sample.

Table 4-10

Maternal Characteristics: Pregnancy-free Interval and Birthweight of Previous Child by IQ Group

	1 Severely Retarded		2 Mildly Retarded		3 Borderline		4 Average		5 Above Average		F	r_{IQ}
	M	S.D.	M	S.D.	M	S.D.	M	S.D.	M	S.D.		
Pregnancy-free Interval (yr.)												
White	2.2	2.5	1.7	2.0	**1.6**	**1.9**	1.8	2.1	1.9	2.1	4.66**	.03***
Black	1.6	2.0	1.3	1.7	*1.7*	*2.2*	2.0	2.4	**2.5**	**2.7**	29.98****	.09****
Group Ns: White -	67		144		1843		8949		1066			
Black -	92		668		5999		7117		112			
Birthweight of Previous Child (g)												
White	3261	649	3270	533	3226	632	3279	579	3319	540	4.16*	.05****
Black	2903	634	2976	641	*3048*	*605*	*3072*	*613*	**3102**	**554**	5.14**	.05****
Group Ns: White -	61		124		1598		7721		898			
Black -	76		575		5214		6050		102			

Differs from severely retarded in D.F.
Differs from mildly retarded in D.F.
Differs from severely and mildly retarded in D.F.s
  *p<.05
  **p<.01
  ***p<.001
  ****p<.00001

Many of the prenatal factors related to severe retardation were also related to mild retardation. These relationships are examined in a later section. Risk factors unique to the severely retarded were the pregnancy complications of seizures, low weight gain, rubella, and rheumatic fever, and prior reproductive loss.

Obstetric Factors

With one exception, the white and black samples differed in the obstetric factors associated with severe retardation (Table 4-20). The exception was breech delivery, a major discriminator between the severely retarded and non-retarded groups. From maximum values of 9% among whites and 7% among

Table 4-11
Maternal Weight Gain in Pounds by IQ Group

	1 Severely Retarded		2 Mildly Retarded		3 Borderline		4 Average		5 Above Average		F	r_{IQ}
	M	S.D.	M	S.D.	M	S.D.	M	S.D.	M	S.D.		
White	20.9	10.5	**24.2**	**11.8**	**23.4**	**10.7**	**23.5**	**9.6**	22.6	8.1	5.53***	−.02*
Black	22.8	11.6	21.8	12.3	22.7	11.5	23.0	10.7	23.8	8.3	3.04*	.02**

Group Ns: White- 86 186 2385 12446 1851
Black- 119 845 8009 9604 149
Differs from severely retarded in D.F.
*p <.05
**p <.01
***p <.001

Table 4-12
Maternal Age at Menarche by IQ Group

	1 Severely Retarded		2 Mildly Retarded		3 Borderline		4 Average		5 Above Average		F	r_{IQ}
	M	S.D.	M	S.D.	M	S.D.	M	S.D.	M	S.D.		
White	12.6	1.3	**13.3**	**1.7**	*12.8*	*1.6*	*12.6*	*1.5*	*12.6*	*1.4*	12.53**	−.04**
Black	12.9	1.4	12.7	1.5	12.7	1.5	12.7	1.6	12.5	1.5	4.75*	−.03**

Differs from severely retarded in D.F.
Differs from mildly retarded in D.F.
*p <.001
**p <.00001

Standard Score

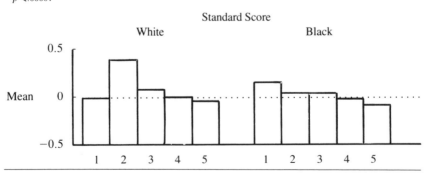

Note. Group Ns: White- 89 195 2430 12620 1871
Black- 127 886 8225 9839 155

Table 4-13

Housing Density by IQ Group

	1 Severely Retarded		2 Mildly Retarded		3 Borderline		4 Average		5 Above Average		F	r_{IQ}
	M	S.D.	M	S.D.	M	S.D.	M	S.D.	M	S.D.		
White	1.2	0.6	1.4	0.9	*1.3*	*0.6*	*1.1*	*0.5*	*0.9*	*0.4*	120.95*	−.18*
Black	1.6	0.8	**1.9**	**1.0**	1.7	0.9	*1.5*	*0.8*	1.2	0.6	97.90*	−.16*

Differs from severely retarded in D.F.
Differs from mildly retarded in D.F.
$*p < .00001$

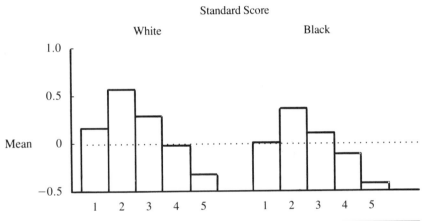

Standard Score

White   Black

Mean

Note. Group Ns: White-   86   193   2400   12493   1862
Black-   128   877   8173   9724   152

blacks, the relative frequency of breech delivery decreased with increasing IQ level (Table 4-21). Negative correlations with IQ were significant but less than .05. Midforceps delivery and low fetal heart rate were important discriminators in the white sample. Midforceps, defined as application of forceps when biparietal diameter of head is engaged but skull is not on perineal floor, were used in almost one fourth of the deliveries of the severely retarded, discriminating between them and the mildly retarded, borderline, and average groups (Table 4-22). The dramatically lower fetal heart rate in the first stage of labor among the severely retarded white children is shown in Table 4-23. These values were the lowest recorded during monitoring at intervals of 30 minutes or less.

Table 4-14

Urinary Tract Infection in Pregnancy by IQ Group

	1 Severely Retarded	2 Mildly Retarded	3 Borderline	4 Average	5 Above Average	χ^2	r_{IQ}
			Percent				
White	14.29	19.30	13.92	*12.07*	*9.38*	25.21**	−.05***
Black	14.42	**24.18**	**24.03**	21.96	17.78	16.31*	−.02*

Differs from severely retarded in D.F.

Differs from mildly retarded in D.F.

 *p <.01

 **p <.0001

 ***p <.00001

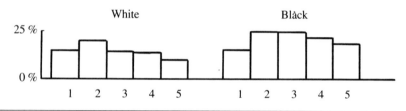

Note. Group Ns: White-   77   171 1976 10312 1504

Black- 104   761 7078   8407   135

Major discriminators in the black sample were intravenous anesthetics at delivery, meconium staining, and low placental weight. General anesthetics were administered via the intravenous route to approximately 3% of the severely retarded compared with less than 1% of the mildly retarded, borderline, or average groups (Table 4-24). Although the indications for this rare procedure were not directly assessed, the analyses show that its use made an independent contribution to differentiation between the severely retarded and comparison groups. Meconium staining, a sign of perinatal anoxia, was present most frequently among the severely retarded, discriminating between them and the mildly retarded, borderline, and average groups. Placental weight, which increased linearly with IQ level, was significantly lower for the severely retarded than for any nonretarded group (Table 4-25).

Other discriminating characteristics of labor were identified in comparisons with the average group: a shorter second stage among severely retarded whites and a lower value for the highest fetal heart rate in the first stage among severely retarded blacks (Table 4-26). In the latter group, augmentation of labor by

Table 4-15

Pregnancy Complications: Rubella and Rheumatic Fever by IQ Group

	1 Severely Retarded	2 Mildly Retarded	3 Borderline	4 Average	5 Above Average	χ^2	r_{IQ}
			Percent				
			Rubella in Pregnancy				
White	2.17	1.00	**0.28**	0.40	0.58	10.80*	−.00
Black	0.81	0.56	0.46	0.38	0.00	2.30	−.01
Group Ns: White -	92	200	2468	12740	1883		
Black -	124	891	8262	9853	156		
			Rheumatic Fever in Pregnancy				
White	0.00	0.00	0.13	0.08	0.05	0.96	−.00
Black	0.83	0.00	**0.02**	0.07	0.00	16.10**	−.01
Group Ns: White -	91	192	2345	12148	1824		
Black -	120	865	8009	9529	151		

Differs from severely retarded in D.F.
 *$p<.05$
**$p<.01$

Table 4-16

Fetal or Neonatal Death at Last Delivery by IQ Group

	1 Severely Retarded	2 Mildly Retarded	3 Borderline	4 Average	5 Above Average	χ^2	r_{IQ}
			Percent				
White	13.24	14.48	15.57	15.01	16.75	2.64	.02
Black	23.66	15.69	**15.38**	17.38	13.91	13.72*	.02

Group Ns: White -   68 145 1830 8899 1057
          Black -   93 663 5981 7078 115

Differs from severely retarded in D.F.
 *$p<.01$

Table 4-17
Maternal Age by IQ Group

	1 Severely Retarded	2 Mildly Retarded	3 Borderline	4 Average	5 Above Average	F	r_{IQ}
	M S.D.	M S.D.	M S.D.	M S.D.	M S.D.		
White	25.6 6.6	25.3 6.2	24.7 6.1	24.9 5.9	24.9 5.2	1.32	.01
Black	25.0 7.6	23.8 6.4	**23.4 6.2**	24.1 6.3	*26.6 6.3*	22.40*	.05*

Differs from severely retarded in D.F.
Differs from mildly retarded in D.F.
*$p < .00001$

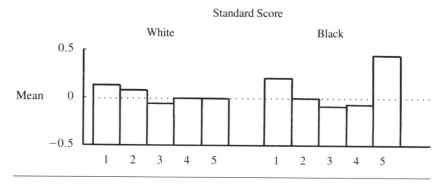

Standard Score

Note. Group Ns: White-   92   201   2473   12777   1889
               Black-   128   895   8319   9919   158

amniotomy or use of oxytocic drugs was less frequent than in the average group (Table 4-27). At delivery, type of presentation was related to severe retardation. Among whites, the occiput posterior position was more frequent in the severely retarded and the more common occiput anterior position less frequent (Table 4-28), factors significant in comparisons with the above-average and borderline groups, respectively. In the black sample, a higher frequency of rare presentations classified as abnormal (face, chin, brow, or shoulder) discriminated between the severely retarded and the average group.

Other significant events during delivery were use of anesthetic agents and the presence of certain abnormalities. More frequent exposure to inhalation anesthetics discriminated between the severely retarded and the above-average in the white sample (Table 4-29). The moderately low negative correlation between this variable and IQ was .14. An opposite trend was found in the black sample where the correlation between inhalation anesthetics and IQ was

Table 4-18

Toxemia in Pregnancy by IQ Group

	1 Severely Retarded	2 Mildly Retarded	3 Borderline	4 Average	5 Above Average	χ^2	r_{IQ}
			Percent				
White	13.51	11.24	10.00	9.90	9.54	1.67	−.01
Black	16.83	14.29	*10.43*	**9.34**	11.20	26.46**	−.03*

Group Ns: White-   74 169 2091 10724 1614
          Black- 101 756 7409   8932   125
Differs from mildly retarded in D.F.
Differs from severely and mildly retarded in D.F.s
*$p <.001$
**$p <.0001$

only .05, but positive. Less frequent use of anesthetics of any type discriminated between the severely retarded and the above-average among blacks. Higher frequencies of polyhydramnios and single umbilical artery among severely retarded whites were significant in the comparison with the average group (Table 4-30). Polyhydramnios, present in 7% of the deliveries of the severely retarded, is an excess of amniotic fluid sometimes associated with fetal malformations. A lower frequency of cord complications discriminated between the severely retarded blacks and the borderline and average groups.

Table 4-19

Mother Employed by IQ Group

	1 Severely Retarded	2 Mildly Retarded	3 Borderline	4 Average	5 Above Average	χ^2	r_{IQ}
			Percent				
White	9.30	8.16	9.09	16.70	31.94	414.35*	.17*
Black	6.25	8.49	11.21	**15.29**	23.08	101.15*	.08*

Group Ns: White-   86 196 2408 12566 1869
          Black- 128 883 8209   9780   156
Differs from severely retarded in D.F.
*$p <.00001$

Table 4-20
Standardized Coefficients for Obstetric Discriminators Between
the Severely Retarded and Comparison Groups

Variable	Comparison Group							
	White				Black			
	MR	BL	AV	AA	MR	BL	AV	AA
Breech delivery	—	—	.24	.36	—	.42	.37	.37
Midforceps delivery	1.00	.40	.37	—	—	—	—	—
Lowest FHR in 1st stage of labor	—	−.69	−.57	−.59	—	—	—	—
Occiput anterior presentation	—	−.43	—	—	—	—	—	—
Polyhydramnios	—	—	.56	—	—	—	—	—
Single umbilical artery	—	—	.35	—	—	—	—	—
Inhalation anesthetic at delivery	—	—	—	.55	—	—	—	—
Occiput posterior presentation	—	—	—	.36	—	—	—	—
Length of 2nd stage of labor	—	—	—	−.31	—	—	—	—
Intravenous anesthetic at delivery	—	—	—	—	.79	.52	.32	—
Meconium staining	—	—	—	—	.59	.40	.33	—
Placental weight	—	—	—	—	—	−.52	−.57	−.55
Cord complications	—	—	—	—	—	−.32	−.32	—
Abnormal presentation at delivery[a]	—	—	—	—	—	—	.31	—
Augmentation of labor	—	—	—	—	—	—	−.23	—
Anesthetics at delivery	—	—	—	—	—	—	—	−.48
Highest FHR in 1st stage of labor	—	—	—	—	—	—	—	−.41
Canonical correlation	*.25**￼*	*.12***￼*	*.07***￼*	*.17***￼*	*.11*￼*	*.07***￼*	*.08***￼*	*.37***￼*

[a]Face, chin, brow, or shoulder

*$p<.01$

**$p<.001$

***$p<.00001$

Table 4-21

Breech Delivery by IQ Group

	1 Severely Retarded	2 Mildly Retarded	3 Borderline	4 Average	5 Above Average	χ^2	r_{IQ}
			Percent				
White	8.89	6.50	4.62	*3.17*	**2.86**	28.87**	−.04***
Black	7.03	3.37	**2.59**	**2.34**	**0.63**	17.12*	−.03**

Group Ns: White-   90 200 2465 12756 1887
          Black- 128 890 8292 9892   158
Differs from severely retarded in D.F.
Differs from severely and mildly retarded in D.F.s
  p <.01
  **p* <.0001
  ***p* <.00001

In most of the comparisons, canonical correlations between obstetric factors and the group classification were low, indicating the limited explanatory power of these variables. The best discrimination was between the severely retarded and the above-average groups in the black sample ($R = .37$) and the severely and mildly retarded groups in the white sample ($R = .25$). The latter comparison was unusual in that only a single discriminator, use of midforceps, was

Table 4-22

Midforceps Delivery by IQ Group

	1 Severely Retarded	2 Mildly Retarded	3 Borderline	4 Average	5 Above Average	χ^2	r_{IQ}
			Percent				
White	23.68	**6.32**	**10.54**	**12.85**	*16.07*	40.64*	.05*
Black	4.72	4.91	5.05	5.14	9.93	6.89	.01

Group Ns: White-   76 174 2145 11475 1718
          Black- 106 795 7523   8964   141
Differs from severely retarded in D.F.s
Differs from mildly retarded in D.F.
  p <.00001

Table 4-23

Lowest Fetal Heart Rate in First Stage of Labor by IQ Group

	1 Severely Retarded	2 Mildly Retarded	3 Borderline	4 Average	5 Above Average	F	r_{IQ}
	M S.D.	M S.D.	M S.D.	M S.D.	M S.D.		
White	119.4 20.1	125.5 14.9	**125.9 13.2**	**125.6 12.9**	**125.3 12.6**	4.08*	−.00
Black	130.6 12.3	131.4 12.7	131.2 13.3	130.8 13.2	129.0 16.0	1.93	−.03*

Differs from severely retarded in D.F.
*p <.01

Standard Score

Note. Group Ns: White- 64 142 1770 9417 1397
Black- 90 655 6275 7652 112

retained. In other analyses, canonical correlations ranged from .07 to .17. It is of considerable importance to identify obstetric risk factors for severe cognitive deficit, even though they may be rare occurrences. Those unique to the severely retarded were midforceps delivery, occiput posterior presentation, intravenous anesthetics, meconium staining, polyhydramnios, and single umbilical artery. In the following section, obstetric factors are combined with indices of socioeconomic status and other significant prenatal factors.

Summary Analyses

The prenatal and obstetric discriminators were analyzed together to determine their combined effectiveness and the robustness of individual variables as contributors to group differences in the period prior to birth. The canonical correla-

Table 4-24

**Obstetric Complications: Intravenous Anesthetic and Meconium Staining
by IQ Group**

	1 Severely Retarded	2 Mildly Retarded	3 Borderline	4 Average	5 Above Average	χ^2	r_{IQ}
			Percent				
		Intravenous Anesthetic at Delivery					
White	2.22	1.00	1.64	1.22	0.96	5.18	$-.02**$
Black	3.15	**0.57**	**0.74**	**0.97**	1.90	13.08*	.02*
Group Ns: White -	90	200	2441	12661	1878		
Black -	127	880	8226	9837	158		
		Meconium Staining					
White	24.72	21.50	19.11	19.43	17.01	8.65	$-.02*$
Black	28.33	**19.91**	**19.59**	**20.05**	22.73	6.73	.00
Group Ns: White -	89	200	2439	12686	1875		
Black -	120	879	8085	9604	154		

Differs from severely retarded in D.F.
*$p<.05$
**$p<.01$

tions from the summary analyses were highly similar to those for prenatal factors alone (Table 4-31). The largest increase was from .34 to .39 in the comparison between the severely and mildly retarded white children. All but one of the 21 prenatal factors and 12 of the 17 obstetric factors were retained. Those eliminated were discriminators between the severely retarded and the above-average group with one exception: among whites, hospitalization in early pregnancy, length of the second stage of labor, inhalation anesthetics at delivery, and occiput posterior presentation were no longer significant. In the black sample, the negative risk factors of less frequent administration of anesthesia and less augmentation of labor were not retained in comparisons with the above-average and average group, respectively. The most important of the combined discriminators included both maternal and family characteristics and complications of pregnancy and delivery.

Table 4-25

Placental Weight in Grams by IQ Group

	1 Severely Retarded		2 Mildly Retarded		3 Borderline		4 Average		5 Above Average		F	r_{IQ}
	M	S.D.	M	S.D.	M	S.D.	M	S.D.	M	S.D.		
White	432.4	104.0	445.0	114.5	440.5	100.7	449.5	96.0	448.3	89.8	4.56*	.03*
Black	396.7	123.2	409.0	100.7	*421.1*	*96.0*	*431.0*	*94.4*	*449.6*	*94.1*	19.97**	.08**

Differs from severely and mildly retarded in D.F.s
*p <.01
**p <.00001

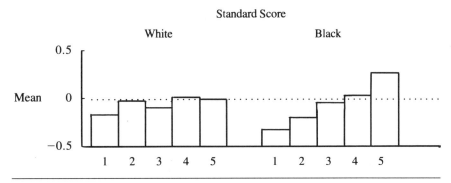

Note. Group Ns: White-   82   171 2206 11565 1726
Black- 110   753 6794   7942   121

THE MILDLY RETARDED

Prenatal Factors

Major discriminators between the mildly retarded and higher IQ groups in the prenatal period were indices of maternal intelligence, education, socioeconomic status, and amount of prenatal care (Table 4-32). As shown in tables presented earlier, values for each of these variables increased across IQ level from the mildly retarded to the above average. In both samples, mothers of the mildly retarded had lower scores on the SRA, a brief test of nonverbal intelligence, than did mothers of children in the three higher IQ groups. Less maternal education, lower socioeconomic index scores, and fewer prenatal clinic visits discriminated between the mildly retarded and all higher IQ groups except for the borderline among whites.

Table 4-26

Obstetric Conditions: Length of Labor and Fetal Heart Rate by IQ Group

	1 Severely Retarded		2 Mildly Retarded		3 Borderline		4 Average		5 Above Average		F	r_{IQ}
	M	S.D.	M	S.D.	M	S.D.	M	S.D.	M	S.D.		

Length of Second Stage of Labor (min.)

White	29.8	36.9	30.1	38.8	30.5	37.8	33.8	38.3	*40.4*	*41.0*	17.21****	.07****
Black	22.3	29.8	21.9	30.5	21.1	27.0	23.1	29.9	29.4	37.3	6.11**	.03*

Group Ns: White -   75   174   2138   11448   1725

Black -   99   680   6150   7417   128

Highest Fetal Heart Rate in First Stage of Labor

White	147.3	10.5	147.4	9.9	148.8	11.7	*150.0*	*12.0*	*150.2*	*11.5*	6.50***	.04***
Black	148.2	10.9	149.2	10.3	149.6	10.5	*150.2*	*10.7*	*151.5*	*11.8*	4.20*	.03*

Group Ns: White -   64   142   1770   9417   1397

Black -   90   655   6275   7652   112

Differs from mildly retarded in D.F.

Differs from severely and mildly retarded in D.F.s

   *$p<.01$

  **$p<.001$

 ***$p<.0001$

****$p<.00001$

Table 4-27

Augmentation of Labor by IQ Group

	1 Severely Retarded	2 Mildly Retarded	3 Borderline	4 Average	5 Above Average	χ^2	r_{IQ}
			Percent				
White	36.78	26.49	28.94	36.33	38.98	63.22*	.07*
Black	21.19	29.07	30.00	**32.04**	33.57	15.61*	.03*

Group Ns: White -   87   185   2308   12022   1811

Black -   118   829   7824   9325   143

Differs from severely retarded in D.F.

*$p<.00001$

Table 4-28
Presentation at Delivery by IQ Group

	1 Severely Retarded	2 Mildly Retarded	3 Borderline	4 Average	5 Above Average	χ^2	r_{IQ}
			Percent				
Occiput Anterior Presentation							
White	75.00	88.14	**86.96**	88.82	89.53	24.51***	.03***
Black	84.00	88.25	89.51	89.46	86.93	6.15	.01
Occiput Posterior Presentation							
White	12.50	4.12	7.23	7.02	**6.42**	7.71	− .01
Black	4.80	7.26	7.08	7.29	11.11	4.85	.01
Abnormal Presentation at Delivery							
White	2.27	0.52	0.76	0.76	0.49	4.69	− .02*
Black	2.40	1.27	0.64	*0.59*	0.65	11.53*	− .02**

Group Ns: White -   88 194 2378 12457 1853
Black - 125 868 8134 9675   153

Differs from severely retarded in D.F.
Differs from severely and mildly retarded in D.F.s
  *p<.05
 **p<.01
***p<.0001

Other characteristics of the mildly retarded common to both samples were higher housing density, higher maternal parity, and more hospitalizations early in pregnancy. Housing density had the largest coefficients and was consistently significant in the white sample. Maternal risk factors unique to the mildly retarded were a higher frequency of self-reported retardation (Table 4-33), and, of less importance among whites, shorter stature as compared with the average and above-average groups (Table 4-34).

In the white sample only, mothers of the mildly retarded reported an age at menarche that was significantly older than in any other IQ group. Higher frequencies of urinary tract infection in pregnancy, anemia, and the unique complication of toxoplasmosis (Table 4-35) discriminated between the mildly

Table 4-29

Anesthetics at Delivery: Inhalation and All Agents Combined by IQ Group

	1 Severely Retarded	2 Mildly Retarded	3 Borderline	4 Average	5 Above Average	χ^2	r_{IQ}
			Percent				
			Inhalation Anesthetic at Delivery				
White	33.33	47.00	*37.94*	*27.53*	**16.51**	280.61*	−.14*
Black	38.58	36.14	*39.70*	*43.80*	*48.73*	46.26*	.05*

Group Ns: White - 90 200 2441 12661 1878

Black - 127 880 8224 9836 158

			Anesthetics at Delivery				
White	90.00	90.00	90.91	93.55	95.69	46.04*	.05*
Black	72.44	66.70	73.46	79.33	**89.87**	148.51*	.10*

Group Ns: White - 90 200 2442 12665 1879

Black - 127 880 8229 9840 158

Differs from severely retarded in D.F.
Differs from mildly retarded in D.F.
Differs from severely and mildly retarded in D.F.s
*p<.00001

retarded and the average and/or above-average groups. Maternal reports of retardation in the father (Table 4-36) and, as shown earlier, in the older siblings of the mildly retarded were significant in the average group comparison. Several negative risk factors were identified: fewer of the mothers of the mildly retarded reported any exposure to abdomino-pelvic x-rays (Table 4-37), they smoked less in pregnancy than mothers of children in the borderline or average groups (Table 4-38), and fewer of them reported recent illnesses at registration for prenatal care.

Among blacks, a lower hematocrit in pregnancy discriminated between mothers of the mildly retarded and those of children in all higher IQ groups (Table 4-39). Other significant pregnancy complications were higher frequencies of toxemia, and the unique conditions of heart disease and unspecified bacterial infection (Table 4-40). Characteristics of reproductive history related to mild retardation were a shorter pregnancy-free interval, lower birthweight of the last child, and, as compared with the borderline group only, a higher

Table 4-30

Obstetric Complications: Polyhydramnios, Umbilical Artery, and Cord by IQ Group

	1 Severely Retarded	2 Mildly Retarded	3 Borderline	4 Average	5 Above Average	χ^2	r_{IQ}
			Percent				
			Polyhydramnios				
White	6.78	2.17	2.29	**1.72**	2.31	11.19*	−.02
Black	3.28	1.56	1.24	1.81	1.61	6.87	.01
Group Ns: White -	59	92	1443	7734	1212		
Black -	61	514	5075	5750	62		
			Single Umbilical Artery				
White	3.61	2.29	1.07	**0.89**	0.86	10.61*	−.02**
Black	1.72	0.73	0.38	0.42	0.00	7.38	−.01
Group Ns: White -	83	175	2237	11698	1736		
Black -	116	821	7610	9022	133		
			Cord Complications				
White	31.46	32.82	31.19	32.75	32.89	2.42	.00
Black	16.80	23.89	**24.80**	**26.60**	28.48	14.93**	.03***
Group Ns: White -	89	195	2424	12654	1873		
Black -	125	879	8156	9739	158		

Differs from severely retarded in D.F.
*$p<.05$
**$p<.01$
***$p<.0001$

frequency of prior fetal death (Table 4-41). Mothers of the mildly retarded were younger than those of the above-average group. As shown earlier in Table 4-17, the correlation between maternal age and IQ was only .05 in the black sample and insignificant among whites. Less edema in pregnancy was the only negative risk factor for mild retardation in the black sample (Table 4-40).

Prenatal characteristics, especially maternal and demographic ones, were effective discriminators between the mildly retarded and the above average. Canonical correlations were .58 and .62 in the white and black samples, respec-

Table 4-31
Standardized Coefficients for Prenatal and Obstetric Discriminators Between the Severely Retarded and Comparison Groups

Variable	White				Black			
	MR	BL	AV	AA	MR	BL	AV	AA
Seizures in pregnancy	—	—	.29	.25	.45	.43	.39	—
Socioeconomic index	—	.26	−.05	−.23	.35	—	—	−.44
Maternal SRA score	—	—	−.33	−.27	—	—	−.19	−.62
Maternal education	.58	.25	—	−.26	—	—	−.44	—
Breech delivery	—	—	.21	.18	—	.23	.27	—
Pregnancy-free interval	—	.24	—	—	—	—	—	−.18
Midforceps delivery	.58	.26	.31	—	—	—	—	—
Weight gain during pregnancy	−.35	−.27	−.17	—	—	—	—	—
Lowest FHR in 1st stage of labor	—	−.39	−.39	−.28	—	—	—	—
Retarded siblings	—	.42	.46	.36	—	—	—	—
Number of prenatal visits	—	—	−.30	−.25	—	—	—	—
Age at menarche	−.39	—	—	—	—	—	—	—
Rubella in pregnancy	—	.30	—	—	—	—	—	—
Occiput anterior presentation	—	−.28	—	—	—	—	—	—
Polyhydramnios	—	—	.30	—	—	—	—	—
Single umbilical artery	—	—	.27	—	—	—	—	—
Parity	—	—	—	.15	—	—	—	—
Anemia in pregnancy	—	—	—	.14	—	—	—	—
Intravenous anesthetic at delivery	—	—	—	—	.44	.31	.24	—
Meconium staining	—	—	—	—	.29	.22	.21	—
Cord complications	—	—	—	—	—	−.22	−.23	—
Placental weight	—	—	—	—	—	−.18	−.37	—
Birthweight of last child	—	—	—	—	—	−.19	—	−.20
Urinary tract infection in pregnancy	—	—	—	—	−.43	−.29	—	—
Housing density	—	—	—	—	−.37	—	—	—

(continued)

Table 4-31 (continued)

Variable	Comparison Group							
	White				Black			
	MR	BL	AV	AA	MR	BL	AV	AA
Rheumatic fever in pregnancy	—	—	—	—	—	.49	—	—
Maternal age	—	—	—	—	—	.30	—	—
Fetal or neonatal death at last delivery	—	—	—	—	—	.23	—	—
Mother employed	—	—	—	—	—	—	−.24	—
Toxemia	—	—	—	—	—	—	.22	—
Abnormal presentation at delivery[a]	—	—	—	—	—	—	.18	—
Highest FHR in 1st stage of labor	—	—	—	—	—	—	—	−.23
Canonical correlation	*.39**	*.17**	*.11**	*.37**	*.21**	*.11**	*.11**	*.58**

[a]Face, chin, brow, or shoulder

*$p < .00001$

tively. In other comparisons, the best discrimination was obtained between the mildly retarded and the average group in the black sample.

Obstetric Factors

Events of labor and delivery related to mild retardation are shown in Table 4-42. The highest fetal heart rate recorded in the first stage of labor was significantly lower for the mildly retarded than the average or above-average groups in both samples (see Table 4-26). A higher frequency of placenta previa discriminated between the mildly retarded and the borderline group and, among whites, the above-average group. Values for this discriminator and the four other obstetric ones unique to the mildly retarded are shown in Table 4-43. More frequent administration of inhalation anesthetics was a major discriminator between mildly retarded white children and all higher IQ groups. Among blacks, however, inhalation anesthetics were given less frequently to mothers of the mildly retarded (see Table 4-29). The effects of socioeconomic status and other prenatal characteristics on these relationships are assessed in summary analyses of

Table 4-32
Standardized Coefficients for Prenatal Discriminators Between
the Mildly Retarded and Comparison Groups

Variable	Comparison Group					
	White			Black		
	BL	AV	AA	BL	AV	AA
Maternal SRA score	−.53	−.32	−.36	−.38	−.38	−.41
Maternal education	—	−.21	−.20	−.43	−.39	−.18
Socioeconomic index	—	−.19	−.37	−.18	−.18	−.45
Number of prenatal visits	—	−.17	−.12	−.20	−.23	−.17
Retarded mother	.35	.33	.15	—	.11	—
Housing density	.31	.23	.15	—	.22	—
Parity	—	—	.08	.08	—	.27
Hospitalizations since LMP	—	.13	.09	—	.06	—
Maternal height	—	−.05	−.04	—	−.10	—
Age at menarche	.37	.21	.12	—	—	—
Cigarettes per day in pregnancy	−.33	−.21	—	—	—	—
Abdomino-pelvic x-rays	−.33	−.13	—	—	—	—
Urinary tract infection in pregnancy	—	.13	.09	—	—	—
Toxoplasmosis in pregnancy	—	.25	—	—	—	—
Retarded father	—	.19	—	—	—	—
Retarded siblings	—	.16	—	—	—	—
Anemia in pregnancy	—	—	.10	—	—	—
Recent maternal illnesses	—	—	−.08	—	—	—
Hematocrit in pregnancy	—	—	—	−.16	−.08	−.07
Pregnancy-free interval	—	—	—	−.33	−.25	—
Toxemia	—	—	—	.22	.15	—
Birthweight of last child	—	—	—	−.18	−.15	—
Organic heart disease in pregnancy	—	—	—	.17	.11	—
Maternal age	—	—	—	—	—	−.47
Prior fetal death	—	—	—	.21	—	—
Bacterial infection in pregnancy	—	—	—	—	.08	—
Edema in pregnancy	—	—	—	—	−.07	—
Canonical correlation	*.16**	*.18**	*.58**	*.17**	*.29**	*.62**

*p<.00001

Table 4-33
Retarded Mother by IQ Group

	1 Severely Retarded	2 Mildly Retarded	3 Borderline	4 Average	5 Above Average	χ^2	r_{IQ}
			Percent				
White	0.00	4.71	*1.42*	*0.41*	*0.11*	102.68*	−.06*
Black	2.46	3.13	1.76	*0.73*	0.00	64.37*	−.06*

Group Ns: White-　87　191　2401　12502　1864
　　　　　 Black-　122　863　8068　9622　154
Differs from mildly retarded in D.F.
$p < .00001$

Table 4-34
Maternal Height in Inches by IQ Group

	1 Severely Retarded		2 Mildly Retarded		3 Borderline		4 Average		5 Above Average		F	r_{IQ}
	M	S.D.	M	S.D.	M	S.D.	M	S.D.	M	S.D.		
White	63.3	2.3	62.8	2.3	63.2	2.7	*63.6*	*2.6*	*64.3*	*2.5*	46.35*	.13*
Black	63.3	2.5	63.1	2.6	63.4	2.6	*63.5*	*2.6*	63.8	3.1	10.48*	.05*

Differs from mildly retarded in D.F.
$p < .00001$

Standard Score

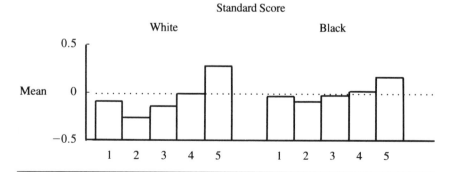

Note. Group Ns: White-　79　185　2246　11332　1665
　　　　　　　　 Black-　123　867　8084　9560　142

Table 4-35
Toxoplasmosis in Pregnancy by IQ Group

	1 Severely Retarded	2 Mildly Retarded	3 Borderline	4 Average	5 Above Average	χ^2	r_{IQ}
			Percent				
White	0.00	1.80	0.00	*0.19*	0.14	18.07*	−.01
Black	1.33	0.00	0.30	0.29	0.00	4.43	−.01

Group Ns: White - 32 111 1114 5132 696
Black - 75 419 3625 4547 102

Differs from mildly retarded in D.F.
*$p<.01$

discriminators from the two epochs. Conduction anesthetics were also given less frequently to mothers of mildly retarded black children (Table 4-43). Negative risk factors in the white sample were induction of labor and midforceps delivery. Both of these procedures were used less frequently among the mildly retarded than in the average or above-average group.

Other obstetric factors were positively related to mild retardation in the white or black sample. Among whites, abruptio placenta and the presence of any placental complication discriminated between the mildly retarded and the

Table 4-36
Retarded Father by IQ Group

	1 Severely Retarded	2 Mildly Retarded	3 Borderline	4 Average	5 Above Average	χ^2	r_{IQ}
			Percent				
White	0.00	2.26	0.74	*0.18*	0.00	56.18**	−.05**
Black	0.00	1.12	0.58	0.38	0.00	11.23*	−.02*

Group Ns: White - 85 177 2306 12271 1851
Black - 107 802 7650 9211 149
Differs from mildly retarded in D.F.
*$p<.05$
**$p<.00001$

Table 4-37
Abdomino-pelvic X-rays by IQ Group

	1 Severely Retarded	2 Mildly Retarded	3 Borderline	4 Average	5 Above Average	χ^2	r_{IQ}
			Percent				
White	29.55	19.59	*27.62*	*27.47*	25.67	8.80	− .01
Black	14.84	18.45	17.75	18.90	20.92	5.66	.02*

Group Ns: White - 88 194 2422 12579 1870
          Black - 128 878 8204 9822 153

Differs from mildly retarded in D.F.
*p<.01

Table 4-38
Pregnancy Complications: Cigarette Smoking and Recent Illnesses by IQ Group

	1 Severely Retarded		2 Mildly Retarded		3 Borderline		4 Average		5 Above Average		F	r_{IQ}
	M	S.D.	M	S.D.	M	S.D.	M	S.D.	M	S.D.		
				Number of Cigarettes per Day in Pregnancy								
White	7.2	9.0	6.4	9.1	*9.4*	*11.2*	*8.4*	*10.7*	5.4	8.9	43.99*	− .09*
Black	3.8	6.8	3.6	6.6	3.9	6.9	3.7	6.7	2.9	5.5	1.79	− .01

Group Ns: White - 90 200 2451 12686 1881
          Black - 127 885 8257 9849 156

	M	S.D.	M	S.D.	M	S.D.	M	S.D.	M	S.D.	F	r_{IQ}
				Number of Recent Maternal Illnesses								
White	0.5	0.7	0.4	0.7	0.6	0.8	0.6	0.8	*0.7*	*0.9*	9.33*	.05*
Black	0.4	0.7	0.4	0.7	0.5	0.7	0.5	0.7	0.4	0.7	0.39	− .00

Group Ns: White - 87 192 2405 12524 1861
          Black - 128 877 8159 9756 155

Differs from mildly retarded in D.F.
*p<.00001

Table 4-39
Maternal Hematocrit in Pregnancy by IQ Group

	1 Severely Retarded		2 Mildly Retarded		3 Borderline		4 Average		5 Above Average		F	r_{IQ}
	M	S.D.	M	S.D.	M	S.D.	M	S.D.	M	S.D.		
White	34.2	3.6	34.5	3.6	34.1	3.6	34.6	3.5	35.2	3.2	26.51*	.09*
Black	31.7	3.7	31.2	3.6	*31.6*	*3.4*	*31.9 3.4*		*33.0 3.2*		23.13*	.08*

Group Ns: White -   90   200   2449   12723   1880

Black -   126   885   8242   9848   155

Differs from mildly retarded in D.F.
*p<.00001

borderline and average groups, respectively (Table 4-43). The proportion of breech deliveries was significantly higher than in the average group. A shorter second stage of labor discriminated between the mildly retarded and the above average. In the black sample, lower placental weight among the mildly retarded was a major discriminator in comparisons with all higher IQ groups. The proportion of abnormal presentations at delivery was significantly higher than in the average group.

Obstetric factors were not effective discriminators between the mildly retarded and the borderline or average group. They were more effective, but only moderately so, in discriminating between the mildly retarded and the above average. Canonical correlations in these extreme group comparisons were .26 in both samples.

Summary Analyses

When prenatal and obstetric discriminators were combined, the most important were the earlier maternal characteristics of SRA score, socioeconomic status, education, and number of clinic visits made (Table 4-44). Canonical correlations were identical or highly similar to those in the prenatal analyses although 8 of the 12 obstetric factors were retained along with 24 of the 27 prenatal ones. Eliminated from the prenatal period were anemia in pregnancy and fewer reported maternal illnesses (significant in the comparison with the above-average group among whites) and less edema in pregnancy (a discriminator in the com-

Table 4-40

Pregnancy Complications: Heart Disease, Bacterial Infection, and Edema by IQ Group

	1 Severely Retarded	2 Mildly Retarded	3 Borderline	4 Average	5 Above Average	χ^2	r_{IQ}
			Percent				
		Organic Heart Disease in Pregnancy					
White	0.00	1.02	1.80	1.48	0.85	8.50	−.02*
Black	2.42	3.16	*1.72*	*1.55*	1.28	13.12*	−.02*
Group Ns: White -	92	197	2445	12683	1876		
Black -	124	886	8215	9787	156		
		Bacterial Infection in Pregnancy					
White	8.99	8.51	7.38	7.22	7.19	0.93	−.01
Black	3.45	8.90	7.47	*6.82*	7.28	9.03	−.01
Group Ns: White -	89	188	2371	12357	1836		
Black -	116	843	7987	9543	151		
		Edema in Pregnancy					
White	42.53	36.79	42.47	42.99	41.20	4.84	−.00
Black	25.62	19.27	22.15	*25.46*	27.81	37.56**	.04**
Group Ns: White -	87	193	2352	12150	1784		
Black -	121	851	7996	9467	151		

Differs from mildly retarded in D.F.
*p<.05
**p<.00001

parison with the average group among blacks). Obstetric factors not retained in the white sample were shorter second stage of labor and less frequent use of midforceps (significant in the comparison with the above-average group) and breech delivery (a discriminator between the mildly retarded and the average group). Among blacks, abnormal presentation at delivery was dropped from the comparison with the average group.

Inhalation anesthetics remained positively associated with mild retardation among whites in comparisons with the average and above-average groups. Nega-

Table 4-41
Prior Fetal Death by IQ Group

	1 Severely Retarded	2 Mildly Retarded	3 Borderline	4 Average	5 Above Average	χ^2	r_{IQ}
			Percent				
White	5.80	6.76	7.04	6.28	4.72	6.40	−.02*
Black	11.58	11.74	8.10	8.82	9.40	12.07*	−.00

Group Ns: White - 69 148 1876 9103 1081

Black - 95 690 6176 7304 117

Differs from mildly retarded in D.F.
*p<.05

Table 4-42
Standardized Coefficients for Obstetric Discriminators Between the Mildly Retarded and Comparison Groups

	Comparison Group					
Variable	White			Black		
	BL	AV	AA	BL	AV	AA
Inhalation anesthetic at delivery	.58	.73	.84	−.49	−.57	−.50
Highest FHR in 1st stage of labor	—	−.33	−.22	—	−.14	−.28
Placenta previa	.54	—	.23	.41	—	—
Induction of labor	—	−.34	−.20	—	—	—
Abruptio placenta	.54	—	—	—	—	—
Placental complications	—	.31	—	—	—	—
Breech delivery	—	.27	—	—	—	—
Midforceps delivery	—	—	−.17	—	—	—
Length of 2nd stage of labor	—	—	−.16	—	—	—
Conduction anesthetic at delivery	—	—	—	−.60	−.66	−.70
Placental weight	—	—	—	−.60	−.60	−.55
Abnormal presentation at delivery[a]	—	—	—	—	.21	—
Canonical correlation	.08*	.07**	.26**	.07**	.11**	.26**

[a]Face, chin, brow or shoulder

*p<.001

**p<.00001

Table 4-43
Obstetric Conditions: Placental Complications, Conduction Anesthetic, and Induction of Labor by IQ Group

	1 Severely Retarded	2 Mildly Retarded	3 Borderline	4 Average	5 Above Average	χ^2	r_{IQ}
			Percent				
			Placenta Previa				
White	1.12	2.08	*0.53*	0.69	*0.37*	9.43	.02*
Black	1.57	0.91	*0.33*	0.61	0.64	12.99*	.00
Group Ns: White -	89	192	2432	12653	1878		
Black -	127	879	8223	9806	157		
			Abruptio Placenta				
White	1.12	4.06	*1.67*	2.11	2.82	10.69*	.02*
Black	2.34	1.13	1.30	1.44	3.16	5.66	.00
Group Ns: White -	89	197	2456	12726	1882		
Black -	128	886	8262	9862	158		
			Placental Complications				
White	2.25	7.33	3.52	*3.76*	4.01	7.91	− .00
Black	4.76	3.21	2.69	3.15	3.16	4.89	− .00
Group Ns: White -	89	191	2416	12605	1872		
Black -	126	872	8145	9724	158		
			Conduction Anesthetic at Delivery				
White	72.22	59.50	67.27	78.05	87.33	289.16****	.14****
Black	47.24	40.11	*45.40*	*49.58*	*60.76*	62.07****	.06****
Group Ns: White -	90	200	2441	12663	1879		
Black -	127	880	8223	9838	158		
			Induction of Labor				
White	10.34	4.32	8.75	*11.17*	*10.77*	19.84***	.03**
Black	2.54	5.31	4.42	5.18	6.29	7.68	.02*
Group Ns: White -	87	185	2308	12022	1811		
Black -	118	829	7824	9325	143		

Differs from mildly retarded in D.F.
  *p<.05
  **p<.01
  ***p<.001
  ****p<.00001

Table 4-44
Standardized Coefficients for Prenatal and Obstetric Discriminators Between the Mildly Retarded and Comparison Groups

Variable	White			Black		
	BL	AV	AA	BL	AV	AA
Maternal SRA score	−.50	−.31	−.36	−.37	−.37	−.41
Socioeconomic index	—	−.18	−.37	−.18	−.17	−.43
Maternal education	—	−.20	−.20	−.43	−.38	−.18
Number of prenatal visits	—	−.15	−.11	−.18	−.21	−.15
Retarded mother	.35	.32	.14	—	.11	—
Housing density	.30	.21	.15	—	.21	—
Parity	—	—	.07	.09	—	.29
Inhalation anesthetic at delivery	—	.12	.10	—	−.10	—
Maternal height	—	−.06	−.05	—	−.09	—
Hospitalizations since LMP	—	.13	—	—	.05	—
Age at menarche	.37	.20	.12	—	—	—
Cigarettes per day in pregnancy	−.33	−.21	—	—	—	—
Abdomino-pelvic x-rays	−.23	−.11	—	—	—	—
Induction of labor	—	−.12	−.08	—	—	—
Urinary tract infection in pregnancy	—	.13	.10	—	—	—
Highest FHR in 1st stage of labor	—	−.08	−.07	—	—	—
Abruptio placenta	.26	—	—	—	—	—
Toxoplasmosis in pregnancy	—	.24	—	—	—	—
Retarded father	—	.18	—	—	—	—
Retarded siblings	—	.16	—	—	—	—
Placental complications	—	.12	—	—	—	—
Placenta previa	—	—	.07	—	—	—
Placental weight	—	—	—	−.17	−.16	−.13
Hematocrit in pregnancy	—	—	—	−.17	−.10	−.08
Pregnancy-free interval	—	—	—	−.32	−.25	—
Toxemia	—	—	—	.21	.15	—
Birthweight of last child	—	—	—	−.14	−.10	—
Organic heart disease in pregnancy	—	—	—	.17	.10	—
Prior fetal death	—	—	—	.20	—	—
Bacterial infection in pregnancy	—	—	—	—	.08	—
Conduction anesthetic at delivery	—	—	—	—	−.07	—
Maternal age	—	—	—	—	—	−.46
Canonical correlation	*.17**	*.18**	*.58**	*.17**	*.29**	*.62**

*$p < .00001$

tive relationships in the black sample for both inhalation and conduction anesthetics were significant in the comparison with the average group.

The discriminating power of factors prior to birth was not increased by the addition of obstetric variables. As in the prenatal analyses, the highest canonical correlations were obtained in the comparisons between the mildly retarded children and those in the above-average group.

5
The Neonatal
Period

From the events and conditions occurring after delivery and in the newborn nursery, 52 variables were screened for their relationship to severe or mild retardation. Of these, 37 differed in univariate comparisons between retarded and higher IQ groups and were entered in the appropriate two-group discriminant function analysis. The syndromes and major malformations of the central nervous system diagnosed in this period were validated against diagnoses made at 1 and 7 years. Specific syndromes other than Down's that are grouped together as a single variable and the individual CNS malformations are listed in Chapter 3. Neonatal seizures were defined as occurring at any time during the first month of life.

THE SEVERELY RETARDED

The most important of the neonatal discriminators were the presence of Down's syndrome, other genetic or postinfection syndromes, seizures, and major CNS malformations (Table 5-1). Down's syndrome affected 16% of the severely retarded in the white sample and 14% in the black sample (Table 5-2). Other genetic syndromes or those resulting from prenatal or postnatal infection were present in 15% of the white group and 7% of the black group. Major malformations of the central nervous system accounted for another 10% of severely retarded white children but only 2% of those in the black sample (Table 5-3). The specific syndromes and malformations are shown in Table 3-7. Generalized seizures in the first month of life were more prevalent among severely retarded whites than blacks and were rare in all nonretarded groups. Except for major CNS malformations in the black sample, these conditions were discriminators in all comparisons.

Table 5-1
Standardized Coefficients for Neonatal Discriminators Between
the Severely Retarded and Comparison Groups

Variable	Comparison Group							
	White				Black			
	MR	BL	AV	AA	MR	BL	AV	AA
Down's syndrome	.53	.57	.64	.48	.77	.75	.73	.48
Other genetic or post-infection syndromes	.46	.45	.53	.50	.30	.38	.45	.34
Neonatal seizures	.43	.22	.16	.25	.39	.18	.18	.32
Major CNS malformations	.27	.26	.30	.36	—	.18	.22	—
Brain abnormality	—	.14	.09	.10	—	.13	.08	—
Percent male	.26	—	—	.06	—	.05	.05	.23
Major eye malformations	—	.07	.06	—	.21	.17	.15	—
Head circumference at birth	—	—	—	−.08	—	−.09	−.09	−.59
Apgar score at 5 min.	—	—	—	−.04	—	−.03	—	—
Minor musculoskeletal malformations	.28	.19	.10	.13	—	—	—	—
Minor ear malformations	—	.10	.07	.13	—	—	—	—
Apneic episode	—	.11	.04	—	—	—	—	—
Peripheral nerve abnormality	—	.07	.08	—	—	—	—	—
Apgar score at 1 min.	—	—	−.03	−.06	—	—	—	—
Resuscitation up to 5 min.	—	.05	—	—	—	—	—	—
Major upper respiratory or mouth malformations	—	—	.09	—	—	—	—	—
Primary apnea	—	—	.06	—	—	—	—	—
Major alimentary tract malformations	—	—	.05	—	—	—	—	—
Major genitourinary malformations	—	—	.05	—	—	—	—	—
Length at birth	—	—	−.02	—	—	—	—	—

(continued)

Table 5-1 (continued)

Variable	Comparison Group							
	White				Black			
	MR	BL	AV	AA	MR	BL	AV	AA
Birthweight	—	—	−.01	—	—	—	—	—
Respiratory difficulty	—	—	—	—	—	.05	.08	.21
Dysmaturity	—	—	—	—	.17	.06	—	—
Major musculoskeletal malformations	—	—	—	—	—	.08	.05	—
Major thoracic malformations	—	—	—	—	—	.11	.11	—
Major cardiovascular malformations	—	—	—	—	—	.05	—	—
Multiple birth	—	—	—	—	—	—	.06	—
Canonical correlation	.56*	.61*	.59*	.68*	.44*	.46*	.49*	.54*

*$p < .00001$

Independently of specific neurological disorders, a clinical diagnosis of brain abnormality contributed to discrimination between the severely retarded and the nonretarded groups. This judgment was made following a review of nursery records for signs of seizures, clonic spasms, hypertonia or hypotonia, hyperactivity, lethargy, paralysis/paresis, or asymmetrical or abnormal reflexes. Approximately twice as many severely retarded whites than blacks received the diagnosis of brain abnormality, which was given only rarely to nonretarded children. In the white sample, the presence of peripheral or cranial nerve abnormalities discriminated between the severely retarded and the borderline and average groups (see Table 5-2).

Malformations other than those of the central nervous system were more prevalent among the severely retarded (Table 5-4). The presence of major eye malformations (cataract, corneal opacity, exophthalmos and proptosis) was a discriminator in both samples. Among whites, major malformations of the upper respiratory tract or mouth (cleft lip or palate and micrognathia), the alimentary tract (inguinal hernia, pyloric stenosis, and umbilical hernia), and the genitourinary tract (hypospadias, urethral meatal stenosis, and hydroureter or megaloureter) had significantly higher frequencies among the severely retarded than the average group. Minor malformations of the musculoskeletal system (polydac-

Table 5-2
Neonatal Conditions: Syndromes and Nervous System Abnormalities by IQ Group

	1 Severely Retarded	2 Mildly Retarded	3 Borderline	4 Average	5 Above Average	χ^2	r_{IQ}
			Percent				

Down's Syndrome

White	16.30	**1.49**	*0.00*	*0.00*	*0.00*	2396.31**	−.14**
Black	14.06	**0.00**	**0.01**	*0.00*	*0.00*	2570.70**	−.13**

Group Ns: White - 92 201 2473 12777 1889

Black - 128 895 8319 9919 158

Other Genetic or Post-Infection Syndromes

White	15.22	**1.00**	**0.28**	*0.04*	**0.00**	1326.42**	−.13**
Black	7.03	**0.89**	**0.08**	*0.01*	**0.00**	527.42**	−.10**

Group Ns: White - 92 201 2473 12777 1889

Black - 128 895 8319 9919 158

Neonatal Seizures

White	10.87	**0.00**	**0.36**	**0.25**	**0.11**	343.37**	−.06**
Black	6.25	**0.34**	**0.29**	**0.25**	**0.00**	148.34**	−.04**

Group Ns: White - 92 201 2473 12777 1889

Black - 128 895 8319 9919 158

Brain Abnormality

White	20.65	2.55	**0.41**	**0.30**	**0.16**	900.11**	−.11**
Black	11.02	0.79	**0.35**	**0.33**	0.63	335.04**	−.06**

Group Ns: White - 92 196 2447 12684 1879

Black - 127 888 8261 9872 158

Peripheral Nerve Abnormality

White	5.43	0.51	**0.58**	**0.42**	0.59	48.50**	−.02*
Black	1.60	0.45	0.55	0.45	*1.90*	10.02*	−.01

Group Ns: White - 92 195 2434 12662 1879

Black - 125 886 8253 9865 158

Differs from severely retarded in D.F.
Differs from mildly retarded in D.F.
Differs from severely and mildly retarded in D.F.s
 *p<.05
**p<.00001

Table 5-3

Major CNS Malformations by IQ Group

	1 Severely Retarded	2 Mildly Retarded	3 Borderline	4 Average	5 Above Average	χ^2	r_{IQ}
			Percent				
White	9.78	**2.99**	*0.36*	*0.10*	**0.05**	470.41*	−.09*
Black	2.34	0.45	**0.06**	*0.02*	0.00	113.13*	−.05*

Differs from severely retarded in D.F.
Differs from severely and mildly retarded in D.F.s
*p <.00001

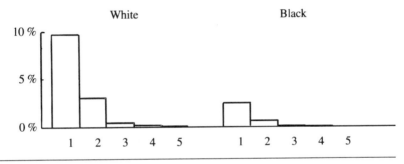

Note. Group Ns: White-   92   201   2473   12777   1889
            Black-   128   895   8319   9919   158

tyly, syndactyly, abnormal fingers or toes, and adduction of the foot) and of the ear (branchial cleft anomaly, deformed ear pinna, and low-set ears) were consistent discriminators between the severely retarded and higher IQ groups. In the black sample, higher frequencies of major thoracic malformations (pectus excavatum and hypoplasia or immaturity of the lungs) and major malformations of the musculoskeletal system (metatarsus adductus, talipes equinovarus, dislocation of the hip, and torticollis) and of the cardiovascular system (cardiac enlargement, ventricular septal defect, patent ductus arteriosis, and atrial septal defect) discriminated between the severely retarded and the borderline and average groups.

The severely retarded differed from other IQ groups in sex ratio, size at birth, and indices of physiological status. More than 60% of the children were male, a characteristic that was significant in comparisons with the mildly retarded and above-average among whites and with all nonretarded groups among blacks (Table 5-5). Correlations between sex of child and IQ score were only .03 and

Table 5-4
Other Malformations by IQ Group

	1 Severely Retarded	2 Mildly Retarded	3 Borderline	4 Average	5 Above Average	χ^2	r_{IQ}
			Percent				

Major Eye Malformations

White	5.43	0.50	**0.16**	**0.16**	0.16	135.90*****	−.04*****
Black	5.47	**0.78**	*0.20*	*0.11*	0.00	182.40*****	−.06*****

Major Upper Respiratory or Mouth Malformations

White	5.43	3.48	*0.65*	**0.16**	*0.16*	169.19*****	−.07*****
Black	0.78	0.34	0.12	0.09	0.00	9.14	−.02*

Major Alimentary Tract Malformations

White	8.70	3.98	1.94	**1.86**	1.96	26.81****	−.02*
Black	4.69	3.02	1.98	1.79	2.53	11.88*	−.01

Major Genitourinary Malformations

White	5.43	1.99	0.81	*0.45*	*0.42*	53.97*****	−.03*****
Black	1.56	0.56	0.48	0.37	0.63	5.46	−.02**

Minor Musculoskeletal Malformations

White	14.13	**1.49**	**0.89**	**0.89**	**0.95**	166.53*****	−.04*****
Black	3.91	2.23	1.92	1.69	1.90	5.30	−.01

Minor Ear Malformations

White	9.78	3.48	**1.01**	*0.77*	**0.48**	107.77*****	−.05*****
Black	7.81	2.91	2.86	2.26	1.90	21.30***	−.03***

Major Thoracic Malformations

White	2.17	0.50	0.32	0.47	0.79	10.37*	.01
Black	2.34	0.34	**0.16**	**0.10**	0.00	45.23*****	−.03****

(continued)

Table 5-4 (continued)

	1 Severely Retarded	2 Mildly Retarded	3 Borderline	4 Average	5 Above Average	χ^2	r_{IQ}
				Percent			

Major Musculoskeletal Malformations

White	9.78	1.99	2.26	2.32	3.34	28.13****	.01
Black	7.81	3.91	*2.63*	**3.62**	1.27	26.26****	.01

Major Cardiovascular Malformations

White	4.35	1.99	*0.32*	*0.21*	*0.16*	83.52*****	− .05*****
Black	3.91	0.67	**0.18**	*0.16*	0.63	90.29*****	− .03*****

Group Ns: White -   92 201 2473 12777 1889

Black -   128 895 8319 9919   158

Differs from severely retarded in D.F.

Differs from mildly retarded in D.F.

Differs from severely and mildly retarded in D.F.s

  *$p<.05$
  **$p<.01$
  ***$p<.001$
  ****$p<.0001$
  *****$p<.00001$

in opposite directions in the two samples. Among blacks, multiple birth was a minor discriminator between the severely retarded and the average group and a higher frequency of dysmaturity (a diagnosis based on signs of malnutrition, meconium staining, or prolonged gestation) was significant in comparisons with the mildly retarded and the borderline.

Of three physical measurements recorded at birth, head circumference was the most sensitive. Values increased linearly with IQ level and correlations with IQ score were .14 and .12 in the white and black samples, respectively (Table 5-6). A smaller head circumference among the severely retarded was a discriminator in the comparison with the above-average group among whites and with all nonretarded groups among blacks. Lower birthweight and shorter length at birth were minor discriminators in the white sample in the comparison with the average group. In both samples, weight and length at birth tended to increase across IQ level and were positively correlated with IQ score (Table 5-7). White infants were heavier than black infants. For example, in the average IQ groups the difference in mean birthweight was nearly 200 grams.

Table 5-5

Neonatal Characteristics: Sex, Multiple Birth, and Dysmaturity by IQ Group

	1 Severely Retarded	2 Mildly Retarded	3 Borderline	4 Average	5 Above Average	χ^2	r_{IQ}
				Percent			
Sex (Percent Male)							
White	63.04	**45.77**	49.37	51.15	**55.59**	25.18**	.03**
Black	61.72	53.63	*50.17*	*48.47*	**51.27**	19.63*	−.03**
Group Ns: White -	92	201	2473	12777	1889		
Black -	128	895	8319	9919	158		
Multiple Birth							
White	2.17	3.98	2.99	1.78	*0.85*	32.96***	−.04***
Black	5.47	5.36	*2.70*	*1.46*	1.27	83.62***	−.07***
Group Ns: White -	92	201	2473	12777	1889		
Black -	128	895	8319	9919	158		
Dysmaturity							
White	26.83	16.05	19.96	19.59	19.87	4.21	.00
Black	23.85	**13.85**	**13.72**	16.52	*22.61*	36.18***	.04***
Group Ns: White -	82	162	2164	11205	1681		
Black -	109	780	7381	8509	115		

Differs from severely retarded in D.F.
Differs from mildly retarded in D.F.
Differs from severely and mildly retarded in D.F.s
*p<.001
**p<.0001
***p<.00001

A lower Apgar score at 5 minutes after delivery discriminated between the severely retarded groups and the above-average among whites and the borderline among blacks. Means and standard scores are shown in Table 5-8. There was essentially no correlation between this variable and IQ. Among whites, lower Apgar score at 1 minute discriminated between the severely retarded and the average and above-average groups (Table 5-9). More frequent occurrences of primary apnea, single apneic episode, and resuscitation up to 5 minutes were

Table 5-6
Head Circumference in Centimeters at Birth by IQ Group

	1 Severely Retarded	2 Mildly Retarded	3 Borderline	4 Average	5 Above Average	F	r_{IQ}
	M S.D.	M S.D.	M S.D.	M S.D.	M S.D.		
White	33.2 2.5	33.3 1.9	33.6 1.7	*34.0 1.5*	***34.2 1.4***	71.78*	.14*
Black	32.6 2.3	32.9 2.0	**33.3 1.7**	***33.5 1.6***	**34.0 1.6**	60.59*	.12*

Differs from severely retarded in D.F.
Differs from mildly retarded in D.F.
Differs from severely and mildly retarded in D.F.s
*p <.00001

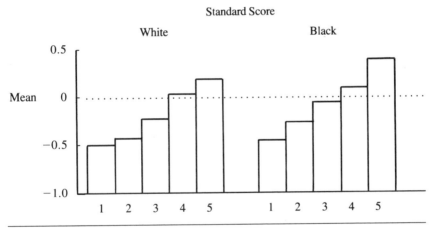

Standard Score

Note. Group Ns: White-   90 194 2415 12599 1866
                Black-   122 880 8197 9791 158

significant in comparisons with the average and/or borderline groups in the white sample (Table 5-10). Primary apnea was a failure to develop spontaneous respiration within 2 minutes after birth. An apneic episode was defined as cessation of breathing for approximately 20 seconds or more with cyanosis, pallor, or collapse. Correlations between these signs of anoxia in the newborn and IQ were uniformly low ($r < .05$). A summary diagnosis of moderate or marked respiratory difficulty in the newborn nursery discriminated between the severely retarded black children and all nonretarded groups. The frequency of this clinical judgment decreased linearly with increasing IQ level in both sam-

Table 5-7
Weight and Length at Birth by IQ Group

	1 Severely Retarded	2 Mildly Retarded	3 Borderline	4 Average	5 Above Average	F	r_{IQ}
	M S.D.	M S.D.	M S.D.	M S.D.	M S.D.		

Birthweight (g)

	1	2	3	4	5	F	r_{IQ}
White	3015 714	3191 647	3184 585	**3291 522**	3354 473	38.18*	.11*
Black	2863 736	2906 605	3014 540	3096 514	3219 521	52.08*	.12*
Group Ns: White -	90	200	2466	12770	1888		
Black -	128	889	8299	9911	158		

Length at Birth (cm)

	1	2	3	4	5	F	r_{IQ}
White	49.0 3.7	49.5 3.3	49.9 2.9	**50.4 2.7**	50.6 2.5	30.24*	.09*
Black	48.3 3.7	48.5 3.2	*49.1 2.8*	49.6 2.7	*50.4 2.4*	69.58*	.13*
Group Ns: White -	88	194	2407	12541	1857		
Black -	122	879	8174	9766	158		

Differs from severely retarded in D.F.
Differs from mildly retarded in D.F.
*p<.00001

ples. However, negative correlations with IQ score were only .06 and .05 in the white and black samples.

Neonatal characteristics were relatively powerful discriminators for the severely retarded, especially among whites. In both samples, the canonical correlations tended to increase systematically with the IQ level of the comparison group. Values ranged from .56 to .68 among whites and .44 to .54 among blacks.

In summary analyses of all precursors of severe retardation through the perinatal period, the seriously handicapping syndromes and neurological abnormalities present in the newborn were the major discriminators between the severely retarded and higher IQ groups (Table 5-11). Maternal characteristics retained in both samples were seizures in pregnancy, SRA score, socioeconomic status, and education. Other complications of pregnancy were low weight gain, less prenatal care, and anemia among whites, and rheumatic fever and toxemia among blacks. The obstetric risk factors retained were midforceps and breech delivery in the white sample and intravenous anesthetics, meconium staining,

Table 5-8

Apgar Score at Five Minutes by IQ Group

	1 Severely Retarded	2 Mildly Retarded	3 Borderline	4 Average	5 Above Average	F	r$_{IQ}$
	M S.D.	M S.D.	M S.D.	M S.D.	M S.D.		
White	8.0 2.0	8.8 1.1	8.9 1.1	8.9 1.1	**8.9 0.9**	16.91**	.02*
Black	8.6 1.9	9.0 1.5	**9.1 1.3**	9.1 1.2	9.1 1.0	7.43**	.00

Differs from severely retarded in D.F.
 *p < .05
**p < .00001

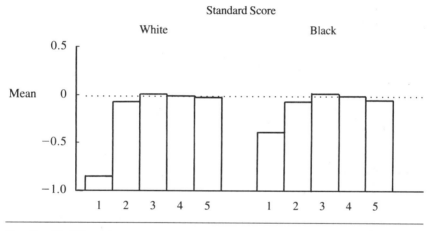

Standard Score

Note. Group Ns: White-   84 189 2267 12210 1842
                 Black- 115 822 7747   9231   149

and low fetal heart rate in the black sample. All but one of the 27 neonatal discriminators and 22 of the 33 prenatal and obstetric factors were included in the summary analyses.

The addition of prenatal and obstetric factors to the significant neonatal ones improved discrimination between extreme groups in the black sample, and, to a lesser extent, discrimination between the two retarded groups in the white sample. Maternal and demographic factors were important in the former comparison and complications of pregnancy and delivery in the latter. Canonical correlations from the summary analyses ranged from .63 to .71 among whites and from .46 to .70 among blacks.

Table 5-9
Apgar Score at One Minute by IQ Group

	1 Severely Retarded		2 Mildly Retarded		3 Borderline		4 Average		5 Above Average		F	r_{IQ}
	M	S.D.	M	S.D.	M	S.D.	M	S.D.	M	S.D.		
White	6.3	2.8	7.2	2.1	7.6	2.0	**7.7**	**1.9**	**7.7**	**1.8**	15.29*	.04*
Black	7.2	2.4	7.8	2.2	8.0	1.9	7.9	1.9	8.0	1.6	7.60*	.00

Group Ns: White-   85   185   2266   12093   1824
            Black-   116   807   7504   8981   144
Differs from severely retarded in D.F.
Differs from mildly retarded in D.F.
Differs from severely and mildly retarded in D.F.s
*p <.00001

THE MILDLY RETARDED

Many of the neonatal conditions related to mild retardation were the same as those related to severe retardation, but they were less effective discriminators for the mildly retarded. Higher frequencies of major cardiovascular malformations, malformations of the CNS, and syndromes other than Down's were significant in comparisons with higher IQ groups in both samples (Table 5-12). Down's syndrome was a major discriminator among whites. All of these conditions were rare among the mildly retarded. In both samples, head circumference at birth was smaller among the mildly retarded and multiple birth was more frequent. Among whites, major malformations of the upper respiratory system or mouth and of the genitourinary tract, and minor malformations of the ear were more common among the mildly retarded than the nonretarded groups. The unique discriminators of lower hemoglobin and metabolic disease were significant in comparisons with the borderline and average groups, respectively (Tables 5-13 and 5-14). The mildly retarded white children had a lower Apgar score at one minute than nonretarded children and a significantly higher frequency of respiratory difficulty in the newborn nursery (see Tables 5-9 and 5-10).

Other neonatal conditions related to mild retardation among blacks were major malformations of the eye and of the musculoskeletal system, and rare spinal cord abnormalities, a unique discriminator. Minor skin malformations and dysmaturity were less frequent among the mildly retarded than the above average. Shorter length at birth was a major discriminator in all comparisons with higher IQ groups. A slightly lower gestational age (Table 5-15) and a

Table 5-10
Respiratory Complications in the Newborn by IQ Group

	1 Severely Retarded	2 Mildly Retarded	3 Borderline	4 Average	5 Above Average	χ^2	r_{IQ}
				Percent			
			Primary Apnea				
White	6.52	1.53	1.19	**0.60**	**0.59**	55.39*****	−.04*****
Black	3.94	2.70	*1.37*	*1.44*	0.63	16.00**	−.02*
			Apneic Episode				
White	4.35	0.51	0.61	**0.50**	0.37	26.99****	−.02*
Black	2.36	0.56	0.62	0.58	0.63	6.68	−.01
			Resuscitation up to Five Minutes				
White	19.57	7.65	**6.46**	5.60	5.22	37.32*****	−.03***
Black	11.02	5.86	4.81	5.13	3.16	12.98*	−.00
			Respiratory Difficulty				
White	8.70	5.10	2.25	*1.45*	*0.59*	67.10*****	−.06*****
Black	8.66	3.38	**1.90**	**1.40**	**0.00**	60.31*****	−.05*****

Group Ns: White -   92 196 2447 12684 1879
　　　　　 Black - 127 888 8261   9872   158

Differs from severely retarded in D.F.
Differs from mildly retarded in D.F.
　*p<.05
　**p<.01
　***p<.001
　****p<.0001
　*****p<.00001

higher proportion of males were significant factors in comparisons with the borderline and average groups. The mildly retarded black children had a higher frequency of primary apnea and of multiple apneic episodes (Table 5-16) than those in the nonretarded groups.

The discriminating power of the neonatal characteristics was only moderate.

Table 5-11
Standardized Coefficients for Prenatal, Obstetric, and Neonatal Discriminators
Between the Severely Retarded and Comparison Groups

Variable	White				Black			
	MR	BL	AV	AA	MR	BL	AV	AA
Down's syndrome	.43	.57	.63	.43	.71	.74	.72	.29
Other genetic or post-infection syndromes	.37	.45	.52	.46	.27	.36	.44	.19
Neonatal seizures	.33	.22	.16	.24	.38	.17	.18	.28
Major CNS malformations	.18	.26	.30	.32	—	.18	.21	—
Major eye malformations	—	.07	.06	—	.20	.17	.15	—
Brain abnormality	—	.14	.09	.10	—	.13	.08	—
Seizures in pregnancy	—	—	.03	.09	.18	.10	.10	—
Maternal SRA score	—	—	−.04	−.10	—	—	−.02	−.47
Head circumference at birth	—	—	—	−.05	—	−.09	−.09	−.29
Percent male	.24	—	—	—	—	.04	.06	—
Socioeconomic index	—	—	−.01	−.09	—	—	—	−.26
Maternal education	.20	—	—	−.08	—	—	−.10	—
Minor musculoskeletal malformations	.23	.19	.10	.12	—	—	—	—
Midforceps delivery	.29	.09	.03	—	—	—	—	—
Minor ear malformations	—	.10	.07	.11	—	—	—	—
Weight gain in pregnancy	−.21	−.05	—	—	—	—	—	—
Peripheral nerve abnormality	—	.07	.08	—	—	—	—	—
Apneic episode	—	.11	.04	—	—	—	—	—
Number of prenatal visits	—	—	−.03	−.07	—	—	—	—
Age at menarche	−.19	—	—	—	—	—	—	—
Major upper repiratory or mouth malformations	—	—	.09	—	—	—	—	—

(continued)

Table 5-11 (continued)

Variable	White				Black			
	MR	BL	AV	AA	MR	BL	AV	AA
Primary apnea	—	—	.06	—	—	—	—	—
Retarded siblings	—	—	.05	—	—	—	—	—
Major alimentary tract malformations	—	—	.05	—	—	—	—	—
Major genitourinary malformations	—	—	.05	—	—	—	—	—
Apgar score at 1 min.	—	—	−.03	—	—	—	—	—
Length at birth	—	—	−.01	—	—	—	—	—
Birthweight	—	—	−.01	—	—	—	—	—
Parity	—	—	—	.06	—	—	—	—
Anemia in pregnancy	—	—	—	.06	—	—	—	—
Breech delivery	—	—	—	.05	—	—	—	—
Apgar score at 5 min.	—	—	—	−.05	—	—	—	—
Respiratory difficulty	—	—	—	—	—	.05	.07	.24
Intravenous anesthetic at delivery	—	—	—	—	.15	.06	.04	—
Major thoracic malformations	—	—	—	—	—	.11	.11	—
Dysmaturity	—	—	—	—	.16	.05	—	—
Urinary tract infection in pregnancy	—	—	—	—	−.12	−.04	—	—
Major musculoskeletal malformations	—	—	—	—	—	.08	.05	—
Cord complications	—	—	—	—	—	−.05	−.05	—
Meconium staining	—	—	—	—	—	.04	.04	—
Housing density	—	—	—	—	−.17	—	—	—
Fetal or neonatal death at last delivery	—	—	—	—	—	.06	—	—
Rheumatic fever in pregnancy	—	—	—	—	—	.06	—	—
Major cardiovascular malformations	—	—	—	—	—	.06	—	—
Multiple birth	—	—	—	—	—	—	.06	—
Toxemia	—	—	—	—	—	—	.04	—
Mother employed	—	—	—	—	—	—	−.04	—
Highest FHR in 1st stage of labor	—	—	—	—	—	—	—	−.27
Canonical correlation	*.63**	*.61**	*.59**	*.71**	*.46**	*.46**	*.50**	*.70**

*$p < .00001$

Table 5-12

**Standardized Coefficients for Neonatal Discriminators Between
the Mildly Retarded and Comparison Groups**

Variable	Comparison Group					
	White			Black		
	BL	AV	AA	BL	AV	AA
Major cardiovascular malformations	.34	.20	.26	.19	.11	—
Major CNS malformations	.46	.45	.40	—	.18	—
Head circumference at birth	—	−.25	−.48	—	−.24	—
Multiple birth	—	—	.23	.26	.33	—
Down's syndrome	.63	.59	.33	—	—	—
Other genetic or post-infection syndromes	—	.18	—	.41	.40	—
Major upper respiratory or mouth malformations	.38	.39	.37	—	—	—
Respiratory difficulty	—	.12	.31	—	—	—
Apgar score at 1 min.	−.23	−.11	—	—	—	—
Major genitourinary malformations	—	.09	.14	—	—	—
Lowest hemoglobin	−.13	—	—	—	—	—
Metabolic diseases[a]	—	.17	—	—	—	—
Minor ear malformations	—	.14	—	—	—	—
Length at birth	—	—	—	−.36	−.37	−.86
Spinal cord abnormality	—	—	—	.34	.14	—
Gestational age	—	—	—	−.26	−.21	—
Percent male	—	—	—	.19	.24	—
Major eye malformations	—	—	—	.19	.17	—
Primary apnea	—	—	—	.22	.11	—
Multiple apneic episodes	—	—	—	.23	—	—
Major musculoskeletal malformations	—	—	—	.17	—	—
Minor skin malformations	—	—	—	—	—	−.37
Dysmaturity	—	—	—	—	—	−.26
Canonical correlation	*.19**	*.20**	*.33**	*.13**	*.18**	*.24**

[a]Hypothyroidism, cystic fibrosis

*p<.00001

Table 5-13

Lowest Hemoglobin of Newborn by IQ Group

	1 Severely Retarded		2 Mildly Retarded		3 Borderline		4 Average		5 Above Average		F	r_{IQ}
	M	S.D.	M	S.D.	M	S.D.	M	S.D.	M	S.D.		
White	17.0	4.0	17.0	3.4	_17.7_	_3.5_	17.5	2.9	17.3	2.9	3.72**	− .02*
Black	17.2	5.1	17.3	3.8	18.0	3.4	17.9	3.2	17.3	3.0	6.02***	.00

Group Ns: White - 56 111 1281 7556 1118

Black - 58 353 3295 4061 80

Differs from mildly retarded in D.F.
*p<.05
**p<.01
***p<.0001

Canonical correlations ranged from .19 to .33 in the white sample and .13 to .24 in the black sample. The higher values were obtained in comparisons between the mildly retarded and the above-average.

All of the prenatal and perinatal characteristics related to mild retardation are shown in Table 5-17. The major discriminators were maternal SRA score, education and socioeconomic status, and the presence of cardiovascular and CNS malformations in the neonate. Housing density, maternal retardation, parity, and maternal height were also significant factors in both samples. Other important neonatal characteristics were smaller head circumference among the mildly retarded and the presence of genetic and postinfection syndromes. The positive relationship between inhalation anesthetics at delivery and mild retardation among whites and the negative relationships of both inhalants and conduction agents to mild retardation among blacks were unaffected by the addition of neonatal factors.

The summary analyses included 27 of the 32 prenatal and obstetric factors entered. Not retained were retardation among older siblings, birthweight of last child, hospitalizations early in pregnancy, placenta previa, and placental weight. All of the 23 neonatal discriminators were included with the exception of the negative risk factors of dysmaturity and minor skin malformations among blacks. Unlike the results for the severely retarded, canonical correlations in the summary analyses were consistently higher than those for neonatal factors alone. Discriminating power was at least doubled in comparisons between the mildly retarded and the above average where canonical correlations were .63 and .62 in the white and black samples, respectively.

Table 5-14

Neonatal Conditions: Metabolic, Spinal Cord, and Skin by IQ Group

	1 Severely Retarded	2 Mildly Retarded	3 Borderline	4 Average	5 Above Average	χ^2	r_{IQ}
			Percent				

Metabolic Diseases

White	0.00	0.50	0.04	*0.02*	0.05	16.77**	− .01
Black	0.78	0.11	0.05	0.00	0.00	29.12****	− .03***
Group Ns: White -	92	200	2470	12768	1888		
Black -	128	894	8314	9914	158		

Spinal Cord Abnormality

White	0.00	0.00	0.00	0.00	0.00	—	—
Black	0.00	0.23	*0.00*	*0.00*	0.00	41.48****	− .02**
Group Ns: White -	92	196	2447	12684	1879		
Black -	127	888	8261	9872	158		

Minor Skin Malformations

White	8.70	3.98	4.73	4.34	5.08	6.42	.01
Black	3.13	1.90	3.10	2.94	*6.33*	10.17*	.01
Group Ns: White -	92	201	2473	12777	1889		
Black -	128	895	8319	9919	158		

Differs from mildly retarded in D.F.
  *$p<.05$
  **$p<.01$
  ***$p<.0001$
  ****$p<.00001$

Table 5-15
Gestational Age in Weeks by IQ Group

	1 Severely Retarded		2 Mildly Retarded		3 Borderline		4 Average		5 Above Average		F	r_{IQ}
	M	S.D.	M	S.D.	M	S.D.	M	S.D.	M	S.D.		
White	39.2	3.6	39.6	3.2	39.8	2.8	40.0	2.4	40.1	2.1	6.26*	.04**
Black	38.3	3.9	38.1	3.8	*38.8*	*3.4*	*39.0*	*3.0*	39.5	2.7	23.72**	.07**

Differs from mildly retarded in D.F.
*p<.0001
**p<.00001

Standard Score

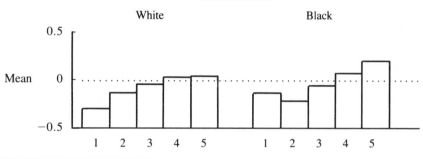

Note. Group Ns: White- 91 201 2441 12719 1882
Black- 122 882 8174 9803 156

Table 5-16
Multiple Apneic Episodes in Newborn by IQ Group

	1 Severely Retarded	2 Mildly Retarded	3 Borderline	4 Average	5 Above Average	χ^2	r_{IQ}
			Percent				
White	2.17	1.02	0.41	0.32	0.43	11.97*	−.02*
Black	1.57	1.35	*0.34*	0.40	0.00	24.60**	−.02*

Group Ns: White- 92 196 2447 12684 1879
Black- 127 888 8261 9872 158
Differs from mildly retarded in D.F.
*p<.05
**p<.0001

Table 5-17

Standardized Coefficients for Prenatal, Obstetric, and Neonatal Discriminators Between the Mildly Retarded and Comparison Groups

Variable	Comparison Group					
	White			Black		
	BL	AV	AA	BL	AV	AA
Maternal SRA score	−.35	−.14	−.28	−.29	−.30	−.40
Maternal education	—	−.19	−.19	−.38	−.35	−.17
Socioeconomic index	—	−.14	−.36	−.16	−.15	−.43
Major cardiovascular malformations	.31	.17	.13	.10	.05	—
Major CNS malformations	.35	.33	.20	—	.14	—
Housing density	.27	.18	.15	—	.20	—
Retarded mother	.23	.20	.15	—	.11	—
Head circumference at birth	—	−.20	−.18	—	−.16	—
Parity	—	—	.08	.09	—	.29
Inhalation anesthetic at delivery	—	.09	.09	—	−.10	—
Maternal height	—	—	−.03	—	−.07	—
Down's syndrome	.44	.44	.15	—	—	—
Other genetic or post- infection syndromes	—	.14	—	.23	.19	—
Major upper respiratory or mouth malformations	.24	.28	.12	—	—	—
Age at menarche	.21	.13	.11	—	—	—
Cigarettes per day in pregnancy	−.23	−.17	—	—	—	—
Abdomino-pelvic x-rays	−.18	−.08	—	—	—	—
Apgar score at 1 min.	−.16	−.07	—	—	—	—
Urinary tract infection in pregnancy	—	.10	.10	—	—	—
Respiratory difficulty	—	.08	.13	—	—	—
Induction of labor	—	−.09	−.08	—	—	—
Major genitourinary malformations	—	.08	.07	—	—	—
Lowest neonatal hemoglobin	−.21	—	—	—	—	—
Abruptio placenta	.18	—	—	—	—	—
Toxoplasmosis in pregnancy	—	.15	—	—	—	—
Retarded father	—	.13	—	—	—	—
Metabolic diseases	—	.13	—	—	—	—
Minor ear malformations	—	.11	—	—	—	—
Highest FHR in 1st stage of labor	—	−.08	—	—	—	—
Placental complications	—	.07	—	—	—	—
Length at birth	—	—	—	−.21	−.18	−.15

(continued)

Table 5-17 (continued)

Variable	Comparison Group					
	White			Black		
	BL	AV	AA	BL	AV	AA
Hematocrit in pregnancy	—	—	—	−.12	−.07	−.07
Pregnancy-free interval	—	—	—	−.29	−.22	—
Multiple birth	—	—	—	.15	.17	—
Toxemia	—	—	—	.14	.13	—
Number of prenatal visits	—	—	—	—	−.13	−.13
Percent male	—	—	—	.13	.14	—
Organic heart disease in pregnancy	—	—	—	.12	.08	—
Primary apnea	—	—	—	.13	.06	—
Major eye malformations	—	—	—	.12	.08	—
Spinal cord abnormality	—	—	—	.24	—	—
Multiple apneic episodes	—	—	—	.15	—	—
Prior fetal death	—	—	—	.14	—	—
Gestational age	—	—	—	−.14	—	—
Major musculoskeletal malformations	—	—	—	.13	—	—
Conduction anesthetic at delivery	—	—	—	—	−.08	—
Bacterial infection in pregnancy	—	—	—	—	.07	—
Maternal age	—	—	—	—	—	−.47
Canonical correlation	*.26**	*.27**	*.63**	*.21**	*.32**	*.62**

*$p < .00001$

6
Infancy

Growth and development during infancy were evaluated with physical measurements, psychomotor scales, medical histories, and pediatric examinations at 4 and 12 months. Of 44 variables screened from the period following nursery discharge to age 1 year, 42 were related to severe or mild mental retardation and were retained for further analysis.

THE SEVERELY RETARDED

Discriminators between the severely retarded and the four higher IQ groups are shown in Table 6-1. Important factors in both samples were diagnoses of delayed motor development and hypotonia at age 1, lower scores on the Bayley Mental and Motor Scales at age 8 months, the occurrence of nonfebrile seizures, and the presence of congenital heart disease. Delayed motor development, defined as failure to walk with support or abnormal gait or posture, was found in 51% of severely retarded whites and 43% of severely retarded blacks (Table 6-2). Less than 1% of average or above-average children were judged to be delayed. Moderate negative correlations with IQ were .20 in both samples. Hypotonia was a less frequent diagnosis, especially among the severely retarded black children. The markedly poorer performance of the severely retarded on the research version of the Bayley Mental and Motor Scales given at 8 months is shown in Tables 6-3 and 6-4. Mean raw scores, or number of items passed, were at about the 5-month level on each scale. Within-group variability is indicated by the large standard deviations. The standard scores, reflecting deviation from the mean in each sample, were lower among severely retarded whites than blacks, and lower on the Mental than the Motor Scale for both groups. The two scales had intercorrelations of .50 and .60 in the white and black samples respectively,

Table 6-1

Standardized Coefficients for Infancy Discriminators Between
the Severely Retarded and Comparison Groups

	Comparison Group							
Variable	White				Black			
	MR	BL	AV	AA	MR	BL	AV	AA
Non-febrile seizures in 1st year	.11	.15	.14	.05	.37	.32	.23	.10
Hypotonia at 1 yr.	.21	.14	.19	.11	.11	.21	.12	—
Delayed motor development at 1 yr.	—	.30	.37	.47	.26	.38	.57	—
Bayley motor score at 8 mo.	−.28	−.10	−.02	−.21	—	—	−.07	−.87
Bayley mental score at 8 mo.	—	−.13	−.14	−.16	−.36	−.19	−.25	—
Congenital heart disease at 1 yr.	—	.16	.12	.10	.12	.15	.11	—
Undescended testicles at 1 yr.	—	.06	.10	.07	.16	.25	.11	—
Head circumference at 1 yr.	—	—	−.05	−.04	−.17	−.07	−.10	−.10
Cerebral palsy at 1 yr.	.31	.49	.47	.21	—	.18	—	—
Percent male	.36	—	.05	.10	.14	—	.07	—
Intensity of social response at 8 mo.	—	−.02	−.02	−.04	—	−.04	−.01	—
Visual impairment at 1 yr.	—	.13	.12	—	—	.14	.12	—
Strabismus at 1 yr.	—	—	.05	—	.21	.09	.08	—
Nystagmus at 1 yr.	—	—	.10	—	—	.11	.10	—
Dyskinesia or ataxia at 1 yr.	—	—	.05	.12	—	.10	—	—
Head circumference at 4 mo.	—	—	−.01	−.05	—	—	—	−.09
Prolonged or recurrent hospitalization in 1st year	—	—	.08	—	—	.01	.07	—
Failure to thrive at 1 yr.	—	.004	.06	—	—	—	.01	—

(continued)

Table 6-1 (continued)

Variable	White				Black			
	MR	BL	AV	AA	MR	BL	AV	AA
Intensity of response at 8 mo.	−.43	−.04	—	−.02	—	—	—	—
Loss of one or both parents in 1st year	—	—	.05	.08	—	—	—	—
Adduction or contracture of hip at 1 yr.	—	.05	—	—	—	—	—	—
Speed of response at 8 mo.	—	−.002	—	—	—	—	—	—
Activity level at 8 mo.	—	—	—	−.02	—	—	—	—
Height at 1 yr.	—	—	—	−.01	—	—	—	—
Weight at 4 mo.	—	—	—	−.006	—	—	—	—
Febrile seizures in 1st year	—	—	—	—	.22	.11	.08	.07
Duration of response at 8 mo.	—	—	—	—	−.08	−.03	−.04	—
Head trauma in 1st year	—	—	—	—	—	.10	.07	—
Cord disease at 1 yr.	—	—	—	—	—	.10	.07	—
CNS infection or inflammation in 1st year	—	—	—	—	—	.06	.04	—
Unfavorable emotional environment in 1st year	—	—	—	—	—	—	.03	—
Canonical correlation	*.52**	*.55**	*.53**	*.73**	*.51**	*.49**	*.55**	*.76**

*$p < .00001$

but each made an important contribution to discrimination between severely retarded and comparison groups. Correlations between mental and motor scores and IQ at age 7 ranged from .22 to .26 in the two samples. Nonfebrile seizures occurred after the first month of life among more than 10% of the severely retarded in each sample, discriminating consistently between them and higher

Table 6-2

Delayed Motor Development and Hypotonia at One Year by IQ Group

	1 Severely Retarded	2 Mildly Retarded	3 Borderline	4 Average	5 Above Average	χ^2	r_{IQ}
			Percent				
			Delayed Motor Development				
White	50.59	17.55	*3.33*	*0.86*	*0.49*	1704.02*	− .20*
Black	42.62	**7.37**	**1.55**	*0.50*	0.65	1626.14*	− .20*
			Hypotonia				
White	21.18	**5.32**	**1.43**	*0.36*	*0.16*	669.43*	− .12*
Black	6.56	**1.43**	**0.15**	*0.09*	0.65	282.88*	− .07*

Group Ns: White - 85 188 2309 12352 1843

Black - 122 841 7941 9627 155

Differs from severely retarded in D.F.

Differs from severely and mildly retarded in D.F.s

*$p<.00001$

IQ groups (Table 6-5). Congenital heart disease, present among 7% of severely retarded whites and 10% of severely retarded blacks, affected less than 1% of children in nonretarded groups (Table 6-6).

Cerebral palsy of mild, moderate, or marked degree was associated with severe retardation in both samples. This diagnosis at age 1 was made more frequently in the white group where it was a significant factor in all comparisons (Table 6-7). The much rarer motor disorder of dyskinesia or ataxia was also a discriminator in both samples. Other significant 1-year conditions among the severely retarded were undescended testicles (Table 6-8), visual impairment or partial or total blindness, strabismus, and nystagmus (Table 6-9). Head circumference was smaller at both 4 and 12 months (Tables 6-10 and 6-11). Among blacks, the later measurement was the more important discriminator. Failure to thrive at age 1 and prolonged or recurrent hospitalization during the first year were related to severe retardation in both samples (Table 6-12).

Five of eight infant behaviors rated following administration of the Bayley Scales were discriminators between the severely retarded and higher IQ groups. Scores on the 5-point rating scales indicated a less intense social response in both samples; less overall response intensity, slower responses, and a lower

Table 6-3

Bayley Mental Scale Score at Eight Months by IQ Group

	1 Severely Retarded		2 Mildly Retarded		3 Borderline		4 Average		5 Above Average		F	r_{IQ}
	M	S.D.	M	S.D.	M	S.D.	M	S.D.	M	S.D.		
White	57.7	22.8	72.5	12.3	*78.4*	*6.3*	*80.1*	*4.4*	*80.4*	*3.8*	401.80*	.22*
Black	59.7	20.1	**75.1**	**9.5**	*78.3*	*6.4*	*79.8*	*4.7*	81.5	3.9	383.87*	.26*

Differs from severely retarded in D.F.
Differs from severely and mildly retarded in D.F.s
*$p < .00001$

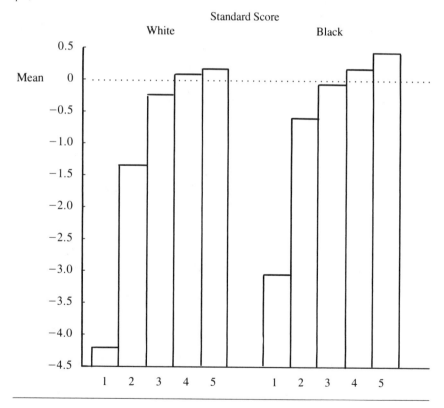

Standard Score

Note. Group Ns: White-   56   140   1858   10668   1613
Black-   92   653   6701   8289   135

Table 6-4

Bayley Motor Scale Score at Eight Months by IQ Group

	1 Severely Retarded	2 Mildly Retarded	3 Borderline	4 Average	5 Above Average	F	r_{IQ}
	M S.D.	M S.D.	M S.D.	M S.D.	M S.D.		
White	20.0 8.3	**27.4 6.5**	*31.6 5.2*	***33.3 4.4***	***34.3 4.0***	267.20*	.24*
Black	22.7 7.2	30.0 6.0	*32.6 4.6*	***33.7 4.1***	***35.2 3.7***	280.73*	.25*

Differs from severely retarded in D.F.
Differs from mildly retarded in D.F.
Differs from severely and mildly retarded in D.F.s
*$p < .00001$

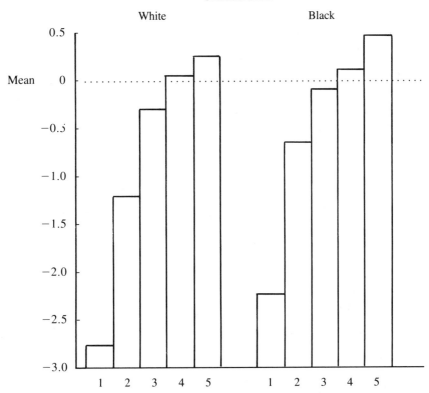

Note. Group Ns: White- 58 140 1858 10666 1613
Black- 92 657 6704 8287 135

Table 6-5

Non-febrile Seizures in First Year by IQ Group

	1 Severely Retarded	2 Mildly Retarded	3 Borderline	4 Average	5 Above Average	χ^2	r_{IQ}
			Percent				
White	11.96	**1.49**	**0.36**	*0.19*	*0.00*	487.59*	−.09*
Black	10.16	**0.34**	**0.14**	**0.19**	**0.00**	526.13*	−.07*

Group Ns: White-   92 201 2473 12777 1889
          Black-   128 895 8319 9919   158

Differs from severely retarded in D.F.
Differs from severely and mildly retarded in D.F.s
*$p < .00001$

activity level among whites; and shorter duration of response among blacks (Tables 6-13 and 6-14). Correlations between the five behavior ratings and IQ ranged from .06 to .14 in the two samples.

Height and weight during the first year (Table 6-15) and adduction or contracture of the hip at age 1 (Table 6-16) were minor discriminators between the severely retarded and nonretarded groups in the white sample. Separation from parents in the first year was more frequent among these infants (Table 6-17). In

Table 6-6

Congenital Heart Disease at One Year by IQ Group

	1 Severely Retarded	2 Mildly Retarded	3 Borderline	4 Average	5 Above Average	χ^2	r_{IQ}
			Percent				
White	7.06	2.66	**0.65**	*0.30*	*0.16*	130.15*	−.06*
Black	9.84	**1.19**	**0.54**	**0.33**	0.65	216.77*	−.06*

Group Ns: White-   85 188 2309 12352 1843
          Black-   122 841 7941 9627   155

Differs from severely retarded in D.F.
Differs from severely and mildly retarded in D.F.s
*$p < .00001$

Table 6-7
Cerebral Palsy and Dyskinesia or Ataxia at One Year by IQ Group

	1 Severely Retarded	2 Mildly Retarded	3 Borderline	4 Average	5 Above Average	χ^2	r_{IQ}
				Percent			
			Cerebral Palsy				
White	28.74	**4.00**	**0.45**	*0.15*	**0.16**	1942.44**	− .16**
Black	18.85	2.47	**0.47**	0.26	0.00	798.16**	− .12**
			Dyskinesia or Ataxia				
White	2.30	0.00	0.12	**0.07**	**0.05**	50.61**	− .02*
Black	1.64	0.34	*0.00*	*0.01*	0.00	132.86**	− .05**

Group Ns: White -   87 200 2470 12767 1886
        Black - 122 890 8304 9897 158

Differs from severely retarded in D.F.
Differs from mildly retarded in D.F.
Differs from severely and mildly retarded in D.F.s
 *$p<.01$
**$p<.00001$

Table 6-8
Undescended Testicles at One Year by IQ Group

	1 Severely Retarded	2 Mildly Retarded	3 Borderline	4 Average	5 Above Average	χ^2	r_{IQ}
				Percent			
White	6.90	2.17	**0.90**	**0.38**	**0.19**	61.68*	− .06*
Black	5.06	**0.83**	**0.14**	**0.23**	0.00	78.94*	− .05*

Group Ns: White-   58   92 1219 6532 1049
        Black-   79 480 4171 4806   81
Differs from severely retarded in D.F.
*$p<.00001$

Table 6-9
Visual and Oculomotor Abnormalities at One Year by IQ Group

	1 Severely Retarded	2 Mildly Retarded	3 Borderline	4 Average	5 Above Average	χ^2	r_{IQ}
			Percent				
			Visual Impairment				
White	8.24	0.53	**0.09**	**0.03**	0.11	600.06*	− .08*
Black	3.28	0.24	**0.05**	*0.01*	0.00	223.59*	− .06*
			Strabismus				
White	16.47	4.79	2.30	**1.73**	1.68	108.72*	− .04*
Black	12.30	**1.66**	**1.30**	**1.06**	0.65	124.41*	− .04*
			Nystagmus				
White	7.06	0.53	0.30	**0.09**	0.33	228.87*	− .05*
Black	10.66	0.83	**0.53**	**0.34**	0.00	256.17*	− .06*

Group Ns: White - 85 188 2309 12352 1843
Black - 122 841 7941 9627 155

Differs from severely retarded in D.F.
Differs from severely and mildly retarded in D.F.s
*p < .00001

Table 6-10
Head Circumference in Centimeters at Four Months by IQ Group

	1 Severely Retarded		2 Mildly Retarded		3 Borderline		4 Average		5 Above Average		F	r_{IQ}
	M	S.D.	M	S.D.	M	S.D.	M	S.D.	M	S.D.		
White	40.2	3.0	40.0	1.9	40.4	1.6	**40.9**	**1.4**	**41.3**	**1.4**	114.64*	.19*
Black	39.4	2.2	39.8	1.8	40.2	1.6	40.6	1.5	*41.2*	*1.6*	89.93*	.16*

Group Ns: White- 79 174 2118 11757 1777
Black- 112 784 7515 9232 150

Differs from severely retarded in D.F.
Differs from severely and mildly retarded in D.F.s
*p < .00001

Table 6-11

Head Circumference in Centimeters at One Year by IQ Group

	1 Severely Retarded		2 Mildly Retarded		3 Borderline		4 Average		5 Above Average		F	r_{IQ}
	M	S.D.	M	S.D.	M	S.D.	M	S.D.	M	S.D.		
White	45.1	3.2	44.6	2.0	*45.3*	*1.6*	**45.8**	**1.5**	**46.3**	**1.4**	131.60*	.21*
Black	44.3	2.0	**45.1**	**1.8**	**45.4**	**1.5**	*45.8*	*1.5*	**46.2**	**1.3**	99.95*	.16*

Differs from severely retarded in D.F.
Differs from mildly retarded in D.F.
Differs from severely and mildly retarded in D.F.s
*p <.00001

Standard Score

White   Black

Note. Group Ns: White- 72 145 2019 11117 1620
Black- 104 734 7194 8843 145

the black sample, febrile seizures was a discriminator of moderate importance. More than 8% of the severely retarded were affected in the first year (Table 6-18). The occurrence of an infection or inflammation of the central nervous system and the very rare events of head trauma and of cord disease were other significant factors. A judgment of an unfavorable emotional environment at age 1, made during the pediatric examination, discriminated between the severely retarded and the average group (Table 6-19).

Characteristics in infancy had moderately high canonical correlations with the group classification when the severely retarded and the mildly retarded, borderline, or average children were compared. Comparisons with the above-

Table 6-12

Failure to Thrive and Hospitalization in the First Year by IQ Group

	1 Severely Retarded	2 Mildly Retarded	3 Borderline	4 Average	5 Above Average	χ^2	r_{IQ}
			Percent				
			Failure to Thrive				
White	3.53	2.66	**0.74**	*0.16*	0.16	92.52*	−.05*
Black	3.28	2.14	0.89	*0.22*	0.00	82.71*	−.07*
			Prolonged or Recurrent Hospitalization				
White	7.06	2.66	0.48	*0.17*	0.11	196.66*	−.07*
Black	2.46	0.48	**0.26**	**0.07**	0.00	46.99*	−.04*

Group Ns: White -   85 188 2309 12352 1843

Black - 122 841 7941   9627   155

Differs from severely retarded in D.F.

Differs from severely and mildly retarded in D.F.s

*$p<.00001$

average group resulted in high canonical correlations of .73 and .76 in the white and black samples, respectively. In summary analyses of development through the first year of life, 61 discriminators for the severely retarded were retained (Table 6-20). They included 36 of the 48 factors from the combined prenatal and perinatal periods and 25 of the 31 infancy characteristics. Syndromes and major CNS malformations diagnosed in the neonatal period and seizures occurring throughout the first year were major discriminators. Also important in the white sample was cerebral palsy at age 1. Risk factors from the periods of pregnancy and delivery were lower maternal weight gain, use of midforceps, and breech delivery among whites, and maternal seizures, intravenous anesthetics, and lower fetal heart rate among blacks. Respiratory problems in the neonate were significant in both samples but neither the Apgar scores nor birthweight (traditional indices of neonatal status) were retained. Maternal education, intelligence, and socioeconomic status made independent contributions to the summary analyses in both samples. Canonical correlations ranged from .66 to .80 among whites and .59 to .82 blacks. The early development of the severely retarded was most clearly differentiated from that of children in the above-average group.

Table 6-13

Intensity of Social Response Rating at Eight Months by IQ Group

	1 Severely Retarded		2 Mildly Retarded		3 Borderline		4 Average		5 Above Average		F	r_{IQ}
	M	S.D.	M	S.D.	M	S.D.	M	S.D.	M	S.D.		
White	2.5	1.2	2.8	0.8	*3.0*	*0.6*	*3.1*	*0.5*	*3.1*	*0.5*	22.63*	.07*
Black	2.7	0.9	2.9	0.7	*3.0*	*0.6*	*3.0*	*0.5*	3.0	0.6	19.16*	.06*

Differs from severely retarded in D.F.
Differs from severely and mildly retarded in D.F.s
*$p < .00001$

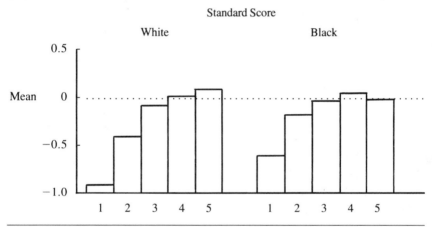

Standard Score

Note. Group Ns: White- 48 129 1756 10042 1520
Black- 87 623 6361 7767 111

THE MILDLY RETARDED

Many characteristics of the mildly retarded in infancy were shared with the severely retarded (Table 6-21). Important discriminators in comparisons with higher IQ groups were lower scores on the Bayley Mental and Motor Scales at 8 months and, at 1 year, delayed motor development and a smaller head circumference. Other factors significant in both samples were a less intense social response at 8 months among the mildly retarded and higher frequencies of hypotonia and failure to thrive. A unique discriminator was the rare occurrence of hypoxic episodes reported during the first year (Table 6-22).

Table 6-14

Ratings of Response Characteristics and Activity Level at Eight Months by IQ Group

	1 Severely Retarded		2 Mildly Retarded		3 Borderline		4 Average		5 Above Average		F	r_{IQ}
	M	S.D.	M	S.D.	M	S.D.	M	S.D.	M	S.D.		

					Intensity of Response							
White	2.1	1.0	**2.9**	**0.9**	**3.2**	**0.7**	3.3	0.7	**3.3**	**0.7**	59.16*	.11*
Black	2.5	1.0	3.0	0.7	3.1	0.6	3.2	0.6	3.5	0.6	64.52*	.13*
Group Ns: White -	51	130	1755	10022	1524							
Black -	87	624	6375	7775	111							

					Speed of Response							
White	2.0	1.0	2.7	0.9	**3.0**	**0.7**	**3.1**	**0.7**	3.2	0.7	66.03*	.12*
Black	2.1	1.0	2.8	0.8	3.0	0.7	*3.1*	*0.6*	3.3	0.7	82.67*	.14*
Group Ns: White -	52	129	1738	9962	1512							
Black -	87	621	6357	7771	111							

					Duration of Response							
White	2.2	1.2	2.8	0.9	3.1	0.7	3.2	0.6	3.2	0.6	43.89*	.10*
Black	2.3	1.0	**3.0**	**0.8**	**3.1**	**0.6**	**3.2**	**0.6**	3.3	0.6	72.40*	.13*
Group Ns: White -	50	130	1733	9978	1513							
Black -	86	626	6356	7756	111							

					Activity Level							
White	2.2	1.0	2.8	0.7	3.0	0.6	3.1	0.6	**3.2**	**0.6**	50.11*	.11*
Black	2.4	1.0	2.9	0.7	3.0	0.5	3.1	0.5	3.2	0.5	71.32*	.13*
Group Ns: White -	53	128	1750	9996	1515							
Black -	88	620	6358	7760	112							

Differs from severely retarded in D.F.
Differs from mildly retarded in D.F.
*$p < .00001$

Table 6-15
Weight at Four Months and Height at One Year by IQ Group

	1 Severely Retarded		2 Mildly Retarded		3 Borderline		4 Average		5 Above Average		F	r_{IQ}
	M	S.D.	M	S.D.	M	S.D.	M	S.D.	M	S.D.		

Weight at Four Months (g)

White	5857	1276	6002	1014	6204	953	6456	863	**6625**	**810**	78.05*	.16*
Black	5597	1185	5671	1030	*6025*	*919*	*6238*	*864*	6591	855	129.10*	.19*

Group Ns: White - 76 171 2107 11684 1767
Black - 112 782 7478 9168 149

Height at One Year (cm)

White	72.8	4.3	73.3	3.4	74.0	3.3	74.6	3.2	**75.2**	**2.9**	46.06*	.13*
Black	72.3	4.0	72.7	3.5	73.4	3.4	74.0	3.2	74.9	3.3	54.48*	.13*

Group Ns: White - 71 144 2010 11083 1618
Black - 105 733 7187 8836 145

Differs from severely retarded in D.F.
Differs from mildly retarded in D.F.
*$p < .00001$

Table 6-16
Adduction or Contracture of Hip at One Year by IQ Group

	1 Severely Retarded	2 Mildly Retarded	3 Borderline	4 Average	5 Above Average	χ^2	r_{IQ}
			Percent				
White	2.17	0.50	**0.24**	0.39	0.42	9.14	− .00
Black	0.78	0.00	0.05	0.17	1.27	27.95*	.01

Group Ns: White - 92 200 2470 12768 1888
Black - 128 894 8314 9914 158

Differs from severely retarded in D.F.
*$p < .0001$

Table 6-17

Loss of One or Both Parents in First Year by IQ Group

	1 Severely Retarded	2 Mildly Retarded	3 Borderline	4 Average	5 Above Average	χ^2	r_{IQ}
			Percent				
White	8.24	2.13	3.90	**2.68**	**0.98**	43.87*	−.05*
Black	2.46	1.07	0.74	0.74	0.00	7.02	−.01

Group Ns: White - 85 188 2309 12352 1843

Black - 122 841 7941 9627 155

Differs from severely retarded in D.F.
*$p<.00001$

Conditions significant in the white sample only included undescended testicle (Table 6-23) and congenital heart disease. Cerebral palsy, affecting 4% of the mildly retarded, was a moderately important discriminator in the comparison with the average group. Nonfebrile seizures in the first year occurred among 1.5% of the mildly retarded and was a significant factor in comparisons with the average and above-average groups. Both prolonged or recurrent hospitalization and an unfavorable emotional environment were associated with mild retardation in the white sample.

Among blacks, sex of child (a control variable) was a moderately important discriminator, with the higher proportion of males among the mildly retarded a significant factor in all comparisons. Smaller size at 4 months (weight and head circumference) and lower weight at age 1 (Table 6-24) were significant in comparisons between the mildly retarded and higher IQ groups. The very rare conditions of cord disease, dyskinesia or ataxia, and visual impairment were discriminators in comparisons with the borderline and average children.

Infant behavior, especially social response to the examiner, was related to mild retardation among blacks. Infants in this group were less responsive to the psychologist during the 8-month examination than those in all higher IQ groups (Table 6-25). They interacted less with their mothers than those in the above-average group (Table 6-26). Slower speed of response was a minor discriminator in the comparison with the average group.

Not unexpectedly, the mildly retarded were less well identified in infancy than the severely retarded. In the comparisons with higher IQ groups, canonical correlations between infancy discriminators and the group classification ranged from .30 to .57 among whites and .21 to .45 among blacks.

Summary analyses of all factors related to mild retardation through the first

Table 6-18

Infancy Conditions: Febrile Seizures, CNS Infection, Cord Disease, and Head Trauma by IQ Group

	1 Severely Retarded	2 Mildly Retarded	3 Borderline	4 Average	5 Above Average	χ^2	r_{IQ}
			Percent				

Febrile Seizures in First Year

White	4.35	1.99	1.50	0.84	0.64	25.37**	−.04**
Black	8.59	**1.56**	**1.14**	**0.95**	**0.00**	71.72**	−.04**

Group Ns: White - 92 201 2473 12777 1889
Black - 128 895 8319 9919 158

CNS Infection or Inflammation in First Year

White	1.18	0.00	0.26	0.16	0.11	6.82	−.02*
Black	3.28	1.07	**0.39**	**0.29**	0.65	38.85**	−.04**

Group Ns: White - 85 188 2309 12352 1843
Black - 122 841 7941 9627 155

Cord Disease at One Year

White	0.00	0.00	0.00	0.00	0.00	—	—
Black	0.82	0.24	*0.00*	*0.00*	0.00	77.69**	−.04**

Group Ns: White - 85 188 2309 12352 1843
Black - 122 841 7941 9627 155

Head Trauma in First Year

White	0.00	0.00	0.00	0.01	0.00	0.36	.00
Black	0.82	0.00	**0.00**	**0.00**	0.00	152.17**	−.03**

Group Ns: White - 85 188 2309 12352 1843
Black - 122 841 7941 9627 155

Differs from severely retarded in D.F.
Differs from severely and mildly retarded in D.F.s
  *$p < .05$
 **$p < .00001$

Table 6-19

Unfavorable Emotional Environment in First Year by IQ Group

	1 Severely Retarded	2 Mildly Retarded	3 Borderline	4 Average	5 Above Average	χ^2	r_{IQ}
			Percent				
White	8.24	9.04	8.49	5.76	2.88	63.08***	−.06***
Black	5.74	2.97	1.93	**1.69**	1.29	17.55*	−.03**

Group Ns: White -   85 188 2309 12352 1843

         Black - 122 841 7941 9627   155

Differs from severely retarded in D.F.

Differs from mildly retarded in D.F.

  *$p<.01$

 **$p<.0001$

***$p<.00001$

year of life are shown in Table 6-27. Forty of the 48 combined prenatal and perinatal characteristics and 19 of the 24 infancy characteristics were retained. Major discriminators were maternal intelligence, education, and socioeconomic status, and indices of motor, mental, and social development in the first year. Syndromes and major malformations from the neonatal period, and neurological abnormalities and smaller head size at age 1 were significant in both samples. Pregnancy risk factors were maternal urinary tract infection and toxoplasmosis among whites and low hematocrit, toxemia, and heart disease among blacks. Inhalation anesthetics at delivery and low fetal heart rate in the first stage of labor were risk factors for mild retardation in the white sample. A lower Apgar score at 1 minute in that sample and primary apnea in the newborn among blacks remained significant in the summary analyses.

Comparisons between the mildly retarded and the borderline and average groups produced only moderate canonical correlations ranging from .26 to .39. Although higher values of .65 and .69 were obtained in the comparisons with the above-average group, the discrimination was little improved over that based on prenatal and perinatal factors alone.

Table 6-20

**Standardized Coefficients for All Discriminators Through the First Year
Between the Severely Retarded and Comparison Groups**

Variable	Comparison Group							
	White				Black			
	MR	BL	AV	AA	MR	BL	AV	AA
Non-febrile seizures[a]	.18	.15	.12	.08	.30	.29	.21	.09
Down's syndrome	.38	.56	.52	.28	.49	.60	.44	—
Other genetic or post-infection syndromes	.30	.23	.31	.21	.09	.19	.22	—
Major CNS malformations	.18	.16	.17	.16	—	.11	.14	—
Bayley mental score at 8 mo.	—	−.04	−.06	−.08	−.38	−.23	−.20	—
Bayley motor score at 8 mo.	−.05	−.06	−.003	−.08	—	—	−.06	−.69
Neonatal seizures	.25	.12	.10	.11	.16	—	.07	—
Percent male	.27	—	.02	.05	—	.04	.05	—
Head circumference at 1 yr.	—	—	−.01	−.01	—	−.06	−.06	−.05
Cerebral palsy at 1 yr.	—	.38	.32	.16	—	.21	—	—
Delayed motor development at 1 yr.	—	—	.18	.31	.04	—	.37	—
Strabismus at 1 yr.	—	—	.03	—	.16	.09	.10	—
Major eye malformations	—	.10	.02	—	—	.07	.10	—
Maternal SRA score	—	—	−.03	−.06	—	—	−.003	−.25
Intensity of social response at 8 mo.	—	−.003	−.01	−.003	—	—	−.004	—
Maternal education	.18	—	—	−.06	—	—	−.07	—
Visual impairment at 1 yr.	—	.09	.06	—	—	.13	—	—
Dyskinesia or ataxia at 1 yr.	—	—	.05	.10	—	.08	—	—
Neonatal brain abnormality	—	—	.05	.04	—	.09	—	—
Head circumference at birth	—	—	—	−.03	—	—	—	−.08

(continued)

113

Table 6-20 (continued)

Variable	Comparison Group							
	White				Black			
	MR	BL	AV	AA	MR	BL	AV	AA
Socioeconomic index	—	—	−.01	−.08	—	—	—	−.18
Minor musculoskeletal malformations	.20	.12	.07	.05	—	—	—	—
Intensity of response at 8 mo.	−.26	−.03	—	−.04	—	—	—	—
Midforceps delivery	.23	.04	.02	—	—	—	—	—
Undescended testicles at 1 yr.	—	.10	.07	.08	—	—	—	—
Congenital heart disease at 1 yr.	—	.02	.02	.02	—	—	—	—
Peripheral nerve abnormality	—	.06	.05	—	—	—	—	—
Loss of one or both parents	—	—	.03	.05	—	—	—	—
Number of prenatal visits	—	—	−.01	−.06	—	—	—	—
Minor ear malformations	—	—	.04	.07	—	—	—	—
Weight gain in pregnancy	−.20	—	—	—	—	—	—	—
Apneic episode	—	.09	—	—	—	—	—	—
Adduction or contracture of hip	—	.04	—	—	—	—	—	—
Speed of response at 8 mo.	—	−.02	—	—	—	—	—	—
Major upper respiratory or mouth malformations	—	—	.07	—	—	—	—	—
Prolonged or recurrent hospitalization	—	—	.06	—	—	—	—	—
Nystagmus at 1 yr.	—	—	.05	—	—	—	—	—
Primary apnea	—	—	.02	—	—	—	—	—
Breech delivery	—	—	—	.04	—	—	—	—
Parity	—	—	—	.01	—	—	—	—
Febrile seizures[a]	—	—	—	—	.16	.07	.06	.04

(continued)

Table 6-20 (continued)

Variable	White				Black			
	MR	BL	AV	AA	MR	BL	AV	AA
Duration of response at 8 mo.	—	—	—	—	−.11	−.05	−.04	—
Seizures in pregnancy	—	—	—	—	.09	.06	.05	—
Head trauma in 1st year	—	—	—	—	—	.12	.09	—
Dysmaturity	—	—	—	—	13	.05	—	—
Major thoracic malformations	—	—	—	—	—	.07	.07	—
Respiratory difficulty	—	—	—	—	—	—	.02	.10
Meconium staining	—	—	—	—	—	.05	.05	—
Intravenous anesthetic at delivery	—	—	—	—	—	.04	.03	—
Housing density	—	—	—	—	−.15	—	—	—
Cord disease at 1 yr.	—	—	—	—	—	.08	—	—
Fetal or neonatal death at last delivery	—	—	—	—	—	.06	—	—
CNS infection or inflammation in 1st year	—	—	—	—	—	.04	—	—
Major musculoskeletal malformations	—	—	—	—	—	.04	—	—
Urinary tract infection in pregnancy	—	—	—	—	—	−.03	—	—
Major cardiovascular malformations	—	—	—	—	—	.002	—	—
Cord complications	—	—	—	—	—	—	−.04	—
Failure to thrive	—	—	—	—	—	—	.03	—
Unfavorable emotional environment in 1st year	—	—	—	—	—	—	.03	—
Toxemia	—	—	—	—	—	—	.03	—
Highest FHR in 1st stage of labor	—	—	—	—	—	—	—	−.09
Canonical correlation	.66*	.70*	.68*	.80*	.59*	.56*	.62*	.82*

[a]Occurring between 1 and 12 months.

*$p < .00001$

Table 6-21
**Standardized Coefficients for Infancy Discriminators Between
the Mildly Retarded and Comparison Groups**

Variable	Comparison Group					
	White			Black		
	BL	AV	AA	BL	AV	AA
Bayley motor score at 8 mo.	−.29	−.18	−.38	−.44	−.32	−.48
Delayed motor development at 1 yr.	.33	.43	.31	.29	.33	—
Bayley mental score at 8 mo.	−.35	−.35	−.24	−.06	−.29	—
Intensity of social response at 8 mo.	−.14	−.11	−.16	−.13	−.09	—
Head circumference at 1 yr.	−.30	−.30	−.40	—	−.21	—
Hypoxia in 1st year	.29	.18	—	.18	—	—
Hypotonia at 1 yr.	—	.09	—	.20	.05	—
Failure to thrive at 1 yr.	—	.10	—	—	.08	—
Undescended testicle at 1 yr.	.25	.20	.17	—	—	—
Congenital heart disease at 1 yr.	—	.11	.10	—	—	—
Non-febrile seizures in 1st year	—	.06	.12	—	—	—
Cerebral palsy at 1 yr.	—	.21	—	—	—	—
Prolonged or recurrent hospitalization in 1st year	—	.11	—	—	—	—
Unfavorable emotional environment in 1st year	—	—	.10	—	—	—
Percent male	—	—	—	.20	.23	.25
Weight at 1 yr.	—	—	—	−.19	−.08	−.44
Social response to examiner at 8 mo.	—	—	—	−.12	−.06	−.28
Weight at 4 mo.	—	—	—	−.24	−.24	—
Cord disease at 1 yr.	—	—	—	.19	.13	—
Dyskinesia or ataxia at 1 yr.	—	—	—	.16	.10	—
Visual impairment at 1 yr.	—	—	—	—	.09	—
Speed of response at 8 mo.	—	—	—	—	−.004	—
Head circumference at 4 mo.	—	—	—	—	—	−.29
Social response to mother at 8 mo.	—	—	—	—	—	−.17
Canonical correlation	*.30**	*.29**	*.57**	*.21**	*.32**	*.45**

*$p<.00001$

Table 6-22
Hypoxia in First Year by IQ Group

	1 Severely Retarded	2 Mildly Retarded	3 Borderline	4 Average	5 Above Average	χ^2	r_{IQ}
			Percent				
White	0.00	1.06	*0.04*	*0.04*	0.00	41.79***	−.02*
Black	0.82	0.24	*0.00*	0.03	0.00	37.26***	−.03**

Group Ns: White -   85 188 2309 12352 1843

Black - 122 841 7941 9627 155

Differs from mildly retarded in D.F.
  *p<.01
 **p<.001
***p<.00001

Table 6-23
Undescended Testicle at One Year by IQ Group

	1 Severely Retarded	2 Mildly Retarded	3 Borderline	4 Average	5 Above Average	χ^2	r_{IQ}
			Percent				
White	3.45	5.43	*1.64*	*0.80*	*0.48*	34.23*	−.05*
Black	6.33	0.62	0.86	0.71	0.00	31.55*	−.03

Group Ns: White -   58   92 1219 6532 1049

Black - 79 480 4171 4806 81

Differs from mildly retarded in D.F.
*p<.00001

Table 6-24

Weight in Kilograms at One Year by IQ Group

	1 Severely Retarded	2 Mildly Retarded	3 Borderline	4 Average	5 Above Average	F	r_{IQ}
	M S.D.	M S.D.	M S.D.	M S.D.	M S.D.		
White	9.2 1.6	9.2 1.3	9.6 1.3	9.9 1.2	10.1 1.1	66.40*	.15*
Black	8.8 1.4	9.1 1.2	*9.4 1.2*	*9.7 1.2*	*10.1 1.2*	95.65*	.17*

Differs from mildly retarded in D.F.
$p < .00001$

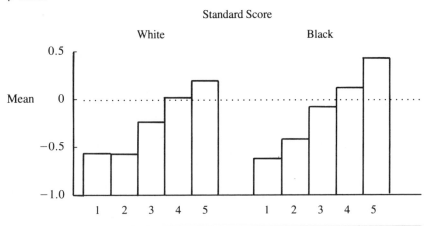

Standard Score

Note. Group Ns: White-   70 145 2007 11085 1616
             Black-   104 731 7184   8832   145

Table 6-25

Social Response to Examiner Rating at Eight Months by IQ Group

	1 Severely Retarded		2 Mildly Retarded		3 Borderline		4 Average		5 Above Average		F	r_{IQ}
	M	S.D.	M	S.D.	M	S.D.	M	S.D.	M	S.D.		
White	2.8	0.6	2.9	0.6	3.1	0.6	3.1	0.7	3.3	0.8	21.96*	.09*
Black	3.0	0.5	2.9	0.6	*3.0*	*0.6*	*3.1*	*0.6*	3.2	0.7	21.46*	.07*

Differs from mildly retarded in D.F.
*$p < .00001$

Standard Score

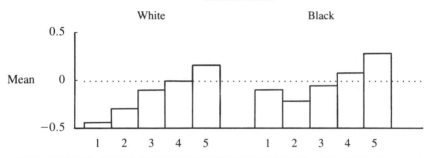

Note. Group Ns: White- 49 127 1751 10001 1515
Black- 80 617 6349 7739 111

Table 6-26

Social Response to Mother Rating at Eight Months by IQ Group

	1 Severely Retarded		2 Mildly Retarded		3 Borderline		4 Average		5 Above Average		F	r_{IQ}
	M	S.D.	M	S.D.	M	S.D.	M	S.D.	M	S.D.		
White	3.0	0.6	3.2	0.6	3.2	0.5	3.3	0.5	3.3	0.5	7.03*	.04**
Black	3.2	0.6	3.2	0.6	3.2	0.5	3.3	0.5	*3.4*	*0.6*	9.42**	.05**

Group Ns: White- 49 127 1748 10005 1521
Black- 83 618 6346 7754 109
Differs from mildly retarded in D.F.
*$p < .0001$
**$p < .00001$

Table 6-27

Standardized Coefficients for All Discriminators Through the First Year Between the Mildly Retarded and Comparison Groups

Variable	Comparison Group					
	White			Black		
	BL	AV	AA	BL	AV	AA
Maternal SRA score	−.24	−.10	−.19	−.23	−.24	−.35
Delayed motor development at 1 yr.	.24	.34	.19	.24	.26	—
Bayley mental score at 8 mo.	−.45	−.35	−.17	−.06	−.19	—
Maternal education	—	−.13	−.15	−.28	−.25	−.17
Socioeconomic index	—	−.08	−.28	−.12	−.11	−.38
Intensity of social response at 8 mo.	−.12	−.09	−.08	−.10	−.06	—
Bayley motor score at 8 mo.	—	—	−.15	−.29	−.23	−.28
Head circumference at 1 yr.	−.25	−.20	−.21	—	−.16	—
Retarded mother	.13	.14	.09	—	.09	—
Housing density	.09	.08	.11	—	.11	—
Maternal height	—	—	−.03	—	−.03	—
Down's syndrome	.30	.30	.08	—	—	—
Major CNS malformations	.23	.19	.11	—	—	—
Age at menarche	.12	.09	.08	—	—	—
Hypoxia in 1st year	.22	.15	—	—	—	—
Cigarettes per day in pregnancy	−.16	−.12	—	—	—	—
Major upper respiratory or mouth malformations	—	.19	.09	—	—	—
Abdomino-pelvic x-rays	−.13	−.07	—	—	—	—
Congenital heart disease at 1 yr.	—	.08	.08	—	—	—
Urinary tract infection in pregnancy	—	.07	.08	—	—	—
Apgar score at 1 min.	−.10	−.05	—	—	—	—
Non-febrile seizures[a]	—	.05	.10	—	—	—
Inhalation anesthetic at delivery	—	.06	.07	—	—	—
Major genitourinary malformations	—	.06	.07	—	—	—
Induction of labor	—	−.06	−.07	—	—	—
Major cardiovascular malformations	.15	—	—	—	—	—
Abruptio placenta	.11	—	—	—	—	—
Cerebral palsy at 1 yr.	—	.15	—	—	—	—
Toxoplasmosis in pregnancy	—	.14	—	—	—	—
Undescended testicle at 1 yr.	—	.14	—	—	—	—
Retarded father	—	.08	—	—	—	—
Failure to thrive at 1 yr.	—	.08	—	—	—	—

(continued)

120

Table 6-27 (continued)

Variable	White			Black		
	BL	AV	AA	BL	AV	AA
Highest FHR in 1st stage of labor	—	−.04	—	—	—	—
Prolonged or recurrent hospitalization	—	.05	—	—	—	—
Unfavorable emotional environment in 1st year	—	—	.07	—	—	—
Head circumference at birth	—	—	−.01	—	—	—
Weight at 1 yr.	—	—	—	−.14	−.05	−.14
Hematocrit in pregnancy	—	—	—	−.10	−.06	−.06
Weight at 4 mo.	—	—	—	−.15	−.15	—
Percent male	—	—	—	.14	.16	—
Pregnancy-free interval	—	—	—	−.15	−.13	—
Hypotonia at 1 yr.	—	—	—	.21	.07	—
Other genetic or post-infection syndromes	—	—	—	.14	.11	—
Cord disease at 1 yr.	—	—	—	.16	.10	—
Toxemia	—	—	—	.13	.11	—
Parity	—	—	—	.02	—	.22
Organic heart disease in pregnancy	—	—	—	.10	.06	—
Dyskinesia or ataxia at 1 yr.	—	—	—	.16	.06	—
Primary apnea	—	—	—	.05	.03	—
Prior fetal death	—	—	—	.11	—	—
Major musculoskeletal malformations	—	—	—	.10	—	—
Multiple apneic episodes	—	—	—	.09	—	—
Gestational age	—	—	—	−.02	—	—
Multiple birth	—	—	—	—	.08	—
Bacterial infection in pregnancy	—	—	—	—	.05	—
Major eye malformations	—	—	—	—	.05	—
Number of prenatal visits	—	—	—	—	−.04	—
Maternal age	—	—	—	—	—	−.41
Head circumference at 4 mo.	—	—	—	—	—	−.09
Canonical correlation	.35*	.35*	.69*	.26*	.39*	.65*

aOccurring between 1 and 12 months

*$p < .00001$

7
The Preschool Period

Tests of speech, language, and hearing were given to approximately one half of the study population at age 3 (Lassman et al., 1980). A battery of psychological tests was administered in all study centers at age 4 as described in an earlier monograph (Broman et al., 1975). From the 3-year examination, summary evaluations of normal or abnormal performance in four areas were screened. Language expression was coded as abnormal if the child failed to name presented objects or to produce short sentences or meaningful phrases. Abnormal language reception was defined as failure to identify familiar objects or to understand action words or words indicating relationships and direction in space. A code of abnormal speech production reflected problems in intelligibility or fluency and unusual voice quality or poor articulation. Abnormal hearing was defined by failure on both a speech–hearing test and a three-frequency pure tone test at 20 db. All four evaluations were related to severe or mild retardation in the univariate screen.

At age 4, intelligence was assessed with the abbreviated version of the Stanford–Binet Intelligence Scale. Test–retest reliability of the IQ scores was .83 in a random sample of 140 children reexamined after 3 months by a visiting psychologist from another study center. Concept formation ability was evaluated with the Graham–Ernhart Block Sort, a test requiring the children to group blocks differing in color, size, and shape. The maximum score on sorting tasks at three levels of difficulty was 45. Test–retest reliability was .43 in the sample of 140 children. The four fine motor subtests in the battery were bead stringing from the Stanford–Binet, Wallin Pegboard B, Porteus Maze IV, and copying a circle, cross, and square. Gross motor skills were evaluated with a line-walking task, hopping, and catching a ball. Fine and gross motor scores, ranging from 0 to 100, were derived from the number of subtests passed in each area (Broman et al., 1975). Hand dominance was determined from performance on the pegboard

Table 7-1

Standardized Coefficients for Preschool Discriminators Between the Severely Retarded and Comparison Groups

Variable[a]	Comparison Group							
	White				Black			
	MR	BL	AV	AA	MR	BL	AV	AA
Abnormal behavior summary rating	.30	.57	.59	.26	.33	.67	.79	.11
Stanford-Binet IQ	−.56	−.37	−.09	−.01	−.67	−.26	−.11	−.36
Abnormal language expression at age 3	.19	.05	.25	.49	—	.15	.15	.30
Abnormal speech production at age 3	—	.12	.22	.02	.15	.26	.17	—
Abnormal language reception at age 3	—	.07	.28	.29	—	.03	.05	.16
Verbal communication	−.18	−.25	−.12	—	−.05	−.09	−.02	—
Height	—	−.11	−.05	−.01	—	−.05	−.03	—
Socioeconomic index	—	.06	—	−.04	—	.03	−.004	−.07
Head circumference	—	—	−.07	—	−.17	−.08	−.02	—
Impulsivity	—	.11	.08	—	—	.12	.02	—
Goal orientation	—	—	—	−.01	—	—	−.03	−.16
Right handedness	—	−.02	−.02	—	—	—	−.01	—
Response to directions	—	—	−.02	—	—	—	−.04	—
Attention span	−.08	−.07	−.10	−.02	—	—	—	—
Activity level	.19	—	—	—	—	—	—	—
Dependency	—	—	—	—	—	—	.02	—
Canonical correlation	*.70**	*.59**	*.57**	*.96**	*.63**	*.55**	*.76**	*.96**

[a]All preschool measures were taken at age 4 except where indicated.

*$p < .00001$

and copying tasks. If different hands were used, dominance was considered indeterminate. Overall dominance was based on agreement among hand, foot, and eye dominance with lack of agreement coded as indeterminate. Foot dominance was established by kicking a ball and eye dominance by looking at a toy through a hole cut in a shoe box.

A behavior profile was completed by the examining psychologist following

Table 7-2

Abnormal Behavior Summary Rating at Age Four by IQ Group

	1 Severely Retarded	2 Mildly Retarded	3 Borderline	4 Average	5 Above Average	x^2	r_{IQ}
			Percent				
White	87.50	**28.48**	*6.58*	*1.59*	*0.62*	2222.31*	−.26*
Black	74.16	**13.20**	*2.00*	*0.32*	*0.00*	3003.67*	−.26*

Group Ns: White-   64 158 2006 10890 1454
            Black-   89 712 6989 8773   145
Differs from severely retarded in D.F.
Differs from severely and mildly retarded in D.F.s
*$p < .00001$

the testing session at age 4. Ten behaviors, which included activity level, attention span, goal orientation, and verbal communication, were rated on 5-point scales with a "normal" midpoint of 3. An overall rating of normal, suspect, or abnormal behavior was also given. All 17 of the psychological variables passed the univariate screen. Height, weight, and head circumference measured at age 4 were also related to severe or mild retardation. A total of 24 preschool characteristics were screened, all of which were retained for multivariate analyses.

THE SEVERELY RETARDED

Most of the differentiating preschool factors were significant in both samples (Table 7-1). Major discriminators between the severely retarded and higher IQ groups were the summary behavior rating at age 4 and IQ score. The rating of abnormal behavior was given more often to the severely retarded white than black children (Table 7-2). In both samples, the frequency of this rating decreased sharply as IQ level increased; the negative correlation with IQ score at age 7 was .26 in both samples. Mean IQ at age 4 in the severely retarded groups was 42, about 10 points higher than the mean score at age 7 (Table 7-3). Correlations between the 4 and 7-year IQ scores were .63 and .59 in the white and black samples, respectively. As shown in the graph of standard scores computed within each sample, the relationships between preschool IQ and later cognitive level were highly similar in the two samples.

Evaluations of language expression, language reception, and speech production at age 3 were independent discriminators of moderate importance. In each

Table 7-3

Stanford-Binet IQ at Age Four by IQ Group

	1 Severely Retarded		2 Mildly Retarded		3 Borderline		4 Average		5 Above Average		F	r_{IQ}
	M	S.D.	M	S.D.	M	S.D.	M	S.D.	M	S.D.		
White	41.8	14.2	**68.5**	**13.0**	*89.2*	*12.8*	*105.7*	*13.3*	*122.4*	*14.8*	1821.30*	.63*
Black	42.1	14.7	**72.1**	**11.8**	*86.2*	*11.9*	*97.1*	*11.7*	*111.8*	*13.2*	1737.07*	.59*

Differs from severely retarded in D.F.
Differs from severely and mildly retarded in D.F.s
*$p < .00001$

Standard Score

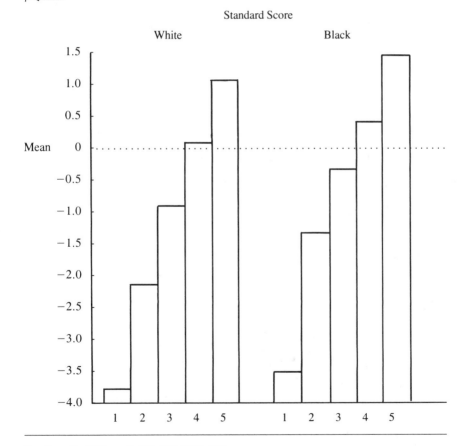

Note. Group Ns: White-   46   147   1968   10846   1451
                    Black-   73   682   6957   8759   145

Table 7-4

Language and Speech Abnormalities at Age Three by IQ Group

	1 Severely Retarded	2 Mildly Retarded	3 Borderline	4 Average	5 Above Average	χ^2	r_{IQ}
			Percent				

Abnormal Language Expression

White	93.94	**42.31**	*15.76*	*3.15*	*0.24*	1098.32*	−.30*
Black	86.05	23.22	*5.98*	*2.29*	**0.00**	973.10*	−.23*
Group Ns: White -	33	104	1250	5967	817		
Black -	43	422	4316	5293	80		

Abnormal Language Reception

White	89.29	35.24	**12.74**	*2.33*	*0.24*	1009.03*	−.27*
Black	80.43	28.64	**14.17**	*6.76*	**0.00**	514.43*	−.21*
Group Ns: White -	28	105	1248	5957	818		
Black -	46	447	4405	5322	80		

Abnormal Speech Production

White	81.25	30.77	**10.92**	*2.71*	*0.86*	804.96*	−.24*
Black	77.27	**17.55**	*3.97*	*1.91*	1.27	927.07*	−.20*
Group Ns: White -	32	104	1236	5951	816		
Black -	44	416	4229	5233	79		

Differs from severely retarded in D.F.
Differs from severely and mildly retarded in D.F.s
*p<.00001

of these areas, four fifths or more of the severely retarded were rated as abnormal. Negative correlations with IQ at age 7 ranged from .20 to .30 (Table 7-4).

Ratings of specific behaviors at age 4 as well as the overall summary rating were significant in the group comparisons. The most important was the low score for verbal communication among the severely retarded (Table 7-5). Other ratings retained in the analyses in both samples indicated a relatively high level of impulsiveness, poor goal orientation, and unresponsiveness to directions. A higher rating for dependency was a minor discriminator for the severely retarded black children. Among whites, the shorter attention span of the severely re-

Table 7-5
Behavior Ratings at Age Four by IQ Group

	1 Severely Retarded		2 Mildly Retarded		3 Borderline		4 Average		5 Above Average		F	r$_{IQ}$
	M	S.D.	M	S.D.	M	S.D.	M	S.D.	M	S.D.		

Verbal Communication

	M	S.D.	M	S.D.	M	S.D.	M	S.D.	M	S.D.	F	r$_{IQ}$
White	1.7	1.2	**2.7**	**1.0**	*2.9*	*0.8*	**2.9**	**0.6**	3.1	0.5	77.24*	.13*
Black	1.9	1.3	**2.6**	**0.9**	*2.8*	*0.7*	**2.9**	**0.6**	*3.1*	*0.6*	124.89*	.17*

Group Ns: White - 50 157 1993 10814 1450
Black - 78 709 6976 8752 145

Impulsivity

	M	S.D.	M	S.D.	M	S.D.	M	S.D.	M	S.D.	F	r$_{IQ}$
White	3.4	1.3	3.0	1.0	**3.0**	**0.6**	**3.0**	**0.4**	3.0	0.3	10.14*	− .00
Black	3.3	1.2	2.9	0.8	**3.0**	**0.5**	*3.0*	*0.3*	3.0	0.2	27.40*	.05*

Group Ns: White - 52 154 1984 10804 1448
Black - 81 708 6963 8743 145

Goal Orientation

	M	S.D.	M	S.D.	M	S.D.	M	S.D.	M	S.D.	F	r$_{IQ}$
White	1.8	0.7	2.1	0.6	2.6	0.6	*2.9*	*0.4*	**3.0**	**0.4**	437.60*	.34*
Black	1.6	0.5	2.3	0.6	*2.7*	*0.5*	*2.9*	*0.4*	3.0	0.4	629.14*	.37*

Group Ns: White - 52 156 1987 10802 1450
Black - 84 709 6971 8746 145

Response to Directions

	M	S.D.	M	S.D.	M	S.D.	M	S.D.	M	S.D.	F	r$_{IQ}$
White	1.6	0.8	2.3	0.9	2.7	0.7	**2.9**	**0.5**	3.0	0.4	218.93*	.21*
Black	1.6	0.7	2.4	0.9	2.8	0.7	*3.0*	*0.5*	3.0	0.3	328.18*	.26*

Group Ns: White - 58 159 2001 10836 1452
Black - 85 713 6987 8752 145

Dependency

	M	S.D.	M	S.D.	M	S.D.	M	S.D.	M	S.D.	F	r$_{IQ}$
White	3.9	1.3	3.7	0.9	3.4	0.7	3.2	0.6	3.0	0.6	149.23*	− .23*
Black	4.2	1.1	3.7	0.8	*3.3*	*0.6*	*3.1*	*0.5*	3.0	0.5	338.57*	− .27*

Group Ns: White - 50 156 1995 10822 1450
Black - 79 706 6959 8750 145

Differs from severely retarded in D.F.
Differs from mildly retarded in D.F.
Differs from severely and mildly retarded in D.F.s
*p<.00001

Table 7-6

Attention Span Rating at Age Four by IQ Group

	1 Severely Retarded		2 Mildly Retarded		3 Borderline		4 Average		5 Above Average		F	r_{IQ}
	M	S.D.	M	S.D.	M	S.D.	M	S.D.	M	S.D.		
White	1.4	0.6	**2.1**	**0.8**	*2.6*	*0.7*	*2.9*	*0.4*	*3.0*	*0.4*	407.58*	.31*
Black	1.7	1.1	2.3	0.9	2.7	0.6	*2.9*	*0.4*	2.9	0.3	385.60*	.29*

Differs from severely retarded in D.F.
Differs from mildly retarded in D.F.
Differs from severely and mildly retarded in D.F.s
p <.00001

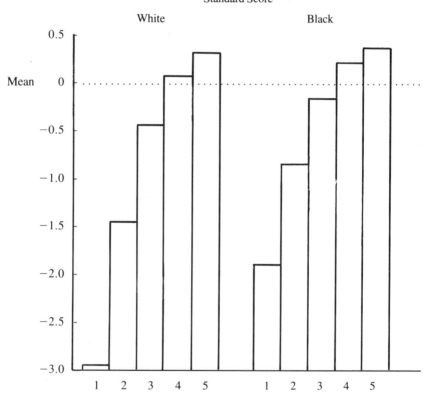

Standard Score

Note. Group Ns: White- 54 154 1984 10802 1446
Black- 81 710 6966 8748 145

Table 7-7

Activity Level Rating at Age Four by IQ Group

	1 Severely Retarded		2 Mildly Retarded		3 Borderline		4 Average		5 Above Average		F	r_{IQ}
	M	S.D.	M	S.D.	M	S.D.	M	S.D.	M	S.D.		
White	3.7	1.3	**3.2**	**1.0**	3.1	0.7	3.0	0.6	3.0	0.5	35.48*	−.07*
Black	3.4	1.3	3.1	0.9	3.0	0.7	3.0	0.5	3.0	0.4	11.08*	−.03*

Differs from severely retarded in D.F.
*$p < .00001$

Standard Score

Note. Group Ns: White-   58   158   1995   10831   1450
              Black-   84   711   6977   8751   145

tarded was a consistent discriminator and a higher level of activity was significant in the comparison with the mildly retarded group (Tables 7-6 and 7-7).
The four-year behavior ratings most highly correlated with IQ at age 7 were
those of goal orientation and attention span.

The smaller stature and head circumference of the severely retarded were
discriminating factors in both samples. Correlations between these physical
measurements at age 4 and IQ at age 7 ranged from .15 to .22 (Tables 7-8 and
7-9). Fewer of the severely retarded were classified as right-handed, a minor

Table 7-8
Height in Centimeters at Age Four by IQ Group

	1 Severely Retarded	2 Mildly Retarded	3 Borderline	4 Average	5 Above Average	F	r_{IQ}
	M S.D.	M S.D.	M S.D.	M S.D.	M S.D.		
White	95.4 7.4	98.4 5.2	**99.9 4.6**	**100.8 4.4**	**101.8 4.4**	61.52*	.15*
Black	97.3 5.7	100.4 4.9	**101.6 4.5**	*102.4 4.4*	*104.1 4.7*	74.76*	.16*

Group Ns: White-   47   129   1734   9515   1295
Black-   78   634   6344   7712   106

Differs from severely retarded in D.F.
Differs from mildly retarded in D.F.
Differs from severely and mildly retarded in D.F.s
*p <.00001

discriminator in both samples (Table 7-10). The control variable of prenatal socioeconomic index was significant in five of the six comparisons between the severely retarded and nonretarded groups in the two samples. Scores were higher than those of families of borderline children and lower than those of average and/or above-average children.

Development in the preschool period was highly predictive of severe cognitive deficit at age 7. Comparisons between the extreme groups produced a canonical correlation of .96 in each sample. The comparison with average children among blacks and with the mildly retarded among whites resulted in high correlations of .76 and .70, respectively.

Table 7-11 presents a summary of all discriminators for the severely retarded through age 4. They include 45 of the 61 factors significant through age 1 and all of the 15 preschool characteristics. Canonical correlations ranged from .65 to .96 in the two samples, reflecting moderately high to high explanatory power. The best discriminators were the marked impairments in intelligence, behavior, and use of language in the preschool period; the presence of major syndromes and CNS malformations at birth; and seizures and cerebral palsy in the first year of life. From the perspective of 4 years after delivery, prenatal factors were of little importance. Indices of relatively low socioeconomic status among mothers of the severely retarded were retained, but pregnancy complications were not. The significant obstetric risk factors were midforceps delivery, intravenous anesthetics, and low fetal heart rate. Malformations of systems other than the CNS, seizures in the first month, and signs of perinatal anoxia were additional neonatal discriminators in the 4-year summary analyses. Smaller

Table 7-9
Head Circumference in Centimeters at Age Four by IQ Group

	1 Severely Retarded		2 Mildly Retarded		3 Borderline		4 Average		5 Above Average		F	r_{IQ}
	M	S.D.	M	S.D.	M	S.D.	M	S.D.	M	S.D.		
White	48.5	3.2	48.8	2.3	*49.6*	*1.6*	**50.1**	**1.5**	*50.7*	*1.5*	131.95*	.22*
Black	48.4	2.0	**49.5**	**1.7**	**49.7**	**1.6**	**50.1**	**1.6**	*50.8*	*1.4*	85.06*	.17*

Differs from severely retarded in D.F.
Differs from mildly retarded in D.F.
Differs from severely and mildly retarded in D.F.s
*$p < .00001$

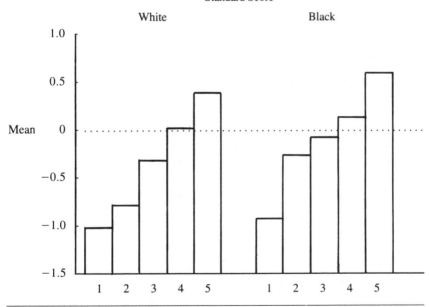

Standard Score

Note. Group Ns: White- 48 128 1727 9464 1285
Black- 81 630 6330 7677 107

Table 7-10

Right Handedness at Age Four by IQ Group

	1 Severely Retarded	2 Mildly Retarded	3 Borderline	4 Average	5 Above Average	χ^2	r_{IQ}
			Percent				
White	50.00	66.67	**75.52**	**79.07**	78.34	45.70**	.04**
Black	62.30	76.30	79.50	**80.88**	82.64	23.89*	.04**

Group Ns: White- 44 153 1973 10800 1450
          Black- 61 692 6955   8752   144
Differs from severely retarded in D.F.
*p <.001
**p <.00001

head size was a robust risk factor for the severely retarded. The period of infancy was characterized by delayed mental and motor development.

THE MILDLY RETARDED

Preschool discriminators between the mildly retarded and higher IQ groups are shown in Table 7-12. The most important were the Stanford–Binet IQ score, fine motor and concept formation scores, and a rating of expressive language. Mean IQ scores in the white and black groups were 68 and 72 (see Table 7-3). At age 7, the mean score on the WISC was 63 in each group. The fine motor scores of the mildly retarded were approximately 50 on a scale with a maximum value of 100; correlations with IQ at age 7 were .38 and .41 in the white and black samples (Table 7-13). The Graham–Ernhart Block Sort, a test of concept formation ability, had similar correlations with school-age IQ (Table 7-14). The low mean scores of the mildly retarded had large standard deviations indicating considerable within-group variability. At age 3, 42% of mildly retarded white children and 23% of the black group were classified as having abnormal language expression (see Table 7-4). Comparable proportions in the average IQ groups were between 2% and 3%.

Other consistent discriminators between the mildly retarded and nonretarded groups were behavior and gross motor skills at age 4. As was the case with language expression, more of the mildly retarded white than black children had an abnormal rating or score. The summary rating of abnormal behavior was given to 28% of mildly retarded white children but to only 13% of those in the

Table 7-11

Standardized Coefficients for All Discriminators Through Age Four Between the Severely Retarded and Comparison Groups

Variable	Comparison Group							
	White				Black			
	MR	BL	AV	AA	MR	BL	AV	AA
Abnormal behavior summary rating at age 4	.22	.27	.29	.22	.27	.43	.63	.11
Stanford-Binet IQ at age 4	− .44	− .18	− .05	—	− .42	− .11	− .06	− .34
Non-febrile seizures[a]	.09	.09	.08	—	.16	.18	.06	.004
Down's syndrome	.28	.46	.43	—	.32	.44	.21	—
Other genetic or post-infection syndromes	.16	.16	.22	.08	—	.13	.06	—
Abnormal language expression at age 3	.20	—	.12	.37	—	.09	.12	.28
Abnormal language reception at age 3	—	.03	.13	.39	—	.04	.05	.18
Abnormal speech production at age 3	—	.06	.10	.03	.14	.19	.13	—
Verbal communication at age 4	− .06	− .11	− .04	—	− .04	− .05	− .02	—
Major CNS malformations	—	.14	.16	.05	—	.10	.08	—
Neonatal seizures	.08	.07	.06	—	.11	—	.04	—
Bayley motor score at 8 months	− .01	− .002	—	− .01	—	—	− .02	− .01
Bayley mental score at 8 months	—	—	− .02	—	− .13	− .13	− .07	—
Impulsivity at age 4	—	.09	.05	—	—	.07	.01	—
Socioeconomic index	—	—	—	− .03	—	− .004	− .002	− .07
Cerebral palsy at 1 year	—	.32	.25	—	—	.12	—	—
Goal orientation at age 4	—	—	—	− .03	—	—	− .03	− .16

(continued)

Table 7-11 (continued)

Variable	Comparison Group							
	White				Black			
	MR	BL	AV	AA	MR	BL	AV	AA
Head circumference at age 4	—	—	−.02	—	−.08	−.04	—	—
Height at age 4	—	—	−.005	—	—	−.01	−.02	—
Delayed motor development at 1 year	—	—	.13	—	—	—	.12	—
Dyskinesia or ataxia at 1 year	—	—	.04	—	—	.04	—	—
Response to directions at age 4	—	—	−.009	—	—	—	−.03	—
Undescended testicles at 1 year	—	.07	.06	.05	—	—	—	—
Attention span at age 4	−.005	−.01	−.02	—	—	—	—	—
Midforceps delivery	.19	—	.02	—	—	—	—	—
Minor musculoskeletal malformations	—	.08	.06	—	—	—	—	—
Intensity of response at 8 months	−.02	−.04	—	—	—	—	—	—
Activity level at age 4	.20	—	—	—	—	—	—	—
Apneic episode	—	.09	—	—	—	—	—	—
Major eye malformations	—	.07	—	—	—	—	—	—
Congenital heart disease at 1 year	—	.02	—	—	—	—	—	—
Major upper respiratory or mouth malformations	—	—	.06	—	—	—	—	—
Visual impairment at 1 year	—	—	.04	—	—	—	—	—
Prolonged or recurrent hospitalization in 1st year	—	—	.04	—	—	—	—	—

(continued)

Table 7-11 (continued)

Variable	Comparison Group							
	White				Black			
	MR	BL	AV	AA	MR	BL	AV	AA
Intensity of social response at 8 months	—	—	−.01	—	—	—	—	—
Neonatal brain abnormality	—	—	—	.04	—	—	—	—
Minor ear malformations	—	—	—	.04	—	—	—	—
Parity	—	—	—	.03	—	—	—	—
Maternal SRA score	—	—	—	−.03	—	—	—	—
Strabismus at 1 year	—	—	—	—	.09	.06	.03	—
Febrile seizures[a]	—	—	—	—	.12	—	.04	—
Head trauma in 1st year	—	—	—	—	—	.05	.02	—
Major thoracic malformations	—	—	—	—	—	.04	.02	—
Duration of response at 8 months	—	—	—	—	—	.02	−.001	—
Housing density	—	—	—	—	−.07	—	—	—
Fetal or neonatal death at last delivery	—	—	—	—	—	.04	—	—
Meconium staining	—	—	—	—	—	.04	—	—
CNS infection or inflammation in 1st year	—	—	—	—	—	.04	—	—
Intravenous anesthetic at delivery	—	—	—	—	—	.03	—	—
Dysmaturity	—	—	—	—	—	.03	—	—
Major musculoskeletal malformations	—	—	—	—	—	.03	—	—
Urinary tract infection in pregnancy	—	—	—	—	—	−.01	—	—
Cord disease at 1 year	—	—	—	—	—	.01	—	—
Maternal education	—	—	—	—	—	—	−.02	—

(continued)

Table 7-11 (continued)

Variable	White				Black			
	MR	BL	AV	AA	MR	BL	AV	AA
Cord complications	—	—	—	—	—	—	− .02	—
Dependency at age 4	—	—	—	—	—	—	− .02	—
Right handedness at age 4	—	—	—	—	—	—	− .001	—
Head circumference at birth	—	—	—	—	—	—	—	− .03
Head circumference at 1 year	—	—	—	—	—	—	—	− .02
Highest FHR in 1st stage of labor	—	—	—	—	—	—	—	− .01
Canonical correlation	*.75**	*.75**	*.74**	*.96**	*.69**	*.65**	*.80**	*.96**

[a]Occurring between 1 and 12 months

$*p<.00001$

black sample. Mean gross motor scores were 32 and 53 in the two groups (Table 7-14). Correlations between this index of gross motor development and IQ at age 7 were .24 and .25 in the two samples.

A shorter attention span, poorer goal orientation, and less verbal communication were specific behaviors that discriminated between the mildly retarded and higher IQ groups in both samples. The mildly retarded black children were rated as more dependent, less responsive to directions, and less impulsive than children in the average group. Less impulsiveness, or perhaps more apprehension in the testing situation, contrasted with the greater impulsiveness at age 4 of the severely retarded in both samples.

Poorer verbal skills at age 3 were reflected in receptive language and in speech as well as in expressive language. Abnormal ratings in the two areas were given more frequently to the white than to the black mildly retarded children (see Table 7-4). Impaired hearing at this age, detected among 12% of mildly retarded whites and 7% of mildly retarded blacks, was a significant factor in the comparison with the borderline group in each sample (Table 7-15).

A lower frequency of right dominance at age 4 (hand, eye, and foot) discriminated between the mildly retarded and all higher IQ groups among whites. The

Table 7-12

Standardized Coefficients for Preschool Discriminators Between the Mildly Retarded and Comparison Groups

Variable[a]	Comparison Group					
	White			Black		
	BL	AV	AA	BL	AV	AA
Stanford-Binet IQ	−.56	−.26	−.20	−.42	−.34	−.65
Fine motor score	−.07	−.15	−.21	−.26	−.21	−.21
Graham-Ernhart Block Sort score	−.25	−.22	−.24	−.06	−.10	−.05
Abnormal language expression at age 3	.06	.29	.24	.20	.17	—
Abnormal behavior summary rating	.13	.27	.07	.19	.20	—
Gross motor score	−.26	−.12	−.06	−.13	−.06	—
Socioeconomic index	—	−.01	−.15	−.12	−.08	−.22
Head circumference	−.14	−.14	−.09	—	−.05	−.08
Attention span	−.04	−.12	−.08	—	−.11	—
Goal orientation	—	−.02	−.06	−.07	−.08	—
Verbal communication	−.05	—	—	−.05	−.06	−.05
Abnormal language reception at age 3	—	.26	.10	—	−.05	—
Abnormal speech production at age 3	—	.15	—	.13	.07	—
Weight	—	—	−.02	−.09	—	—
Abnormal hearing at age 3	.05	—	—	.03	—	—
Percent male	−.26	−.16	−.10	—	—	—
Right dominance	−.12	−.05	−.05	—	—	—
Height	—	—	—	—	−.06	−.04
Dependency	—	—	—	.18	.12	—
Response to directions	—	—	—	—	−.12	—
Impulsivity	—	—	—	—	−.10	—
Canonical correlation	.44*	.45*	.86*	.39*	.59*	.82*

[a]All preschool measures were taken at age 4 except where indicated.

*$p < .00001$

proportion of children with established right dominance at this age tended to increase with IQ level in both samples (Table 7-16). At age 4, the smaller size of the mildly retarded was reflected in head circumference (the most sensitive of the three measurements), weight, and, among blacks, height. The relationship between weight and IQ level is shown in Table 7-17. The control variables of socioeconomic index and sex of child were retained in the analyses of preschool

Table 7-13

Fine Motor Score at Age Four by IQ Group

	1 Severely Retarded		2 Mildly Retarded		3 Borderline		4 Average		5 Above Average		F	r_{IQ}
	M	S.D.	M	S.D.	M	S.D.	M	S.D.	M	S.D.		
White	18.7	20.8	49.4	20.8	69.6	18.8	83.3	14.7	90.4	11.1	620.02*	.38*
Black	18.5	21.4	50.5	18.5	65.8	17.1	76.6	16.3	86.1	13.5	732.22*	.41*

Differs from mildly retarded in D.F.
*$p < .00001$

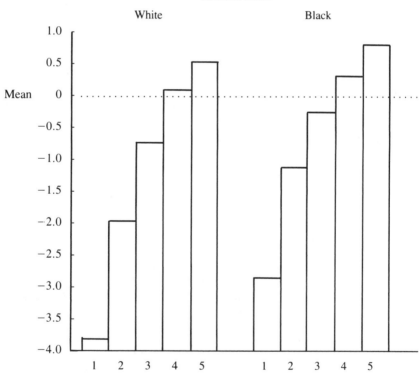

Standard Score

Note. Group Ns: White-   18   106   1711   10094   1404
              Black-   32   617   6617   8407   138

Table 7-14

Block Sort and Gross Motor Scores at Age Four by IQ Group

	1 Severely Retarded		2 Mildly Retarded		3 Borderline		4 Average		5 Above Average		F	r_{IQ}
	M	S.D.	M	S.D.	M	S.D.	M	S.D.	M	S.D.		

Graham-Ernhart Block Sort Score

White	11.4	10.8	21.1	11.6	*31.1*	*9.1*	*36.4*	*6.5*	*39.5*	*4.5*	537.39*	.36*
Black	9.1	9.2	22.2	11.2	*29.3*	*9.5*	*33.8*	*7.7*	*37.9*	*4.9*	515.78*	.35*

Group Ns: White - 17 124 1797 10409 1414

Black - 32 621 6711 8516 143

Gross Motor Score

White	12.6	15.9	31.6	25.3	*61.5*	*25.8*	*73.6*	*21.6*	*77.9*	*20.0*	229.08*	.24*
Black	10.9	16.0	53.3	27.2	*70.0*	*21.3*	*76.3*	*18.8*	79.4	17.4	303.50*	.25*

Group Ns: White - 18 94 1430 8907 1279

Black - 33 563 6269 8165 140

Differs from mildly retarded in D.F.
$*p<.00001$

Table 7-15

Abnormal Hearing at Age Three by IQ Group

	1 Severely Retarded	2 Mildly Retarded	3 Borderline	4 Average	5 Above Average	χ^2	r_{IQ}
			Percent				
White	33.33	12.33	*4.64*	2.67	1.87	84.88*	−.08*
Black	33.33	6.81	*2.47*	1.60	1.28	165.63*	−.09*

Group Ns: White- 15 73 1142 5804 804

Black- 27 382 4134 5188 78

Differs from mildly retarded in D.F.
$*p<.00001$

Table 7-16

Right Dominance at Age Four by IQ Group

	1 Severely Retarded	2 Mildly Retarded	3 Borderline	4 Average	5 Above Average	χ^2	r_{IQ}
			Percent				
White	19.35	23.45	*39.94*	*45.50*	*47.16*	58.58*	.05*
Black	21.15	36.98	41.65	43.82	43.36	26.32*	.04*

Group Ns: White-   31   145   1933   10727   1442
            Black-   52   676   6895   8716   143
Differs from mildly retarded in D.F.
*$p < .00001$

factors. Lower socioeconomic status among the mildly retarded was significant in five of the six comparisons with higher IQ groups in the two samples. Among whites, the lower proportion of males in the mildly retarded group was a consistent discriminator.

Preschool characteristics were highly correlated with the group classification when the mildly retarded and above-average children were compared ($R > .80$). They were least effective in discriminating between the mildly retarded and the borderline group in the black sample ($R = .39$).

Summary analyses of all factors related to mild retardation from the period of gestation through age 4 are shown in Table 7-18. The 61 variables included 43 of the 59 discriminators from the earlier 1-year summaries and 18 of the 19 preschool characteristics. Canonical correlations in the black and white samples increased from moderate values of .41 and .46 in the borderline group comparison to high values of .83 and .87 in the above-average group comparison. The best discriminators were performance at age 4 on the Stanford–Binet, the fine motor tasks, and the block sort test.

Risk factors were primarily, but not exclusively, socioenvironmental. Mothers of the mildly retarded were characterized by lower intelligence test scores, lower socioeconomic status, less education, and shorter stature. In the black sample, mothers of this group were also younger and of higher parity; pregnancies were more closely spaced and they had experienced prior fetal loss. Urinary tract infection in pregnancy and inhalation anesthetics at delivery were risk factors for mild retardation among whites. Heart disease, toxemia, and low hematocrit in pregnancy were risk factors among blacks. Postnatally, serious neurological abnormalities were present in the group of mildly retarded children in the white sample. In both samples, infancy was marked by delays in physical growth and psychomotor development.

Table 7-17

Weight in Kilograms at Age Four by IQ Group

	1 Severely Retarded		2 Mildly Retarded		3 Borderline		4 Average		5 Above Average		F	r_{IQ}
	M	S.D.	M	S.D.	M	S.D.	M	S.D.	M	S.D.		
White	14.9	3.4	15.6	2.7	16.1	2.2	16.6	2.2	*17.0*	*2.2*	45.79*	.13*
Black	14.8	2.4	15.5	2.1	*16.1*	*2.2*	16.5	2.2	17.4	2.8	62.13*	.15*

Differs from mildly retarded in D.F.
*$p < .00001$

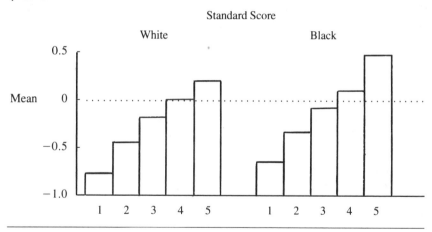

Note. Group Ns: White-   47 128 1728 9514 1294
              Black-   80 635 6355 7707   106

Variable	White			Black		
	BL	AV	AA	BL	AV	AA
Stanford-Binet IQ at age 4	−.51	−.19	−.18	−.36	−.29	−.61
Fine motor score at age 4	−.06	−.11	−.19	−.21	−.18	−.20
Graham-Ernhart Block Sort score at age 4	−.20	−.16	−.22	−.07	−.10	−.06
Maternal SRA score	−.09	−.05	−.04	−.06	−.08	−.07
Abnormal language expression at age 3	.08	.26	.24	.18	.17	—
Abnormal behavior summary rating at age 4	.12	.23	.07	.18	.18	—
Gross motor score at age 4	−.17	−.06	−.05	−.11	−.05	—
Socioeconomic index	—	—	−.12	−.04	−.01	−.18
Attention span at age 4	−.03	−.10	−.07	—	−.10	—
Goal orientation at age 4	—	−.03	−.07	−.06	−.08	—
Intensity of social response at 8 months	−.04	−.04	−.02	—	−.04	—
Verbal communication at age 4	−.03	—	—	−.02	−.05	−.03
Delayed motor development at 1 year	.21	.24	—	—	.08	—
Abnormal language reception at age 3	—	.21	.10	—	.05	—
Head circumference at 1 year	−.15	—	−.09	—	−.07	—
Abnormal speech production at age 3	—	.13	—	.11	.05	—
Maternal education	—	−.02	—	−.14	−.10	—
Bayley motor score at 8 months	—	—	−.06	−.05	−.06	—
Head circumference at age 4	—	−.12	—	—	—	−.08
Bayley mental score at 8 months	—	−.10	—	—	−.02	—
Retarded mother	—	.08	—	—	.02	—
Abnormal hearing at age 3	.05	—	—	.04	—	—
Maternal height	—	—	−.02	—	−.01	—
Percent male	−.20	−.12	−.09	—	—	—
Right dominance at age 4	−.11	−.04	−.05	—	—	—
Major CNS malformations	.13	.14	—	—	—	—
Cigarettes per day in pregnancy	−.06	−.09	—	—	—	—
Age at menarche	.09	—	.04	—	—	—

(continued)

Table 7-18 (continued)

| | Comparison Group | | | | | |
| | White | | | Black | | |
Variable	BL	AV	AA	BL	AV	AA
Abdomino-pelvic x-rays	−.07	−.04	—	—	—	—
Non-febrile seizures[a]	—	.02	.05	—	—	—
Housing density	—	.04	.03	—	—	—
Inhalation anesthetic at delivery	—	.04	.02	—	—	—
Major upper respiratory or mouth malformations	—	.11	—	—	—	—
Cerebral palsy at 1 year	—	.10	—	—	—	—
Down's syndrome	—	.09	—	—	—	—
Hypoxia in 1st year	—	.06	—	—	—	—
Retarded father	—	.05	—	—	—	—
Induction of labor	—	−.04	—	—	—	—
Urinary tract infection in pregnancy	—	—	.06	—	—	—
Unfavorable emotional environment in 1st year	—	—	.02	—	—	—
Head circumference at birth	—	—	−.01	—	—	—
Parity	—	—	—	.10	—	.18
Major musculoskeletal malformations	—	—	—	.07	.11	—
Pregnancy-free interval	—	—	—	−.09	−.07	—
Weight at 4 months	—	—	—	−.08	−.05	—
Organic heart disease in pregnancy	—	—	—	.08	.04	—
Weight at 1 year	—	—	—	−.04	−.01	—
Dependency at age 4	—	—	—	.17	—	—
Hypotonia at 1 year	—	—	—	.16	—	—
Primary apnea	—	—	—	.04	—	—
Prior fetal death	—	—	—	.04	—	—
Gestational age	—	—	—	−.03	—	—
Response to directions at age 4	—	—	—	—	−.12	—
Impulsivity at age 4	—	—	—	—	−.09	—
Toxemia	—	—	—	—	.06	—
Hematocrit in pregnancy	—	—	—	—	−.03	—
Number of prenatal visits	—	—	—	—	−.02	—
Multiple birth	—	—	—	—	.01	—
Major eye malformations	—	—	—	—	.01	—
Height at age 4	—	—	—	—	−.01	—
Maternal age	—	—	—	—	—	−.18
Canonical correlation	*.46**	*.50**	*.87**	*.41**	*.61**	*.83**

[a]Occurring between 1 and 12 months.

*p<.00001

143

8

The School-Age Period

At age 7, when the criterion IQ scores were obtained, children in the study were given other psychological tests and a pediatric-neurological examination. Their mothers were interviewed about current social and medical conditions in the family and about changes that had taken place since the birth of the study child. Results of the medical examination were combined with events recorded in interval histories into a medical summary of years 2 through 7.[1] The three sets of data reflecting primarily the concurrent characteristics of the retarded groups were analyzed in the same manner as were the antecedent factors. Of 30 family characteristics screened, including a new socioeconomic index, 28 differed in univariate comparisons between a retarded and higer IQ group and were entered in discriminant function analyses. Similarly, 91 of 120 biomedical charac- teristics and all of 24 psychological measures passed the univariate screen and were analyzed multivariately.

THE SEVERELY RETARDED

Demographic and Family Characteristics

From information collected in the maternal interview, major discriminators between the severely retarded and higher IQ groups were the socioeconomic index in the white sample and maternal education in the black sample (Table 8-1. The curvilinear relationship between the 7-year socioeconomic index and IQ level is shown clearly in the white sample where discriminant coefficients were positive in comparisons with the mildly retarded and borderline groups

---

[1]Seizures were reviewed separately and were included if they occurred after the first 28 days.

Table 8-1
Standardized Coefficients for Seven-Year Family and Demographic Discriminators Between the Severely Retarded and Comparison Groups

Variable	Comparison Group							
	White				Black			
	MR	BL	AV	AA	MR	BL	AV	AA
Socioeconomic index	.78	.48	−.14	−.67	.18	—	—	—
Maternal education	—	—	−.16	−.08	—	−.61	−.68	−.58
Mother employed	—	−.57	−.41	−.21	—	—	−.25	—
Number of subsequent pregnancies	−.53	—	—	—	—	—	.37	.29
Public assistance	—	—	—	.08	—	—	.21	.43
Retardation in siblings	—	—	—	.16	—	—	—	.24
Reported mental illness in study child	—	.56	.83	.47	—	—	—	—
Number of children under 8 in household	—	−.44	−.26	—	—	—	—	—
Family size	—	—	—	.17	—	—	—	—
Study child adopted or in foster home	—	—	—	.07	—	—	—	—
Paternal age	—	—	—	—	—	.67	.29	—
Housing density	—	—	—	—	−.65	—	—	—
Number of changes in residence	—	—	—	—	−.50	—	—	—
Father present	—	—	—	—	.43	—	—	—
Canonical correlation	*.33***	*.15***	*.08***	*.32***	*.16**	*.05**	*.09***	*.55***

*$p < .0001$
**$p < .00001$

(indicating higher status among the severely retarded) and negative in comparisons with the average and above-average groups. In the black sample, the socioeconomic index discriminated between the severely and mildly retarded children. A lower level of education among mothers of the severely retarded was an important factor in comparisons with all nonretarded groups among blacks and was significant in comparisons with the average and above-average children

Table 8-2
Socioeconomic Index and Maternal Education by IQ Group

	1 Severely Retarded		2 Mildly Retarded		3 Borderline		4 Average		5 Above Average		F	r_{IQ}
	M	S.D.	M	S.D.	M	S.D.	M	S.D.	M	S.D.		
					Socioeconomic Index							
White	51.0	25.3	**37.5**	**20.1**	*43.2*	*19.9*	*57.8*	*22.5*	*77.1*	*19.3*	680.24*	.42*
Black	33.5	19.2	**28.5**	**16.8**	34.8	17.8	*42.5*	*19.5*	56.7	22.7	287.96*	.27*
Group Ns: White -	91		201		2407		12580		1867			
Black -	127		895		7889		9471		156			
					Maternal Education (yr.)							
White	10.8	2.8	9.6	2.5	10.1	2.3	***11.5***	***2.4***	***13.8***	***2.5***	657.44*	.40*
Black	9.3	2.8	9.3	2.4	***10.2***	***2.1***	***10.8***	***2.0***	***12.1***	***2.5***	206.07*	.23*
Group Ns: White -	62		192		2351		12376		1857			
Black -	103		831		7781		9357		154			

Differs from severely retarded in D.F.
Differs from mildly retarded in D.F.
Differs from severely and mildly retarded in D.F.s
*p<.00001

among whites. Differences between the samples in socioeconomic index score and amount of maternal education replicated those found in the prenatal period (Table 8-2). Mean values were lower among blacks than whites and the two variables were less highly related in IQ in the black sample.

Other family characteristics of the severely retarded in both samples were a lower frequency of maternal employment since birth of the study child (a consistent discriminator among whites), a higher frequency of public financial assistance than in the average and/or above-average groups, and more reported retardation among siblings, a factor significant in the comparison with the above-average group in each sample. Fewer subsequent pregnancies discriminated between mothers of the severely retarded and the mildly retarded among whites; however, a different finding of more pregnancies in the retarded group than in the average and above-average groups was significant in the black sample. Both maternal employment and public assistance were more common among blacks than whites in all IQ groups (Table 8-3). The small positive

Table 8-3

Maternal Employment and Public Assistance by IQ Group

	1 Severely Retarded	2 Mildly Retarded	3 Borderline	4 Average	5 Above Average	χ^2	r_{IQ}
			Percent				
			Mother Employed				
White	36.21	44.00	*57.79*	*59.48*	*60.69*	33.30**	.03*
Black	63.83	63.44	74.47	*80.53*	78.67	180.43**	.10**
Group Ns: White -	58	175	2227	12089	1842		
Black -	94	774	7355	9024	150		
			Public Assistance				
White	20.34	32.00	29.94	15.30	*4.03*	549.45**	−.20**
Black	47.31	**54.44**	*41.24*	*28.06*	**12.08**	487.78**	−.18**
Group Ns: White -	59	175	2231	12101	1834		
Black -	93	777	7361	9007	149		

Differs from severely retarded in D.F.
Differs from mildly retarded in D.F.
Differs from severely and mildly retarded in D.F.s
 *$p<.0001$
 **$p<.00001$

correlation between maternal employment and IQ was higher among blacks than whites; negative correlations between public assistance and IQ were similar in the two samples. Number of subsequent pregnancies was also negatively related to IQ with the larger correlation in the black sample (Table 8-4). Frequencies for reported retardation in siblings are shown in Table 8-5. This interview item was very broadly defined because it could be based on a formal diagnosis, special school placement, or maternal impression alone.

Discriminators unique to the white sample were a history of treatment for mental illness among the severely retarded, fewer younger children in the household but larger family size or total number of children, and adoption or foster home placement. These characteristics were identified in comparisons with nonretarded groups. Treatment for mental illness, the most important of the discriminators, was reported for 7% of the severely retarded white children (Table 8-6). The number of children in the household under the age of 8 was significantly lower than in the borderline and average groups, but was negatively

Table 8-4
Number of Subsequent Pregnancies by IQ Group

	1 Severely Retarded		2 Mildly Retarded		3 Borderline		4 Average		5 Above Average		F	r_{IQ}
	M	S.D.	M	S.D.	M	S.D.	M	S.D.	M	S.D.		
White	1.0	1.1	**1.7**	**1.5**	1.5	1.3	*1.3*	*1.2*	1.2	*1.1*	19.39*	− .05*
Black	1.6	1.6	1.8	1.5	*1.5*	*1.3*	**1.2**	**1.2**	**0.8**	**0.9**	105.77*	− .16*

Group Ns: White - 57 176 2232 12098 1839
Black - 94 775 7350 9027 150

Differs from severely retarded in D.F.
Differs from mildly retarded in D.F.
Differs from severely and mildly retarded in D.F.s
p<.00001

correlated with IQ in both samples, with a higher value among blacks than whites (Table 8-7). Family size, larger among the severely retarded than the above-average, also had negative correlations with IQ score in the two samples (Table 8-8). The inverted U-shaped relationship between family size and IQ level is clearly illustrated in the graphs of standard scores computed within each sample. At the time of the 7-year interview, 7% of the severely retarded white

Table 8-5
Retardation in Siblings by IQ Group

	1 Severely Retarded	2 Mildly Retarded	3 Borderline	4 Average	5 Above Average	χ^2	r_{IQ}
			Percent				
White	14.04	26.14	*15.65*	7.73	**3.69**	281.15*	− .14*
Black	13.83	17.48	*10.05*	7.46	**3.33**	113.08*	− .09*

Group Ns: White - 57 176 2236 12103 1842
Black - 94 778 7362 9038 150

Differs from severely retarded in D.F.
Differs from mildly retarded in D.F.
Differs from severely and mildly retarded in D.F.s
p<.00001

Table 8-6
Reported Mental Illness in Study Child by IQ Group

	1 Severely Retarded	2 Mildly Retarded	3 Borderline	4 Average	5 Above Average	χ^2	r_{IQ}
			Percent				
White	7.41	0.71	**1.18**	**0.51**	**0.48**	51.21**	−.04*
Black	0.00	0.59	0.28	0.21	0.75	5.03	−.00

Group Ns: White- 54 140 1775 9776 1470
Black- 78 675 6442 7965 134
Differs from severely retarded in D.F.
*p <.0001
**p <.00001

children were living with adoptive or foster parents or a guardian, as compared to 1% of the above-average group (Table 8-9).

In the black sample, a more advanced paternal age discriminated between the severely retarded and the borderline and average groups; lower housing density, fewer household moves, and presence of the father were significant in the comparison with the mildly retarded. Paternal age, although older among the severely retarded, was uncorrelated with IQ score in the black sample; there was, however, a slight negative relationship among whites (Table 8-10). Housing density, number of changes in residence since birth, and presence of the father

Table 8-7
Number of Children Under Age Eight in Household by IQ Group

	1 Severely Retarded		2 Mildly Retarded		3 Borderline		4 Average		5 Above Average		F	r_{IQ}
	M	S.D.	M	S.D.	M	S.D.	M	S.D.	M	S.D.		
White	1.8	0.9	2.3	1.3	**2.2**	**1.2**	**2.1**	**1.0**	2.0	0.9	13.99*	−.05*
Black	2.3	1.3	2.5	1.4	2.3	1.3	2.0	1.1	1.7	0.9	89.95*	−.15*

Group Ns: White - 62 196 2391 12556 1869
Black - 104 843 7859 9446 156
Differs from severely retarded in D.F.
*p<.00001

Table 8-8
Family Size by IQ Group

	1 Severely Retarded		2 Mildly Retarded		3 Borderline		4 Average		5 Above Average		F	r_{IQ}
	M	S.D.	M	S.D.	M	S.D.	M	S.D.	M	S.D.		
White	4.2	2.4	4.6	2.2	4.3	2.0	3.8	1.8	*3.1*	*1.4*	130.58*	−.19*
Black	4.8	2.5	5.6	2.9	4.7	2.4	*4.1*	*2.2*	*3.5*	*1.8*	109.44*	−.17*

Differs from mildly retarded in D.F.

Differs from severely and mildly retarded in D.F.s

$p < .00001$

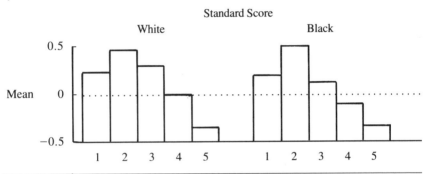

Standard Score

Note. Group Ns: White- 53 170 2178 11895 1826

Black- 92 756 7180 8803 146

Table 8-9
Study Child Adopted or in Foster Home by IQ Group

	1 Severely Retarded	2 Mildly Retarded	3 Borderline	4 Average	5 Above Average	χ^2	r_{IQ}
			Percent				
White	6.90	9.60	*6.36*	*3.08*	**1.23**	119.62*	−.09*
Black	8.91	8.48	*6.06*	4.38	3.85	45.40*	−.05*

Group Ns: White- 58 198 2404 12584 1870

Black- 101 849 7883 9472 156

Differs from severely retarded in D.F.

Differs from mildly retarded in D.F.

$p < .00001$

150

Table 8-10
Paternal Age, Housing Density, and Changes in Residence by IQ Group

	1 Severely Retarded		2 Mildly Retarded		3 Borderline		4 Average		5 Above Average		F	r_{IQ}
	M	S.D.	M	S.D.	M	S.D.	M	S.D.	M	S.D.		
					Paternal Age (yr.)							
White	36.0	6.9	36.7	7.3	35.9	7.3	35.5	6.8	34.7	5.8	7.77**	−.05**
Black	38.5	9.5	36.3	8.8	**35.4**	**7.9**	**35.8**	**7.7**	37.6	8.1	5.55*	.02
Group Ns: White -	51		135		1702		10330		1690			
Black -	57		371		3981		5482		109			
					Housing Density							
White	1.1	0.4	1.3	0.6	1.3	0.5	*1.1*	*0.4*	0.9	0.3	224.21**	−.24**
Black	1.5	0.6	**1.7**	**0.8**	*1.5*	*0.7*	1.3	0.6	1.1	0.4	108.46**	−.16**
Group Ns: White -	63		196		2392		12561		1870			
Black -	104		844		7863		9447		156			
					Number of Changes in Residence							
White	3.1	3.2	3.4	3.0	3.2	3.4	*2.5*	*2.7*	2.5	2.3	33.27**	−.07**
Black	1.8	1.9	**2.4**	**2.1**	*2.1*	*1.9*	*1.9*	*1.7*	1.5	1.6	26.97**	−.08**
Group Ns: White -	59		176		2242		12172		1844			
Black -	95		778		7386		9050		150			

Differs from severely retarded in D.F.
Differs from mildly retarded in D.F.
  *$p<.001$
  **$p<.00001$

at age 7 all had the familiar curvilinear relationship to IQ level of other social class-related factors. The first two variables were negatively correlated with IQ score in both samples, and the presence of the father, a factor of considerable interest in family constellation studies, had low positive correlations with IQ (Table 8-11).

Demographic and family characteristics were moderately good discriminators between the severely retarded and above-average black children ($R = .55$). Maximum explanatory power was less among whites, where family charac-

Table 8-11

Father Present by IQ Group

	1 Severely Retarded	2 Mildly Retarded	3 Borderline	4 Average	5 Above Average	χ^2	r_{IQ}
			Percent				
White	84.75	76.84	75.77	84.69	91.61	205.91*	.12*
Black	60.00	**47.06**	53.72	60.52	74.00	127.83*	.10*

Group Ns: White-   59 177 2253 12205 1848
           Black-   95 782 7407   9070   150
Differs from severely retarded in D.F.
*$p < .00001$

teristics were equally effective in discriminating between the extreme groups and the two retarded groups ($Rs = .32$ and $.33$).

Biomedical Characteristics

Physical findings at age 7 and events from medical histories after the age of 1 were highly related to severe retardation in both samples. A wide range of discriminating conditions was identified that included Down's and other major syndromes, cerebral palsy, epilepsy, malformations of the CNS and other systems, seizures, sensory abnormalities, trauma, and infections (Table 8-12). Minor neurological signs, head circumference, and height were also related to severe retardation. The control variables of socioeconomic status and sex of child were retained in some analyses. Canonical correlations between the biomedical characteristics and the group classification ranged from .65 and .66 in comparisons with the mildly retarded in each sample to .82 and .84 in comparisons with the above average.

The most important factors were among the group of 24 common to both samples. The discriminating power of the severe abnormalities of Down's syndrome, major malformations of the CNS, and, to a lesser extent, other genetic and postinfection syndromes changed little from that in the neonatal period. Distributions and univariate statistics for these "primary" conditions were presented in an earlier chapter (see Tables 5-2 and 5-3). Cerebral palsy diagnosed at age 7 was second in importance only to Down's syndrome. Approximately one third of the severely retarded white children and 23% of the severely retarded black children were affected with a mild, moderate, or severe degree of this chronic motor disability (Table 8-13). Subtypes of the disorder included in the

Table 8-12

Standardized Coefficients for Seven-Year Pediatric Discriminators in the Severely Retarded and Comparison Groups

Variable	Comparison Group							
	White				Black			
	MR	BL	AV	AA	MR	BL	AV	AA
Down's syndrome	.44	.52	.55	.39	.47	.52	.48	.13
Cerebral palsy	.26	.30	.39	.22	.25	.29	.36	.07
Abnormal gait	.17	.06	.07	.16	.28	.19	.24	.44
Diagnostic or other medical procedures	.22	.06	.10	.04	.12	.06	.07	.22
Other genetic or pre- natal infection syndromes	.30	.24	.31	.19	—	.09	.07	—
Major CNS malformations	.20	.20	.17	.17	—	.12	.12	—
Asymptomatic gen- eralized seizures	—	.14	.05	.11	.14	.15	.06	—
Mirror or other ab- normal movements	—	.10	.04	.05	.16	.11	.10	—
Major eye malformations	—	—	.04	.07	.22	.11	.11	.14
Minor ear malformations	—	.05	.03	.04	.10	.03	—	.10
Right handedness	—	—	− .01	− .03	− .06	− .03	− .02	− .19
Abnormal shape of skull	—	.14	.07	.09	—	.09	.08	—
Minor motor seizures	—	.18	—	.10	.21	.25	.20	—
Asymptomatic partial seizures	—	.09	.03	.10	—	.09	.09	—
Minor musculoskeletal malformations	—	—	.04	—	.12	.06	.04	.12
Failure to thrive	—	.05	.11	.09	—	.02	.06	—
Head circumference	—	—	− .01	− .04	—	− .06	− .05	− .20
Height	—	—	− .02	− .02	− .06	− .02	− .02	—
Minor upper respira- tory or mouth malformations	—	.09	.02	—	—	.06	.05	—
Hypoxia without unconsciousness	—	.07	.02	—	—	.04	.03	—
Socioeconomic index	—	—	—	− .14	—	—	− .05	− .27
Epilepsy	.27	—	.16	—	—	—	.05	—
Abnormal reflexes	—	—	—	.05	—	.02	—	—

(continued)

153

Table 8-12 (continued)

Variable	White				Black			
	MR	BL	AV	AA	MR	BL	AV	AA
Encephalitis	—	—	.03	—	—	.01	—	—
Petit mal	—	.14	.13	.10	—	—	—	—
Dyskinesia or ataxia	—	.09	.13	.10	—	—	—	—
Major genitourinary malformations	—	.08	.04	.04	—	—	—	—
Major thoracic malformations	—	.10	.04	—	—	—	—	—
Hypothyroidism	—	—	.06	.07	—	—	—	—
Major upper respiratory or mouth malformations	—	—	.03	.06	—	—	—	—
Cranial nerve abnormality[a]	—	—	.03	.05	—	—	—	—
Percent male	.22	—	—	—	—	—	—	—
Color blindness	−.18	—	—	—	—	—	—	—
Right dominance	−.11	—	—	—	—	—	—	—
Minor skin malformations	—	—	.02	—	—	—	—	—
Bilateral deafness	—	—	—	.06	—	—	—	—
Binocular blindness	—	—	—	—	—	.17	.13	—
Major musculoskeletal malformations	—	—	—	—	.14	.05	—	—
Post traumatic deficit	—	—	—	—	—	.13	.07	—
Coma	—	—	—	—	—	.01	.02	—
Liver infection	—	—	—	—	—	.08	—	—
Minor CNS malformations	—	—	—	—	—	.04	—	—
Bacterial meningitis	—	—	—	—	—	.03	—	—
Chorioretinitis	—	—	—	—	—	.03	—	—
Subdural hematoma or effusion	—	—	—	—	—	—	.08	—
Documented cardiovascular disorder	—	—	—	—	—	—	.06	—
Hemoglobinopathy	—	—	—	—	—	—	.04	—
Canonical correlation	.66*	.71*	.70*	.82*	.65*	.64*	.70*	.84*

[a]Other than auditory nerve

*$p < .00001$

Table 8-13

Cerebral Palsy by IQ Group

	1 Severely Retarded	2 Mildly Retarded	3 Borderline	4 Average	5 Above Average	χ^2	r_{IQ}
			Percent				
White	32.61	**5.47**	**1.01**	*0.15*	*0.11*	2060.62*	−.19*
Black	22.83	**1.79**	**0.24**	*0.03*	**0.00**	1922.21*	−.18*

Differs from severely retarded in D.F.
Differs from severely and mildly retarded in D.F.s
*$p <$ .00001

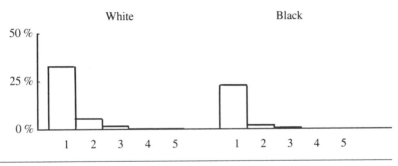

Note. Group Ns: White- 92 201 2473 12776 1889
Black- 127 893 8308 9899 158

diagnosis were hemiparesis, monoparesis, paraparesis, quadriplegia, and atonic diplegia. Negative correlations between cerebral palsy and IQ score were .18 and .19 in the two samples.

Frequencies for the clinical types of seizures related to severe retardation are shown in Table 8-14. All but petit mal were significant in both samples. Asymptomatic generalized seizures, the most consistent of the discriminators, occurred at least once among 15% of the severely retarded in each sample. These clinically generalized seizures were not associated with any known trauma or acute neurological illness. Minor motor seizures (tonic, hemitonic, myoclonic, akinetic, or a mixture) were almost entirely confined to the severely retarded, occurring among 14% of the white group and 11% of the black group. Asymptomatic partial seizures (focal motor or focal sensory of unknown etiology) were less common among the severely retarded, affecting approximately 6% in each sample. Epilepsy, defined as the spontaneous recurrence of at least one non-

Table 8-14
Seizure Disorders by IQ Group

	1 Severely Retarded	2 Mildly Retarded	3 Borderline	4 Average	5 Above Average	χ^2	r_{IQ}
			Percent				
		Asymptomatic Generalized Seizures					
White	15.22	1.99	**0.81**	**0.32**	**0.21**	446.66*	−.09*
Black	14.84	**1.90**	*0.41*	**0.34**	0.63	527.59*	−.09*
			Minor Motor Seizures				
White	14.13	0.00	**0.20**	0.02	**0.00**	1592.00*	−.13*
Black	10.94	**0.22**	**0.06**	**0.03**	0.00	1223.26*	−.11*
			Asymptomatic Partial Seizures				
White	5.43	1.49	**0.28**	*0.10*	**0.05**	181.73*	−.06*
Black	6.25	0.56	**0.19**	**0.09**	0.00	252.17*	−.07*
			Epilepsy				
White	27.17	**3.48**	1.01	**0.43**	0.32	1003.52*	−.12*
Black	23.44	2.57	0.58	*0.31*	0.63	1042.56*	−.13*
			Petit Mal				
White	1.09	0.50	**0.00**	*0.00*	**0.00**	136.11*	−.04*
Black	0.00	0.11	0.01	0.00	0.00	10.01	−.02*

Group Ns: White -   92   201   2473   12777   1889

Black -   128   895   8319   9919   158

Differs from severely retarded in D.F.
Differs from severely and mildly retarded in D.F.s
*$p<.00001$

Table 8-15
Major Malformations by IQ Group

	1 Severely Retarded	2 Mildly Retarded	3 Borderline	4 Average	5 Above Average	χ^2	r_{IQ}
			Percent				
Major Eye Malformations							
White	6.52	2.99	**1.09**	**0.67**	**0.64**	56.88****	− .04****
Black	14.06	**2.01**	**1.03**	**0.80**	**0.63**	225.04****	− .06****
Abnormal Shape of Skull							
White	4.35	3.98	*0.36*	*0.32*	*0.32*	105.62****	− .04****
Black	5.47	1.34	**0.58**	**0.45**	0.00	66.06****	− .04****
Major Genitourinary Malformations							
White	13.04	4.48	*1.21*	**1.70**	**2.17**	82.13****	− .01
Black	7.03	1.34	1.02	1.07	1.90	43.06****	− .02*
Major Thoracic Malformations							
White	14.13	2.99	**1.29**	**1.04**	1.27	138.90****	− .04****
Black	3.13	0.56	0.25	0.23	0.00	42.11****	− .04****
Major Upper Respiratory or Mouth Malformations							
White	15.22	6.47	*2.63*	*1.99*	*1.16*	107.26****	− .05****
Black	7.81	3.24	2.66	2.12	0.63	26.21****	− .03**
Major Musculoskeletal Malformations							
White	18.48	5.97	3.19	2.75	2.33	90.44****	− .05****
Black	14.84	**2.57**	**1.84**	1.84	4.43	117.25****	− .03***

Group Ns: White -   92 201 2473 12777 1889
Black - 128 895 8319 9919 158

Differs from severely retarded in D.F.
Differs from mildly retarded in D.F.
Differs from severely and mildly retarded in D.F.s
*p<.05
**p<.001
***p<.0001
****p<.00001

Table 8-16
Minor Malformations by IQ Group

	1 Severely Retarded	2 Mildly Retarded	3 Borderline	4 Average	5 Above Average	χ^2	r_{IQ}
			Percent				
Minor Ear Malformations							
White	13.04	5.97	*1.70*	**0.86**	**0.69**	184.83****	− .07****
Black	11.72	**2.68**	**2.72**	2.04	**1.27**	57.40****	− .04****
Minor Musculoskeletal Malformations							
White	14.13	5.97	2.10	*1.46*	2.01	113.23****	− .04****
Black	10.94	**2.01**	**1.48**	**1.45**	**0.63**	77.19****	− .03***
Minor Upper Respiratory or Mouth Malformations							
White	9.78	2.99	**0.81**	**0.89**	0.79	87.41****	− .03***
Black	5.47	1.56	*0.59*	*0.31*	0.63	87.63****	− .05****
Minor Skin Malformations							
White	8.70	3.48	4.08	**3.31**	4.87	20.30**	− .00
Black	7.03	6.26	6.11	6.49	5.06	1.67	.00
Minor CNS Malformations							
White	1.09	0.50	0.49	0.35	0.21	3.70	− .01
Black	2.34	0.45	**0.34**	0.35	0.63	14.45*	− .01

Group Ns: White -   92 201 2473 12777 1889
             Black - 128 895 8319   9919   158

Differs from severely retarded in D.F.
Differs from mildly retarded in D.F.
Differs from severely and mildly retarded in D.F.s
  *$p<.01$
 **$p<.001$
 ***$p<.0001$
****$p<.00001$

Table 8-17
Minor Neurological Signs by IQ Group

	1 Severely Retarded	2 Mildly Retarded	3 Borderline	4 Average	5 Above Average	χ^2	r_{IQ}
			Percent				
			Abnormal Gait				
White	65.12	**24.50**	*9.63*	*4.47*	*3.04*	502.88*	−.17*
Black	59.50	**13.10**	*4.14*	*2.02*	*1.29*	721.77*	−.19*
Group Ns: White -	86	200	2450	12688	1873		
Black -	121	870	8120	9705	155		
		Mirror or Other Abnormal Movements					
White	40.91	**13.20**	**7.00**	**5.40**	**4.91**	231.16*	−.08*
Black	28.33	**5.52**	**2.50**	**2.10**	**0.65**	360.68*	−.09*
Group Ns: White -	88	197	2444	12678	1872		
Black -	120	870	8118	9700	154		
			Abnormal Reflexes				
White	61.11	33.00	18.65	13.41	**13.13**	260.26*	−.10*
Black	45.08	22.30	*12.59*	*11.41*	10.97	203.79*	−.08*
Group Ns: White -	90	200	2450	12688	1873		
Black -	122	870	8120	9705	155		

Differs from severely retarded in D.F.
Differs from mildly retarded in D.F.
Differs from severely and mildly retarded in D.F.s
*$p<.00001$

Table 8-18
Right Handedness and Right Dominance by IQ Group

	1 Severely Retarded	2 Mildly Retarded	3 Borderline	4 Average	5 Above Average	χ^2	r_{IQ}
			Percent				
Right Handedness							
White	65.71	78.57	85.02	**86.90**	**87.76**	45.39**	.03*
Black	69.61	**83.64**	**87.81**	**88.87**	**93.51**	60.16**	.05**
Group Ns: White -	70	196	2444	12665	1871		
Black -	102	868	8108	9693	154		
Right Dominance							
White	16.36	**36.79**	44.20	47.98	51.47	53.88**	.05**
Black	28.41	38.13	41.64	44.58	46.75	32.86**	.05**
Group Ns: White -	55	193	2448	12674	1873		
Black -	88	868	8114	9702	154		

Differs from severely retarded in D.F.
Differs from severely and mildly retarded in D.F.s
*$p < .0001$
**$p < .00001$

febrile seizure in the interval between 1 month and 7 years, was diagnosed among about one fourth of the severely retarded in each sample, as compared with 3% of the mildly retarded and less than .5% of the average children. The four types of seizures had low negative correlations with IQ score ranging from approximately .06 for asymptomatic partial seizures to .13 for epilepsy and minor motor seizures.

Malformations in the study children were reassessed at age 7 (Myriantho-poulos, 1985). In addition to major malformations of the CNS, other malformations, both major and minor, were related to severe retardation in both samples. A group of major eye malformations, primarily ptosis and cataract, was a consistent discriminator among blacks, affecting 14% of the severely retarded in that sample and 6.5% in the white sample (Table 8-15). Abnormal skull shape, mainly cranial asymmetry, was present among approximately 5% of the severely retarded in each sample, discriminating between them and the nonretarded groups. Minor malformations of the ear (deformed ear pinna, branchial cleft

Table 8-19

Head Circumference and Height by IQ Group

	1 Severely Retarded		2 Mildly Retarded		3 Borderline		4 Average		5 Above Average		F	r_{IQ}
	M	S.D.	M	S.D.	M	S.D.	M	S.D.	M	S.D.		

Head Circumference (cm)

	M	S.D.	M	S.D.	M	S.D.	M	S.D.	M	S.D.	F	r_{IQ}
White	50.4	5.3	50.3	2.1	*50.9*	*1.6*	**51.5**	**1.5**	**52.1**	**1.4**	191.98*	.24*
Black	49.5	2.5	50.6	1.7	**51.0**	**1.6**	**51.4**	**1.5**	**52.1**	**1.6**	144.21*	.19*

Group Ns: White - 88 199 2439 12646 1869

  Black - 117 870 8093 9676 151

Height (cm)

	M	S.D.	M	S.D.	M	S.D.	M	S.D.	M	S.D.	F	r_{IQ}
White	114.5	8.6	118.1	7.7	119.6	6.2	**120.7**	**5.5**	**122.0**	**5.4**	78.74*	.15*
Black	117.6	9.1	**121.6**	**7.5**	**122.6**	**6.8**	**123.3**	**6.1**	124.4	6.3	41.58*	.10*

Group Ns: White - 79 198 2441 12653 1869

  Black - 113 870 8088 9675 153

Differs from severely retarded in D.F.
Differs from mildly retarded in D.F.
Differs from severely and mildly retarded in D.F.s
*$p<.00001$

anomaly) and of the musculoskeletal system (clinodactyly, syndactyly) affected between 11% and 14% of the severely retarded (Table 8-16). The group of musculoskeletal conditions was a more consistent discriminator among blacks than whites. Minor malformations of the upper respiratory system or mouth (missing and malformed teeth, cleft uvula) had a higher prevalence among white than black severely retarded children, but was a discriminator in both samples in comparisons with the borderline and average groups.

Minor neurological signs were frequent among the severely retarded, especially in the white sample. Abnormal gait, observed during walking, running, or hopping, was the most consistent of three discriminating "soft" signs. Relative frequencies decreased sharply from 65% and 60% in the white and black severely retarded groups (at least twice the proportion of children with cerebral palsy) to 3% or less in the above-average groups (Table 8-17). Negative correlations between abnormal gait and IQ score were .17 and .19 in the two samples. The higher prevalence of mirror or other abnormal movements and of abnormal

Table 8-20

Failure to Thrive by IQ Group

	1 Severely Retarded	2 Mildly Retarded	3 Borderline	4 Average	5 Above Average	χ^2	r_{IQ}
			Percent				
White	6.67	2.00	**0.61**	*0.09*	*0.05*	228.26*	−.08*
Black	3.28	1.49	*0.41*	*0.12*	0.00	83.42*	−.06*

Group Ns: White-   90 200 2450 12688 1873
          Black- 122 870 8120   9705   155
Differs from severely retarded in D.F.
Differs from severely and mildly retarded in D.F.s
*$p < .00001$

reflexes among the severely retarded white children was striking although each of the signs had similar discriminating power in the two samples. Abnormal movements included fasciculation, myoclonus, tremor, and athetosis; abnormal reflexes were hypoactive, hyperactive, or asymmetric.

Fewer of the severely retarded children were right-handed at age 7, a minor discriminator in both samples but one that was retained consistently among blacks. Hand preference was established on the basis of use of a pencil in five trials given during the neurological examination. Frequencies for right-handedness by IQ group are shown in Table 8-18; positive correlations with IQ score, although significant, were only .03 and .05 in the two samples.

Smaller head circumference at age 7 discriminated between the severely retarded and at least two of the three nonretarded groups in each sample. Large standard deviations, particularly among whites, were associated with mean values of 50 centimeters in each severely retarded group (Table 8-19). Correlations between head circumference and IQ score were in the low moderate range. Shorter stature was also associated with severe retardation in both samples; mean height was approximately 6 centimeters below that in the average group in each sample. Height was less highly related to IQ score than was head circumference. Failure to thrive in the period between 1 and 7 years was a discriminator between the severely retarded and nonretarded groups in both samples. This syndrome, which could have resulted from chronic illness, malnutrition, or neglect, was diagnosed among 7% of the severely retarded white children and 3% of those in the black sample (Table 8-20).

Other discriminators from the medical summary common to both samples were encephalitis, or inflammation of the brain resulting from infectious disease,

Table 8-21
Encephalitis and Hypoxia by IQ Group

	1 Severely Retarded	2 Mildly Retarded	3 Borderline	4 Average	5 Above Average	χ^2	r_{IQ}
			Percent				
			Encephalitis				
White	2.22	0.00	0.29	**0.09**	0.16	34.14***	−.02*
Black	2.44	0.46	**0.07**	**0.08**	0.00	71.76***	−.03***

Group Ns: White -   90 200 2450 12688 1873
          Black - 123 870 8120   9705   155

			Hypoxia Without Unconsciousness				
White	5.81	1.52	**0.21**	**0.32**	0.27	86.27***	−.04***
Black	1.64	0.35	**0.12**	**0.06**	0.00	32.40***	−.03**

Group Ns: White -   86 197 2384 12349 1835
          Black - 122 869 8105   9680   155

Differs from severely retarded in D.F.
 *$p<.01$
 **$p<.0001$
***$p<.00001$

Table 8-22
Diagnostic or Other Medical Procedures by IQ Group

	1 Severely Retarded	2 Mildly Retarded	3 Borderline	4 Average	5 Above Average	χ^2	r_{IQ}
			Percent				
White	70.00	**31.50**	*18.20*	*13.34*	*12.87*	315.63*	−.10*
Black	52.46	**22.07**	*11.90*	*9.30*	*8.39*	350.42*	−.11*

Group Ns: White -   90 200 2450 12688 1873
          Black - 122 870 8120   9705   155

Differs from severely retarded in D.F.
Differs from severely and mildly retarded in D.F.s
*$p<.00001$

Table 8-23

Dyskinesia or Ataxia by IQ Group

	1 Severely Retarded	2 Mildly Retarded	3 Borderline	4 Average	5 Above Average	χ^2	r_{IQ}
			Percent				
White	8.70	1.00	**0.32**	**0.07**	**0.05**	438.54*	$-.08*$
Black	3.15	0.78	*0.07*	*0.03*	0.00	160.54*	$-.06*$

Group Ns: White-   92 201 2473 12776 1889
          Black- 127 893 8308   9899   158

Differs from severely retarded in D.F.
Differs from mildly retarded in D.F.
*$p < .00001$

and episodes of hypoxia without unconsciousness caused by accidents such as aspiration of a foreign body. Encephalitis after the age of 1 was diagnosed in 2% of the severely retarded children in each sample (Table 8-21). Hypoxia was reported more frequently among the severely retarded white than black children.

Not unexpectedly, in view of the large number of disorders affecting the severely retarded, a consistent discriminator in both samples was the high frequency with which diagnostic and other medical procedures were performed

Table 8-24

Hypothyroidism by IQ Group

	1 Severely Retarded	2 Mildly Retarded	3 Borderline	4 Average	5 Above Average	χ^2	r_{IQ}
			Percent				
White	1.11	0.50	0.04	**0.03**	**0.00**	36.96**	$-.02*$
Black	0.82	0.00	0.00	0.00	0.00	154.51**	$-.04**$

Group Ns: White -   90 200 2450 12688 1873
          Black - 122 870 8120   9705   155

Differs from severely retarded in D.F.
 *$p < .01$
**$p < .00001$

Table 8-25

Cranial Nerve Abnormality by IQ Group

	1 Severely Retarded	2 Mildly Retarded	3 Borderline	4 Average	5 Above Average	χ^2	r_{IQ}
			Percent				
White	12.22	8.50	*1.39*	**0.49**	**0.32**	349.53*	−.09*
Black	5.74	1.61	0.71	0.31	0.65	87.19*	−.06*

Group Ns: White-   90 200 2450 12688 1873
 Black- 122 870 8120 9705   155
Differs from mildly retarded in D.F.
Differs from severely and mildly retarded in D.F.s
*p <.00001

(Table 8-22). These included EEGs, spinal and ventricular punctures, and parenteral fluids. Lower socioeconomic status of the severely retarded groups was retained as a significant factor in comparisons with the average and/or above-average children.

Several biomedical characteristics of the severely retarded were unique to either whites or blacks. In the white sample, 11 such conditions were identified in the discriminant function analyses. Dyskinesia or ataxia, impairments of voluntary movement or muscular coordination, was diagnosed in 9% of the severely retarded white children at age 7 (Table 8-23). One of the children had experienced petit mal seizures in the interval between 1 month and 7 years (see Table 8-14). Major genitourinary, thoracic, and upper respiratory or mouth malformations were significant factors among whites. Relative frequencies ranged from 13% to 15% among the severely retarded (see Table 8-15). Minor malformations of the skin were present among 9% of the group (see Table 8-18).

Other significant conditions in the white sample were hypothyroidism, present in one of the severely retarded children; abnormalities of the cranial nerves other than the auditory one (primarily the 12th and 7th nerves); and bilateral deafness, a greater than 30 decibel hearing loss in each ear, diagnosed in two of the severely retarded white children. The absence of or failure to detect color blindness in this group was a discriminator in the comparison with the mildly retarded, among whom approximately 10% were affected (Tables 8-24 through 8-26). Also significant in the comparison with the mildly retarded was a lower frequency of right dominance among the severely retarded (hand, eye, and foot; see Table 8-18) and a higher proportion of male children, sex of child having been entered in the analyses as a control variable.

Table 8-26
Sensory Abnormalities by IQ Group

	1 Severely Retarded	2 Mildly Retarded	3 Borderline	4 Average	5 Above Average	χ^2	r_{IQ}
			Percent				

Bilateral Deafness

White	2.17	0.50	0.57	0.09	**0.00**	54.63*	−.05*
Black	3.91	1.01	*0.18*	*0.10*	0.00	122.04*	−.06*

Group Ns: White -   92 201 2473 12777 1889
          Black -   128 895 8319   9919   158

Color Blindness

White	0.00	**10.50**	6.20	*3.29*	*3.10*	79.48*	−.05*
Black	2.46	7.59	*4.14*	2.60	0.65	81.02*	−.06*

Group Ns: White -   90 200 2450 12688 1873
          Black -   122 870 8120   9705   155

Binocular Blindness

White	5.43	1.00	*0.04*	*0.02*	0.05	453.43*	−.08*
Black	6.25	0.11	**0.02**	**0.00**	0.00	874.99*	−.10*

Group Ns: White -   92 201 2473 12777 1889
          Black -   128 895 8319   9919   158

Differs from severely retarded in D.F.
Differs from mildly retarded in D.F.
*$p<.00001$

There were 11 discriminators from the 7-year medical summary that were unique to the severely retarded in the black sample. Although present in similar proportions in both severely retarded groups, binocular blindness, or lack of functional vision in both eyes, was a significant factor among blacks only (Table 8-26). Major malformations of the musculoskeletal system were also present in elevated frequencies among the severely retarded in both samples, but was a discriminator among blacks only in comparisons with the mildly retarded and borderline groups (see Table 8-15). These conditions included metatarsus adductus, talipes equinovarus and calcaneovalgus, dislocation of the hip, and

Table 8-27

Trauma, Coma, and Hematoma by IQ Group

	1 Severely Retarded	2 Mildly Retarded	3 Borderline	4 Average	5 Above Average	χ^2	r_{IQ}
			Percent				
			Post Traumatic Deficit				
White	1.09	0.00	0.04	0.01	0.00	62.97****	− .02*
Black	2.34	0.34	*0.00*	**0.00**	0.00	216.31****	− .06****
Group Ns: White -	92	201	2473	12777	1889		
Black -	128	895	8319	9919	158		
			Coma				
White	2.22	0.00	0.24	0.11	0.05	33.55****	− .02*
Black	2.46	0.57	**0.12**	**0.12**	0.00	52.07****	− .03***
Group Ns: White -	90	200	2450	12688	1873		
Black -	122	870	8120	9705	155		
			Subdural Hematoma or Effusion				
White	0.00	0.00	0.04	0.01	0.00	2.21	− .01
Black	0.82	0.11	0.04	**0.01**	0.00	27.39***	− .03**
Group Ns: White -	90	200	2450	12688	1873		
Black -	122	870	8120	9705	155		

Differs from severely retarded in D.F.

Differs from severely and mildly retarded in D.F.s

*p<.01
**p<.001
***p<.0001
****p<.00001

scoliosis. Minor malformations of the central nervous system (frontal bossing, palpable sutures, pilonidal sinus) were detected in 2% of the severely retarded children compared with less than .5% of those in the comparison groups (see Table 8-16).

Severe head injury resulting in cognitive impairment, and histories of coma and of subdural hematoma or effusion discriminated between the severely retarded and the borderline and/or average groups among blacks; only the latter

Table 8-28
Bacterial Meningitis by IQ Group

	1 Severely Retarded	2 Mildly Retarded	3 Borderline	4 Average	5 Above Average	χ^2	r_{IQ}
			Percent				
White	0.00	0.50	0.20	0.16	0.16	1.74	− .00
Black	1.63	0.23	**0.18**	0.20	0.65	13.80*	− .00

Group Ns: White -   90 200 2450 12688 1873

Black -   123 870 8120 9705 155

Differs from severely retarded in D.F.
*$p<.01$

condition was absent among the severely retarded in the white sample. (Table 8-27). Two children had a history of bacterial meningitis, a significant factor in the comparison with the borderline group (Table 8-28). Infection of the liver was rarer among the severely retarded black than white children but was a discriminator in the former sample only (Table 8-29). Chorioretinitis, inflammation of the choroid and retina, was more frequent among the severely retarded (Table 8-30). On the basis of laboratory tests, cardiovascular disorders were identified in two of the severely retarded children and hemoglobinopathies in four of the group (Table 8-31). Neither of these conditions was present among the severely retarded white children.

Table 8-29
Liver Infection by IQ Group

	1 Severely Retarded	2 Mildly Retarded	3 Borderline	4 Average	5 Above Average	χ^2	r_{IQ}
			Percent				
White	4.44	0.00	0.29	0.09	0.00	141.02**	− .05**
Black	0.82	0.00	**0.02**	0.05	0.00	18.72*	− .00

Group Ns: White -   90 200 2446 12670 1871

Black -   122 870 8119 9703 155

Differs from severely retarded in D.F.
 *$p<.001$
**$p<.00001$

Table 8-30

Chorioretinitis by IQ Group

	1 Severely Retarded	2 Mildly Retarded	3 Borderline	4 Average	5 Above Average	χ^2	r_{IQ}
			Percent				
White	0.00	0.50	0.04	0.04	0.05	9.11	.00
Black	1.64	0.00	**0.04**	0.01	0.00	101.53*	− .04*

Group Ns: White - 90 200 2450 12688 1873

Black - 122 870 8120 9705 155

Differs from severely retarded in D.F.

*$p<.00001$

Table 8-31

Cardiovascular Disorder and Hemoglobinopathy by IQ Group

	1 Severely Retarded	2 Mildly Retarded	3 Borderline	4 Average	5 Above Average	χ^2	r_{IQ}
			Percent				
			Documented Cardiovascular Disorder				
White	0.00	0.00	0.16	0.05	0.00	6.21	− .01
Black	1.64	0.00	0.10	**0.06**	0.00	36.65****	− .02*
			Hemoglobinopathy				
White	0.00	0.00	0.00	0.06	0.00	2.54	− .00
Black	3.28	0.80	0.59	**0.46**	1.29	20.41***	− .02**

Group Ns: White - 90 200 2450 12688 1873

Black - 122 870 8120 9705 155

Differs from severely retarded in D.F.

*$p<.05$

**$p<.01$

***$p<.001$

****$p<.00001$

Table 8-32

Standardized Coefficients for Seven-Year Psychological Discriminators Between the Severely Retarded and Comparison Groups

Variable	Comparison Group							
	White				Black			
	MR	BL	AV	AA	MR	BL	AV	AA
Abnormal behavior summary rating	.36	.76	.93	.81	.65	.88	.91	.10
Auditory-Vocal Association score	−.19	−.01	−.01	−.04	−.11	−.03	−.04	−.23
Goal orientation	−.02	−.06	−.06	−.01	−.12	−.09	−.08	−.04
Fearfulness	−.22	−.34	−.19	−.09	−.28	−.20	−.07	—
Verbal communication	−.37	−.41	−.15	−.09	−.25	−.15	−.05	—
Draw-A-Person score	−.16	−.02	—	−.03	−.06	−.04	−.01	−.13
Attention span	−.14	−.09	−.05	−.13	—	−.08	−.04	−.06
Dependency	—	.15	.03	.08	.16	.09	.06	.11
Tactile finger recognition, right hand	−.06	−.04	−.02	−.04	—	−.03	−.02	−.09
Assertiveness	.34	.04	—	.05	.03	—	—	—
WRAT arithmetic score	—	—	−.02	−.07	—	—	−.01	−.42
Self-confidence	.12	.13	—	—	.06	—	—	—
Activity level	—	—	.05	—	.08	.02	—	—
Percent male	.23	—	—	—	—	—	—	—
Socioeconomic index	.20	—	—	—	—	—	—	—
WRAT spelling score	—	−.03	—	—	—	—	—	—
Impulsivity	—	.01	—	—	—	—	—	—
Separation anxiety	—	—	.06	—	—	—	—	—
Tactile finger recognition, left hand	—	—	−.01	—	—	—	—	—
Frustration tolerance	—	—	—	−.02	—	—	—	—
Hostility	—	—	—	—	−.22	−.12	−.06	—
Emotionality	—	—	—	—	.16	—	—	—
WRAT reading score	—	—	—	—	—	—	—	−.03
Canonical correlation	.69*	.58*	.66*	.86*	.59*	.66*	.82*	.95*

*p<.00001

Table 8-33

Abnormal Behavior Summary Rating by IQ Group

	1 Severely Retarded	2 Mildly Retarded	3 Borderline	4 Average	5 Above Average	χ^2	r_{IQ}
			Percent				
White	73.68	**20.90**	*3.48*	*0.33*	*0.11*	3878.48*	$-.27*$
Black	78.45	**14.25**	*1.05*	*0.17*	**0.00**	5207.46*	$-.31*$

Differs from severely retarded in D.F.
Differs from severely and mildly retarded in D.F.s
*$p < .00001$

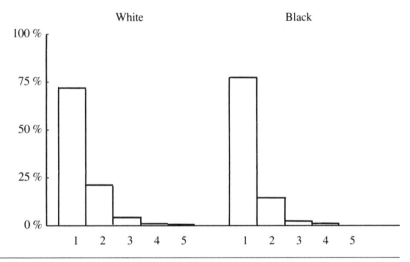

Note. Group Ns: White-   76 201 2468 12757 1887
                   Black- 116 891 8307   9909   158

Psychological Test Scores and Behavior Ratings

Many of the severely retarded, especially in the white sample, could not be evaluated with the full psychological test battery administered at age 7. As noted earlier, approximately two thirds of these children were given IQ tests other than the WISC and 18% could not be tested. The most complete psychological data were ratings of behavior observed during the testing session. For the discriminators shown in Table 8-32, the proportion of known cases among the

Table 8-34

Auditory-Vocal Association and Draw-A-Person Scores by IQ Group

	1 Severely Retarded		2 Mildly Retarded		3 Borderline		4 Average		5 Above Average		F	r_{IQ}
	M	S.D.	M	S.D.	M	S.D.	M	S.D.	M	S.D.		

Auditory-Vocal Association Score

White	33.0	15.1	**54.2**	**13.8**	*73.1*	*12.1*	*88.2*	*12.4*	*106.2*	*15.7*	2176.25*	.63*
Black	26.7	17.1	**51.0**	**12.0**	*67.0*	*12.1*	*78.5*	*11.0*	*93.9*	*13.7*	2175.42*	.60*
Group Ns: White -	23		181		2421		12667		1873			
Black -	47		841		8104		9772		156			

Draw-A-Person Score

White	60.5	8.3	**75.9**	**10.2**	*86.9*	*10.4*	96.4	12.4	*105.9*	*14.4*	810.42*	.43*
Black	62.1	10.0	**77.8**	**10.6**	*88.6*	*11.4*	*96.2*	*12.7*	*109.6*	*15.4*	907.06*	.43*
Group Ns: White -	21		187		2465		12753		1886			
Black -	43		867		8272		9887		157			

Differs from severely retarded in D.F.
Differs from mildy retarded in D.F.
Differs from severely and mildly retarded in D.F.s
*p<.00001

severely retarded in the white and black samples decreased from 83% and 91% for the behavior summary rating to averages of 23% and 34% for the psychological test scores retained in the analyses. Average proportions known for the 5-point individual behavior ratings were 65% and 73% in the white and black severely retarded groups.

The summary rating of abnormal behavior was the largest and most consistent discriminator between the severely retarded and comparison groups. Approximately three quarters of the children in each sample were placed in that category (Table 8-33). Negative correlations between the dichotomous rating (suspect and normal ratings were combined) and IQ score were in the moderate range. Language age scores on the Auditory–Vocal Association Test, part of the Illinois Test of Psycholinguistic Abilities, and standard scores on the Goodenough Harris Draw-A-Person Test are shown by IQ group in Table 8-34. The former scores, based on ability to complete simple verbal analogies orally, were highly correlated with IQ in both samples. Mean scores were consistently higher among whites than blacks with a difference as large as 12 months between the

Table 8-35

Goal Orientation Rating by IQ Group

	1 Severely Retarded		2 Mildly Retarded		3 Borderline		4 Average		5 Above Average		F	r_{IQ}
	M	S.D.	M	S.D.	M	S.D.	M	S.D.	M	S.D.		
White	1.9	0.6	**2.3**	**0.6**	**2.7**	**0.5**	**3.0**	**0.4**	**3.2**	**0.4**	656.72*	.39*
Black	1.8	0.6	**2.5**	**0.6**	**2.8**	**0.4**	**3.0**	**0.3**	**3.2**	**0.4**	762.14*	.37*

Differs from severely retarded in D.F.
Differs from severely and mildly retarded in D.F.s
*$p < .00001$

Standard Score

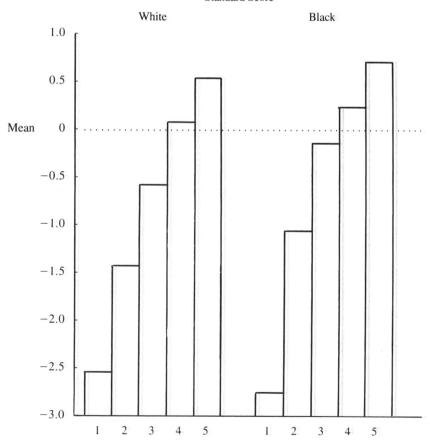

Note. Group Ns: White- 59 200 2446 12686 1874
Black- 100 885 8241 9870 156

Table 8-36
Behavior Ratings by IQ Group

	1 Severely Retarded		2 Mildly Retarded		3 Borderline		4 Average		5 Above Average		F	r_{IQ}
	M	S.D.	M	S.D.	M	S.D.	M	S.D.	M	S.D.		

Fearfulness

	M	S.D.	M	S.D.	M	S.D.	M	S.D.	M	S.D.	F	r_{IQ}
White	2.2	1.0	**3.0**	**0.8**	*3.1*	*0.7*	3.0	0.6	**2.7**	**0.6**	149.64****	$-$.15****
Black	2.3	1.3	**3.0**	**0.8**	**3.0**	**0.6**	2.9	0.5	2.7	0.5	91.23****	$-$.08****

Group Ns: White - 67 200 2455 12694 1873
Black - 105 888 8273 9875 156

Verbal Communication

	M	S.D.	M	S.D.	M	S.D.	M	S.D.	M	S.D.	F	r_{IQ}
White	2.2	1.4	**2.7**	**1.0**	2.7	0.8	**2.9**	**0.6**	*3.1*	*0.5*	132.34****	.19****
Black	2.1	1.4	**2.5**	**0.9**	**2.6**	**0.6**	2.8	0.6	*3.2*	*0.6*	172.02****	.21****

Group Ns: White - 64 199 2455 12689 1873
Black - 102 887 8266 9877 155

Attention Span

	M	S.D.	M	S.D.	M	S.D.	M	S.D.	M	S.D.	F	r_{IQ}
White	1.6	0.9	**2.5**	**0.9**	2.8	0.6	*3.0*	*0.4*	3.1	0.3	318.76****	.25****
Black	1.7	1.1	2.6	0.8	**2.9**	**0.5**	*3.0*	*0.4*	3.0	0.3	310.02****	.21****

Group Ns: White - 59 198 2438 12680 1873
Black - 97 871 8219 9863 156

Dependency

	M	S.D.	M	S.D.	M	S.D.	M	S.D.	M	S.D.	F	r_{IQ}
White	4.1	1.0	3.8	0.8	*3.3*	*0.6*	*3.1*	*0.5*	2.9	0.5	387.44****	$-$.31****
Black	4.4	0.9	**3.6**	**0.8**	*3.2*	*0.5*	*3.0*	*0.4*	2.8	0.5	592.45****	$-$.32****

Group Ns: White - 61 199 2449 12689 1873
Black - 98 888 8272 9876 156

Assertiveness

	M	S.D.	M	S.D.	M	S.D.	M	S.D.	M	S.D.	F	r_{IQ}
White	3.4	1.1	**2.6**	**0.7**	*2.7*	*0.6*	2.8	0.4	**2.9**	**0.3**	80.01****	$-$.10****
Black	3.0	1.2	**2.6**	**0.7**	2.7	0.5	2.8	0.4	2.8	0.4	56.97****	$-$.10****

Group Ns: White - 60 199 2452 12679 1873
Black - 92 884 8271 9882 155

(continued)

174

Table 8-36 (continued)

	1 Severely Retarded		2 Mildly Retarded		3 Borderline		4 Average		5 Above Average		F	r_{IQ}
	M	S.D.	M	S.D.	M	S.D.	M	S.D.	M	S.D.		

Self-confidence

| White | 3.0 | 0.8 | **2.5** | **0.7** | **2.6** | **0.6** | 2.8 | 0.5 | 3.1 | 0.5 | 243.93**** | .26**** |
| Black | 2.8 | 0.8 | **2.5** | **0.6** | 2.7 | 0.5 | *2.9* | *0.4* | *3.1* | *0.4* | 249.92**** | .23**** |

Group Ns: White - 43 193 2445 12681 1870

Black - 61 872 8248 9871 156

Activity Level

| White | 3.8 | 1.2 | 3.1 | 0.9 | 3.0 | 0.7 | **3.0** | **0.5** | 3.0 | 0.4 | 52.70**** | −.03*** |
| Black | 3.5 | 1.3 | **2.9** | **0.9** | **2.9** | **0.6** | *3.0* | *0.5* | 3.0 | 0.4 | 42.08**** | .02** |

Group Ns: White - 68 201 2456 12700 1873

Black - 105 887 8278 9874 156

Impulsivity

| White | 3.3 | 1.2 | 2.8 | 0.8 | *2.9* | *0.5* | *3.0* | *0.3* | 3.0 | 0.2 | 49.70**** | .07**** |
| Black | 2.9 | 1.4 | 2.8 | 0.7 | *2.9* | *0.4* | *3.0* | *0.3* | 3.0 | 0.1 | 103.96**** | .13**** |

Group Ns: White - 60 197 2449 12691 1874

Black - 97 884 8267 9877 156

Separation Anxiety

| White | 3.1 | 1.1 | 3.1 | 0.8 | *2.9* | *0.6* | **2.8** | **0.5** | 2.7 | 0.5 | 65.65**** | −.14**** |
| Black | 2.7 | 1.1 | 2.9 | 0.6 | 2.8 | 0.5 | 2.8 | 0.5 | 2.7 | 0.5 | 14.69**** | −.05**** |

Group Ns: White - 47 150 2019 10512 1581

Black - 77 716 6462 7742 139

Frustration Tolerance

| White | 2.5 | 1.2 | 2.5 | 0.7 | 2.6 | 0.6 | 2.8 | 0.4 | ***3.0*** | ***0.3*** | 197.18**** | .24**** |
| Black | 2.4 | 1.2 | 2.5 | 0.7 | 2.7 | 0.5 | *2.9* | *0.4* | 3.0 | 0.1 | 203.98**** | .21**** |

Group Ns: White - 57 195 2453 12687 1872

Black - 84 884 8260 9872 156

(continued)

Table 8-36 (continued)

	1 Severely Retarded	2 Mildly Retarded	3 Borderline	4 Average	5 Above Average	F	r_{IQ}
	M S.D.	M S.D.	M S.D.	M S.D.	M S.D.		
			Hostility				
White	3.1 0.6	2.9 0.5	*3.0 0.4*	*3.0 0.3*	*3.0 0.3*	10.08****	.03****
Black	2.9 0.7	**3.0 0.4**	**3.0 0.3**	**3.0 0.3**	2.9 0.3	3.82*	.01
Group Ns: White -	58	199	2452	12683	1874		
Black -	85	889	8273	9880	155		
			Emotionality				
White	3.2 1.4	2.8 0.8	2.8 0.7	*2.9 0.4*	3.0 0.3	33.84****	.07****
Black	3.1 1.4	**2.6 0.9**	2.8 0.6	*2.9 0.4*	3.0 0.2	121.11****	.14****
Group Ns: White -	70	200	2456	12693	1873		
Black -	102	888	8272	9879	156		

Differs from severely retarded in D.F.
Differs from mildly retarded in D.F.
Differs from severely and mildly retarded in D.F.s
　*$p<.01$
　**$p<.001$
　***$p<.0001$
　****$p<.00001$

two above-average IQ groups. Language age for the severely retarded was below the 3 year level. Standard scores, or IQ equivalents, on the free drawing of a human figure task were less highly correlated with IQ. Differences between the samples in mean scores were minimal. The severely retarded had unexpectedly high scores of approximately 60.

For goal orientation, the behavior rating most highly correlated with IQ, graphs of the standard scores in each sample are presented to illustrate the separation among IQ groups not apparent from inspection of the raw scores (Table 8-35). The mean rating for the severely retarded corresponded to the scale point of "briefly attempts to achieve goal." On other discriminating behavior ratings in both samples, the severely retarded were characterized as less fearful, less communicative, less attentive, and more dependent than children in higher IQ groups (Table 8-36). In comparisons primarily with the mildly retarded and the borderline, ratings of greater assertiveness and self-confidence

Table 8-37
Tactile Finger Recognition by IQ Group

	1 Severely Retarded	2 Mildly Retarded	3 Borderline	4 Average	5 Above Average	F	r_{IQ}
	M S.D.	M S.D.	M S.D.	M S.D.	M S.D.		
			Right Hand				
White	2.1 1.6	**3.8 1.2**	*4.5 0.8*	*4.7 0.6*	*4.8 0.4*	288.56*	.21*
Black	3.2 1.6	4.0 1.1	*4.5 0.8*	*4.6 0.6*	*4.8 0.4*	210.39*	.18*
			Left Hand				
White	2.5 1.8	3.7 1.3	*4.5 0.8*	*4.7 0.6*	4.8 0.5	264.00*	.20*
Black	3.3 1.5	4.1 1.1	*4.5 0.8*	4.7 0.6	4.8 0.4	165.74*	.17*

Group Ns: White - 19 190 2449 12716 1882
Black - 41 876 8268 9882 157

Differs from severely retarded in D.F.
Differs from mildly retarded in D.F.
Differs from severely and mildly retarded in D.F.s
*$p < .00001$

and a higher activity level were retained. Self-confidence, but not assertiveness, was positively correlated with IQ score in the total samples. Activity level was essentially unrelated to IQ. Among whites only, impulsiveness, separation anxiety, and withdrawal from frustrating tasks were discriminating behaviors for the severely retarded. In the black sample, less hostility and, as compared with the mildly retarded, more variability in emotional responses characterized the severely retarded.

On other psychometric tests, poor tactile finger recognition on the right hand was a consistent discriminator for the severely retarded in both samples; low scores on the left hand were retained in the comparison with the average group among whites. Correlations between Tactile Finger Recognition scores and IQ were in the low–moderate range (Table 8-37).

The severely retarded children were performing at approximately the beginning prekindergarten level on the arithmetic subtest of the Wide Range Achievement Test, a discriminating factor in both samples (Table 8-38). A similarly low spelling score and a slightly higher, but still prekindergarten level, reading score were retained in one comparison among whites and blacks, respec-

Table 8-38
Wide Range Achievement Test Scores by IQ Group

	1 Severely Retarded		2 Mildly Retarded		3 Borderline		4 Average		5 Above Average		F	r_{IQ}
	M	S.D.	M	S.D.	M	S.D.	M	S.D.	M	S.D.		

Arithmetic Score

	M	S.D.	M	S.D.	M	S.D.	M	S.D.	M	S.D.	F	r_{IQ}
White	3.3	3.0	10.2	5.9	*17.8*	*4.3*	**21.9**	**2.9**	24.4	2.9	1998.76*	.56*
Black	3.9	4.1	12.7	5.8	*18.2*	*4.2*	**21.3**	**3.5**	24.1	3.1	1614.62*	.51*

Group Ns: White - 20 190 2455 12730 1881
Black - 43 872 8275 9881 157

Spelling Score

	M	S.D.	M	S.D.	M	S.D.	M	S.D.	M	S.D.	F	r_{IQ}
White	3.3	4.9	13.4	6.7	**21.3**	**5.4**	26.8	5.3	32.0	5.8	1430.68*	.53*
Black	5.9	8.4	15.4	6.7	*21.3*	*5.2*	25.3	5.2	31.1	6.0	1311.14*	.49*

Group Ns: White - 20 188 2454 12722 1880
Black - 42 874 8274 9872 157

Reading Score

	M	S.D.	M	S.D.	M	S.D.	M	S.D.	M	S.D.	F	r_{IQ}
White	5.3	6.3	17.4	10.3	29.0	10.5	39.9	11.3	51.8	12.1	1331.79*	.53*
Black	7.5	9.2	20.3	10.3	29.5	9.6	36.3	9.9	**47.6**	**11.6**	1054.43*	.46*

Group Ns: White - 20 186 2449 12729 1882
Black - 42 872 8280 9881 156

Differs from severely retarded in D.F.
Differs from mildly retarded in D.F.
Differs from severely and mildly retarded in D.F.s
*p<.00001

tively. WRAT subtest scores, especially spelling and reading, were higher among the severely retarded black than white children. The moderately high positive correlations between the achievement scores and IQ ranged from .46 to .56 in the two samples. Sex of child and socioeconomic status at age 7, entered as control variables, were retained as discriminators between the severely and mildly retarded white children.

As expected, canonical correlations between the psychological markers and the group classification were high, reaching maximum values in the extreme group comparisons of .86 among whites and .95 among blacks.

Table 8-39

Standardized Coefficients for Seven-Year Family and Demographic Discriminators Between the Mildly Retarded and Comparison Groups

Variable	Comparison Group					
	White			Black		
	BL	AV	AA	BL	AV	AA
Socioeconomic index	−.48	−.47	−.53	—	−.17	−.64
Retardation in siblings	.50	.40	.26	.26	.18	—
Maternal education	—	−.25	−.22	−.40	−.30	−.27
Mother's additional schooling	−.36	−.11	−.03	−.13	−.13	—
Housing density	—	.13	.10	.42	.25	—
Mother employed	−.44	−.19	−.08	—	−.16	—
Number of changes in residence	—	.25	.20	.17	.14	—
Number of subsequent pregnancies	—	.21	.10	.16	.25	—
Maternal age	—	.16	.05	—	—	−.40
Family size	—	—	.09	—	.15	.38
Public assistance	—	—	.14	.22	.21	—
Study child adopted or in foster home	—	.15	—	.06	—	—
Subsequent siblings live-born now dead	—	—	—	.13	.07	—
Father employed	—	—	—	−.10	−.08	—
Child care	—	—	—	−.24	—	—
Canonical correlation	*.13**	*.15**	*.59**	*.18**	*.29**	*.56**

*p<.00001

THE MILDLY RETARDED

Demographic and Family Characteristics

At the time of the 7-year evaluations, families of the mildly retarded in both samples had lower socioeconomic index scores than those of comparison group children, a higher rate of retardation among siblings, less educated and less frequently employed mothers, and more crowded and less stable housing (Table 8-39). Other discriminating characteristics common to the two samples were more subsequent pregnancies among mothers of the mildly retarded, a larger family size, and more frequent public financial assistance. Adoption or foster home placement occurred more often among the mildly retarded than non-retarded groups. These variables were also related to severe retardation; distributions and univariate statistics are shown in Tables 8-2–8-5 and 8-8–8-10.

Table 8-40

Additional Maternal Schooling by IQ Group

	1 Severely Retarded	2 Mildly Retarded	3 Borderline	4 Average	5 Above Average	χ²	r_IQ
			Percent				
White	8.62	4.00	*11.60*	*17.25*	*30.78*	298.89*	.14*
Black	24.47	20.80	*28.30*	*34.88*	34.00	126.45*	.09*

Differs from mildly retarded in D.F.
*p <.00001

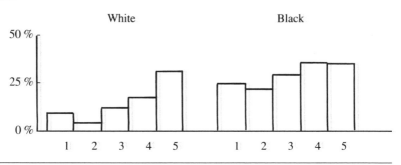

White   Black

Note. Group Ns: White-   58   175   2225   12087   1842
                 Black-   94   774   7353   9022   150

Table 8-41

Maternal Age by IQ Group

	1 Severely Retarded		2 Mildly Retarded		3 Borderline		4 Average		5 Above Average		F	r_IQ
	M	S.D.	M	S.D.	M	S.D.	M	S.D.	M	S.D.		
White	34.9	7.7	34.3	7.7	33.0	7.1	*32.8*	*6.3*	*32.7*	*5.3*	5.67**	− .02*
Black	34.5	9.0	33.0	8.5	32.2	7.9	32.5	7.3	*34.7*	*6.9*	9.00***	.01

Group Ns: White -   82   198   2424   12611   1871
          Black -   119   851   7908   9498   156

Differs from mildly retarded in D.F.
  *p<.01
  **p<.001
***p<.00001

Table 8-42
Sibling Death, Father Employed, and Child Care by IQ Group

	1 Severely Retarded	2 Mildly Retarded	3 Borderline	4 Average	5 Above Average	χ^2	r_{IQ}
			Percent				
			Subsequent Sibling Death				
White	1.75	5.68	3.40	3.06	2.55	6.84	−.02**
Black	6.38	8.48	*4.99*	*3.92*	3.33	40.15***	−.05***
Group Ns: White -	57	176	2234	12105	1842		
Black -	94	778	7360	9033	150		
			Father Employed				
White	86.54	86.86	87.49	92.42	96.66	109.98***	.10***
Black	82.81	80.15	*86.55*	*91.08*	94.74	89.89***	.10***
Group Ns: White -	52	137	1742	10472	1706		
Black -	64	408	4305	5883	114		
			Child Care				
White	36.21	40.00	52.57	53.86	53.42	21.16**	.02*
Black	61.29	60.67	*71.84*	76.90	72.00	136.26***	.08***
Group Ns: White -	58	175	2216	12064	1840		
Black -	93	773	7334	9001	150		

Differs from mildly retarded in D.F.
  *$p<.05$
  **$p<.001$
  ***$p<.00001$

Five factors were unique to the mildly retarded. Fewer of the mothers in either sample had received additional schooling or training since birth of the study child (Table 8-40). Among whites, mothers were older than in the average and above-average groups but, among blacks, younger than in the highest IQ group. There was little or no relationship between maternal age and IQ score (Table 8-41). Deaths among younger siblings, a lower rate of paternal employment, and less utilization of child care related to mild retardation in the black sample (Table 8-42).

The significant demographic and family characteristics were consistent with

Table 8-43
**Standardized Coefficients for Seven-Year Pediatric Discriminators
in the Mildly Retarded and Comparison Groups**

	Comparison Group					
	White			Black		
Variable	BL	AV	AA	BL	AV	AA
Socioeconomic index	−.27	−.27	−.63	−.40	−.47	−.76
Abnormal gait	.24	.21	.21	.38	.38	.19
Head circumference	−.22	−.25	−.29	−.25	−.27	−.35
Diagnostic or other medical procedures	.11	.08	.08	.21	.18	.12
Color blindness	—	.13	.14	.16	.18	.12
Cyanotic congenital heart disease	.18	—	.08	.17	.12	—
Failure to thrive	—	.17	.12	.12	.14	—
Major CNS malformations	—	.20	.14	.13	.08	—
Strabismus	.17	.11	—	.16	.12	—
Cerebral palsy	—	.28	.12	—	.16	—
Major cardiovascular malformations	—	.08	.06	—	.08	—
Abnormal shape of skull	.32	.19	.12	—	—	—
Cranial nerve abnormality[a]	.25	.22	.17	—	—	—
Minor ear malformations	.20	.11	.12	—	—	—
Major upper respiratory or mouth malformations	.13	.07	.06	—	—	—
Ear infection	.12	.09	.05	—	—	—
Down's syndrome	.34	.34	—	—	—	—
Binocular blindness	.19	.14	—	—	—	—
Acyanotic congenital heart disease	.21	.09	—	—	—	—
CNS infection[b]	.20	.07	—	—	—	—
Nystagmus	.18	.09	—	—	—	—
Major genitourinary malformations	.13	—	—	—	—	—
Petit mal	—	.20	—	—	—	—
Gonadal dysgenesis	—	.19	—	—	—	—
Minor musculoskeletal malformations	—	.09	—	—	—	—
Symptomatic intoxication[c]	—	.08	—	—	—	—
Asymptomatic partial seizures	—	.08	—	—	—	—
Chickenpox	—	−.07	—	—	—	—
Atypical staring	—	.06	—	—	—	—
Hyperthermia	—	—	.05	—	—	—
Right handedness	—	—	—	−.15	−.10	−.16

(continued)

Table 8-43 (continued)

Variable	White			Black		
	BL	AV	AA	BL	AV	AA
Mumps	—	—	—	−.12	−.08	−.11
Other genetic or prenatal infection syndromes	—	—	—	.16	.16	—
Abnormal reflexes	—	—	—	.21	.14	—
Post traumatic deficit	—	—	—	.16	.10	—
Minor upper respiratory or mouth malformations	—	—	—	.13	.11	—
Dyskinesia or ataxia	—	—	—	.18	.07	—
Bilateral deafness	—	—	—	.11	.06	—
Asymptomatic generalized seizures	—	—	—	.21	—	—
Monocular blindness	—	—	—	.14	—	—
Epilepsy	—	—	—	—	.16	—
Major hemorrhage	—	—	—	—	.07	—
Weight	—	—	—	—	−.07	—
Eye infection	—	—	—	—	—	−.16
Canonical correlation	*.33**	*.33**	*.67**	*.25**	*.36**	*.57**

[a]Other than auditory nerve

[b]Other than meningitis or encephalitis

[c]Agents other than hydrocarbon, lead, or salicylate

*$p < .00001$

the well-established relationship between mild retardation and lower socioeconmic status and its correlates (e.g., Birch et al., 1970). Considered alone, however, they were surprisingly poor discriminators except in the comparison with above-average children. Canonical correlations with the group classification ranged from .13 to .59 among whites and .18 to .56 among blacks.

Biomedical Characteristics

Ten biomedical complications were related to mild retardation in both samples (Table 8-43). All but 3 of these conditions were discriminators for the severely retarded as well. Serious disorders were relatively infrequent especially in the

Table 8-44
Cardiovascular Malformations and Cyanotic Congenital Heart Disease by IQ Group

	1 Severely Retarded	2 Mildly Retarded	3 Borderline	4 Average	5 Above Average	χ^2	r_{IQ}
			Percent				
			Major Cardiovascular Malformations				
White	3.26	2.49	0.49	*0.23*	*0.32*	59.34***	−.04***
Black	3.13	1.45	0.49	*0.28*	0.00	48.55***	−.04***

Group Ns: White - 92 201 2473 12777 1889
Black - 128 895 8319 9919 158

			Cyanotic Heart Disease				
White	0.00	1.00	*0.08*	0.07	*0.00*	24.30**	−.02*
Black	0.82	0.46	*0.04*	*0.01*	0.00	49.62***	−.03***

Group Ns: White - 90 200 2450 12688 1873
Black - 122 870 8120 9705 155

Differs from mildly retarded in D.F.
  *$p<.01$
 **$p<.0001$
***$p<.00001$

black sample. Milder disorders were also less frequent among blacks than whites. As reported earlier, major malformations of the central nervous system (hydrocephaly, microcephaly, and cerebellar astrocytoma) were present in 3% of the mildly retarded white children and .5% of the mildly retarded black children (see Tables 5-3 and 3-11). Major cardiovascular malformations were identified in 2.5% of the group among whites and 1.5% among blacks (Table 8-44). The proportion of mildly retarded children with cerebral palsy at age 7 was 5.5% in the white sample and 2% in the black sample (see Table 8-13).

The minor neurological sign of abnormal gait was a highly consistent discriminator. Almost one fourth of the mildly retarded among whites and 13% among blacks were observed to have awkward or restricted gait at age 7 (see Table 8-17). Smaller head circumference was also a consistent discriminator. Mean values for the mildly retarded were at least 1.5 centimeters below that for the above-average group in each sample (see Table 8-19). A history of failure to thrive after the first year, although infrequent, discriminated between the mildly

Table 8-45
Oculomotor Disorders by IQ Group

	1 Severely Retarded	2 Mildly Retarded	3 Borderline	4 Average	5 Above Average	χ^2	r_{IQ}
				Percent			
			Strabismus				
White	31.11	24.00	*11.39*	*7.76*	6.25	169.85*	−.09*
Black	21.31	16.55	*10.02*	*8.18*	9.03	92.79*	−.07*
			Nystagmus				
White	14.44	6.50	*1.63*	*1.02*	0.96	184.05*	−.06*
Black	11.48	1.72	0.89	0.70	0.00	167.03*	−.06*

Group Ns: White -   90 200 2450 12688 1873
        Black - 122 870 8120 9705   155

Differs from mildly retarded in D.F.
*p<.00001

retarded and higher IQ groups in both samples (see Table 8-20). Two of the children in the white sample and four in the black sample had cyanotic congenital heart disease (Table 8-44).

Sensory abnormalities among the mildly retarded included strabismus, or impaired extraocular movements, more prevalent among whites (Table 8-45), and, as mentioned earlier, color blindness (see Table 8-26). Like the severely retarded, the mildly retarded had undergone more diagnostic or other medical procedures between the age of 1 and 7 than children in the comparison groups (see Table 8-22). A final common discriminator was the major one of socioeconomic status.

Other biomedical factors were confined to one sample. Among whites, three of the mildly retarded children had Down's syndrome (see Table 5-2). Abnormal skull shape and major malformations of the upper respiratory and genitourinary systems were more frequent than in nonretarded groups (see Table 8-15). Minor malformations of the ear and of the musculoskeletal system were also more frequent (see Table 8-16). One case of gonadal dysgenesis, the only occurrence of this syndrome in the study cohort, was identified among the mildly retarded white children. Two of the children were blind in both eyes (see Table 8-26), and 8.5% had cranial nerve abnormalities, a discriminator in all comparisons

Table 8-46

Atypical Staring by IQ Group

	1 Severely Retarded	2 Mildly Retarded	3 Borderline	4 Average	5 Above Average	χ^2	r_{IQ}
			Percent				
White	3.26	1.00	0.24	*0.11*	0.05	73.44*	− .04*
Black	1.56	0.45	0.06	0.06	0.00	46.73*	− .03*

Group Ns: White - 92 201 2473 12777 1889

Black - 128 895 8319 9919 158

Differs from mildly retarded in D.F.
*p<.00001

(see Table 8-25). Although present in elevated frequencies among the severely retarded, nystagmus, or involuntary rapid movement of the eyeball, was a discriminator unique to the mildly retarded white children (Table 8-45). Rarely occurring seizure states, significant in the comparison with the average group, were asymptomatic partial seizures, petit mal, and atypical staring (Tables 8-14 and 8-46).

Other conditions related to mild retardation among whites were congenital heart disease without cyanosis (Table 8-47), CNS infections exclusive of meningitis and encephalitis, reported episodes of symptomatic intoxication (from

Table 8-47

Acyanotic Congenital Heart Disease by IQ Group

	1 Severely Retarded	2 Mildly Retarded	3 Borderline	4 Average	5 Above Average	χ^2	r_{IQ}
			Percent				
White	8.89	3.50	*0.61*	*0.40*	0.48	160.00*	− .05*
Black	5.74	1.49	0.60	0.28	0.00	95.52*	− .05*

Group Ns: White- 90 200 2450 12688 1873

Black- 122 870 8120 9705 155

Differs from mildly retarded in D.F.
*p <.00001

Table 8-48

CNS Infection, Symptomatic Intoxication, and Hyperthermia by IQ Group

	1 Severely Retarded	2 Mildly Retarded	3 Borderline	4 Average	5 Above Average	χ^2	r_{IQ}
			Percent				

CNS Infection

White	1.11	1.00	*0.04*	*0.06*	0.00	40.74****	− .03****
Black	0.00	0.00	0.04	0.01	0.00	1.74	.00
Group Ns: White -	90	200	2450	12688	1873		
Black -	122	870	8120	9705	155		

Symptomatic Intoxication

White	0.00	2.01	0.62	*0.40*	0.38	13.95**	− .02*
Black	2.48	1.03	1.03	0.74	0.00	9.09	− .03***
Group Ns: White -	89	199	2435	12600	1864		
Black -	121	870	8094	9665	153		

Hyperthermia

White	4.44	5.00	2.45	2.52	*2.14*	7.56	− .01
Black	0.82	1.84	1.96	1.88	0.65	2.27	.00
Group Ns: White -	90	200	2450	12688	1873		
Black -	122	870	8120	9705	155		

Differs from mildly retarded in D.F.
   *$p<.05$
  **$p<.01$
 ***$p<.001$
****$p<.00001$

agents other than hydrocarbon, lead, or salicylate), and hyperthermia (Table 8-48). Ear infections between the ages of 1 and 7 were more common among the mildly retarded, discriminating between them and all comparison groups. Chickenpox was reported significantly less often than in the average group (Table 8-49).

Biomedical discriminators in the black sample included several major disorders with low prevalence rates. In the group of 895 mildly retarded children, 8 had genetic and postinfection syndromes identified in infancy (see Tables 5-2

Table 8-49
Ear Infection and Chickenpox by IQ Group

	1 Severely Retarded	2 Mildly Retarded	3 Borderline	4 Average	5 Above Average	χ^2	r_{IQ}
			Percent				
			Ear Infection				
White	9.76	13.97	*6.65*	*5.45*	*5.44*	30.36**	− .03*
Black	4.20	3.66	2.83	2.95	2.01	2.98	− .01

Group Ns: White -   82 179 2239 11487 1709
          Black - 119 846 7939   9439   149

			Chickenpox				
White	33.33	28.00	35.80	*41.29*	48.75	90.28*	.08*
Black	23.77	20.11	23.29	26.76	38.06	53.91*	.06*

Group Ns: White -   90 200 2450 12688 1873
          Black - 122 870 8120   9705   155

Differs from mildly retarded in D.F.
 *$p < .001$
 **$p < .00001$

Table 8-50
Monocular Blindness by IQ Group

	1 Severely Retarded	2 Mildly Retarded	3 Borderline	4 Average	5 Above Average	χ^2	r_{IQ}
			Percent				
White	0.00	0.00	0.00	0.11	0.00	5.10	.00
Black	0.00	0.45	*0.05*	0.06	0.00	18.51**	− .02*

Group Ns: White -   92 201 2473 12777 1889
          Black - 128 895 8319   9919   158

Differs from mildly retarded in D.F.
 *$p < .05$
 **$p < .001$

Table 8-51
Major Hemorrhage by IQ Group

	1 Severely Retarded	2 Mildly Retarded	3 Borderline	4 Average	5 Above Average	χ^2	r_{IQ}
			Percent				
White	0.00	0.00	0.00	0.19	0.00	8.73	.01
Black	0.00	0.23	*0.02*	*0.02*	0.65	25.40*	− .00

Group Ns: White - 90 200 2450 12688 1873

Black - 122 870 8120 9705 155

Differs from mildly retarded in D.F.
*p<.0001

Table 8-52
Mumps and Eye Infection by IQ Group

	1 Severely Retarded	2 Mildly Retarded	3 Borderline	4 Average	5 Above Average	χ^2	r_{IQ}
			Percent				
			Mumps				
White	18.89	17.50	20.53	23.59	27.12	30.83***	.05***
Black	8.20	10.80	*15.18*	*16.99*	*21.94*	38.23***	.05***

Group Ns: White - 90 200 2450 12688 1873

Black - 122 870 8120 9705 155

			Eye Infection				
White	2.25	2.02	0.87	0.75	0.60	7.59	− .02*
Black	3.28	0.35	0.64	0.80	*2.60*	21.20**	.00

Group Ns: White - 89 198 2424 12516 1833

Black - 122 866 8090 9663 154

Differs from mildly retarded in D.F.
  *p<.01
 **p<.001
***p<.00001

Table 8-53

Weight in Kilograms by IQ Group

	1 Severely Retarded	2 Mildly Retarded	3 Borderline	4 Average	5 Above Average	F	r_{IQ}
	M S.D.	M S.D.	M S.D.	M S.D.	M S.D.		
White	21.7 6.4	22.4 5.3	23.1 4.3	23.8 4.1	24.4 3.9	37.15*	.11*
Black	22.1 5.7	22.8 4.8	23.7 4.9	24.3 4.8	25.4 5.1	37.76*	.10*

Differs from mildly retarded in D.F.
*p < .00001

Standard Score

Note. Group Ns: White-   79   197   2443   12661   1869
Black-   116   870   8097   9688   153

and 3-11). Three children suffered cognitive deficit following head trauma (see Table 8-27). Dyskinesia or ataxia at age 7 was diagnosed in .8% of the group (see Table 8-23), epilepsy in 2.6%, and 1.9% had had asymptomatic generalized seizures (see Table 8-14). Sensory deficits included bilateral deafness in 1% of the mildly retarded (see Table 8-20) and monocular blindness in .45% (Table 8-50).

Less handicapping conditions among the mildly retarded were a relatively high frequency of abnormal reflexes (see Table 8-17), less right-handedness at age 7 (see Table 8-18), and minor upper respiratory or mouth malformations that were present in 1.6% of the group (see Table 8-16). Two of the children had a history of major hemorrhage (Table 8-51). Negative risk factors for mild retardation in the black sample were mumps, reported less often than in any comparison group, and eye infections, less frequent than in the above-average group (Table 8-52). Mean weight was 1.5 kilograms below that of the average

Table 8-54
**Standardized Coefficients for Seven-Year Psychological Discriminators
Between the Mildly Retarded and Comparison Groups**

Variable	Comparison Group					
	White			Black		
	BL	AV	AA	BL	AV	AA
Auditory-Vocal Association score	−.35	−.20	−.17	−.34	−.37	−.58
Draw-A-Person score	−.23	−.10	−.10	−.32	−.20	−.36
WRAT arithmetic score	−.32	−.51	−.34	−.23	−.26	—
Abnormal behavior summary rating	.18	.38	.05	.27	.14	—
Goal orientation	−.05	−.12	−.07	−.16	−.18	—
Tactile finger recognition, left hand	−.14	−.14	−.08	−.05	−.05	—
Tactile finger recognition, right hand	−.09	−.11	−.07	−.09	−.05	—
Dependency	.10	.09	.05	.13	.12	—
Impulsivity	−.10	−.09	−.04	−.07	−.10	—
Socioeconomic index	—	—	−.12	−.08	−.06	−.16
Percent male	−.12	−.07	−.04	—	.02	—
Bender-Gestalt error score	—	.09	.25	.06	.12	—
Assertiveness	−.12	—	—	−.07	−.04	—
Emotionality	—	−.03	—	−.04	−.05	—
Attention span	—	−.01	−.02	—	−.01	—
WRAT spelling score	−.16	—	—	−.05	—	—
Frustration tolerance	—	—	−.08	—	−.02	—
Verbal communication	—	—	−.01	—	—	−.09
Hostility	−.09	−.08	−.05	—	—	—
Fearfulness	−.16	—	—	—	—	—
Separation anxiety	.08	—	—	—	—	—
Self-confidence	—	—	—	—	−.02	−.11
Activity level	—	—	—	—	−.02	—
Canonical correlation	*.51**	*.53**	*.87**	*.50**	*.70**	*.85**

*$p < .00001$

group at age 7 (Table 8-53). Weight increased in step-wise fashion with IQ level
in both samples but correlations with IQ score were modest.

Concurrent biomedical factors and those reported in histories following infancy were less highly related to mild retardation than to the more severe
cognitive deficit, as expected. These factors (and socioeconomic status) were

effective discriminators, however, between the mildly retarded and above-average children in each sample; canonical correlations were .67 among whites and .57 among blacks. In other comparisons, values were moderate ranging from .25 to .36 in the two samples.

Psychological Test Scores and Behavior Ratings

Performance levels on tests of verbal analogies, drawing a human figure, and arithmetic were major discriminators between the mildly retarded and higher IQ groups (Table 8-54). A summary rating of behavior in the testing situation was also an important discriminator. All but one of the measures had been retained in comparable analyses for the severely retarded, and, except for some behavior ratings, all were significant in both samples. Language age scores on the Auditory–Vocal Association Test were slightly above the 4-year level in both mildly retarded groups (see Table 8-34) and mean standard scores on the Draw-A-Person Test (comparable to IQ scores) were 76 and 78 among whites and blacks, respectively. The mildly retarded were performing at about the mid-kindergarten level on the arithmetic subtest of the Wide Range Achievement Test (see Table 8-36). More than 20% of the children in the white sample and 14% in the black sample were judged to be abnormal in behavior in the summary rating given at age 7 (see Table 8-33).

Other consistent psychometric discriminators were poorer tactile finger recognition on both hands (see Table 8-37) and a higher Koppitz error score on the Bender–Gestalt Test, a task that requires the copying of geometric forms (Table 8-55). As shown in the graph, standardized scores on the Bender were linearly related to IQ level in each sample; correlations between the raw scores and IQ were in the high–moderate range. Low spelling scores among the mildly retarded, at approximately the mid-kindergarten level, discriminated between them and the borderline group in each sample (see Table 8-38).

Ratings of specific behaviors observed during the psychological examination indicated poorer goal orientation among the mildly retarded in both samples (see Table 8-35), a higher degree of dependency, and more rigid, or less impulsive, behavior (see Table 8-36). Retained less consistently in comparisons with higher IQ groups were lower ratings for assertiveness, emotional reactivity, attention span, frustration tolerance, and verbal communication. In addition to these shared behavioral characteristics, mildly retarded children in the white sample were rated as more agreeable (less hostile) than comparison group children and as less cautious or fearful in the testing situation, but more anxious about separation from the caretaker than children in the borderline group. In the black sample, less self-confidence and a lower activity level among the mildly retarded were significant in comparisons with average and above-average groups.

In the analyses of concurrent psychological characteristics of the mildly re-

Table 8-55
Bender-Gestalt Error Score by IQ Group

	1 Severely Retarded		2 Mildly Retarded		3 Borderline		4 Average		5 Above Average		F	r_{IQ}
	M	S.D.	M	S.D.	M	S.D.	M	S.D.	M	S.D.		
White	15.5	3.0	12.9	3.7	8.6	3.6	5.6	2.9	3.4	2.2	1199.52*	−.48*
Black	16.5	3.7	12.8	3.9	9.3	3.6	7.0	3.2	4.6	2.6	995.98*	−.43*

Differs from mildly retarded in D.F.
*$p < .00001$

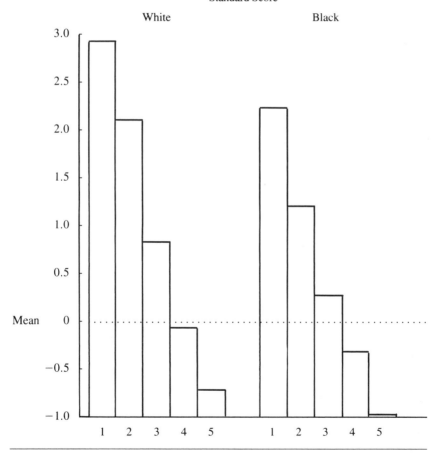

Standard Score

Note. Group Ns: White- 13 177 2462 12761 1885
Black- 31 860 8301 9904 158

Note. Group Ns: White-   13   177   2462   12761   1885
　　　　　　　Black-   31   860   8301   9904   158

193

tarded, socioeconomic status and sex of child were significant in both samples. The socioeconomic index score at age 7 was retained consistently among blacks, and sex ratio (lower in the mildly retarded) among whites. Canonical correlations between the discriminators and the group classification ranged from .50 to values of .85 and .87 in comparisons between the mildly retarded and the above average.

9

Subgroups of the Mentally Retarded

Mentally retarded children differ in presence and degree of biological deficit as well as in severity of cognitive deficit. Because of this heterogeneity, analyses of total groups of retarded children may obscure some antecedent factors and attribute inappropriate generality to others (Birch et al., 1970). In the present study, a majority of the severely retarded and a small minority of the mildly retarded had major neurological disorders (see Tables 3-5, 3-6, and 3-10). As noted earlier, prevalence of these disorders at both levels of retardation was related to ethnicity and to social class, with the highest proportion of neurologically abnormal children (82%) among the severely retarded whites in the highest SES group (see Table 3-5). To the extent that associated neurological abnormalities explain or account for mental retardation (and this differs in degree, as in Down's syndrome and epilepsy), then children without clear clinical signs of CNS pathology pose the largest etiological questions and are the primary focus of this chapter.

RISK FACTORS AND NEUROLOGICAL STATUS

Each retarded group was dichotomized into children with and without major neurological disorders. The two subgroups were compared on characteristics of pregnancy and events occurring in delivery and the neonatal period. Children free of the following conditions were designated as CNS "normals": Down's syndrome, other genetic and post-infection syndromes, post-traumatic deficit, major CNS malformations[1], cerebral palsy, epilepsy, bilateral deafness, and binocular blindness. The distribution of these conditions among the CNS ab-

---

[1]Specific syndromes and CNS malformations are listed in Tables 3-7 and 3-11.

Table 9-1

Standardized Coefficients for Prenatal and Perinatal Discriminators Between Severely Retarded Children With and Without Major CNS Disorders in the White Sample

Variable	Prenatal and Delivery	Neonatal	Prenatal and Perinatal
Urinary tract infection in pregnancy	.88	—	.79
Family income	− .38	—	—
Brain abnormality	—	− .81	− .53
Percent male	—	.58	—
Canonical correlation	*.46*	*.39*	*.51*

Note: Negative coefficients indicate lower means or frequencies in the severely retarded group without major CNS disorders.

Table 9-2

Prenatal and Perinatal Discriminators Between Severely Retarded Children With and Without Major CNS Disorders in the White Sample

Variable	Major CNS Disorders						t or χ²
	With			Without			
	N	Mean or Percent	SD	N	Mean or Percent	SD	
Urinary tract infection in pregnancy	57	5.26%		20	40.00%		11.89***
Brain abnormality	66	28.79%		26	0.00%		7.76**
Percent male	66	56.06%		26	80.78%		3.88*
Family income	58	4966	2296	23	3717	1166	2.48*

Note: Chi-square statistic is underlined.
*p<.05
**p<.01
***p<.001

196

Table 9-3

**Standardized Coefficients for Prenatal and Perinatal Discriminators
Between Severely Retarded Children With and Without
Major CNS Disorders in the Black Sample**

Variable	Prenatal and Delivery	Neonatal	Prenatal and Perinatal
Recent maternal illnesses	.64	—	.39
Socioeconomic index	−.56	—	−.41
Cigarettes smoked per day in pregnancy	.49	—	.35
Lowest neonatal hematocrit	—	−.82	−.54
Brain abnormality	—	−.67	−.56
Apgar score at 5 minutes	—	.50	—
Canonical correlation	*.38*	*.40*	*.48*

normals is shown in Tables 3-6 and 3-10. In the severely retarded groups, 28% of whites ($N=26$) and 46% of blacks ($N=59$) met the criteria for CNS normals. Among the mildly retarded, 86% in the white sample and 94% in the black sample were free of major neurological disorders; the number of CNS abnormal cases was 28 among whites and 56 among blacks. The subgroups within each level of retardation were compared on all prenatal, obstetric, and neonatal variables with differences evaluated by the t or chi-square test. Those that passed the univariate screen ($p < .05$) were entered in a discriminant function analysis of prenatal and delivery or neonatal factors. A third analysis combined the results in a summary of subgroup differences through the perinatal period.

The Severely Retarded

Discriminators between subgroups of the severely retarded in the white sample are shown in Tables 9-1 and 9-2. The prenatal factors were urinary tract infection in pregnancy, approximately eight times as frequent among mothers of CNS normals than those of abnormals, and yearly income, lower among families of the CNS normals. The pregnancy complication of urinary tract infection, which may be accompanied by endotoxemia, has been implicated in other adverse outcomes in the Collaborative Project population including excess perinatal deaths (Naeye, 1979), fetal leukoencephalopathy in infants dying in the first month (Leviton & Gilles, 1979, 1984), and low birthweight (Sever, Ellenberg, & Edmonds, 1977). No differences between subgroups were found in events during labor and delivery. The two prenatal characteristics were moder-

Table 9-4

Prenatal and Perinatal Discriminators Between Severely Retarded Children With and Without Major CNS Disorders in the Black Sample

| Variable | Major CNS Disorders | | | | | | t or χ^2 |
| | With | | | Without | | | |
	N	Mean or Percent	SD	N	Mean or Percent	SD	
Socioeconomic index	68	38.82	20.49	54	30.39	16.80	2.44*
Cigarettes per day in pregnancy	69	2.25	5.28	58	5.40	8.09	2.64**
Recent maternal illness	69	0.28	0.57	59	0.61	0.85	2.61*
Lowest neonatal hematocrit	59	59.64	11.82	54	55.09	11.91	2.04*
Apgar score at 5 minutes	62	8.24	2.32	53	8.98	1.26	2.07*
Brain abnormality	69	17.39%		58	3.44%		4.91*

*$p<.05$
**$p<.01$

Table 9-5

Standardized Coefficients for Prenatal and Perinatal Discriminators Between Severely Retarded Children With and Without Selected Major CNS Disorders in the White Sample

Variable	Prenatal and Delivery	Neonatal	Prenatal and Perinatal
Maternal SRA score	−.61	—	−.61
Family income	−.58	—	−.58
Urinary tract infection in pregnancy	.12	—	.12
Neonatal seizures	—	−1.00	—
Canonical correlation	.77	.38	.77

Note: Negative coefficients indicate lower means or frequencies in the severely retarded group without major CNS disorders.

Table 9-6

**Prenatal and Perinatal Discriminators Between Severely Retarded Children
With and Without Selected Major CNS Disorders in the White Sample**

| Variable | Major CNS Disorders | | | | | | t or χ^{2} [1] |
| | With | | | Without | | | |
	N	Mean or Percent	SD	N	Mean or Percent	SD	
Maternal SRA score	10	41.80	7.98	6	31.67	7.99	3.06**
Family income	21	5595	2256	23	3717	1166	2.48*
Urinary tract infection in pregnancy	24	4.17%		20	40.00%		<u>6.55*</u>
Neonatal seizures	27	25.93%		26	0.00%		<u>5.67*</u>

[1]Chi-square statistic is underlined.
*$p<.05$
**$p<.01$

ately effective as discriminators, having a canonical correlation of .46 with the
subgroup classification. Following birth, the CNS normals were characterized by
an absence of diagnosed brain abnormality in the nursery period (compared with
29% identified among the abnormals) and a high sex ratio with 81% of the
children male. In the summary analysis, maternal urinary tract infection and
neonatal brain abnormality were retained as discriminators. Their canonical
correlation with the subgroup classification was .51.

Table 9-7

**Standardized Coefficients for Prenatal and Perinatal Discriminators
Between Severely Retarded Children With and Without
Selected Major CNS Disorders in the Black Sample**

Variable	Prenatal and Delivery	Neonatal	Prenatal and Perinatal
Early rupture of membranes	− .85	—	− .69
Length of 2nd stage of labor	− .78	—	− .63
Resuscitation after 5 minutes	—	− .68	—
Primary apnea	—	− .65	− .50
Canonical correlation	*.43*	*.36*	*.51*

Table 9-8

**Prenatal and Perinatal Discriminators Between Severely Retarded Children
With and Without Selected Major CNS Disorders in the Black Sample**

| Variable | Major CNS Disorders | | | | | | t or χ^2 |
| | With | | | Without | | | |
	N	Mean or Percent	SD	N	Mean or Percent	SD	
Early rupture of membranes	30	30.00%		47	8.51%		4.59*
Length of 2nd stage of labor	27	32.89	48.05	48	17.38	14.61	2.08*
Resuscitation after 5 minutes	36	16.67%		58	1.72%		5.19*
Primary apnea	36	11.11%		58	0.00%		4.28*

*$p<.05$

Subgroups of the severely retarded in the black sample differed on three prenatal factors (Tables 9-3 and 9-4). Again, no differences in labor or delivery were found. Reported illnesses in the year preceding study registration and cigarette smoking during pregnancy were more frequent among mothers of the CNS normals. These mothers had a lower socioeconomic index score than

Table 9-9

**Standardized Coefficients for Prenatal and Perinatal Discriminators
Between Mildly Retarded Children With and Without
Major CNS Disorders in the White Sample**

Variable	Prenatal and Delivery	Neonatal	Prenatal and Perinatal
Bacterial infection in 1st trimester	−.68	—	−.46
Highest FHR during 1st stage of labor	.53	—	.31
Socioeconomic index	−.49	—	—
Brain abnormality	—	−.56	−.34
Resuscitation up to 5 minutes	—	−.40	−.27
Micrognathia	—	−.44	−.41
Canonical correlation	.36	.39	.47

Table 9-10

Prenatal and Perinatal Discriminators Between Mildly Retarded Children With and Without Major CNS Disorders in the White Sample

Variable	Major CNS Disorders						t or χ^2
	With			Without			
	N	Mean or Percent	SD	N	Mean or Percent	SD	
Bacterial infection in 1st trimester	26	11.54%		150	0.67%		7.41**
Brain abnormality	28	14.29%		168	0.60%		13.01***
Resuscitation up to 5 minutes	28	25.00%		168	4.76%		11.19***
Micrognathia	28	10.71%		172	0.58%		7.97**
Socioeconomic index	28	47.18	23.90	164	39.26	17.64	2.08*
Highest FHR during 1st stage of labor	21	142.67	8.66	121	148.26	9.87	2.44*

*$p<.05$
**$p<.01$
***$p<.001$

mothers of the CNS abnormals, a finding consistent with the one in the white sample for family income. As neonates, the CNS normals had a lower hematocrit (lowest value obtained) than abnormals, but means in both subgroups, accompanied by large standard deviations, were close to the population mean for blacks (57 ± 8, $N=16,995$). Mean Apgar score at 5 minutes was higher in the CNS normals (9 versus 8) and, as among whites, the clinical judgment of brain abnormality in the newborn was validated by its higher frequency in the abnormal subgroup. Neonatal and prenatal factors had similar discriminating power with canonical correlations of .40 and .38, respectively. All variables except the Apgar score were retained in the summary analysis. The highest coefficients were associated with hematocrit and brain abnormality in the neonatal period. The five characteristics had a canonical correlation of .48 with the subgroup classification.

In a further exploration of specificity in risk factors, the severely retarded who were free of major neurological disorders were compared with a smaller, less heterogeneous subgroup. Eliminated from the CNS abnormals were children with conditions considered to be known or highly probable proximate causes of

Table 9-11

**Standardized Coefficients for Prenatal and Perinatal Discriminators
Between Mildly Retarded Children With and Without
Major CNS Disorders in the Black Sample**

Variable	Prenatal and Delivery	Neonatal	Prenatal and Perinatal
Diabetes in pregnancy	− .78	—	− .36
Bacterial infection in 3rd trimester	− .44	—	− .21
Recent maternal illnesses	− .34	—	—
Major eye malformations	—	− .53	− .52
Spinal cord abnormality	—	− .50	− .49
Minor musculoskeletal malformations	—	− .50	− .47
Brain abnormality	—	− .24	− .20
Peripheral nerve abnormality	—	− .23	—
Canonical correlation	*.18*	*.33*	*.34*

their cognitive deficit. These were Down's and other syndromes, post-traumatic deficit, and major CNS malformations. The size of the abnormal subgroup was reduced from 66 to 27 among whites and from 69 to 36 among blacks. The remaining children had diagnoses of cerebral palsy, epilepsy, and severe sensory deficits as shown in Table 3-6. Among whites, the results differed little from the original ones. Prenatal discriminators included a lower nonverbal intelligence test score for mothers of CNS normals in addition to lower family income and a higher frequency of urinary tract infection (Tables 9-5 and 9-6). The canonical correlation of .77 was considerably higher, however, than the one in the first analysis. The neonatal discriminator of seizures in the first month of life, absent in CNS normals and occurring among more than one fourth of the abnormals, "replaced" the more general diagnosis of brain abnormality. Sex of child was no longer a significant factor. In the summary analysis, the three maternal characteristics but not the neonatal one were retained.

Restricting the subgroup of CNS abnormals had larger effects on the pre- and perinatal comparisons in the black sample. In the first analysis, prenatal characteristics of the severely retarded CNS normals (maternal illnesses, cigarette smoking, and SES) were no longer significant. Instead, the discriminators were two complications of delivery among CNS abnormals that had a canonical correlation of .43 with the subgroup classification (Tables 9-7 and 9-8). Rupture of fetal membranes before or at onset of labor occurred in 30% of the deliveries compared with 8.5% among CNS normals. Premature rupture of the membranes

Table 9-12

**Prenatal and Perinatal Discriminators Between Mildly Retarded Children
With and Without Major CNS Disorders in the Black Sample**

| Variable | Major CNS Disorders | | | | | | t or χ^2 |
| | With | | | Without | | | |
	N	Mean or Percent	SD	N	Mean or Percent	SD	
Diabetes in pregnancy	56	3.57%		832	0.12%		9.73**
Bacterial infection in 3rd trimester	49	12.24%		758	4.35%		4.63*
Spinal cord abnormality	55	3.64%		833	0.00%		16.33***
Brain abnormality	55	5.45%		833	0.48%		10.58**
Peripheral nerve abnormality	55	3.64%		831	0.17%		6.76**
Major eye mal-formations	56	7.14%		838	0.36%		22.98****
Minor musculo-skeletal malforma-tions	56	10.71%		838	1.43%		18.46***
Recent maternal illnesses	55	0.64	0.75	822	0.43	0.69	2.17*

*p<.05
**p<.01
***p<.0001
****p<.00001

is associated with amniotic fluid infections, as both cause and consequence, and
with the adverse outcomes of preterm delivery and perinatal death (Naeye &
Peters, 1980). The second risk factor was longer second stage of labor among the
CNS abnormals. Although the mean duration of 33 minutes (versus 17 for the
normals) did not greatly exceed that of the black population (22.3 $\pm$ 28.8,
$N=14,474$), the distribution was highly skewed, as indicated by the standard
deviation, with a median value of only 15 minutes. In four of the CNS abnormal
cases, the second stage of labor was longer than 1 hour. In three of the cases,
duration ranged from 2.3 to 3.1 hours.

In the neonatal period, the following signs of perinatal anoxia among the
CNS abnormals were discriminating factors: primary apnea or failure to develop

Table 9-13
Standardized Coefficients for Prenatal, Obstetric, and Neonatal Discriminators Between the Severely Retarded and Comparison Subgroups

Variable	Comparison Subgroup							
	White				Black			
	MR	BL	AV	AA	MR	BL	AV	AA
Percent male	.59	.27	.20	—	—	.26	.25	—
Maternal SRA score	—	−.16	−.18	−.16	—	—	−.06	−.42
Housing density	—	—	.18	.31	−.30	—	—	—
Highest FHR in 1st stage of labor	—	—	−.18	—	—	—	−.19	—
Socioeconomic index	—	—	—	−.23	—	—	—	−.15
Peripheral nerve abnormality	—	.37	.39	.23	—	—	—	—
Minor musculoskeletal malformations	—	.48	.39	.26	—	—	—	—
Minor ear malformations	—	.43	.41	.41	—	—	—	—
Major eye malformations	—	.42	.34	.28	—	—	—	—
Weight gain in pregnancy	—	−.24	−.20	−.20	—	—	—	—
Urinary tract infection in pregnancy	—	.16	.13	.20	—	—	—	—
Anemia in pregnancy	—	—	.18	.29	—	—	—	—
Induction of labor	.58	—	—	—	—	—	—	—
Maternal occupation	.52	—	—	—	—	—	—	—
Major upper respiratory or mouth malformations	—	—	.32	—	—	—	—	—
Breech delivery	—	—	.16	—	—	—	—	—
Mother married	—	—	—	−.15	—	—	—	—
Number of prenatal visits	—	—	—	−.12	—	—	—	—
Maternal education	—	—	—	—	—	−.31	−.34	−.37
Seizures in pregnancy	—	—	—	—	.26	.41	.35	—
Neonatal seizures	—	—	—	—	.39	.29	.26	—
Meconium staining	—	—	—	—	.17	.23	.25	—
Retarded siblings	—	—	—	—	.41	—	.24	—

(continued)

Table 9-13 (continued)

Variable	White				Black			
	MR	BL	AV	AA	MR	BL	AV	AA
Dysmaturity	—	—	—	—	.33	.30	—	—
Head circumference at birth	—	—	—	—	—	−.33	−.24	—
Length at birth	—	—	—	—	—	—	−.21	−.38
Intravenous anesthetic at delivery	—	—	—	—	.29	.19	—	—
Major musculoskeletal malformations	—	—	—	—	—	.26	—	.17
Multiple birth	—	—	—	—	—	.21	.24	—
Brain abnormality	—	—	—	—	—	.16	.17	—
Diabetes in pregnancy	—	—	—	—	.36	—	—	—
Minor skin malformations	—	—	—	—	.25	—	—	—
Placenta previa	—	—	—	—	—	.32	—	—
Pregnancy-free interval	—	—	—	—	—	—	−.24	—
Erythroblastosis	—	—	—	—	—	—	.22	—
Toxemia	—	—	—	—	—	—	.19	—
Cord complications	—	—	—	—	—	—	−.15	—
Maternal age	—	—	—	—	—	—	—	−.26
Canonical correlation	*.35**	*.22***	*.12***	*.33***	*.29***	*.12***	*.14***	*.67***

*$p<.0001$
**$p<.00001$

spontaneous respiration in the first 2 minutes and resuscitation after the first 5 minutes. Primary apnea was not detected among the CNS normals and resuscitation after 5 minutes was required for only 2%, as compared with 17% of the CNS abnormals. A lower Apgar score at 5 minutes among the abnormals was a discriminator in the original analysis. Hematocrit of the neonate and the diagnosis of brain abnormality were no longer significant. The delivery complications and resuscitation of the newborn were retained in the summary analysis, where the canonical correlation with the subgroup classification was .51.

Table 9-14

Sex by IQ Subgroup

	1 Severely Retarded	2 Mildly Retarded	3 Borderline	4 Average	5 Above Average	χ²	r$_{IQ}$
			Percent Male				
White	80.77	**46.82**	**48.81**	**51.12**	**55.54**	30.03***	.04***
Black	64.41	53.40	*50.09*	*48.48*	*50.96*	15.71*	−.03**

Group Ns: White- 26 173 2391 12667 1878
Black- 59 839 8223 9868 157

Differs from severely retarded in D.F.
Differs from severely and mildly retarded in D.F.s
  *p <.01
  **p <.001
  ***p <.00001

The Mildly Retarded

In comparisons within the mildly retarded groups, no exclusions were made from the small subgroup of CNS abnormals. The most common neurological disorders were cerebral palsy and, among blacks, epilepsy (see Table 3-10). The pre- and perinatal discriminators between subgroups in the white sample are shown in

Table 9-15

Highest Fetal Heart Rate in First Stage of Labor by IQ Subgroup

	1 Severely Retarded		2 Mildly Retarded		3 Borderline		4 Average		5 Above Average		F	r$_{IQ}$
	M	S.D.	M	S.D.	M	S.D.	M	S.D.	M	S.D.		
White	144.0	8.1	148.3	9.9	148.7	11.8	**150.0**	**12.0**	**150.2**	**11.5**	6.36**	.04**
Black	146.7	9.9	149.1	10.1	149.6	10.5	*150.2*	*10.7*	*151.5*	*11.8*	4.95*	.03*

Group Ns: White- 18 121 1718 9336 1391
Black- 43 613 6202 7614 111

Differs from severely retarded in D.F.
Differs from severely and mildly retarded in D.F.s
  *p <.001
  **p <.0001

Table 9-16

SRA Score, Housing Density, and Socioeconomic Index by IQ Subgroup

	1 Severely Retarded		2 Mildly Retarded		3 Borderline		4 Average		5 Above Average		F	r_{IQ}
	M	S.D.	M	S.D.	M	S.D.	M	S.D.	M	S.D.		

Maternal SRA Score

	M	S.D.	M	S.D.	M	S.D.	M	S.D.	M	S.D.	F	r_{IQ}
White	31.7	8.0	34.6	8.5	*38.1*	*8.0*	*41.8*	*7.0*	*45.3*	*5.9*	209.00*	.30*
Black	30.8	7.9	29.9	8.8	*32.7*	*8.4*	*35.1*	*8.1*	*39.2*	*7.4*	90.04*	.20*

Group Ns: White - 6 86 1513 8410 1301
Black - 27 436 4563 5592 84

Housing Density

	M	S.D.	M	S.D.	M	S.D.	M	S.D.	M	S.D.	F	r_{IQ}
White	1.5	0.8	1.4	0.9	*1.3*	*0.6*	*1.1*	*0.5*	*0.9*	*0.4*	122.82*	−.19*
Black	1.6	0.7	*1.9*	*1.0*	1.7	0.9	*1.5*	*0.8*	1.2	0.6	96.37*	−.16*

Group Ns: White - 24 165 2320 12385 1851
Black - 59 822 8078 9675 151

Prenatal Socioeconomic Index Score

	M	S.D.	M	S.D.	M	S.D.	M	S.D.	M	S.D.	F	r_{IQ}
White	45.6	18.1	39.3	17.6	44.3	17.9	*57.1*	*20.5*	*73.2*	*18.1*	575.84*	.41*
Black	30.4	16.8	30.1	14.8	*34.6*	*16.1*	*40.9*	*18.0*	*54.9*	*20.8*	235.39*	.26*

Group Ns: White - 23 164 2303 12376 1853
Black - 54 810 7991 9627 155

Differs from severely retarded in D.F.
Differs from mildly retarded in D.F.
Differs from severely and mildly retarded in D.F.s
*$p < .00001$

Tables 9-9 and 9-10. CNS abnormals had a higher frequency of maternal bacterial infection in the first trimester and a lower fetal heart rate in the first stage of labor (highest value recorded). Among CNS normals, this measure of fetal heart rate was close to the mean of the total white population (150 ± 12, N=12,790). Socioeconomic status was lower among families of the CNS normals. In the neonatal period, resuscitation in the first 5 minutes after delivery was required more frequently among the CNS abnormals, who were more often judged to have definite signs of brain abnormality in the nursery period. Micrognathia, a major

Table 9-17

Pregnancy Complications: Urinary Tract Infection and Anemia by IQ Subgroup

	1 Severely Retarded	2 Mildly Retarded	3 Borderline	4 Average	5 Above Average	χ^2	r_{IQ}
			Percent				

Urinary Tract Infection in Pregnancy

White	40.00	20.55	*13.93*	*12.05*	*9.36*	40.89***	− .06***
Black	20.41	·23.81	24.05	21.95	17.91	11.89*	− .03**
Group Ns: White -	20	146	1909	10224	1496		
Black -	49	714	7002	8368	134		

Anemia in Pregnancy

White	26.92	13.95	13.45	*9.67*	**4.81**	101.35***	− .09***
Black	42.86	39.06	36.72	32.78	27.27	42.97***	− .06***
Group Ns: White -	26	172	2379	12611	1871		
Black -	56	832	8151	9784	154		

Differs from severely retarded in D.F.
Differs from severely and mildly retarded in D.F.s
  *$p<.05$
 **$p<.001$
***$p<.00001$

malformation of the upper respiratory system and mouth, was present in 11% of the CNS abnormal subgroup. In the summary analysis, all of the biomedical characteristics of the CNS abnormals were retained. Canonical correlations between the discriminators and the subgroup classification ranged from .36 for prenatal and delivery factors to .47 for all factors through the perinatal period.

In the black sample, complications in pregnancy and the newborn period were present more often in the CNS abnormal subgroup of the mildly retarded (Tables 9-11 and 9-12). Two discriminators—maternal bacterial infection and neonatal brain abnormality—had been identified earlier among whites. The significant prenatal factors were maternal diabetes, third trimester bacterial infection, and recent confining illnesses reported at registration for prenatal care; all were more frequent among the CNS abnormals. The canonical correlation between these conditions and the subgroup classification was only .18, however. As neonates, the CNS abnormals had higher frequencies of major and minor malformations and abnormalities of the spinal cord and peripheral nerves.

Table 9-18

Weight Gain and Prenatal Visits by IQ Subgroup

	1 Severely Retarded		2 Mildly Retarded		3 Borderline		4 Average		5 Above Average		F	r_{IQ}
	M	S.D.	M	S.D.	M	S.D.	M	S.D.	M	S.D.		

Maternal Weight Gain in Pregnancy (lb.)

	M	S.D.	M	S.D.	M	S.D.	M	S.D.	M	S.D.	F	r_{IQ}
White	18.1	9.8	24.0	11.7	**23.4**	**10.7**	**23.5**	**9.6**	**22.6**	**8.1**	5.43**	− .02*
Black	21.5	12.5	21.7	12.4	22.7	11.5	23.0	10.7	23.8	8.3	3.35*	.03**
Group Ns: White -	22		162		2307		12337		1840			
Black -	54		793		7916		9556		148			

Number of Prenatal Visits

	M	S.D.	M	S.D.	M	S.D.	M	S.D.	M	S.D.	F	r_{IQ}
White	8.5	4.1	8.3	4.1	8.7	4.2	10.0	4.1	*11.3*	*3.6*	114.97***	.19***
Black	7.2	3.7	6.7	3.5	*7.4*	*3.5*	*8.2*	*3.6*	9.2	3.7	78.47***	.14***
Group Ns: White -	26		172		2385		12656		1874			
Black -	59		838		8215		9860		156			

Differs from severely retarded in D.F.
Differs from mildly retarded in D.F.
Differs from severely and mildly retarded in D.F.s
  *p<.01
  **p<.001

The discriminating diagnosis of brain abnormality was made less often among the mildly retarded CNS abnormal blacks than whites (5.5 versus 14%). Prevalence rates for the neonatal complications were low. The most common was minor malformations of the musculoskeletal system present among 11% of the CNS abnormals; major eye malformations affected 7% of the subgroup. The neonatal discriminators and those retained in the summary analysis (all but reported maternal illnesses and peripheral nerve abnormality) had moderate canonical correlations of .33 and .34 with the subgroup classification.

Risk factors for mild retardation were further evaluated in within-group regression analyses for all children with IQs between 50 and 69 in the two samples. As in the examination of subgroups, the objective was to define the etiological roles of pregnancy and perinatal events, in this case, in the relative absence of social factors that dominate comparisons between the mildly retarded and higher IQ groups. In a correlation screen for the selection of antecedents, and in stepwise multiple regressions, the outcome or criterion measure was IQ score of

Table 9-19
Maternal Occupation Score by IQ Subgroup

	1 Severely Retarded		2 Mildly Retarded		3 Borderline		4 Average		5 Above Average		F	r_{IQ}
	M	S.D.	M	S.D.	M	S.D.	M	S.D.	M	S.D.		
White	47.8	25.4	**34.6**	**24.3**	40.4	23.5	51.6	25.0	67.1	22.8	326.93*	.32*
Black	20.7	19.6	22.5	17.0	25.3	18.8	30.1	22.1	44.2	27.0	102.28*	.18*

Group Ns: White-   23   166   2331   12446   1854
          Black-   59   830   8119   9734   154
Differs from severely retarded in D.F.
*$p < .00001$

the mildly retarded. Mean values in the white and black samples were 62.5 ± 5.3 ($N=201$) and 63.5 ± 4.8 ($N=895$), respectively. The significance level was set at $p < 05$.

Only eight variables passed the correlation screen in each sample. Their correlations with IQ ranged from .14 to .27 among whites and .07 to .15 among blacks. In the mildly retarded white group, prenatal and neonatal, but no labor and delivery factors, were selected. Variables retained in the five regression analyses and multiple correlations with IQ (R) are reported. The amount of variance accounted for (R^2) was very small, especially in the black sample.

Prenatal predictors among whites were maternal height and prior child death,

Table 9-20
Mother Married by IQ Subgroup

	1 Severely Retarded	2 Mildly Retarded	3 Borderline	4 Average	5 Above Average	χ^2	r_{IQ}
			Percent				
White	80.77	86.13	84.65	90.08	**96.33**	164.27*	.11*
Black	55.93	61.26	62.56	66.89	79.62	58.86*	.07*

Group Ns: White-   26   173   2391   12666   1878
          Black-   59   839   8223   9868   157
Differs from severely retarded in D.F.
*$p < .00001$

Table 9-21
Induction of Labor and Breech Delivery by IQ Subgroup

	1 Severely Retarded	2 Mildly Retarded	3 Borderline	4 Average	5 Above Average	χ^2	r_{IQ}
				Percent			
			Induction of Labor				
White	16.67	**3.13**	*8.65*	*11.10*	10.78	22.37***	.03***
Black	1.89	5.26	4.42	5.16	6.34	6.99	.02*
Group Ns: White -	24	160	2231	11918	1800		
Black -	53	779	7730	9275	142		
			Breech Delivery				
White	12.00	5.81	4.49	**3.14**	**2.83**	21.96***	− .04****
Black	8.47	3.12	**2.55**	**2.34**	**0.64**	13.42**	− .03***
Group Ns: White -	25	172	2384	12646	1876		
Black -	59	834	8196	9841	157		

Differs from severely retarded in D.F.
Differs from mildly retarded in D.F.
 $*p<.05$
 $**p<.01$
 $***p<.001$
 $****p<.00001$

the latter negatively related to IQ ($R= .28$). In the neonatal period, Down's syndrome and diagnosed brain abnormality were associated with lower IQ scores of the mildly retarded white children ($R= .33$). Among blacks, the only prenatal predictor was nonverbal IQ score (SRA) of the mother ($R= .15$). From the labor and delivery period, single umbilical artery was negatively related to IQ ($R= .07$). Major eye malformations and multiple apneic episodes were significant neonatal factors ($R= .10$). The latter variable had an unexpected positive relationship to IQ within the mildly retarded black group.

Obviously, little variance in IQ within the mildly retarded range was explained by pre- and perinatal factors. Nor did social characteristics of the family contribute to within-group differences. Socioeconomic status, as measured by the prenatal socioeconomic index score, was clearly unrelated to IQ. Correlations of zero were obtained in both samples in the initial variable screen where SES-predictor correlations could also be examined. The only significant finding was a positive relationship between the socioeconomic index score and neonatal brain abnormality among mildly retarded white children ($r= .21$).

DEVELOPMENT OF THE CNS NORMALS

The longterm development of retarded children without major neurological disorders was examined by comparing them with children in higher IQ groups, also restricted to CNS normals. The goals were to determine the discriminating power and relative importance of other risk factors and correlates when serious neurological abnormalities were absent and to identify new relationships not detected in the analyses of the total groups, especially the severely retarded. The proportion of cases removed from the comparison groups because of major neurological abnormalities ranged from 3% of the borderline among whites and 1% among blacks to approximately .6% of the average and above-average children in each sample. As in the earlier analyses, variables from all epochs were screened individually in comparisons between pairs of retarded and higher IQ subgroups in the white and black samples. Those differing at the .05 level were entered in the appropriate two-group discriminant function analysis. Results are reported in this chapter for the combined pre- and perinatal periods, summary analyses through age 4, and social, biomedical, and psychological characteristics at age 7. All significant findings are indicated in the chart in Appendix 1.

The Severely Retarded

Pre- and perinatal discriminators in both samples were the biological characteristics of an excess of males and a lower fetal heart rate in the first stage of labor and the family characteristics of lower maternal intelligence and, as compared with the above average, lower socioeconomic status (Table 9-13). Housing density was higher in families of the severely retarded subgroup among whites but, among blacks, was significantly lower than in families of the mildly retarded. In the white sample, highest fetal heart rate in the first stage of labor and housing density in the prenatal period were discriminators unique to the CNS normals. Descriptive data for these variables are shown in Tables 9-14 through 9-16.

Antecedents of severe retardation among whites only were the pregnancy complications of urinary tract infection, unique to the CNS normals, anemia, and low weight gain. Fewer prenatal visits was a discriminator in the comparison with the above average (Tables 9-17 and 9-18). Prenatal demographic factors, both subgroup characteristics only, were a higher ranked or more prestigious occupation among mothers of the severely than mildly retarded and fewer married mothers than in the above-average subgroup (Tables 9-19 and 9-20). Obstetric risk factors for the severely retarded CNS normals were induction of

Table 9-22
Malformations and Peripheral Nerve Abnormality by IQ Subgroup

	1 Severely Retarded	2 Mildly Retarded	3 Borderline	4 Average	5 Above Average	χ^2	r_{IQ}
				Percent			

Major Eye Malformations

White	3.85	0.00	**0.13**	**0.14**	**0.11**	25.96**	−.01
Black	0.00	0.36	0.19	0.11	0.00	4.54	−.02*
Group Ns: White -	26	173	2391	12667	1878		
Black -	59	839	8223	9868	157		

Major Upper Respiratory or Mouth Malformations

White	3.85	2.31	*0.54*	***0.17***	*0.16*	56.55***	−.04***
Black	0.00	0.12	0.12	0.09	0.00	0.64	−.00
Group Ns: White -	26	173	2391	12667	1878		
Black -	59	839	8223	9868	157		

Minor Musculoskeletal Malformations

White	11.54	1.16	**0.79**	**0.90**	**0.96**	33.08***	−.01
Black	0.00	1.67	1.90	1.69	1.27	2.44	−.00
Group Ns: White -	26	173	2391	12667	1878		
Black -	59	839	8223	9868	157		

Minor Ear Malformations

White	11.54	2.89	**1.00**	*0.78*	*0.48*	49.92***	−.03**
Black	3.39	2.74	2.87	2.27	1.91	7.05	−.02*
Group Ns: White -	26	173	2391	12667	1878		
Black -	59	839	8223	9868	157		

Peripheral Nerve Abnormality in Newborn

White	7.69	0.60	**0.55**	**0.42**	**0.59**	30.47***	−.01
Black	0.00	0.24	0.54	0.44	1.91	8.88	.00
Group Ns: White -	26	167	2356	12553	1868		
Black -	57	831	8157	9815	157		

Differs from severely retarded in D.F.
Differs from mildly retarded in D.F.
Differs from severely and mildly retarded in D.F.s
*p<.05
**p<.0001
***p<.00001

Table 9-23

Pregnancy Complications: Seizures, Diabetes, and Toxemia by IQ Subgroup

	1 Severely Retarded	2 Mildly Retarded	3 Borderline	4 Average	5 Above Average	χ^2	r_{IQ}
				Percent			
			Seizures in Pregnancy				
White	4.17	0.00	1.03	0.56	0.17	19.18***	−.02**
Black	5.45	**0.63**	**0.47**	**0.37**	**0.00**	34.53****	−.02**
Group Ns: White -	24	161	2233	11709	1726		
Black -	55	789	7818	9288	149		
			Diabetes in Pregnancy				
White	3.85	0.59	0.80	0.57	0.54	6.41	−.02*
Black	3.57	**0.12**	0.61	0.61	0.65	11.53*	−.00
Group Ns: White -	26	170	2379	12593	1868		
Black -	56	832	8132	9776	154		
			Toxemia in Pregnancy				
White	16.67	10.49	9.97	9.87	9.53	1.22	−.01
Black	19.57	13.64	*10.36*	**9.35**	11.29	20.58***	−.02**
Group Ns: White -	18	143	2026	10633	1605		
Black -	46	711	7334	8885	124		

Differs from mildly retarded in D.F.
Differs from severely and mildly retarded in D.F.s
*p<.05
**p<.01
***p<.0001
****p<.00001

labor—a unique discriminator—and breech delivery. Labor was induced in 17% of the cases and 12% were delivered by breech. As is evident from Table 9-21, breech delivery was entered as a significant obstetric factor but not retained in some pre- and perinatal summary analyses. Neonatal complications were the most important of the early antecedents in the white sample. The severely retarded CNS normals had higher frequencies of both major and minor malformations and peripheral nerve abnormalities (Table 9-22). Moderately large

Table 9-24

Retarded Siblings by IQ Subgroup

	1 Severely Retarded	2 Mildly Retarded	3 Borderline	4 Average	5 Above Average	χ^2	r_{IQ}
			Percent				
White	5.88	7.63	6.59	3.27	2.12	53.35***	−.08***
Black	14.29	**3.31**	4.04	**3.37**	2.00	13.26*	−.03**

Group Ns: White- 17 118 1562 8112 991
Black- 28 513 4772 5730 100

Differs from severely retarded in D.F.

*$p < .05$

**$p < .01$

***$p < .00001$

discriminant coefficients were associated with these conditions in almost all comparisons with nonretarded subgroups.

In the black sample, the pregnancy complications of maternal seizures, diabetes, and toxemia were more frequent among mothers of the severely retarded CNS normals. Toxemia was by far the most prevalent of the complications (Table 9-23). The occurrence of seizures in the mother, however, was the most consistent discriminator. Diabetes was a risk factor unique to the subgroup. Other prenatal characteristics were a family history of retardation in older siblings (also unique to the CNS normals), less maternal education, a shorter pregnancy-free interval, and, as compared with the above average, younger maternal age (Tables 9-24 and 9-25). Complications of delivery in the severely retarded subgroup were meconium staining, a sign of perinatal anoxia, the rare procedure of general anesthetics administered intravenously, and placenta previa, a discriminator unique to the subgroup; cord complications were relatively infrequent (Table 9-26). Meconium staining, fairly common at all IQ levels, was present in more than one third of the severely retarded cases. The two other complications affected only approximately 3% of the subgroup.

The most important of the neonatal discriminators was seizures in the first month of life occurring among 3% of the severely retarded subgroup in the black sample (Table 9-27). Other newborn complications were dysmaturity, major malformations of the musculoskeletal system, multiple birth (8.5% of the cases), and brain abnormality diagnosed in the nursery period in 3.5% of the subgroup children. Unique neonatal conditions were minor skin malformations and erythroblastosis, which were significant in comparisons with the mildly retarded

Table 9-25
Maternal Characteristics:
Education, Pregnancy-free Interval, and Age by IQ Subgroup

	1 Severely Retarded	2 Mildly Retarded	3 Borderline	4 Average	5 Above Average	F	r_{IQ}
	M S.D.	M S.D.	M S.D.	M S.D.	M S.D.		

Maternal Education (yr.)

White	10.1 3.0	9.2 2.4	9.8 2.3	*11.3 2.3*	**13.5 2.4**	660.38***	.43***
Black	8.9 2.5	9.1 2.3	**9.9 2.1**	**10.6 2.0**	**11.9 2.2**	215.87***	.24***

Group Ns: White - 24 167 2326 12404 1854
         Black - 58 827 8118 9733 155

Pregnancy-free Interval (yr.)

White	1.9 1.7	1.5 1.8	1.6 1.9	1.8 2.1	*1.9 2.1*	4.72**	.04***
Black	1.1 1.0	1.3 1.7	*1.7 2.2*	**2.0 2.4**	**2.5 2.7**	30.01***	.10***

Group Ns: White - 22 125 1786 8869 1057
         Black - 40 628 5928 7086 111

Maternal Age

White	28.0 7.3	**25.2 6.0**	**24.7 6.1**	24.9 5.9	**24.9 5.2**	2.64*	.01
Black	23.5 6.3	23.8 6.4	23.4 6.2	24.1 6.3	***26.6 6.3***	22.05***	.06***

Group Ns: White - 26 173 2391 12667 1878
         Black - 59 839 8223 9868 157

Differs from severely retarded in D.F.
Differs from mildly retarded in D.F.
Differs from severely and mildly retarded in D.F.s
  *p<.05
  **p<.001
  ***p<.00001

and average subgroups, respectively. Shorter length at birth was also a unique characteristic. Smaller head circumference was a risk factor for all severely retarded black children (Table 9-28).

Only in the extreme group comparison among blacks were pre- and perinatal factors effective discriminators for the severely retarded CNS normals (R = .67). Of the six characteristics retained in that comparison, four were mater-

Table 9-26

Obstetric Complications: Meconium, Intravenous Anesthetic, Placenta Previa, and Cord Complications by IQ Subgroup

	1 Severely Retarded	2 Mildly Retarded	3 Borderline	4 Average	5 Above Average	χ^2	r_{IQ}
			Percent				
			Meconium Staining				
White	16.00	21.51	19.35	19.39	17.01	6.82	$-.02*$
Black	33.93	**19.78**	**19.50**	**20.05**	22.88	8.69	.01
Group Ns: White -	25	172	2357	12576	1864		
Black -	56	824	7993	9554	153		
			Intravenous Anesthetic at Delivery				
White	4.17	1.16	1.61	1.21	0.96	5.54	$-.02**$
Black	3.45	**0.48**	**0.73**	0.97	1.91	11.09*	.02**
Group Ns: White -	24	172	2362	12552	1867		
Black -	58	827	8130	9786	157		
			Placenta Previa				
White	0.00	1.82	0.55	0.69	0.37	6.56	$-.01$
Black	3.39	0.97	*0.33*	0.62	0.64	20.01***	$-.00$
Group Ns: White -	25	165	2354	12547	1867		
Black -	59	823	8128	9755	156		
			Cord Complications				
White	24.00	31.55	31.33	32.76	33.03	2.95	.00
Black	14.04	24.03	24.74	**26.63**	28.66	14.23**	.03****
Group Ns: White -	25	168	2346	12544	1862		
Black -	57	824	8063	9689	157		

Differs from severely retarded in D.F.
Differs from severely and mildly retarded in D.F.s
  *$p<.05$
  **$p<.01$
  ***$p<.001$
  ****$p<.0001$

Table 9-27
Neonatal Conditions by IQ Subgroup

	1 Severely Retarded	2 Mildly Retarded	3 Borderline	4 Average	5 Above Average	χ^2	r_{IQ}
				Percent			

Neonatal Seizures

White	0.00	0.00	0.25	0.24	0.11	1.79	.00
Black	3.39	**0.24**	**0.24**	**0.22**	0.00	24.92****	−.02*
Group Ns: White -	26	173	2391	12667	1878		
Black -	59	839	8223	9868	157		

Dysmaturity

White	27.27	17.99	19.79	19.53	19.98	1.27	.01
Black	26.92	**14.13**	**13.71**	16.52	*22.81*	35.18*****	.04*****
Group Ns: White -	22	139	2092	11110	1672		
Black -	52	729	7296	8464	114		

Major Musculoskeletal Malformations

White	7.69	2.31	2.17	2.31	3.30	10.61*	.02**
Black	8.47	3.93	*2.66*	3.62	**1.27**	21.71***	.01
Group Ns: White -	26	173	2391	12667	1878		
Black -	59	839	8223	9868	157		

Multiple Birth

White	0.00	4.62	2.89	1.78	*0.85*	35.52*****	−.04*****
Black	8.47	5.13	*2.69*	*1.47*	1.27	79.24*****	−.07*****
Group Ns: White -	26	173	239!	12667	1878		
Black -	59	839	8223	9868	157		

Brain Abnormality

White	0.00	0.60	0.25	0.27	0.16	1.57	−.01
Black	3.45	0.48	**0.34**	**0.32**	0.64	17.23**	−.02*
Group Ns: White -	26	168	2369	12575	1868		
Black -	58	833	8165	9822	157		

(continued)

Table 9-27 (continued)

	1 Severely Retarded	2 Mildly Retarded	3 Borderline	4 Average	5 Above Average	χ^2	r_{IQ}
			Percent				
			Minor Skin Malformations				
White	7.69	4.05	4.73	4.35	5.11	3.28	.02*
Black	6.78	**1.79**	3.13	2.93	*6.37*	13.85**	.00
Group Ns: White -	26	173	2391	12667	1878		
Black -	59	839	8223	9868	157		
			Erythroblastosis				
White	0.00	0.00	0.72	0.99	1.23	4.87	.02**
Black	3.45	0.60	0.61	**0.56**	*2.55*	17.85**	− .01
Group Ns: White -	26	168	2369	12575	1868		
Black -	58	833	8165	9822	157		

Differs from severely retarded in D.F.
Differs from mildly retarded in D.F.
Differs from severely and mildly retarded in D.F.s
    *$p<.05$
    **$p<.01$
    ***$p<.001$
    ****$p<.0001$
    *****$p<.00001$

nal (intelligence, SES, education, and age) and two were neonatal (length and musculoskeletal malformations). In other comparisons, canonical correlations were moderate (.22 to .35) or low (.12 to .14), a marked contrast to the strong relationships obtained in the corresponding analyses for all severely retarded children (see Table 5-11).

By age 4, discrimination between the CNS normal subgroup of the severely retarded and higher IQ subgroups had improved considerably. Canonical correlations between variables retained in the 4-year summary analyses and the subgroup classification ranged from .34 to .77 among whites and .44 to .93 among blacks (Table 9-29). The variables entered in the summaries were discriminators from the pre- and perinatal, infancy, and preschool periods. The majority of the characteristics from the two later epochs were not unique to the severely retarded subgroup. The most important discriminators were the summary rating of behavior and IQ at age 4. Among whites, the proportion of children

Table 9-28

Head Circumference and Length at Birth by IQ Subgroup

	1 Severely Retarded		2 Mildly Retarded		3 Borderline		4 Average		5 Above Average		F	r_{IQ}
	M	S.D.	M	S.D.	M	S.D.	M	S.D.	M	S.D.		
Head Circumference (cm)												
White	33.8	2.0	33.4	1.8	33.6	1.7	*34.0*	*1.5*	34.2	1.4	60.63*	.13*
Black	32.5	2.3	32.9	1.9	**33.3**	**1.7**	*33.5*	*1.6*	34.0	1.6	56.71*	.12*
Group Ns: White -	26		167		2338		12490		1856			
Black -	58		825		8102		9741		157			
Length (cm)												
White	49.6	4.1	49.7	3.3	50.0	2.8	50.4	2.6	50.6	2.5	20.82*	.08*
Black	47.9	3.8	48.5	3.2	*49.1*	*2.8*	**49.6**	**2.7**	**50.4**	**2.4**	65.37*	.13*
Group Ns: White -	26		167		2331		12434		1847			
Black -	58		825		8079		9716		157			

Differs from severely retarded in D.F.
Differs from mildly retarded in D.F.
Differs from severely and mildly retarded in D.F.s
*p<.00001

rated as abnormal in behavior was slightly lower than in the total group of severely retarded children (Table 9-30). Mean IQ of the subgroup in each sample was only a few points above the mean of 42 in the total groups (Table 9-31). A low rating for verbal communication and a relatively high rating for impulsiveness at age 4 were also discriminators for the severely retarded subgroups (Table 9-32).

Other factors significant in both samples were the medical complications of undescended testicles, visual impairment, and cerebral palsy at 1 year of age. (Table 9-33). Cerebral palsy, absent by definition among CNS normals at age 7, was diagnosed at age 1 in 4% of whites and 5% of blacks in the severely retarded subgroup. Larger head circumference at this age was a discriminator for the white subgroup in comparisons with the mildly retarded and borderline, but a smaller head size was a significant characteristic among blacks (Table 9-34). Low scores at 8 months on the Bayley Mental and Motor Scales were discriminators in both samples (Table 9-35). Large variation within the severely re-

Table 9-29
Standardized Coefficients for All Discriminators Through Age Four
Between the Severely Retarded and Comparison Subgroups

Variable	White				Black			
	MR	BL	AV	AA	MR	BL	AV	AA
Abnormal behavior summary rating at age 4	.34	.47	.67	.73	.40	.71	.88	.22
Stanford-Binet IQ at age 4	−.62	−.32	−.22	−.13	−.42	−.27	−.14	−.58
Bayley motor score at 8 months	—	—	−.01	−.05	−.06	−.06	−.07	−.06
Undescended testicles at 1 year	—	—	.30	—	.20	.20	.09	—
Verbal communication at age 4	—	−.26	—	—	−.19	−.16	−.06	—
Bayley mental score at 8 months	—	−.04	−.06	−.05	—	−.09	—	—
Impulsivity at age 4	—	.30	—	—	—	.17	.04	—
Head circumference at 1 year	.31	.09	—	—	—	—	−.05	—
Visual impairment at 1 year	—	.11	.07	—	—	.01	—	—
Socioeconomic index	—	—	—	−.05	—	—	−.003	−.001
Cerebral palsy at 1 year	—	—	.11	—	—	.08	—	—
Highest FHR in 1st stage of labor	—	—	−.06	—	—	—	−.01	—
Delayed motor development at 1 year	—	.20	.30	.18	—	—	—	—
Attention span at age 4	—	−.04	−.12	−.15	—	—	—	—
Intensity of response at 8 months	−.13	−.05	—	−.01	—	—	—	—
Minor ear malformations	—	.04	.04	.01	—	—	—	—
Peripheral nerve abnormality at 1 year	—	.24	.09	—	—	—	—	—

(continued)

Table 9-29 (continued)

Variable	White				Black			
	MR	BL	AV	AA	MR	BL	AV	AA
Neonatal peripheral nerve abnormality	—	.16	.13	—	—	—	—	—
Urinary tract infection in pregnancy	—	.19	—	.09	—	—	—	—
Minor musculo-skeletal malformations	—	.12	.10	—	—	—	—	—
Maternal SRA score	—	− .04	—	− .03	—	—	—	—
Induction of labor	.26	—	—	—	—	—	—	—
Major eye malformations	—	.19	—	—	—	—	—	—
Activity level at age 4	—	—	.07	—	—	—	—	—
Breech delivery	—	—	.05	—	—	—	—	—
Major upper respiratory or mouth malformations	—	—	.02	—	—	—	—	—
Height at age 4	—	—	—	− .05	—	—	—	—
Strabismus at 1 year	—	—	—	—	.19	.11	.05	—
Neonatal seizures	—	—	—	—	.09	.09	.06	—
Goal orientation at age 4	—	—	—	—	—	− .01	− .05	− .18
Unfavorable emotional environment in 1st year	—	—	—	—	.08	.05	.002	—
Maternal education	—	—	—	—	—	− .04	− .01	− .08
Intravenous anesthetic at delivery	—	—	—	—	.16	.09	—	—
Retarded siblings	—	—	—	—	.19	—	.04	—
Head circumference at age 4	—	—	—	—	− .15	− .07	—	—
Meconium staining	—	—	—	—	—	.08	.03	—
Percent male	—	—	—	—	.09	—	.01	—
Duration of response at 8 months	—	—	—	—	—	− .05	− .02	—

(continued)

Table 9-29 (continued)

Variable	White MR	BL	AV	AA	Black MR	BL	AV	AA
Loss of one or both parents in 1st year	—	—	—	—	—	.03	.02	—
Undescended testicle at 1 year	—	—	—	—	.14	—	—	—
Diabetes in pregnancy	—	—	—	—	.13	—	—	—
Housing density	—	—	—	—	−.11	—	—	—
Seizures in pregnancy	—	—	—	—	—	.11	—	—
Dysmaturity	—	—	—	—	—	.04	—	—
Response to directions at age 4	—	—	—	—	—	—	−.03	—
Cord complications	—	—	—	—	—	—	−.02	—
Erythroblastosis	—	—	—	—	—	—	.01	—
Dependency at age 4	—	—	—	—	—	—	.01	—
Length at birth	—	—	—	—	—	—	—	−.07
Canonical correlation	*.56**	*.43**	*.34**	*.77**	*.61**	*.44**	*.65**	*.93**

Table 9-30
Abnormal Behavior Summary Rating at Age Four by IQ Subgroup

	1 Severely Retarded	2 Mildly Retarded	3 Borderline	4 Average	5 Above Average	χ^2	r_{IQ}
			Percent				
White	80.95	**24.24**	*6.50*	*1.58*	*0.62*	980.57*	−.18*
Black	73.33	**11.33**	*1.96*	*0.32*	*0.00*	1915.49*	−.20*

Group Ns: White- 21 132 1938 10796 1447
Black- 45 662 6904 8730 144

Differs from severely retarded in D.F.

Differs from severely and mildly retarded in D.F.s

*$p <.00001$

Table 9-31
Stanford-Binet IQ at Age Four by IQ Subgroup

	1 Severely Retarded		2 Mildly Retarded		3 Borderline		4 Average		5 Above Average		F	r_{IQ}
	M	S.D.	M	S.D.	M	S.D.	M	S.D.	M	S.D.		
White	47.4	9.7	**69.6**	**12.4**	**89.4**	**12.7**	**105.7**	**13.3**	**122.4**	**14.8**	1548.82*	.62*
Black	45.5	11.7	**72.7**	**11.7**	**86.3**	**11.8**	**97.1**	**11.7**	**111.9**	**13.3**	1508.10*	.58*

Group Ns: White- 15 124 1904 10753 1444
Black- 39 639 6873 8716 144

Differs from severely retarded in D.F.
Differs from severely and mildly retarded in D.F.s
*p <.00001

Table 9-32
Verbal Communication and Impulsivity Ratings at Age Four by IQ Subgroup

	1 Severely Retarded		2 Mildly Retarded		3 Borderline		4 Average		5 Above Average		F	r_{IQ}
	M	S.D.	M	S.D.	M	S.D.	M	S.D.	M	S.D.		

Verbal Communication

White	2.2	1.4	2.8	1.0	**2.9**	**0.8**	2.9	0.6	3.1	0.5	34.27*	.11*
Black	1.8	1.2	**2.6**	**0.9**	**2.8**	**0.7**	**2.9**	**0.6**	**3.1**	**0.6**	101.39*	.16*

Group Ns: White - 18 131 1925 10722 1443
Black - 42 661 6890 8708 144

Impulsivity

White	3.7	1.3	3.0	1.0	**3.0**	**0.6**	3.0	0.4	3.0	0.3	14.23*	.00
Black	3.3	1.1	2.9	0.8	**3.0**	**0.5**	**3.0**	**0.3**	3.0	0.2	24.50*	.06*

Group Ns: White - 20 129 1919 10713 1441
Black - 43 660 6877 8699 144

Differs from severely retarded in D.F.
Differs from mildly retarded in D.F.
Differs from severely and mildly retarded in D.F.s
*p<.00001

224

Table 9-33

Infancy Conditions: Undescended Testicles, Visual Impairment, and Cerebral Palsy at One Year by IQ Subgroup

	1 Severely Retarded	2 Mildly Retarded	3 Borderline	4 Average	5 Above Average	χ^2	r_{IQ}
				Percent			
			Undescended Testicles				
White	9.52	1.23	**0.94**	**0.39**	**0.19**	46.40***	−.05***
Black	5.26	**0.45**	**0.15**	**0.23**	0.00	45.90***	−.02*
Group Ns: White -	21	81	1165	6472	1042		
Black -	38	448	4116	4782	80		
			Visual Impairment				
White	4.00	0.00	**0.04**	**0.02**	0.05	108.77***	−.01
Black	1.85	0.13	**0.04**	**0.01**	0.00	58.61***	−.03**
Group Ns: White -	25	160	2233	12247	1832		
Black -	54	787	7849	9577	154		
			Cerebral Palsy				
White	4.00	0.00	0.21	**0.07**	0.16	40.68***	−.02*
Black	5.17	1.67	**0.32**	0.23	0.00	86.40***	−.05***
Group Ns: White -	25	172	2390	12658	1877		
Black -	58	837	8208	9846	157		

Differs from severely retarded in D.F.
  *$p<.05$
  **$p<.0001$
  ***$p<.00001$

tarded subgroups, particularly on the mental scale, is indicated by the standard deviations. On both scales, mean raw scores correspond to a performance level of approximately 6 months. The only perinatal risk factor retained in both samples was a lower fetal heart rate in the first stage of labor. The prenatal socioeconomic index score was a minor discriminator in comparisons between the severely retarded and the average and above-average subgroups.

Characteristics identified among whites only were short attention span and a relatively high activity level at age 4 and, as compared with the above-average

Table 9-34

Head Circumference at One Year in Centimeters by IQ Subgroup

	1 Severely Retarded		2 Mildly Retarded		3 Borderline		4 Average		5 Above Average		F	r_{IQ}
	M	S.D.	M	S.D.	M	S.D.	M	S.D.	M	S.D.		
White	46.2	1.7	**44.7**	**1.8**	*45.3*	*1.6*	45.8	*1.5*	46.3	*1.4*	120.99*	.20*
Black	44.8	2.0	45.1	1.8	45.4	1.5	*45.8*	*1.5*	**46.2**	**1.3**	83.62*	.15*

Differs from severely retarded in D.F.
Differs from mildly retarded in D.F.
Differs from severely and mildly retarded in D.F.s
*$p < .00001$

Standard Score

Note. Group Ns: White- 21 122 1948 11022 1611
Black- 48 684 7113 8797 144

subgroup, shorter stature (Tables 9-36 and 9-37). At the end of the first year, delayed motor development was the most important biomedical discriminator for the severely retarded subgroup. A unique factor was peripheral nerve abnormalities at this age (Table 9-38). Low intensity of response at 8 months as rated during the administration of the Bayley Scales was significant in comparisons between the severely retarded and three higher IQ subgroups (Table 9-39). The major and minor malformations and peripheral nerve abnormalities identified in the neonatal period were retained in the 4-year summary analyses. The significant prenatal and obstetric risk factors were maternal urinary tract infection,

Table 9-35

Bayley Mental and Motor Scale Scores at Eight Months by IQ Subgroup

	1 Severely Retarded		2 Mildly Retarded		3 Borderline		4 Average		5 Above Average		F	r_{IQ}
	M	S.D.	M	S.D.	M	S.D.	M	S.D.	M	S.D.		
Bayley Mental Scale Score												
White	69.8	14.7	74.4	10.0	*78.7*	*5.6*	*80.1* *4.3*		*80.4* *3.8*		108.31*	.15*
Black	66.8	14.2	75.4	9.0	*78.4*	*6.2*	*79.9* *4.7*		81.5	3.9	188.83*	.22*
Group Ns: White -	19	118	1796	10570	1604							
Black -	46	611	6618	8246	135							
Bayley Motor Scale Score												
White	25.0	6.2	28.1	6.2	*31.7*	*5.0*	*33.4* *4.4*		*34.3* *4.0*		135.36*	.19*
Black	25.0	6.0	**30.2** **5.8**		*32.6*	*4.6*	*33.7* *4.1*		*35.2* *3.7*		179.72*	.21*
Group Ns: White -	19	118	1796	10568	1604							
Black -	45	614	6621	8244	135							

Differs from severely retarded in D.F.
Differs from mildly retarded in D.F.
Differs from severely and mildly retarded in D.F.s
*p<.00001

induction of labor, and breech delivery. Maternal nonverbal intelligence test score was also retained.

In the black sample, discriminators for the severely retarded subgroup were lower ratings at age 4 for goal orientation and response to directions and a higher rating for dependency—all had small coefficients. A smaller head circumference at this age was significant in the comparisons with the mildly retarded and borderline subgroups. These data are shown in Tables 9-40 and 9-41. At 1 year of age, the medical complications of strabismus and the unique minor malformation of undescended testicle were more frequent in the severely retarded subgroup (Table 9-42). Adverse family conditions recorded on the pediatric examination were unfavorable emotional environment and loss of one or both parents (Table 9-43). Parental loss in the first year was a previously unidentified environmental factor. A shorter duration of response at 8 months rated during the

Table 9-36

Attention Span and Activity Level Ratings at Age Four by IQ Subgroup

	1 Severely Retarded		2 Mildly Retarded		3 Borderline		4 Average		5 Above Average		F	r_{IQ}
	M	S.D.	M	S.D.	M	S.D.	M	S.D.	M	S.D.		
					Attention Span							
White	1.6	0.7	2.2	0.8	**2.6**	**0.7**	**2.9**	**0.4**	**3.0**	**0.4**	282.12**	.28**
Black	2.0	1.2	2.3	0.8	2.7	0.6	2.9	0.4	2.9	0.3	320.79**	.28**
Group Ns: White -	21		130		1917		10711		1439			
Black -	43		662		6881		8705		144			
					Activity Level							
White	4.1	1.1	3.2	1.0	3.1	0.7	**3.0**	**0.6**	3.0	0.5	33.10**	− .09**
Black	3.4	1.2	3.1	0.9	3.0	0.7	3.0	0.5	3.0	0.4	7.74**	− .03*
Group Ns: White -	19		133		1927		10740		1443			
Black -	44		663		6891		8707		144			

Differs from severely retarded in D.F.
Differs from mildly retarded in D.F.
Differs from severely and mildly retarded in D.F.s
  *$p < .001$
 **$p < .00001$

Bayley examinations was a discriminator in two comparisons between the severely retarded and nonretarded subgroups (Table 9-44).

The neonatal risk factors retained in the analyses through age 4 were seizures
in the first month of life, the high sex ratio, dysmaturity, erythroblastosis, and
shorter length at birth. Significant pregnancy and obstetric complications were
diabetes and seizures in the mother and use of intravenous anesthetics and
meconium staining at delivery. Other risk factors for the severely retarded subgroup in the black sample were a low level of maternal education at registration
for prenatal care and reported retardation in older children.

At age 7, family and demographic markers unique to the CNS normals
among the severely retarded were maternal age and employment of the father
among whites, and socioeconomic status, family size, and adoption or foster
home placement among blacks. As the canonical correlations in Table 9-45

Table 9-37
Height at Age Four in Centimeters by IQ Subgroup

	1 Severely Retarded		2 Mildly Retarded		3 Borderline		4 Average		5 Above Average		F	r_{IQ}
	M	S.D.	M	S.D.	M	S.D.	M	S.D.	M	S.D.		
White	98.5	7.5	98.7	5.1	100.0	4.5	100.8	4.4	**101.8**	**4.4**	39.01*	.13*
Black	99.6	4.6	100.5	4.9	101.6	4.5	*102.4*	*4.4*	*104.1*	*4.7*	53.80*	.14*

Differs from severely retarded in D.F.
Differs from mildly retarded in D.F.
*p <.00001

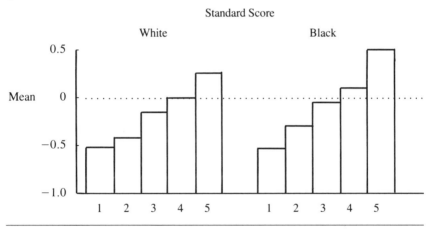

Standard Score

Note. Group Ns: White-   15   107   1674   9438   1289
          Black-   42   593   6271   7671   105

show, variables from this epoch were not highly related to the subgroup classification except in the comparison between the severely retarded and the above
average in the black sample ($R = .61$). Among whites, moderate correlations
were obtained in comparisons with both the mildly retarded and the above
average. Characteristics common to the subgroups in both samples were a lower
level of maternal education, number of subsequent pregnancies (fewer among
whites than in the mildly retarded but more frequent among blacks than in all
nonretarded subgroups), lower socioeconomic status and more public financial
assistance, both retained in comparisons with the above average, and less maternal employment since delivery.

Table 9-38
Delayed Motor Development and Peripheral Nerve Abnormality
at One Year by IQ Subgroup

	1 Severely Retarded	2 Mildly Retarded	3 Borderline	4 Average	5 Above Average	χ^2	r_{IQ}
				Percent			
			Delayed Motor Development				
White	28.00	11.25	*2.64*	*0.82*	*0.38*	362.42**	−.10**
Black	16.67	6.35	*1.44*	*0.49*	0.65	331.61**	−.11**
Group Ns: White-	25	160	2233	12247	1832		
Black-	54	787	7849	9577	154		
			Peripheral Nerve Abnormality				
White	4.00	0.00	*0.09*	*0.19*	0.22	21.57*	.01
Black	0.00	0.00	0.11	0.14	0.65	4.60	.01
Group Ns: White-	25	160	2233	12247	1832		
Black-	54	787	7849	9577	154		

Differs from severely retarded in D.F.
Differs from severely and mildly retarded in D.F.s
 *$p<.001$
**$p<.00001$

In the white sample only, maternal reports of mental illness of the study child was an important discriminator in all comparisons. Older age of the mother was significant in comparisons with the nonretarded. Paternal unemployment discriminated between the severely retarded subgroup and the above average. Among blacks, family size in the severely retarded subgroup was smaller than in the mildly retarded and was the only discriminator in that comparison. Higher rates of reported retardation among siblings and of adoption or foster home placement of the study child were significant in comparisons with the average and above-average subgroups. Distributions of the family and demographic characteristics are shown in Tables 9-46 through 9-49.

The biomedical characteristics of the severely retarded CNS normals at age 7 are shown in Table 9-50. Abnormalities significant in both samples included major malformations of the eye and skull, minor malformations of the ear and musculoskeletal system, abnormal gait, and mirror or other abnormal move-

Table 9-39

Intensity of Response Rating at Eight Months by IQ Subgroup

	1 Severely Retarded		2 Mildly Retarded		3 Borderline		4 Average		5 Above Average		F	r_{IQ}
	M	S.D.	M	S.D.	M	S.D.	M	S.D.	M	S.D.		
White	2.5	0.7	**3.0**	**0.8**	**3.2**	**0.7**	3.3	0.7	**3.3**	**0.7**	59.19*	.08*
Black	2.6	1.0	3.0	0.7	3.2	0.6	3.2	0.6	3.5	0.6	64.53*	.11*

Differs from severely retarded in D.F.
*p < .00001

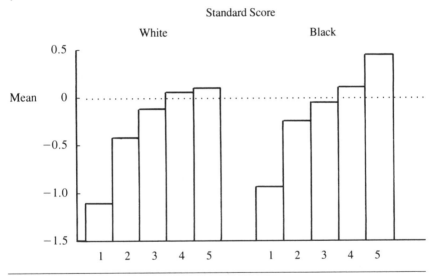

Standard Score

Note. Group Ns: White-   17 109 1680 9874 1503
           Black-   43 581 6297 7735 111

ments (Tables 9-51–9-53). Head circumference among whites was larger than that of mildly retarded and borderline children, but in the black sample, smaller head size was a consistent discriminator in comparisons with higher IQ subgroups. (Table 9-54). In the interval between 1 and 7 years, failure to thrive was diagnosed in 8% of the white and 3.5% of the black severely retarded subgroup (Table 9-55). During this period, diagnostic and other medical procedures were performed frequently, especially among whites (Table 9-56). A lower so-

Table 9-40

Goal Orientation, Response to Directions, and Dependency Ratings
at Age Four by IQ Subgroup

	1 Severely Retarded		2 Mildly Retarded		3 Borderline		4 Average		5 Above Average		F	r_{IQ}
	M	S.D.	M	S.D.	M	S.D.	M	S.D.	M	S.D.		

<table>
<tr><td colspan="13" align="center">Goal Orientation</td></tr>
<tr><td>White</td><td>1.9 1.0</td><td></td><td>2.1 0.6</td><td></td><td>2.6 0.6</td><td></td><td>*2.9 0.4*</td><td></td><td>3.0 0.4</td><td></td><td>364.82*</td><td>.32*</td></tr>
</table>

Goal Orientation

White	1.9 1.0	2.1 0.6	2.6 0.6	*2.9 0.4*	3.0 0.4	364.82*	.32*
Black	1.6 0.6	2.3 0.6	**2.7 0.5**	*2.9 0.4*	**3.0 0.4**	536.67*	.35*

Group Ns: White - 20 130 1920 10710 1443
          Black - 43 661 6886 8703 144

Response to Directions

White	1.6 0.9	2.4 0.9	**2.7 0.7**	2.9 0.5	**3.0 0.4**	156.08*	.19*
Black	1.7 0.8	2.4 0.9	2.8 0.7	**3.0 0.5**	3.0 0.3	255.47*	.24*

Group Ns: White - 21 133 1933 10744 1445
          Black - 44 664 6901 8708 144

Dependency

White	3.6 1.5	3.7 0.9	3.4 0.7	3.2 0.6	3.0 0.6	129.55*	−.22*
Black	4.1 1.1	3.7 0.8	*3.3 0.6*	**3.1 0.5**	3.0 0.5	293.64*	−.26*

Group Ns: White - 17 131 1927 10730 1443
          Black - 42 659 6873 8705 144

Differs from severely retarded in D.F.
Differs from mildly retarded in D.F.
Differs from severely and mildly retarded in D.F.s
*$p < .00001$

cioeconomic index score at age 7 was retained in comparisons between the severely retarded and the average and above average in both samples.

In the white subgroup, major genitourinary and thoracic malformations were distinguishing characteristics (see Table 9-51). Nearly one half of the children had abnormal reflexes (see Table 9-53). There was one case of hypothyroidism, an extremely rare condition, among the severely retarded CNS normals (Table 9-57). Discriminators unique to the subgroup in the white sample were a history

Table 9-41

Head Circumference at Age Four in Centimeters by IQ Subgroup

	1 Severely Retarded	2 Mildly Retarded	3 Borderline	4 Average	5 Above Average	F	r_{IQ}
	M S.D.	M S.D.	M S.D.	M S.D.	M S.D.		
White	49.7 1.8	48.9 2.0	*49.6 1.6*	*50.1 1.5*	*50.7 1.5*	114.65*	.21*
Black	48.6 2.1	**49.4 1.6**	**49.7 1.6**	*50.1 1.6*	*50.8 1.4*	74.52*	.16*

Group Ns: White-   15   106   1668   9386   1279
              Black-   42   589   6256   7637   106

Differs from severely retarded in D.F.
Differs from mildly retarded in D.F.
Differs from severely and mildly retarded in D.F.s
*p <.00001

of ear infections and the visual abnormality of amblyopia (Tables 9-58 and 9-59). The high proportion of males was significant in the comparison with the mildly retarded.

Among blacks, rare cardiovascular and blood disorders were discriminating characteristics of the severely retarded CNS normals (Table 9-60). Of these, hemolytic disease was unique to the subgroup. Another rare complication was liver infection (Table 9-61). Major malformations of the musculoskeletal system and minor central nervous system malformations were more frequent in the severely retarded subgroup (see Tables 9-51 and 9-52). Visual field defect was a rare, and previously unidentified, condition (see Table 9-59). There were fewer children who were right-handed at age 7 among the severely retarded, a factor significant in all comparisons with the nonretarded (Table 9-62). Other characteristics of the subgroup in the black sample were histories of subdural hematoma or effusion, spasmus nutans (a unique condition) and episodes of hypoxia without unconsciousness (Table 9-63).

The medical findings from examination at 7 years and from interval histories after the first year were not powerful discriminators except in the comparison between severely retarded CNS normals and the above average in the black sample (R = .79). In all other comparisons, canonical correlations with the subgroup classification were in the moderate range of .21 to .42.

The behavioral and cognitive markers at age 7 were, as expected, highly related to IQ level (Table 9-64). Maximum canonical correlations in the extreme group comparisons were .83 among whites and .94 among blacks. The most important of the psychological discriminators were the summary rating of

Table 9-42
Strabismus and Undescended Testicle at One Year by IQ Subgroup

	1 Severely Retarded	2 Mildly Retarded	3 Borderline	4 Average	5 Above Average	χ^2	r_{IQ}
			Percent				
			Strabismus				
White	8.00	3.75	1.88	1.71	1.58	10.07*	−.01
Black	14.81	**1.14**	**1.27**	**1.04**	**0.65**	88.32*****	−.02**
Group Ns: White -	25	160	2233	12247	1832		
Black -	54	787	7849	9577	154		
			Undescended Testicle				
White	0.00	4.94	*1.55*	*0.80*	*0.48*	23.18***	−.04****
Black	5.26	**0.45**	0.87	**0.71**	0.00	11.88*	−.01
Group Ns: White -	21	81	1165	6472	1042		
Black -	38	448	4116	4782	80		

Differs from severely retarded in D.F.
Differs from mildly retarded in D.F.
  *$p<.05$
  **$p<.01$
  ***$p<.001$
  ****$p<.0001$
  *****$p<.00001$

behavior and the Auditory–Vocal Association and Draw-A-Person Tests. More than two thirds of the children in the severely retarded subgroup were rated as abnormal in behavior (Table 9-65). For those who could be tested, language age score was about 30 months and DAP standard score was approximately 60 (Table 9-66). Poor tactile finger recognition on both hands, a task not free of cognitive demands, was a fairly consistent discriminator in both samples (Table 9-67).

Twelve of 15 individual behavior ratings were retained in the analyses. Children in the severely retarded subgroup in both samples were given low ratings for goal orientation, verbal communication, and fearfulness and high ratings for dependency and activity level (Table 9-68). Significant among whites only were a low rating for attention span and high ratings for self-confidence, separation

Table 9-43
Unfavorable Emotional Environment and Loss of Parents
in First Year by IQ Subgroup

	1 Severely Retarded	2 Mildly Retarded	3 Borderline	4 Average	5 Above Average	χ^2	r_{IQ}
			Percent				
			Unfavorable Emotional Environment				
White	4.00	9.38	8.42	5.78	*2.89*	59.71****	−.07****
Black	11.11	**3.05**	**1.91**	**1.70**	**1.30**	32.86****	−.03***
			Loss of One or Both Parents				
White	8.00	**1.25**	3.90	2.67	**0.98**	37.28****	−.04****
Black	5.56	1.02	**0.75**	**0.71**	0.00	18.89**	−.02*

Group Ns: White -   25 160 2233 12247 1832

Black -   54 787 7849 9577 154

Differs from severely retarded in D.F.
Differs from mildly retarded in D.F.
  *$p<.05$
 **$p<.001$
 ***$p<.0001$
****$p<.00001$

anxiety, impulsiveness, and assertiveness. In the black sample, the severely retarded subgroup had low ratings for both hostility and frustration tolerance.

Of the three subtests of the Wide Range Achievement Test, arithmetic was the most consistent discriminator. The severely retarded children who could be evaluated were performing within the prekindergarten level (Table 9-69).

The Mildly Retarded

Although few differences were expected between the large CNS normal subgroup and all mildly retarded children, some unique characteristics were identified. Most importantly, these analyses show that biological risk factors for mild cognitive deficit are present after the exclusion of those children with major neurological disorders. The combined prenatal and perinatal discriminators are shown in Table 9-70. The majority of those significant in both samples were

Table 9-44
Duration of Response Rating at Eight Months by IQ Subgroup

	1 Severely Retarded		2 Mildly Retarded		3 Borderline		4 Average		5 Above Average		F	r_{IQ}
	M	S.D.	M	S.D.	M	S.D.	M	S.D.	M	S.D.		
White	2.5	1.0	2.9	0.8	3.1	0.7	3.2	0.6	3.2	0.6	18.15*	.07*
Black	2.3	0.9	**3.0**	**0.8**	**3.1**	**0.6**	**3.2**	**0.6**	3.3	0.6	45.13*	.11*

Group Ns: White-   16   110 1677 9892 1504
          Black-   43   583 6281 7716   111
Differs from severely retarded in D.F.
*$p <.00001$

family and demographic characteristics: intelligence and education of the mother, socioeconomic status, housing density, pregnancy-free interval and parity, and reported retardation of both parents.[2] A shorter pregnancy-free interval among whites and paternal retardation among blacks were unique to the CNS normals. Other discriminators common to the two samples were inhalation anesthetics at delivery, positively related to mild retardation among whites and negatively related among blacks, and the neonatal risk factors of major cardiovascular malformations and smaller head circumference at birth.

Of antecedent factors in the white sample only, later registration for prenatal care was unique to the subgroup. Mothers were older at menarche, more often had urinary tract infection in pregnancy, and reported more hospitalizations in the interval between the last menstrual period and study registration. Negative pregnancy and obstetric risk factors in the white mildly retarded subgroup were higher smoking in pregnancy, fewer abdomino-pelvic x-rays (lifetime history), fewer confining illnesses preceding study registration, fewer induced labors, and less frequent use of midforceps—a discriminator in the extreme group comparison. Significant neonatal complications were major malformations of the upper respiratory system or mouth, minor ear malformations, and respiratory difficulty in the newborn nursery, diagnosed in 3.6% of the subgroup and a discriminator in the comparison with the above average only.

In the black sample, a risk factor unique to the CNS normals among the mildly retarded was self-reported maternal mental illness. Other maternal char-

---

[2]Distributions for discriminators shared with the severely retarded subgroup are shown in the preceding section. Distributions for other discriminators are shown in Appendix 5, Tables 1–15 (pre- and perinatal), Tables 16–22 (infancy and preschool) and Tables 23–35 (7-year).

Table 9-45
Standardized Coefficients for Seven-Year Family and Demographic Discriminators Between the Severely Retarded and Comparison Subgroups

Variable	Comparison Subgroup							
	White				Black			
	MR	BL	AV	AA	MR	BL	AV	AA
Maternal education	—	—	−.33	−.25	—	−.91	−.70	−.36
Number of subsequent pregnancies	−.61	—	—	—	—	.39	.44	.40
Socioeconomic index	—	—	—	−.33	—	—	—	−.31
Public assistance	—	—	—	.31	—	—	—	.21
Mother employed	—	—	—	−.14	—	—	−.25	—
Reported mental illness in study child	.72	.84	.86	.59	—	—	—	—
Maternal age	—	.58	.38	.27	—	—	—	—
Father employed	—	—	—	−.11	—	—	—	—
Family size	—	—	—	—	−1.00	—	—	—
Retardation in siblings	—	—	—	—	—	—	.24	.26
Study child adopted or in foster home	—	—	—	—	—	—	.15	—
Canonical correlation	*.33***	*.12****	*.08****	*.28****	*.08**	*.05***	*.09****	*.61****

*p<.05
**p<.0001
***p<.00001

acteristics were the pregnancy complications of low hematocrit, toxemia, and heart disease; fewer prenatal visits, more prior fetal deaths, shorter stature, and, as compared with the above average, younger maternal age. The only significant obstetric factor was less frequent administration of conduction anesthetics at delivery. The high frequency of male infants and of multiple births in the mildly retarded subgroup were discriminating characteristics. As neonates the children were shorter, and, in the comparison with the borderline subgroup, had significantly higher frequencies of major musculoskeletal malformations, primary apnea and multiple apneic episodes, and a shorter gestational age (Tables 9-84 and 9-85).

Table 9-46

Maternal Education, Socioeconomic Index Score, and Age by IQ Subgroup

	1 Severely Retarded		2 Mildly Retarded		3 Borderline		4 Average		5 Above Average		F	r_{IQ}
	M	S.D.	M	S.D.	M	S.D.	M	S.D.	M	S.D.		

Maternal Education (yr.)

White	9.9	3.2	9.5	2.4	10.1	2.3	*11.5*	*2.4*	*13.8*	*2.5*	653.65***	.43***
Black	8.9	2.8	9.3	2.4	*10.2*	*2.1*	*10.8*	*2.0*	*12.1*	*2.5*	204.85***	.24***

Group Ns: White - 19 166 2271 12276 1847

       Black - 55 778 7689 9310 153

Seven Year Socioeconomic Index

White	43.8	23.1	35.5	18.8	*43.1*	*19.9*	57.8	22.5	*77.1*	*19.3*	675.12***	.44***
Black	29.5	17.8	28.5	16.8	34.8	17.8	*42.5*	*19.5*	*56.7*	*22.8*	283.85***	.29***

Group Ns: White - 25 173 2326 12473 1856

       Black - 59 839 7796 9422 155

Maternal Age

White	38.0	9.3	34.1	7.4	**33.0**	**7.1**	*32.8*	*6.2*	*32.7*	*5.3*	6.59**	−.02*
Black	33.3	8.7	33.0	8.4	32.2	7.8	32.5	7.3	*34.7*	*6.9*	6.83**	.02*

Group Ns: White - 23 171 2343 12503 1860

       Black - 57 796 7815 9449 155

Differs from severely retarded in D.F.
Differs from mildly retarded in D.F.
Differs from severely and mildly retarded in D.F.s
 *p<.05
 **p<.0001
 ***p<.00001

The combined prenatal and perinatal antecedents were fairly effective discriminators between mildly retarded CNS normals and the above average. Canonical correlations with the subgroup classification were .61 and .63 in the two samples. With the exception of a moderate value of .30 obtained in the comparison with the average subgroup among blacks, other comparisons resulted in relatively low canonical correlations of .19.

Table 9-47

Subsequent Pregnancies and Family Size by IQ Subgroup

	1 Severely Retarded		2 Mildly Retarded		3 Borderline		4 Average		5 Above Average		F	r_{IQ}
	M	S.D.	M	S.D.	M	S.D.	M	S.D.	M	S.D.		

Number of Subsequent Pregnancies

White	0.6	1.1	**1.7**	**1.5**	1.5	1.3	*1.3*	*1.2*	*1.2*	*1.1*	20.18*	−.06*
Black	2.0	1.6	1.9	1.5	*1.5*	*1.3*	*1.2*	*1.2*	**0.9**	**0.9**	109.21*	−.18*

Group Ns: White - 16 154 2157 12001 1831
Black - 48 729 7266 8982 149

Family Size

White	3.8	3.1	4.7	2.3	4.3	2.0	3.8	1.8	*3.1*	*1.4*	130.26*	−.20*
Black	4.7	2.2	**5.6**	**2.9**	4.7	2.4	*4.1*	*2.2*	3.5	1.8	108.37*	−.17*

Group Ns: White - 15 149 2104 11798 1818
Black - 47 710 7096 8758 145

Differs from severely retarded in D.F.
Differs from mildly retarded in D.F.
Differs from severely and mildly retarded in D.F.s
*p<.00001

In summary analyses of all discriminators through age 4, the most important were IQ and other measures of preschool abilities, and maternal intelligence as estimated by the SRA score (Table 9-71). Mean Stanford–Binet IQ scores in the white and black subgroups were 70 and 73 (see Table 9-31). The lower SRA scores of the mothers differed from the total sample means by approximately 1 standard deviation among whites and one half of a standard deviation among blacks (see Table 9-16). Scores on the motor and concept formation tests at age 4 and frequencies of abnormal ratings from the speech, language, and hearing evaluations at age 3 are shown in Tables 16 and 17, Appendix 5. Behavioral problems observed during the 4-year examination were reflected in the summary rating and in low ratings for attention span, goal orientation, and response to directions. Smaller head circumference at age 4 was also significant in both samples. Discriminators unique to the CNS normals among the mildly retarded were the preschool characteristics of poor responsiveness to directions among whites and abnormal hearing among blacks. Early risk factors retained in both

Table 9-48

Public Assistance and Parental Employment by IQ Subgroup

	1 Severely Retarded	2 Mildly Retarded	3 Borderline	4 Average	5 Above Average	χ^2	r_{IQ}
			Percent				
			Public Assistance				
White	35.29	33.99	29.84	15.25	*4.00*	545.42***	−.22***
Black	46.94	54.46	*41.25*	27.97	**12.16**	478.99***	−.18***
Group Ns: White -	17	153	2155	11998	1825		
Black -	49	729	7278	8962	148		
			Father Employed				
White	76.92	86.44	87.49	92.42	**96.70**	111.22***	.10***
Black	82.35	79.74	*86.47*	*91.11*	94.69	92.31***	.10***
Group Ns: White -	13	118	1686	10388	1697		
Black -	34	385	4264	5862	113		
			Mother Employed				
White	35.29	41.83	*57.83*	*59.46*	**60.72**	26.89**	.03*
Black	60.42	62.91	74.43	**80.53**	78.52	180.10***	.10***
Group Ns: White -	17	153	2151	11992	1833		
Black -	48	728	7271	8979	149		

Differs from severely retarded in D.F.
Differs from mildly retarded in D.F.
Differs from severely and mildly retarded in D.F.s
   *$p<.001$
  **$p<.0001$
 ***$p<.00001$

samples were delayed motor development and smaller head circumference at age 1, lower scores on the Bayley Scales at 8 months, lower socioeconomic status (retained most consistently among blacks), and the maternal characteristics of less education and self-reported retardation.

In the white sample only, fewer children in the mildly retarded subgroup exhibited right dominance of hand, leg, and eye at age 4. Significant medical

Table 9-49

Mental Illness, Adoption, and Retardation in Siblings by IQ Subgroup

	1 Severely Retarded	2 Mildly Retarded	3 Borderline	4 Average	5 Above Average	χ^2	r_{IQ}
			Percent				
		Reported Mental Illness in Study Child					
White	12.50	**0.81**	**1.11**	**0.51**	**0.48**	47.43**	−.03*
Black	0.00	0.63	0.25	0.21	0.75	5.52	−.00
Group Ns: White -	16	123	1711	9701	1463		
Black -	40	632	6374	7925	133		
		Study Child Adopted or in Foster Home					
White	10.53	8.77	6.37	*3.07*	1.13	114.44**	−.09**
Black	13.21	8.19	*6.01*	**4.36**	3.87	45.00**	−.05**
Group Ns: White -	19	171	2323	12478	1859		
Black -	53	794	7790	9423	155		
		Retardation in Siblings					
White	12.50	25.97	*15.59*	*7.70*	*3.71*	265.35*	−.14*
Black	18.75	17.51	*9.95*	*7.43*	**3.36**	111.89*	−.09*
Group Ns: White -	16	154	2161	12005	1834		
Black -	48	731	7278	8993	149		

Differs from severely retarded in D.F.
Differs from mildly retarded in D.F.
Differs from severely and mildly retarded in D.F.s
 *$p<.01$
 **$p<.00001$

complications were congenital heart disease and undescended testicle at age 1 and major malformations of the upper respiratory system or mouth. A less intense social response at 8 months was a discriminator in all comparisons. The lower sex ratio in the white subgroup, significant in the preschool analysis, was retained in the 4-year summary. Risk factors from pregnancy and delivery were maternal urinary tract infection and the use of inhalation anesthetics. Older

Table 9-50
Standardized Coefficients for Seven-Year Pediatric Discriminators Between the Severely Retarded and Comparison Subgroups

Variable	White				Black			
	MR	BL	AV	AA	MR	BL	AV	AA
Major eye malformations	.50	.24	.20	.16	.40	.28	.30	.17
Diagnostic or other medical procedures	.47	.25	.22	.26	.26	.20	.21	.30
Abnormal gait	—	.15	.20	.30	.41	.45	.57	.46
Head circumference	.47	.16	—	—	−.14	−.14	−.18	−.19
Minor ear malformations	—	.16	.18	.21	.20	.08	.08	—
Abnormal shape of skull	—	.47	.45	.42	—	.30	.27	—
Failure to thrive	—	.28	.48	.44	—	.08	.14	—
Minor musculoskeletal malformations	—	.12	.15	—	.23	.14	.09	—
Mirror or other abnormal movements	—	—	.11	—	.26	.26	.23	.12
Socioeconomic index	—	—	−.12	−.33	—	—	−.13	−.33
Major genitourinary malformations	—	.21	.12	.12	—	—	—	—
Hypothyroidism	——	.45	.38	—	—	—	—	—
Abnormal reflexes	—	—	.12	.16	—	—	—	—
Ear infection	—	—	.07	.09	—	—	—	—
Percent male	.34	—	—	—	—	—	—	—
Major thoracic malformations	—	—	.08	—	—	—	—	—
Amblyopia	—	—	—	.10	—	—	—	—
Documented cardiovascular disorder	—	—	—	—	.27	.23	.11	—
Hemoglobinopathy	—	—	—	—	.21	.11	.13	—
Right handedness	—	—	—	—	—	−.09	−.07	−.22
Liver infection	—	—	—	—	—	.24	.14	—
Subdural hematoma or effusion	—	—	—	—	—	.14	.23	—
Hemolytic disease	—	—	—	—	—	.17	.12	—

(continued)

Table 9-50 (continued)

Variable	White				Black			
	MR	BL	AV	AA	MR	BL	AV	AA
Spasmus nutans	—	—	—	—	—	.14	.07	—
Minor CNS mal-								
formations	—	—	—	—	—	.11	.09	—
Visual field defect	—	—	—	—	—	.11	—	—
Major musculoskeletal								
malformations	—	—	—	—	—	.09	—	—
Hypoxia without								
unconsciousness	—	—	—	—	—	—	.10	—
Canonical correlation	*.42**	*.33**	*.21**	*.42**	*.42**	*.30**	*.34**	*.79**

*$p<.00001$

maternal age at menarche, reported retardation of the father, and higher housing density in the prenatal period were also retained.

Among blacks, the mildly retarded subgroup had low ratings for verbal communication and impulsiveness at age 4 and a high rating for dependency. The children were shorter at that age, a minor discriminator, and weighed less in the first year than those in higher IQ subgroups. Hypotonia at age 1 was diagnosed in 11 cases (Table 22, Appendix 5). The neonatal risk factors of multiple apneic episodes, primary apnea, musculoskeletal malformations, and shorter gestational age were retained in the comparison with the borderline subgroup. Maternal antecedents in the black sample included a shorter pregnancy-free interval, heart disease and toxemia in pregnancy, and prior fetal death. Higher parity and younger maternal age at registration for prenatal care discriminated between the mildly retarded and the above average.

The canonical correlations in the 4-year summary analyses ranged from .43 to .86 among whites and from .39 to .83 among blacks. Maximum values were obtained in the extreme group comparisons between the mildly retarded and the above average. Discriminatory power in the comparison with the average subgroup was greater among blacks than whites.

Differences between the mildly retarded and nonretarded subgroups in family and demographic characteristics at age 7 are shown in Table 9-72. Most of the markers were significant in both samples and were not unique to the CNS

Table 9-51

Major Malformations by IQ Subgroup

	1 Severely Retarded	2 Mildly Retarded	3 Borderline	4 Average	5 Above Average	χ^2	r_{IQ}
			Percent				
		Major Eye Malformations					
White	11.54	**1.16**	**1.00**	**0.66**	**0.59**	47.08****	−.03***
Black	15.25	**1.55**	**1.01**	**0.80**	**0.64**	132.01****	−.03****
		Abnormal Shape of Skull					
White	15.38	4.62	*0.38*	*0.32*	*0.32*	227.99****	−.04****
Black	11.86	1.43	**0.58**	**0.46**	0.00	143.12****	−.04****
		Major Genitourinary Malformations					
White	11.54	3.47	**1.21**	**1.71**	**2.18**	23.96***	.01
Black	3.39	1.19	1.00	1.07	1.91	4.60	−.00
		Major Thoracic Malformations					
White	7.69	2.89	1.34	**1.03**	1.22	17.24**	−.02*
Black	0.00	0.48	0.24	0.23	0.00	2.42	−.02*
		Major Musculoskeletal Malformations					
White	3.85	4.62	2.51	2.68	2.24	4.21	−.01
Black	10.17	2.26	**1.75**	1.80	4.46	29.74****	−.00

Group Ns: White -   26   173   2391   12667   1878

   Black -   59   839   8223   9868   157

Differs from severely retarded in D.F.

Differs from severely and mildly retarded in D.F.s

   *$p<.05$

   **$p<.01$

   ***$p<.0001$

   ****$p<.00001$

Table 9-52

Minor Malformations by IQ Subgroup

	1 Severely Retarded	2 Mildly Retarded	3 Borderline	4 Average	5 Above Average	χ^2	r_{IQ}
			Percent				
			Minor Ear Malformations				
White	11.54	5.78	*1.71*	*0.84*	*0.69*	85.80*****	− .05*****
Black	10.17	**2.38**	**2.68**	**2.04**	1.27	24.57****	− .03***
			Minor Musculoskeletal Malformations				
White	11.54	4.05	**1.88**	*1.45*	2.02	27.67****	− .01
Black	8.47	**1.79**	**1.46**	**1.44**	0.64	21.27***	− .02*
			Minor CNS Malformations				
White	3.85	0.00	0.42	0.32	0.21	11.81*	− .01
Black	3.39	0.48	**0.34**	**0.34**	0.64	15.88**	− .00

Group Ns: White - 26 173 2391 12667 1878
Black - 59 839 8223 9868 157

Differs from severely retarded in D.F.
Differs from severely and mildly retarded in D.F.s
 *p<.05
 **p<.01
 ***p<.001
 ****p<.0001
 *****p<.00001

normal subgroup. Major discriminators were the socioeconomic index score at this age, maternal education, and retardation in siblings. Both socioeconomic status and level of maternal education were lower among the mildly retarded, and maternal reports of retarded siblings were more frequent. Other characteristics of the mildly retarded subgroups were less maternal employment and more pregnancies since birth of the study child, more household moves in that interval, and higher housing density. Fewer of the mothers had received additional education or training since study registration (Table 24, Appendix 5). Larger family size, public financial assistance, and adoption or foster home

Table 9-53
Minor Neurological Signs by IQ Subgroup

	1 Severely Retarded	2 Mildly Retarded	3 Borderline	4 Average	5 Above Average	χ^2	r_{IQ}
			Percent				
			Abnormal Gait				
White	33.33	20.93	*8.48*	*4.27*	*2.90*	213.54*	−.11*
Black	44.83	**11.41**	*3.93*	*1.98*	*1.30*	426.25*	−.13*
Group Ns: White -	24	172	2369	12578	1862		
Black -	58	815	8024	9654	154		
			Mirror or Other Abnormal Movements				
White	24.00	10.00	6.60	**5.25**	4.84	31.78*	−.04*
Black	24.56	**4.66**	**2.38**	**2.07**	**0.65**	145.18*	−.05*
Group Ns: White -	25	170	2364	12568	1861		
Black -	57	815	8022	9650	153		
			Abnormal Reflexes				
White	46.15	27.91	17.73	**13.21**	**12.84**	86.03*	−.06*
Black	32.76	20.12	*12.35*	*11.37*	10.39	77.24*	−.05*
Group Ns: White -	26	172	2369	12578	1862		
Black -	58	815	8024	9654	154		

Differs from severely retarded in D.F.
Differs from mildly retarded in D.F.
Differs from severely and mildly retarded in D.F.s
*p<.00001

placement of the study child were also significant in both samples. Mothers of the mildly retarded were older than those of average children among whites and younger than those of the above average among blacks. Older age of the father in the white sample was a discriminator unique to the subgroup. Among blacks, paternal unemployment and less frequent use of child care were characteristics of the mildly retarded subgroup.

Concurrent family and demographic factors were not effective discriminators

Table 9-54
Head Circumference in Centimeters by IQ Subgroup

	1 Severely Retarded	2 Mildly Retarded	3 Borderline	4 Average	5 Above Average	F	r_{IQ}
	M S.D.	M S.D.	M S.D.	M S.D.	M S.D.		
White	51.7 1.8	**50.4 1.9**	*50.9 1.6*	*51.5 1.5*	*52.1 1.4*	187.04*	.24*
Black	50.0 2.2	**50.6 1.7**	*51.0 1.6*	*51.4 1.5*	*52.1 1.6*	120.43*	.18*

Differs from severely retarded in D.F.
Differs from mildly retarded in D.F.
Differs from severely and mildly retarded in D.F.s
*$p < .00001$

Standard Score

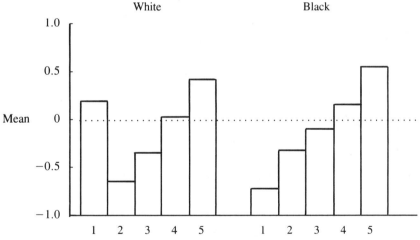

Note. Group Ns: White-   24 172 2358 12537 1858
Black-   56 815 7997 9626 150

between the mildly retarded and higher IQ subgroups except in the comparison with the above average, where the canonical correlations with the subgroup classification were .57 and .59 in the two samples.

Biomedical characteristics of the mildly retarded CNS normals at age 7 are shown in Table 9-73. Consistent discriminators in both samples were smaller head circumference, abnormal gait, a history of failure to thrive, and the rare

Table 9-55
Failure to Thrive by IQ Subgroup

	1 Severely Retarded	2 Mildly Retarded	3 Borderline	4 Average	5 Above Average	χ^2	r_{IQ}
			Percent				
White	7.69	2.33	*0.46*	*0.09*	*0.05*	151.94*	− .06*
Black	3.45	1.47	*0.39*	*0.12*	0.00	68.01*	− .06*

Group Ns: White - 26 172 2369 12578 1862

Black - 58 815 8024 9654 154

Differs from severely retarded in D.F.
Differs from severely and mildly retarded in D.F.s
*$p<.00001$

condition of cyanotic congenital heart disease. Both subgroups had relatively high frequencies of color blindness and strabismus. A larger number of medical procedures performed since infancy was also a significant factor. The control variable of socioeconomic status at age 7 had large coefficients, especially in the extreme group comparisons. In the white sample, abnormal shape of skull (mainly cranial asymmetry), minor malformations of the musculoskeletal system and ear, and major alimentary malformations were discriminators in com-

Table 9-56
Diagnostic or Other Medical Procedures by IQ Subgroup

	1 Severely Retarded	2 Mildly Retarded	3 Borderline	4 Average	5 Above Average	χ^2	r_{IQ}
			Percent				
White	61.54	**26.74**	**16.67**	*12.91*	*12.51*	102.09*	− .06*
Black	44.83	**18.90**	*11.32*	*9.03*	*7.79*	162.25*	− .08*

Group Ns: White - 26 172 2369 12578 1862

Black - 58 815 8024 9654 154

Differs from severely retarded in D.F.
Differs from severely and mildly retarded in D.F.s
*$p<.00001$

Table 9-57
Hypothyroidism by IQ Subgroup

	1 Severely Retarded	2 Mildly Retarded	3 Borderline	4 Average	5 Above Average	χ^2	r_{IQ}
			Percent				
White	3.85	0.00	**0.00**	**0.03**	0.00	130.18*	−.01
Black	0.00	0.00	0.00	0.00	0.00	—	—

Group Ns: White - 26 172 2369 12578 1862
Black - 58 815 8024 9654 154

Differs from severely retarded in D.F.
*$p<.00001$

parisons with higher IQ subgroups. Prevalence rates among the mildly retarded ranged from 4% to 6%. Cranial nerve abnormalities and nystagmus were present in 5% of the subgroup; four children had acyanotic congenital heart disease. Adverse events documented in medical histories were unspecified symptomatic intoxication, burns requiring hospitalization, and ear infections. Chickenpox was reported less frequently than for children in higher IQ subgroups. The discriminators unique to the CNS normals were malformations of the alimentary system and severe burns. Among blacks, abnormal reflexes in 20% of the mildly

Table 9-58
Ear Infection by IQ Subgroup

	1 Severely Retarded	2 Mildly Retarded	3 Borderline	4 Average	5 Above Average	χ^2	r_{IQ}
			Percent				
White	17.39	11.46	6.20	*5.38*	**5.41**	18.92**	−.02*
Black	7.14	3.54	2.82	2.96	2.03	5.33	−.01

Group Ns: White - 23 157 2162 11391 1700
Black - 56 791 7844 9390 148

Differs from severely retarded in D.F.
Differs from severely and mildly retarded in D.F.s
*$p<.05$
**$p<.001$

Table 9-59
Amblyopia and Visual Field Defect by IQ Subgroup

	1 Severely Retarded	2 Mildly Retarded	3 Borderline	4 Average	5 Above Average	χ^2	r_{IQ}
			Percent				
Amblyopia							
White	7.69	3.49	2.32	1.64	**0.75**	25.05**	− .04***
Black	3.45	1.72	2.18	2.03	1.95	1.58	− .00
Visual Field Defect							
White	0.00	0.00	0.00	0.08	0.11	2.31	.01
Black	1.72	0.00	**0.06**	0.08	0.00	22.07*	− .00

Group Ns: White -   26 172 2369 12578 1862
　　　　　　Black -   58 815 8024 9654 154

Differs from severely retarded in D.F.
  *$p<.05$
 **$p<.0001$
***$p<.00001$

retarded and fewer children who were right-handed at age 7 were significant factors. Major malformations of the cardiovascular system and minor malformations of the upper respiratory system or mouth were discriminating conditions with prevalence rates of less than 2%. Three children were blind in one eye and two had a history of major hemorrhage. Lower weight of the mildly retarded at age 7 was retained in the comparison with the average subgroup. Mumps and eye infections were reported less frequently than in histories of the nonretarded.

In comparison between the mildly retarded subgroup and the borderline and average subgroups, canonical correlations between biomedical complications and the subgroup classification were in the low–moderate range of .20 to .32. Higher values of .58 and .63 were obtained in the comparison with the above average in the black and white samples. These summary statistics reflect the contribution of socioeconomic status as a major discriminator in the analyses of concurrent medical characteristics of the mildly retarded CNS normals.

With few exceptions, psychological markers discriminating between the mildly retarded and higher IQ subgroups were the same in both samples. None

Table 9-60

**Cardiovascular Disorder, Hemoglobinopathy, and Hemolytic Disease
by IQ Subgroup**

	1 Severely Retarded	2 Mildly Retarded	3 Borderline	4 Average	5 Above Average	χ^2	r_{IQ}
			Percent				
		Documented Cardiovascular Disorder					
White	0.00	0.00	0.17	0.05	0.00	6.35	− .01
Black	3.45	**0.00**	**0.10**	**0.06**	0.00	78.37***	− .02*
			Hemoglobinopathy				
White	0.00	0.00	0.00	0.05	0.00	2.11	− .00
Black	5.17	**0.86**	**0.60**	**0.47**	1.30	26.64**	− .02*
			Hemolytic Disease				
White	0.00	0.00	0.04	0.02	0.05	0.69	.00
Black	1.72	0.12	**0.05**	**0.05**	0.00	28.21**	− .01

Group Ns: White - 26 172 2369 12578 1862

Black - 58 815 8024 9654 154

Differs from severely retarded in D.F.
   *$p<.05$
  **$p<.0001$
 ***$p<.00001$

was unique to the CNS normals. Canonical correlations ranged from .48 in the comparison with the borderline in both samples to .85 and .86 in the extreme group comparisons (Table 9-74). Separation between the mildly retarded and the average subgroup was greater among blacks than whites. The major discriminators were scores on the Auditory–Vocal Association and Draw-A-Person Tests and the arithmetic subtest of the Wide Range Achievement Test (see Tables 9-66 and 9-69). Tactile finger recognition was less accurate in the mildly retarded subgroups, as was performance on the Bender–Gestalt Test (Table 34, Appendix 5). Lower scores on the spelling subtest of the WRAT was a minor discriminator in both samples. Evaluations of behavior in the testing situation at age 7 indicated more overall abnormality in the mildly retarded subgroups,

Table 9-61
Liver Infection by IQ Subgroup

	1 Severely Retarded	2 Mildly Retarded	3 Borderline	4 Average	5 Above Average	χ^2	r_{IQ}
			Percent				
White	0.00	0.00	0.25	0.09	0.00	7.83	$-.02*$
Black	1.72	0.00	**0.02**	**0.05**	0.00	39.54**	$-.01$

Group Ns: White - 26 172 2366 12560 1860
Black - 58 815 8023 9652 154

Differs from severely retarded in D.F.
*$p<.01$
**$p<.00001$

Table 9-62
Right Handedness by IQ Subgroup

	1 Severely Retarded	2 Mildly Retarded	3 Borderline	4 Average	5 Above Average	χ^2	r_{IQ}
			Percent				
White	76.00	80.59	85.45	86.97	87.74	13.73**	.02*
Black	76.36	83.89	**87.89**	**88.91**	**93.46**	31.53***	.04***

Group Ns: White- 25 170 2364 12555 1860
Black- 55 813 8012 9643 153

Differs from severely and mildly retarded in D.F.s
*$p <.05$
**$p <.01$
***$p <.00001$

Table 9-63
Hematoma, Spasmus Nutans, and Hypoxia by IQ Subgroup

	1 Severely Retarded	2 Mildly Retarded	3 Borderline	4 Average	5 Above Average	χ^2	r_{IQ}
			Percent				

Subdural Hematoma or Effusion

White	0.00	0.00	0.00	0.01	0.00	0.35	−.00
Black	1.72	0.12	**0.04**	**0.01**	0.00	55.41***	−.03**
Group Ns: White -	26	172	2369	12578	1862		
Black -	58	815	8024	9654	154		

Spasmus Nutans

White	0.00	0.00	0.00	0.01	0.00	0.35	.00
Black	1.72	0.12	**0.06**	**0.06**	0.00	23.43**	−.02*
Group Ns: White -	26	172	2369	12578	1862		
Black -	58	815	8024	9654	154		

Hypoxia Without Unconsciousness

White	0.00	1.76	0.22	0.31	0.27	12.53*	−.01
Black	1.72	0.37	0.12	**0.06**	0.00	21.57**	−.02**
Group Ns: White -	26	170	2307	12247	1824		
Black -	58	814	8009	9631	154		

Differs from severely retarded in D.F.
*$p<.05$
**$p<.001$
***$p<.00001$

poorer goal orientation, shorter attention span, lower frustration tolerance, more dependency, and less spontaneity as evidenced by lower ratings for impulsiveness, assertiveness, and emotionality. Among whites, the mildly retarded were rated as less fearful and less hostile than borderline children and among blacks as less self-confident and less communicative than the average and the above average. Control variables retained in the analyses of concurrent psychological characteristics were socioeconomic status and, among whites, sex ratio (fewer males). Both were consistent but relatively minor discriminators.

Table 9-64

Standardized Coefficients for Seven-Year Psychological Discriminators Between the Severely Retarded and Comparison Subgroups

Variable	Comparison Subgroup							
	White				Black			
	MR	BL	AV	AA	MR	BL	AV	AA
Abnormal behavior summary rating	.42	.60	.91	.84	.61	.87	.91	.15
Auditory-Vocal Association score	−.30	−.25	−.08	−.05	−.35	−.11	−.08	−.22
Draw-A-Person score	−.34	−.16	−.03	−.05	−.13	−.08	−.03	−.13
Tactile finger recognition, right hand	−.34	−.22	−.10	−.12	—	−.05	−.03	−.13
Goal orientation	—	−.04	−.07	−.01	−.08	−.15	−.12	−.08
Fearfulness	—	−.27	−.18	−.11	−.29	−.25	−.10	—
Dependency	—	—	.01	.05	.10	.07	.05	.09
WRAT arithmetic score	—	—	−.08	−.08	—	−.05	−.06	−.41
Tactile finger recognition, left hand	—	−.15	−.07	−.02	—	—	−.01	—
Verbal communication	—	—	—	−.07	—	−.12	−.06	—
Activity level	—	—	.03	—	.12	—	—	—
Attention span	−.04	−.06	−.07	−.07	—	—	—	—
Percent male	.29	.03	.004	—	—	—	—	—
Self-confidence	.23	.10	—	—	—	—	—	—
Separation anxiety	—	.17	.10	—	—	—	—	—
Impulsivity	.16	—	—	—	—	—	—	—
WRAT spelling score	—	−.13	—	—	—	—	—	—
Assertiveness	—	—	—	.07	—	—	—	—
Socioeconomic index	—	—	—	−.05	—	—	—	—
Hostility	—	—	—	—	−.29	−.16	−.09	—
Frustration tolerance	—	—	—	—	—	−.05	−.03	—
WRAT reading score	—	—	—	—	—	—	—	−.03
Canonical correlation	.62*	.40*	.48*	.83*	.47*	.50*	.72*	.94*

*$p<.00001$

Table 9-65
Abnormal Behavior Summary Rating by IQ Subgroup

	1 Severely Retarded	2 Mildly Retarded	3 Borderline	4 Average	5 Above Average	χ^2	r_{IQ}
			Percent				
White	72.73	**17.34**	*3.44*	*0.32*	*0.11*	1838.92*	−.18*
Black	67.24	**13.26**	*1.04*	*0.15*	*0.00*	2989.73*	−.23*

Group Ns: White- 22 173 2386 12647 1876
 Black- 58 837 8211 9858 157

Differs from severely retarded in D.F.
Differs from severely and mildly retarded in D.F.s
p <.00001

Table 9-66
Auditory-Vocal Association and Draw-A-Person Scores by IQ Subgroup

	1 Severely Retarded		2 Mildly Retarded		3 Borderline		4 Average		5 Above Average		F	r_{IQ}
	M	S.D.	M	S.D.	M	S.D.	M	S.D.	M	S.D.		

Auditory-Vocal Association Score

	1 Severely Retarded		2 Mildly Retarded		3 Borderline		4 Average		5 Above Average		F	r_{IQ}
White	31.4	16.3	**54.9**	**13.6**	*73.3*	*12.0*	*88.2*	*12.4*	*106.2*	*15.8*	2030.04*	.65*
Black	27.6	17.7	**51.4**	**11.9**	*67.0*	*12.1*	*78.5*	*11.0*	*94.0*	*13.8*	2040.24*	.61*

Group Ns: White- 12 156 2345 12564 1862
 Black - 32 796 8017 9730 155

Draw-A-Person Score

	1 Severely Retarded		2 Mildly Retarded		3 Borderline		4 Average		5 Above Average		F	r_{IQ}
White	60.1	7.9	**76.5**	**10.2**	*87.0*	*10.4*	*96.5*	*12.4*	*105.9*	*14.4*	753.99*	.44*
Black	64.2	10.0	**77.9**	**10.3**	*88.7*	*11.4*	*96.2*	*12.7*	*109.6*	*15.4*	856.06*	.44*

Group Ns: White - 12 166 2383 12645 1875
 Black - 30 817 8177 9837 156

Differs from severely retarded in D.F.
Differs from severely and mildly retarded in D.F.s
p<.00001

Table 9-67

Tactile Finger Recognition Scores by IQ Subgroup

	1 Severely Retarded		2 Mildly Retarded		3 Borderline		4 Average		5 Above Average		F	r_{IQ}
	M	S.D.	M	S.D.	M	S.D.	M	S.D.	M	S.D.		

Tactile Finger Recognition, Right Hand

White	1.7	1.6	**3.8**	**1.2**	**4.5**	**0.8**	**4.7**	**0.6**	**4.8**	**0.4**	242.38*	.21*
Black	3.3	1.5	4.1	1.1	*4.5*	*0.8*	*4.6*	*0.6*	**4.6**	**0.4**	175.63*	.18*

Group Ns: White - 11 166 2367 12610 1871

Black - 29 830 8178 9830 156

Tactile Finger Recognition, Left Hand

White	2.1	2.1	3.7	1.4	*4.5*	*0.8*	*4.7*	*0.6*	**4.8**	**0.5**	238.53*	.20*
Black	3.5	1.5	4.1	1.1	*4.5*	*0.8*	*4.7*	*0.6*	4.8	0.4	140.97*	.16*

Group Ns: White - 11 166 2367 12607 1871

Black - 29 829 8176 9831 156

Differs from severely retarded in D.F.
Differs from mildly retarded in D.F.
Differs from severely and mildly retarded in D.F.s
*p<.00001

Table 9-68
Behavior Ratings by IQ Subgroup

	1 Severely Retarded		2 Mildly Retarded		3 Borderline		4 Average		5 Above Average		F	r$_{IQ}$
	M	S.D.	M	S.D.	M	S.D.	M	S.D.	M	S.D.		

Goal Orientation

	M	S.D.	M	S.D.	M	S.D.	M	S.D.	M	S.D.	F	r$_{IQ}$
White	1.9	0.6	2.4	0.6	*2.7*	*0.5*	*3.0*	*0.4*	*3.2*	*0.4*	550.70***	.38***
Black	1.9	0.7	**2.5**	**0.6**	*2.8*	*0.4*	*3.0*	*0.3*	*3.2*	*0.4*	595.73***	.35***

Group Ns: White - 20 172 2364 12578 1863
Black - 54 830 8145 9819 155

Fearfulness

	M	S.D.	M	S.D.	M	S.D.	M	S.D.	M	S.D.	F	r$_{IQ}$
White	2.3	1.0	3.0	0.8	*3.1*	*0.7*	*3.0*	*0.6*	2.7	0.6	135.51***	−.18***
Black	2.3	1.2	**3.0**	**0.8**	3.0	0.6	**2.9**	**0.5**	2.7	0.5	73.92***	−.10***

Group Ns: White - 22 172 2373 12586 1862
Black - 55 833 8177 9824 155

Dependency

	M	S.D.	M	S.D.	M	S.D.	M	S.D.	M	S.D.	F	r$_{IQ}$
White	4.1	1.0	3.7	0.8	*3.3*	*0.6*	*3.1*	*0.5*	2.9	0.5	322.73***	−.30***
Black	4.2	1.0	**3.6**	**0.8**	*3.2*	*0.5*	*3.0*	*0.4*	2.8	0.5	442.12***	−.30***

Group Ns: White - 20 172 2367 12581 1862
Black - 50 834 8177 9825 155

Verbal Communication

	M	S.D.	M	S.D.	M	S.D.	M	S.D.	M	S.D.	F	r$_{IQ}$
White	2.6	1.6	2.6	1.0	2.7	0.8	2.9	0.6	**3.1**	**0.5**	117.57***	.19***
Black	2.4	1.4	2.5	0.8	**2.6**	**0.6**	**2.8**	**0.6**	*3.2*	*0.6*	156.85***	.20***

Group Ns: White - 21 172 2373 12581 1862
Black - 54 834 8170 9827 154

Activity Level

	M	S.D.	M	S.D.	M	S.D.	M	S.D.	M	S.D.	F	r$_{IQ}$
White	4.0	1.0	3.0	0.8	3.0	0.7	**3.0**	**0.5**	3.0	0.4	30.91*	−.01
Black	3.5	1.2	**2.9**	**0.9**	2.9	0.6	3.0	0.5	3.0	0.4	28.89*	.04*

Group Ns: White - 22 173 2374 12592 1862
Black - 55 832 8182 9823 155

(continued)

Table 9-68 (continued)

	1 Severely Retarded		2 Mildly Retarded		3 Borderline		4 Average		5 Above Average		F	r_{IQ}
	M	S.D.	M	S.D.	M	S.D.	M	S.D.	M	S.D.		

Attention Span

	1		2		3		4		5		F	r_{IQ}
White	1.5	0.9	**2.5**	**0.9**	**2.8**	**0.6**	*3.0*	*0.4*	*3.1*	*0.3*	227.04***	.23***
Black	1.9	1.3	2.6	0.8	2.9	0.5	*3.0*	*0.4*	3.0	0.3	193.67***	.18***

Group Ns: White -   20 170 2357 12572 1862

Black -   53 818 8125 9812 155

Self-confidence

	1		2		3		4		5		F	r_{IQ}
White	2.9	1.0	**2.5**	**0.7**	**2.6**	**0.6**	2.8	0.5	3.1	0.5	246.05***	.27***
Black	2.6	0.7	2.5	0.6	2.7	0.5	*2.9*	*0.4*	*3.1*	*0.4*	247.34***	.24***

Group Ns: White -   16 169 2364 12574 1859

Black -   33 820 8153 9820 155

Separation Anxiety

	1		2		3		4		5		F	r_{IQ}
White	3.4	1.0	3.1	0.8	**2.9**	**0.6**	**2.8**	**0.5**	2.7	0.5	66.11***	− .15***
Black	2.7	1.0	2.9	0.6	2.8	0.5	2.8	0.5	2.7	0.5	14.19***	− .06***

Group Ns: White -   17 126 1957 10427 1575

Black -   44 666 6383 7702 138

Impulsivity

	1		2		3		4		5		F	r_{IQ}
White	3.4	1.2	**2.7**	**0.8**	2.9	0.5	*3.0*	*0.3*	3.0	0.2	45.09***	.08***
Black	2.9	1.3	2.8	0.7	2.9	0.4	*3.0*	*0.3*	3.0	0.1	108.91***	.14***

Group Ns: White -   20 172 2369 12583 1863

Black -   54 830 8171 9826 155

Assertiveness

	1		2		3		4		5		F	r_{IQ}
White	3.4	1.1	2.6	0.7	2.7	0.6	2.8	0.4	**2.9**	**0.3**	69.35***	.13***
Black	2.9	1.2	2.6	0.7	2.7	0.5	2.8	0.4	2.8	0.4	56.92***	.11***

Group Ns: White -   22 171 2370 12571 1862

Black -   50 829 8175 9831 154

(continued)

Table 9-68 (continued)

	1 Severely Retarded		2 Mildly Retarded		3 Borderline		4 Average		5 Above Average		F	r_{IQ}
	M	S.D.	M	S.D.	M	S.D.	M	S.D.	M	S.D.		

Hostility												
White	3.2	0.6	2.9	0.5	*3.0*	*0.4*	3.0	0.3	3.0	0.3	8.06***	−.03*
Black	2.8	0.6	**3.0**	**0.4**	**3.0**	**0.3**	**3.0**	**0.3**	2.9	0.3	6.21**	−.00

Group Ns: White - 21 171 2370 12575 1863
          Black - 46 834 8177 9829 154

Frustration Tolerance												
White	2.3	1.2	2.5	0.7	2.6	0.6	2.8	0.4	*3.0*	*0.3*	192.73***	.25***
Black	2.2	1.0	2.5	0.6	**2.7**	**0.5**	**2.9**	**0.4**	3.0	0.1	215.32***	.22***

Group Ns: White - 20 169 2371 12580 1861
          Black - 46 829 8165 9821 155

Differs from severely retarded in D.F.
Differs from mildly retarded in D.F.
Differs from severely and mildly retarded in D.F.s
  *p<.001
 **p<.0001
***p<.00001

Table 9-69

Wide Range Achievement Test Scores by IQ Subgroup

	1 Severely Retarded		2 Mildly Retarded		3 Borderline		4 Average		5 Above Average		F	r_{IQ}
	M	S.D.	M	S.D.	M	S.D.	M	S.D.	M	S.D.		

WRAT Arithmetic Score

	M	S.D.	M	S.D.	M	S.D.	M	S.D.	M	S.D.	F	r_{IQ}
White	3.5	3.3	10.5	6.1	*17.9*	*4.3*	***21.9***	***2.9***	***24.4***	***2.9***	1769.04*	.57*
Black	4.6	4.5	12.9	5.7	***18.2***	***4.2***	***21.3***	***3.5***	***24.1***	***3.2***	1488.78*	.52*

Group Ns: White -   10   165   2375   12623   1870
          Black -   33   825   8183   9836   156

WRAT Spelling Score

	M	S.D.	M	S.D.	M	S.D.	M	S.D.	M	S.D.	F	r_{IQ}
White	4.5	6.2	14.0	6.6	***21.4***	***5.4***	26.8	5.3	32.0	5.8	1289.77*	.55*
Black	7.4	9.0	15.6	6.6	*21.3*	*5.2*	25.3	5.2	31.1	6.0	1216.71*	.50*

Group Ns: White -   11   164   2373   12615   1869
          Black -   32   826   8182   9826   156

WRAT Reading Score

	M	S.D.	M	S.D.	M	S.D.	M	S.D.	M	S.D.	F	r_{IQ}
White	8.0	7.2	17.9	10.4	29.1	10.5	39.9	11.3	51.8	12.1	1240.72*	.55*
Black	8.8	10.0	20.6	10.2	29.5	9.6	36.3	9.9	**47.6**	**11.6**	997.21*	.47*

Group Ns: White -   11   163   2369   12621   1871
          Black -   32   826   8188   9835   155

Differs from severely retarded in D.F.
Differs from mildly retarded in D.F.
Differs from severely and mildly retarded in D.F.s
*p<.00001

Table 9-70
Standardized Coefficients for Prenatal, Obstetric, and Neonatal Discriminators Between the Mildly Retarded and Comparison Subgroups

Variable	Comparison Subgroup					
	White			Black		
	BL	AV	AA	BL	AV	AA
Maternal SRA score	−.37	−.31	−.33	−.34	−.34	−.39
Maternal education	—	−.18	−.19	−.41	−.35	−.18
Socioeconomic index	—	−.18	−.35	−.15	−.15	−.42
Major cardiovascular malformations	.34	.23	.14	.10	.05	—
Head circumference at birth	—	−.25	−.19	—	−.19	−.18
Housing density	.30	.23	.15	—	.21	—
Retarded mother	.29	.30	.15	—	.11	—
Pregnancy-free interval	—	—	−.17	−.33	−.23	—
Retarded father	.15	.20	—	—	.06	—
Inhalation anesthetic at delivery	—	.15	.12	—	−.10	—
Parity	—	—	.08	—	.02	.30
Age at menarche	.31	.18	.11	—	—	—
Major upper respiratory or mouth malformations	.21	.25	.11	—	—	—
Urinary tract infection in pregnancy	.25	.15	.11	—	—	—
Induction of labor	−.24	−.12	−.09	—	—	—
Cigarettes per day in pregnancy	−.26	−.19	—	—	—	—
Abdomino-pelvic x-rays	−.27	−.13	—	—	—	—
Minor ear malformations	—	.15	—	—	—	—
Gestation at registration	—	.10	—	—	—	—
Recent maternal illnesses	—	—	−.10	—	—	—
Respiratory difficulty in newborn	—	—	.10	—	—	—
Hospitalizations since LMP	—	—	.08	—	—	—
Midforceps delivery	—	—	−.02	—	—	—
Percent male	—	—	—	.13	.14	.09
Hematocrit in pregnancy	—	—	—	−.13	−.08	−.06
Length at birth	—	—	—	−.23	−.18	—
Multiple birth	—	—	—	.15	.16	—
Number of prenatal visits	—	—	—	—	−.15	−.13
Toxemia	—	—	—	.14	.13	—
Organic heart disease in pregnancy	—	—	—	.13	.08	—
Conduction anesthetic at delivery	—	—	—	−.10	−.07	—
Prior fetal death	—	—	—	.19	—	—

(continued)

Table 9-70 (continued)

| | Comparison Subgroup | | | | | |
| Variable | White | | | Black | | |
	BL	AV	AA	BL	AV	AA
Multiple apneic episodes	—	—	—	.19	—	—
Gestational age	—	—	—	−.17	—	—
Major musculoskeletal malformations	—	—	—	.14	—	—
Maternal mental illness	—	—	—	.15	—	—
Primary apnea	—	—	—	.10	—	—
Maternal height	—	—	—	—	−.08	—
Maternal age	—	—	—	—	—	−.46
Canonical correlation	*.19**	*.19**	*.61**	*.19**	*.30**	*.63**

*$p < .00001$

Table 9-71
Standardized Coefficients for All Discriminators Through Age Four
Between the Mildly Retarded and Comparison Subgroups

| Variable | Comparison Subgroup | | | | | |
| | White | | | Black | | |
	BL	AV	AA	BL	AV	AA
Stanford-Binet IQ at age 4	− .48	− .19	− .18	− .35	− .28	− .62
Fine motor score at age 4	− .03	− .12	− .18	− .22	− .19	− .22
Maternal SRA score	− .08	− .06	− .06	− .08	− .09	− .07
Abnormal language expression at age 3	.13	.32	.26	.18	.16	—
Graham-Ernhart Block Sort score at age 4	− .29	− .22	− .24	− .08	− .11	—
Abnormal behavior summary rating at age 4	.07	.21	.05	.15	.17	—
Gross motor score at age 4	− .21	− .07	− .04	− .13	− .06	—
Delayed motor development at 1 year	.15	.18	.08	—	.09	—
Abnormal speech production at age 3	.07	.13	—	.11	.06	—
Socioeconomic index	—	—	− .12	− .02	− .003	− .17
Abnormal language reception at age 3	—	.22	.09	—	.05	—
Head circumference at 1 year	− .13	—	− .09	—	− .08	—
Maternal education	—	− .01	—	− .16	− .11	—
Attention span at age 4	—	− .09	− .09	—	− .10	—
Goal orientation at age 4	—	− .06	—	− .06	− .07	—
Bayley motor score at 8 months	—	—	− .04	− .04	− .06	—
Abnormal hearing at age 3	.08	.02	—	.03	—	—
Bayley mental score at 8 months	—	− .08	—	− .01	− .03	—
Head circumference at age 4	—	− .12	—	—	—	− .09
Response to directions at age 4	—	—	− .07	—	− .12	—
Retarded mother	—	.11	—	—	.02	—
Percent male	− .21	− .14	− .10	—	—	—
Age at menarche	.12	.06	.04	—	—	—
Intensity of social response at 8 months	− .06	− .05	− .02	—	—	—
Induction of labor	− .05	− .05	− .02	—	—	—
Urinary tract infection in pregnancy	.10	—	.07	—	—	—
Right dominance at age 4	− .11	− .05	—	—	—	—
Abdomino-pelvic x-rays	− .10	− .05	—	—	—	—

(continued)

Table 9-71 (continued)

Variable	Comparison Subgroup					
	White			Black		
	BL	AV	AA	BL	AV	AA
Major upper respiratory or mouth malformations	—	.10	.04	—	—	—
Retarded father	.07	.06	—	—	—	—
Housing density	—	.04	.03	—	—	—
Inhalation anesthetic at delivery	—	.05	.02	—	—	—
Cigarettes per day in pregnancy	—	− .09	—	—	—	—
Undescended testicle at 1 year	—	.07	—	—	—	—
Congenital heart disease at 1 year	—	.04	—	—	—	—
Verbal communication at age 4	—	—	—	− .04	− .06	− .05
Dependency at age 4	—	—	—	.19	.12	—
Pregnancy-free interval	—	—	—	− .10	− .07	—
Organic heart disease in pregnancy	—	—	—	.07	.04	—
Weight at 4 months	—	—	—	− .06	− .05	—
Weight at 1 year	—	—	—	− .06	− .01	—
Hypotonia at 1 year	—	—	—	.16	—	—
Multiple apneic episodes	—	—	—	.09	—	—
Major musculoskeletal malformations	—	—	—	.07	—	—
Prior fetal death	—	—	—	.06	—	—
Primary apnea	—	—	—	.04	—	—
Gestational age	—	—	—	− .03	—	—
Impulsivity at age 4	—	—	—	—	− .09	—
Toxemia	—	—	—	—	.05	—
Number of prenatal visits	—	—	—	—	− .03	—
Hematocrit in pregnancy	—	—	—	—	− .03	—
Maternal height	—	—	—	—	− .02	—
Height at age 4	—	—	—	—	− .01	—
Multiple birth	—	—	—	—	.002	—
Maternal age	—	—	—	—	—	− .17
Parity	—	—	—	—	—	.17
Canonical correlation	*.43**	*.44**	*.86**	*.39**	*.59**	*.83**

*$p < .00001$

Table 9-72

Standardized Coefficients for Seven-Year Family and Demographic Discriminators Between the Mildly Retarded and Comparison Subgroups

| Variable | Comparison Subgroup | | | | | |
| | White | | | Black | | |
	BL	AV	AA	BL	AV	AA
Socioeconomic index	−.62	−.53	−.54	—	−.16	−.62
Maternal education	—	−.25	−.21	−.45	−.31	−.29
Retardation in siblings	.44	.38	.24	.27	.18	—
Mother employed	−.52	−.22	−.10	—	−.17	—
Number of subsequent pregnancies	—	.26	.11	.18	.27	—
Number of changes in residence	—	.26	.21	.17	.14	—
Housing density	—	—	.10	.41	.23	—
Family size	—	—	.10	—	.17	.39
Public assistance	—	—	.16	.21	.20	—
Study child adopted or in foster home	—	.11	—	.04	—	—
Maternal age	—	.12	—	—	—	−.41
Mother's additional schooling	—	−.09	—	—	−.13	—
Paternal age	—	.05	.04	—	—	—
Father employed	—	—	—	−.11	−.08	—
Child care	—	—	—	−.28	—	—
Canonical correlation	*.13**	*.15**	*.59**	*.17**	*.29**	*.57**

*$p < .00001$

Table 9-73
Standardized Coefficients for Seven-Year Pediatric Discriminators
in the Mildly Retarded and Comparison Subgroups

| Variable | White | | | Black | | |
	BL	AV	AA	BL	AV	AA
Socioeconomic index	− .38	− .42	− .68	− .48	− .54	− .76
Head circumference	− .23	− .33	− .30	− .29	− .32	− .35
Abnormal gait	.29	.32	.22	.43	.43	.18
Failure to thrive	.20	.28	.15	.16	.17	—
Cyanotic congenital heart disease	.26	.10	.11	.21	.14	—
Color blindness	—	.17	.14	.19	.21	.12
Diagnostic or other medical procedures	—	.11	.08	.24	.20	.10
Strabismus	.21	.16	.12	.17	.13	—
Abnormal shape of skull	.44	.30	.12	—	—	—
Cranial nerve abnormality[a]	.26	.27	.15	—	—	—
Minor ear malformations	.22	.18	.10	—	—	—
Nystagmus	.24	.15	.08	—	—	—
Acyanotic congenital heart disease	.18	.10	—	—	—	—
Major alimentary malformations	.15	—	—	—	—	—
Symptomatic intoxication[b]	—	.13	—	—	—	—
Ear infection	—	.12	—	—	—	—
Minor musculoskeletal malformations	—	.10	—	—	—	—
Chickenpox	—	− .08	—	—	—	—
Severe burns	—	.07	—	—	—	—
Right handedness	—	—	—	− .17	− .11	− .15
Mumps	—	—	—	− .14	− .10	− .13
Abnormal reflexes	—	—	—	.23	.16	—
Minor upper respiratory or mouth malformations	—	—	—	.17	.13	—
Monocular blindness	—	—	—	.15	—	—
Major cardiovascular malformations	—	—	—	—	.09	—
Major hemorrhage	—	—	—	—	.08	—
Weight	—	—	—	—	− .08	—
Eye infection	—	—	—	—	—	− .15
Canonical correlation	.27*	.23*	.63*	.20*	.32*	.58*

[a]Other than auditory nerve

[b]Agents other than hydrocarbon, lead, or salicylate

*$p < .00001$

Table 9-74
Standardized Coefficients for Seven-Year Psychological Discriminators Between the Mildly Retarded and Comparison Subgroups

Variable	Comparison Subgroup					
	White			Black		
	BL	AV	AA	BL	AV	AA
Auditory-Vocal Association score	−.35	−.21	−.17	−.34	−.37	−.57
Draw-A-Person score	−.25	−.12	−.11	−.33	−.20	−.37
WRAT arithmetic score	−.38	−.53	−.32	−.23	−.26	—
Abnormal behavior summary rating	.14	.35	.05	.26	.14	—
Socioeconomic index	−.07	—	−.13	−.09	−.06	−.16
Goal orientation	−.05	−.11	−.07	−.15	−.18	—
Tactile finger recognition, left hand	−.21	−.16	−.09	−.05	−.05	—
Dependency	.11	.09	.05	.13	.12	—
Impulsivity	−.10	−.09	−.04	−.06	−.11	—
Assertiveness	−.14	−.06	−.07	−.07	−.05	—
Bender-Gestalt error score	—	.09	.25	.07	.12	—
Tactile finger recognition, right hand	—	−.11	−.06	−.09	−.06	—
Emotionality	—	−.04	—	−.05	−.06	—
Attention span	—	−.03	−.03	—	−.01	—
Frustration tolerance	—	—	−.09	−.01	−.03	—
WRAT spelling score	−.10	—	—	−.04	—	—
Percent male	−.10	−.07	−.04	—	—	—
Fearfulness	−.10	—	—	—	—	—
Hostility	−.08	—	—	—	—	—
Self-confidence	—	—	—	—	−.02	−.10
Verbal communication	—	—	—	—	—	−.10
Canonical correlation	*.48**	*.49**	*.85**	*.48**	*.69**	*.86**

*p<.00001

10

Familial Patterns
of Mental Retardation

The frequency of retardation, or IQ under 70, was determined among the relatives of the severely and mildly retarded children. Siblings, half siblings, cousins, and twins were identified in the study cohort. In families with two affected individuals, each was counted as both an index and secondary case. This procedure is unbiased in studies such as the Collaborative Project, in which families with more than one affected child were not more likely to be identified than families with only one affected child.

SIBLINGS

The severely retarded white children had 20 siblings in the study. None of these siblings was retarded, and their mean IQ of 103.4 (SD = 12.1) was near that of the white sample. The 58 siblings of the mildly retarded white children showed a different pattern; 12 (20.7%) were retarded, and their mean IQ was only 84.8 (SD = 18.1). Figure 10-1 shows that the distribution of these siblings' IQ scores is clearly shifted downward. The apparent bimodality of the curve for the siblings of the mildly retarded was unrelated to socioeconomic status, sex, or siblings' IQ, and therefore was most likely a random fluctuation due to small sample size.

In contrast to the whites, the siblings of severely and mildly retarded black children did not show a different pattern. Retardation was common among siblings of both the severely and mildly retarded (20.8% of 40 and 21.1% of 327, respectively), and the mean IQs of the siblings were very similar (77.8 and 78.1, respectively). These data suggest a less clear distinction between the severely and mildly retarded groups for blacks than for whites. White children with IQs below 50 were characterized by siblings with normal IQs, average socioeconomic status, and a very high incidence of central nervous system pathology—all

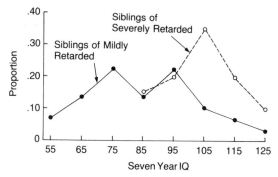

FIGURE 10-1.   IQ distribution for siblings of severely retarded (IQ < 50) and mildly retarded (IQ 50–69) white children.

consistent with previous descriptions of retarded populations (Zigler, 1967, 1978). Part of the overlap between the retarded groups among blacks may have been caused by too high an IQ cutoff because IQ distributions of black populations are generally shifted downward. In support of this hypothesis, only 6 of 37 (16%) severely retarded black children with IQs between 40 and 49 had any major CNS disorders, compared to 63 of 91 (69%) with IQs below 40. Also, the mean socioeconomic index score of the latter group was significantly higher (37.6 vs. 23.5, $p < .001$) and comparable to the mean score of 38.6 in the total black sample).

In an additional analysis, the IQ cutoffs for blacks were shifted, redefining severe retardation as an IQ below 40 and mild retardation as an IQ between 40 and 59. The distributions of the IQs of the two new groups of siblings did differ slightly (Figure 10-2). The 20 siblings of the severely retarded had a mean IQ of 77.8, with a large standard deviation of 20.2. The 73 siblings of the mildly retarded had a similar mean (76.0), but a lower standard deviation (13.7). The greater variability among the siblings of the severely retarded children resulted from two brothers with IQs of 25 and 38; both had epilepsy. Without this

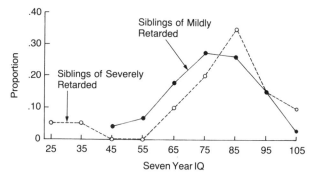

FIGURE 10-2.   IQ distribution for siblings of severely retarded (IQ < 40) and mildly retarded (IQ 40–59) black children.

Table 10-1

Reported Retardation Among Siblings of Severely Retarded White Children

Study Child's Diagnosis	Sibling's Diagnosis
Phenylketonuria	Phenylketonuria
Aminoaciduria	Aminoaciduria (died age 9 months)
Cerebral palsy	Cerebral palsy, epilepsy, severe retardation
Epilepsy	Epilepsy, severe retardation, institutionalized
Carnosinemia	Epilepsy, severe encephalopathy
Epilepsy	Hydrocephaly
Chromosomal translocation	Post-meningitic encephalopathy
Undifferentiated	Educably retarded, in special classes
Undifferentiated	In special classes, could print name at age 10

family, the difference between the two group means (76.0 vs. 83.1, SD = 13.4) was nearly significant ($p = .055$).

The familial incidence of severe retardation is thought to be due largely to the presence of specific abnormalities, none of which was present among the 20 study siblings of the severely retarded white children. There was, however, limited information available for nonstudy siblings because mothers were asked during both prenatal and 7-year interviews about retardation in all family members including their associated diagnoses. The frequency of retardation could then be determined for all siblings of severely retarded white children. Excluded were any children 1 year of age or less, except one child who died at age 9 months, apparently from the same aminoaciduria as his brother in the study. Based on this analysis, there was fairly good evidence that 9 of 196 siblings were retarded. The diagnoses of these 9 sibling pairs are shown in Table 10-1. This frequency of retardation among siblings (4.6%) was higher than in the total white sample (1.7%), but should be interpreted with caution because it is based on maternal report. There were, however, several instances of the same diagnosis for siblings within a family. The two cases in the study classified as undifferentiated had relatively high IQs and the retardation in these families appeared to be cultural–familial.

HALF SIBLINGS

The half siblings in this study were all maternal. Different fathers were reported by the mother in family history interviews. The severely retarded white children had no half siblings in the study, and the mildly retarded white children had only seven. None of the seven was retarded, and their mean IQ was 89.1 (SD = 9.4). The severely retarded black children had four half siblings in the study. One was retarded (25.0%), and their mean IQ was 81.3. The mildly retarded blacks had 78 half siblings, 20 of whom were retarded (25.6%). Their mean IQ was 79.5 (SD = 11.4). Thirteen of the mildly retarded black children had both full and half siblings in the study. Two of their 16 full siblings were retarded; their mean IQ was 79.0 (SD = 9.9). Five of their 19 half siblings were retarded; their mean IQ was 76.7 (SD = 11.9). One might expect more retardation and a lower mean IQ among the more closely related full siblings, but this was not the case.

COUSINS

The severely retarded white children had 23 first cousins in the study. None was retarded, and their mean IQ was 102.4 (SD = 14.9). Four of 58 first cousins of the mildly retarded white children were retarded (6.9%), and the cousins' mean IQ was 92.1 (SD = 15.0).

Like the full siblings, the cousins of the severely and mildly retarded black children had similar scores. Four of 35 first cousins of the severely retarded blacks were retarded (11.4%), and the mean IQ of the 35 was 86.5 (SD = 17.8). Twenty of 316 first cousins of the mildly retarded were retarded (6.3%); the mean IQ of the first cousins was 87.3 (SD = 12.9). The cousins of both the severely and mildly retarded had mean IQs similar to that of the black sample, whereas the full siblings of both retarded groups had scores below the sample mean.

TWINS

The number of retarded twins in the cohort was too small for classical twin studies of severe and mild retardation. Of 65 retarded twins in the Collaborative Project, only 53 could be used for pair-wise analyses because the co-twin had died or, in three cases, the zygosity had not been established. The twins were identified as monozygotic (MZ) or dizygotic (DZ) from the comparison of nine blood groups, finger and palm prints, and gross and microscopic examination of the placenta (Myrianthopoulos, 1970). The IQs of the 53 retarded twins are shown with the scores of their co-twins in Table 10-2. The only severely retarded MZ twin had an IQ of 48, 2 points lower than her co-twin, who was classified as mildly retarded. The analyses for DZ twins showed that five co-twins of severely retarded black children had a mean IQ of 79.2 (SD = 13.9) compared to 74.3 (SD = 17.6) for 23 co-twins of the mildly retarded. For the very small sample of white DZ pairs, the two co-twins of the severely retarded had a

Table 10-2

IQs of Twin Pairs, One or Both Retarded, by Zygosity, Ethnicity, and Sex

	Monozygotic Twins				Dizygotic Twins			
	IQ Scores	Sex	IQ Scores	Sex	IQ Scores	Sex	IQ Scores	Sex
Black	48,50	G	65,71	B	21,88	BG	62,88	BG
	50,54	G	68,82	B	25,72	BG	64,73	BG
	51,57	G	68,85	G	25,83	BG	64,74	BG
	59,69	B	69,73	G	34,59	GB	64,83	BG
	60,62	G	69,80	G	37,94	BG	66,95	GB
	63,83	G			52,60	BG	67,73	GG
					59,73	BB	67,74	BG
					60,61	GB	67,99	GG
					64,67	BB	68,73	GG
					64,69	BB	68,82	BG
					52,80	BG	68,92	GB
					62,120	BG		
White	60,62	G			25,94	BB	64,67	GB
					47,88	BG	64,70	GB
					63,69	GB		

mean IQ of 91.0, much higher than the mean of 66.6 for the three co-twins of the mildly retarded.

Overall, 12 co-twins of the 18 retarded MZ twins and 14 co-twins of the 35 DZ twins were retarded. There was a greater resemblance between MZ than DZ pairs but, because of the small samples, concordance for retardation was not significantly different between the twin types. Assessing risks to the co-twins is complicated by the fact that retardation was more frequent in twins than singletons by a factor of 2.7 in blacks and 1.9 in whites.

Retardation and mean IQ among various types of relatives of the retarded children are summarized in Table 10-3. As noted earlier, families with more than one affected child were not overrepresented in the study; therefore, all affected individuals could be used.

These unique data provide an opportunity to compare familial patterns by severity of retardation and ethnic group. Among whites, the data show a clear distinction between relatives of the severely and the mildly retarded children. This finding agrees with the results of Roberts (1952) that siblings of severely retarded children have higher IQs and less retardation than those of mildly

Table 10-3
Frequency of Retardation and Mean IQ Among Relatives of
Severely and Mildly Retarded

Relationship to Retarded	Severely Retarded				Mildly Retarded			
	N	Percent Retarded	WISC IQ		N	Percent Retarded	WISC IQ	
			Mean	SD			Mean	SD
White								
Monozygotic twin	0	—	—	—	2	100.0	61.0	1.4
Dizygotic twin	2	0.0	91.0	4.2	5	80.0	66.6	3.0
Full sibling	20	0.0	103.4	12.1	58	20.7	84.8	18.1
Half sibling	0	—	—	—	7	0.0	89.1	9.4
First cousin	23	0.0	102.4	14.9	58	6.9	92.1	15.0
Black								
Monozygotic twin	1	100.0	50.0	0.0	15	60.0	65.6	12.9
Dizygotic twin	5	20.0	79.2	13.9	23	39.1	74.3	17.6
Full sibling	40	20.8	77.8	20.2	327	21.1	78.1	13.2
Half sibling	4	25.0	81.3	10.6	78	25.6	79.5	11.4
First cousin	35	11.4	86.5	17.8	316	6.3	87.3	12.9

retarded children. Kamin (1974) pointed out that Roberts' striking results were due to the fact that he separated his severely and mildly retarded children based on their siblings' rather than their own IQs, but his results are not unique. In an earlier study, Roberts (1940) had found higher IQs among siblings of severely than mildly retarded children. Åkesson (1961) reported high frequencies of retardation among the relatives of "high-grade" mental defectives but not among the relatives of "low-grade" defectives. In the present study, both the sibling and first cousin data in the white sample suggest a qualitative difference between severe and mild retardation.

Although there was no retardation among the study siblings of severely retarded whites, additional information on nonstudy siblings revealed a frequency of 4.6%, which was significantly higher than the frequency of 1.7% in the white sample (severe plus mild). Many of these cases were caused by specific genetic abnormalities or associated with major neurological disorders, as would be expected in the two-group theory of retardation (Zigler, 1967).

There is more speculation than evidence in the literature concerning the etiology of mild or cultural–familial retardation (Zigler, 1978). In the current study, the 12-fold increase in the frequency of retardation among full siblings of mildly retarded whites (to 20.7%), compared with the 4-fold increase among first cousins (to 6.9%), could be consistent with genetic or environmental influences. The data for blacks lead to different conclusions. First, the family patterns do not show a clear distinction between the relatives of the severely and mildly retarded. The data support a hypothesis that the entire IQ distribution is shifted downward in the black population so that severely retarded black children with IQs in the 40s are similar to the mildly retarded in terms of central nervous system pathology, socioeconomic status, and familial patterns. Only if the IQ cutoffs for defining severe and mild retardation are shifted downward are the distributions of siblings' IQs at all consistent with the two-group theory.

None of the results of these analyses supports a genetic etiology for familial retardation in blacks. The increased risk of retardation to all types of relatives living with a retarded child—full siblings, half siblings, and even the twins after considering the increased frequency of retardation in all twins (an increase which, of course, must be environmental)—was of the same order of magnitude, about four times the population frequency. On the other hand, first cousins, who lived apart from the retarded children, did not have increased frequencies of retardation or lower mean IQs. Among retarded children with both full and half siblings in the study, half siblings did not have a higher IQ than full siblings, as would be expected under a polygenic hypothesis. Although the samples were small, there was not even a trend in this direction.

In summary, the family data presented in this chapter strongly support the traditional two-group theory of mental retardation in the white sample. In the black sample where most retardation appeared to be of the cultural–familial type, environmental factors were strongly implicated in the etiology, a finding consistent with the concept that the downward shift in the IQ distribution also has an environmental basis.

11

Summary and Conclusions

In modern history, severe mental retardation has been attributed to central nervous system pathology, and mild mental retardation to environmental factors or to an interaction between genetic and environmental factors (Zigler, 1967, 1978). In the 1950s, epidemiological studies identified a high frequency of perinatal complications in the birth records of mentally retarded children; the more severe retardation was associated with the most complications, the less severe with fewer and less pathogenic complications. This research led to the hypothesis of a continuum of reproductive casualty (Lilienfeld & Pasamanick, 1955; Pasamanick & Lilienfeld, 1955).

To investigate the contribution of perinatal events to mental retardation and other abnormal outcomes, a population large enough to sample relatively rare events would have to be drawn. Just so, the Collaborative Perinatal Project was designed to examine enough pregnancies and their outcomes to determine the relationship between perinatal complications and developmental disabilities.

In this study, the mentally retarded were identified in a population of 17,000 white and 19,000 black children followed from gestation to age 7. Severe mental retardation was found in 92 children representing .5% of the white sample. In the black sample, .7%, or 128 children, were severely retarded. Previously reported prevalence rates in children are about .4% (Willerman, 1979). Mild retardation was identified in 1% or 201 of the white children, and in 5% or 895 of the black children.

More than 350 antecedent and concurrent factors were screened for association with severe and mild retardation. The potential predictors included prenatal social and demographic characteristics of the family, events in pregnancy and delivery, and indices of the development of the children from the neonatal period through age 4. Also examined were the concomitant social, physical, and psychological characteristics at age 7. Within each developmental epoch, and for the different types of information collected at age 7, discriminant analyses were performed to identify those variables independently related to each level of mental retardation in the two samples.

As expected, in the period from gestation through infancy, the factors most highly related to severe retardation were the rare but devastating conditions exemplified by Down's syndrome, malformations of the central nervous system, and cerebral palsy. Altogether, 72% of the severely retarded in the white sample and 54% in the black sample had 1 or more of the 26 major CNS disorders identified in these groups. Neonatal and postneonatal seizures and delayed psychomotor development were other major predictors of severe retardation.

Some complications of pregnancy and delivery were relatively important within-epoch discriminators but had little explanatory power. These included seizures in pregnancy, which occurred in less than 4% of mothers of the severely retarded, breech delivery, and midforceps delivery. Other risk factors for severe retardation confirmed in the study were anemia, toxemia, and low weight gain in pregnancy; low fetal heart rate in labor; and meconium staining at delivery. Again, while these events made independent contributions to outcome, their effects were small.

Neonatal characteristics of the severely retarded included congenital malformations (other than those of the CNS), apnea, clinical signs of brain abnormality, and smaller size than children in the comparison groups.

Given the data at hand, it appears reasonable to believe that the locus of cause in idiopathic severe mental retardation lies in anomalies of embryologic or fetal development as yet inaccessible. In order to identify precursors of this "unaccounted for" condition, the severely retarded children without major CNS disorders were compared with the CNS positives and with groups of higher functioning children also without major CNS disorders. These analyses were performed for the mildly retarded as well.

A major finding for the severely retarded "CNS normal" subgroup was a high frequency of maternal urinary tract infection in pregnancy, a complication which, in pathological studies in this population, has been linked to endotoxemia and fetal leukoencephalopathy (Leviton & Gilles, 1979, 1984). Important neonatal characteristics of this subgroup were the presence of congenital malformations and the very high proportion of males. By age 7, several of these children had been diagnosed as autistic or as having other childhood psychoses (Torrey, Hersh, & McCabe, 1975), lending further credence to the hypothesis of undetected variations in fetal development as causal in severe mental retardation.

There were very important differences between the risk factors for the severely and the mildly retarded children. Prominent among the discriminators for the mildly retarded were socioeconomic variables, including socioeconomic index and maternal education. The maternal nonverbal intelligence score, reflecting a combination of experiential and perhaps genetic influences, was the only discriminator retained throughout the first year in all comparisons in both samples. Maternal intelligence, clearly a confounded variable, is also a powerful one.

Early risk factors for mild retardation through the neonatal period were the maternal characteristics of short stature and late age at menarche, and the pregnancy complications of urinary tract infection, anemia, and toxemia, complications also related to severe retardation. Neonatal characteristics of the mildly retarded included non-CNS malformations, small size, respiratory difficulty, low Apgar score, and multiple birth. Major CNS disorders were, as expected, much less important as discriminators for the mildly retarded and, when they occurred, were mostly confined to the white sample.

The Bayley psychomoter scores at 8 months were highly related to intellectual level at age 7, as was the diagnosis of delayed motor development at 1 year. These variables discriminated not only between the retarded and normal groups but between the severely and mildly retarded. Although the correlations between the Bayley scores at 8 months and IQ at 7 years were only approximately .25, the Bayley Scales appear to be an excellent determinant of risk for later mental retardation.

Given the size of the population, and the size of the samples of severely and mildly retarded children, the study provides strong comfirmation of the two-group theory of mental retardation. Severe retardation was associated with major CNS abnormalities, and even when not detected, their presence was suggested by certain risk factors and also by the developmental anomalies found in other systems. These children came largely from families of average to low socioeconomic status and, typically, not from families with other retarded members.

The mildly retarded children, on the other hand, were from families of very low socioeconomic status with a relatively high incidence of familial mental retardation and few had major CNS disorders. The cognitive development of this group was related primarily to adverse or nonfacilitating environmental conditions.

The IQ cutoff of 50, however, produced some overlap between "organic" and cultural–familial mental retardation. Those children with an IQ below 50 without a diagnosed major CNS disorder were in some ways similar to the mildly retarded groups. Their IQs were usually at the top of the severely retarded range, and their socioeconomic status was very low. On the other hand, the small subgroup of mildly retarded children with major CNS disorders often had high socioeconomic index scores, suggesting a higher level of environmental press for academic readiness, a characteristic of middle class families.

These results confirm many previously reported findings. Perhaps the most comparable study was the epidemiological investigation of mental subnormality by Birch et al. (1970). These investigators also compared the frequency of CNS abnormalities among the severely and mildly retarded (using an IQ score of 60 as a cutoff). In both studies, many more severely than mildly retarded children had signs of CNS damage. Birch and his colleagues, including among their criteria "soft" neurological signs, found a virtual lack of mild retardation without CNS signs in their upper socioeconomic group.

Many of their other results were consistent with the current study. Mild retardation, but not severe, was much more frequent in lower socioeconomic status groups. Associations were found between retardation and large family size, high housing density, breech delivery, multiple birth, and toxemia and anemia in pregnancy. Short maternal stature was associated with mild retardation, not severe. On the other hand, some of the associations found by Birch were not supported by the multivariate analyses in this study. Examples of these were the influence of low birthweight and gestational age. Not surprisingly, the sample in the Birch study, from Aberdeen, Scotland, showed greater similarities to the Collaborative Perinatal Project white children than to the black children.

The major unanswered etiological question is the cause of so-called cultural–familial retardation. Explanations have ranged from its representing the low end of the polygenetically determined distribution of IQs (Penrose, 1963) to its being caused by cultural deprivation leading to lower IQ scores (Kennedy, 1973; Stein & Susser, 1960).

More recently, Costeff et al. (1983) and Hagberg et al. (1981) have suggested that perinatal complications resulting in CNS damage are a major cause of mild retardation. Hagberg claims to have rejected "the myth that MMR (mild mental retardation) is mainly a polygenic problem" (p. 450). Their Swedish sample, in which .4% were mildly retarded, was similar to the upper SES white group in the Collaborative Perinatal Project, in which .3% were mildly retarded. In both cases, 43% of the mildly retarded children had major CNS abnormalities. Upper SES level whites, however, are not a typical sample from which to draw conclusions about mild retardation. Within the Collaborative Project sample, 90% of mildly retarded white children were not in the top SES level, and, of these, only 10% had a major CNS disorder. For the large group of black children in this IQ range, among whom there was also little evidence for polygenetic transmission, this figure was even lower. Although some perinatal complications were found to be associated with mild retardation, socioeconomic factors were of much greater importance.

In understanding the full scope of the problem of mild or cultural–familial retardation, one must take note of one very important difference between the subjects in this study who were of lower socioeconomic status and the population from which they were drawn. Beginning in pregnancy, the mothers and children in the Collaborative Project received excellent medical care, including a heroic effort to encourage the use of this care; free transportation, reminder calls, and rescheduled appointments were an important part of the administration of the Collaborative Project centers. In the general population, lower class mothers are often severely stressed by their environment and unable or at times unwilling to obtain the level of medical care that can prevent or treat some conditions associated with childhood retardation, such as anemia, that are very prevalent in the black population. There are, then, very likely fewer medical complications among mothers and children in this study than in the population that they represent.

It is clear that in the United States, mental retardation of a mild type, sometimes characterized as a learning disability, is highly correlated with socioeconomic status and with related variables such as the mothers' education and intelligence. On the other hand, mental retardation of a severe type, associated with training as an alternative to traditional schooling, is highly correlated with number and severity of clinical signs of central nervous system pathology.

The Collaborative Perinatal Project has confirmed the catastrophic nature of major chromosomal abnormalities, malformations of the CNS, and cerebral palsy and the importance as risk factors of complicated deliveries, early seizures, signs of perinatal anoxia, and several complications of pregnancy.

It has identified urinary tract infection in pregnancy as being more significant than previously believed, and demonstrated a lower incidence of hard neurological signs in the mildly retarded than has been reported.

It has made a good case for perinatal and follow-up medical care as an essential public health practice for mothers of low socioeconomic status and it has left unanswered the question of the specific causes of mild mental retardation, particularly in children of lower-class parents, leaving that answer to a treatment study.

Appendix 1:
Variables Associated
with Retardation

Variables Associated with Mental Retardation in
Univariate (○) and Multivariate (●) Analyses

Variable	Severely Retarded				Mildly Retarded			
	White		Black		White		Black	
	Total	CNS Normal	Total	CNS Normal	Total	CNS Normal	Total	CNS Normal
THE PRENATAL PERIOD								
Family and Demographic								
Socioeconomic index	●	●	●	●	●	●	●	●
Mother married	○	●	○	○	○	○	○	○
Maternal education	●	●	●	●	●	●	●	●
Paternal education	○	●	○	○	○	○	○	○
Mother employed	○	○	●	○	○	○	○	○
Father present	○	○	○	○	○	○	○	○
Maternal occupation	○	●	○	○	○	○	○	○
Paternal occupation	○	○	○	○	○	○	○	○
Family income	○	○	○	○	○	○	○	○
Housing density	○	●	●	●	●	●	●	●
Retarded siblings	●	—	—	●	●	○	—	—
Retarded mother	—	—	—	—	●	●	●	●
Retarded father	—	—	—	—	●	●	○	●
Maternal mental illness	—	—	—	—	—	—	○	●
Paternal mental illness	—	—	—	—	—	—	—	—
Consanguinity	—	—	—	—	—	—	—	—
Maternal								
Twin birth	—	—	—	—	—	—	—	—
Age	—	●	●	●	—	—	●	●
Weight	—	—	—	—	○	○	—	—
Height	○	—	—	—	●	●	●	●
Age at menarche	●	—	○	—	●	●	—	—
Parity	●	○	○	—	●	●	●	●
Prior fetal death	—	—	—	—	—	—	●	●
Last child fetal death	—	—	—	●	—	—	—	—
Birthweight of last child	—	—	●	—	—	—	●	●
Neonatal death at last delivery	—	—	—	—	—	—	—	—
Childhood death last delivery	—	—	—	—	—	—	—	—
Fetal or neonatal death at last delivery	—	—	●	○	—	—	—	—
Smoking history	—	—	—	—	○	○	—	—
SRA score	●	●	●	●	●	●	●	●

(continued)

Appendix 1 (continued)

Variable	Severely Retarded				Mildly Retarded			
	White		Black		White		Black	
	Total	CNS Normal	Total	CNS Normal	Total	CNS Normal	Total	CNS Normal
THE PRENATAL PERIOD								
Pregnancy								
Cigarettes per day	—	—	—	●	●	●	—	—
Gestation at registration	○	○	○	○	○	●	○	○
Pregnancy-free interval	●	—	●	●	—	●	●	●
Recent maternal illnesses	—	—	—	—	●	●	—	—
Hospitalizations since LMP	●	—	○	○	●	●	●	●
Abdomino-pelvic x-rays	—	—	—	—	●	●	—	—
Number of prenatal visits	●	●	○	○	●	●	●	●
Weight gain	●	●	—	—	○	○	○	○
Hemoglobin	○	○	○	○	○	○	○	○
Hematocrit	○	○	○	○	○	○	●	●
Inadequate pelvis	—	—	—	—	—	—	—	—
Vomiting	—	—	—	—	—	—	—	—
Fever	—	—	—	○	—	—	—	—
Jaundice	—	—	—	—	—	—	—	—
Edema	—	—	—	—	—	○	●	●
Vaginal bleeding	—	—	—	—	—	—	—	—
Seizures	●	—	●	●	—	—	—	—
Organic heart disease	—	—	—	—	—	—	●	●
Rheumatic fever	—	—	●	—	—	—	—	—
Asthma	—	—	—	—	—	—	—	—
Anemia	●	●	○	—	●	○	○	○
Diabetes	—	—	—	●	—	—	—	—
Syphilis	—	—	—	—	—	—	—	—
Glomerulonephritis	—	—	—	—	—	—	—	—
Urinary tract infection	—	●	●	—	●	●	—	—
Toxoplasmosis	—	—	—	—	●	—	—	—
Rubella	●	—	—	—	—	—	—	—
Herpes hominus infection	—	—	—	—	—	—	—	—
Other viral infection	—	—	—	—	—	—	—	—
Other parasitic infection	—	—	—	—	—	—	—	—
Fungal infection	—	—	—	—	—	—	—	—
Bacterial infection	—	—	—	—	—	—	●	—

(continued)

Appendix 1 (continued)

Variable	Severely Retarded				Mildly Retarded			
	White		Black		White		Black	
	Total	CNS Normal	Total	CNS Normal	Total	CNS Normal	Total	CNS Normal
THE PRENATAL PERIOD								
Pregnancy								
Toxemia	—	—	●	●	—	—	—	—
Hypotension	—	—	—	—	—	—	—	—
LABOR AND DELIVERY								
Lowest FHR in 1st stage of labor	●	—	—	—	—	—	—	—
Highest FHR in 1st stage of labor	—	●	●	●	●	—	●	●
Lowest FHR in 2nd stage of labor	—	—	—	—	—	—	—	—
Highest FHR in 2nd stage of labor	—	—	—	—	—	—	—	—
Meconium staining	—	—	●	●	—	—	—	—
Vaginal bleeding at admission for delivery	—	—	—	—	—	—	—	—
Length of 1st stage of labor	—	—	—	—	—	—	—	—
Length of 2nd stage of labor	●	—	—	○	●	●	○	○
Vertex delivery	○	○	○	○	○	—	—	—
Breech delivery	●	●	●	●	●	—	—	—
Caesarean section	—	—	—	—	—	—	—	—
Midforceps delivery	●	—	—	—	●	●	○	—
Induction of labor	—	●	—	—	●	●	—	—
Augmentation of labor	—	—	●	○	○	○	—	—
Placental complications	—	—	—	○	●	—	—	—
Abruptio placenta	—	—	—	—	●	—	—	—
Placenta previa	—	—	—	●	●	—	●	●
Marginal sinus rupture	—	—	—	—	—	—	—	—
Cord complications	—	—	●	●	—	—	—	—
Placental weight	—	—	●	●	—	—	●	●
Early rupture of membranes	—	—	—	○	—	—	—	—

(continued)

Appendix 1 (continued)

| Variable | Severely Retarded | | | | Mildly Retarded | | | |
| | White | | Black | | White | | Black | |
	Total	CNS Normal	Total	CNS Normal	Total	CNS Normal	Total	CNS Normal
LABOR AND DELIVERY								
Polyhydramnios	●	—	—	—	—	—	—	—
Single umbilical artery	●	—	—	—	—	—	—	—
Arrested progress of labor	—	—	—	—	—	—	○	—
Occiput anterior presentation	●	—	—	—	—	—	—	—
Occiput posterior presentation	●	○	—	—	—	—	—	—
Abnormal presentation at delivery	—	—	●	—	—	—	●	—
Anesthetics at delivery	○	○	●	●	○	—	○	○
Inhalation anesthetics at delivery	●	—	—	—	●	●	●	●
Intravenous anesthetics at delivery	—	—	●	●	—	—	—	—
Conduction anesthetics at delivery	○	○	○	—	○	○	●	●
THE NEONATAL PERIOD								
Sex of child	●	●	●	●	○	○	●	●
Gestational age	○	—	○	○	○	○	●	●
Apgar score at 1 minute	●	—	○	○	●	●	○	○
Apgar score at 5 minutes	●	—	●	—	—	—	○	○
Positive direct Coombs test	—	—	—	—	—	—	—	—
Highest serum bilirubin	○	—	○	—	○	—	○	○
Peripheral nerve abnormality	●	●	—	—	—	—	—	—
Fractured skull	—	—	—	—	—	—	—	—
Cephalohematoma	—	—	—	—	—	—	—	—
Intracranial hemorrhage	○	—	—	—	—	—	—	—
Spinal cord abnormality	—	—	—	—	—	—	●	—
CNS infection	—	—	—	—	—	—	—	—
Respiratory difficulty	○	—	●	○	●	●	○	○
Brain abnormality	●	—	●	●	○	—	—	—
Erythroblastosis	—	—	—	●	—	—	—	●

(continued)

Appendix 1 (continued)

Variable	Severely Retarded				Mildly Retarded			
	White		Black		White		Black	
	Total	CNS Normal	Total	CNS Normal	Total	CNS Normal	Total	CNS Normal
THE NEONATAL PERIOD								
Primary apnea	●	—	○	—	—	—	●	●
Apneic episode	●	—	○	—	—	—	—	—
Multiple apneic episodes	○	—	—	—	—	—	●	●
Resuscitation up to 5 minutes	●	—	○	—	—	—	○	○
Resuscitation after 5 minutes	○	—	○	—	—	—	○	○
Lowest hematocrit	—	—	—	—	—	●	○	○
Lowest hemoglobin	—	—	—	—	●	—	○	○
Dysmaturity	—	—	●	●	—	—	●	●
Length at birth	●	○	○	●	○	○	●	●
Birthweight	●	○	○	○	○	○	○	○
Head circumference at birth	●	—	●	●	●	●	●	●
Metabolic diseases	—	—	○	—	●	—	—	—
Down's syndrome	●	—	●	—	●	—	—	—
Other genetic or post-infection syndromes	●	—	●	—	●	—	●	—
Neonatal seizures	●	—	●	●	—	—	—	—
Multiple birth	—	—	●	●	●	●	●	●
Major Malformations								
CNS	●	—	●	—	●	—	●	—
Musculoskeletal	○	—	●	●	—	—	●	●
Eye	●	●	●	—	—	—	●	—
Ear	—	—	—	—	—	—	—	—
Upper respiratory or mouth	●	●	—	—	●	●	—	—
Thoracic	—	—	●	—	—	—	—	—
Cardiovascular	○	—	●	—	●	●	●	●
Alimentary	●	—	○	—	—	—	○	○
Liver	—	—	—	—	—	—	—	—

(continued)

Appendix 1 (continued)

Variable	Severely Retarded				Mildly Retarded			
	White		Black		White		Black	
	Total	CNS Normal	Total	CNS Normal	Total	CNS Normal	Total	CNS Normal
Major Malformations								
Genitourinary	●	—	—	—	●	—	—	—
Tumors	—	—	—	—	—	—	—	—
Skin	—	—	—	—	—	—	—	—
Minor Malformations								
CNS	—	—	—	—	—	—	—	—
Musculoskeletal	●	●	—	—	—	—	—	—
Eye	—	—	—	—	—	—	—	—
Ear	●	●	○	—	●	●	—	—
Upper respiratory or mouth	—	—	—	—	—	—	—	—
Alimentary	—	—	—	—	—	—	—	—
Genitourinary	—	—	—	—	—	—	—	—
Skin	—	—	—	●	—	—	●	●
Tumor	—	—	—	—	—	—	—	—
INFANCY								
Four Months								
Height	○	—	○	○	○	○	○	○
Weight	●	○	○	○	○	○	●	●
Head circumference	●	—	●	●	○	○	●	●
Eight Months								
Bayley mental score	●	●	●	●	●	●	●	●
Bayley motor score	●	●	●	●	●	●	●	●
Speed of response	●	○	○	○	○	○	●	○
Intensity of response	●	●	○	○	○	○	○	○
Duration of response	○	○	●	●	○	○	○	○
Persistence in pursuit	○	○	○	○	○	○	○	○
Intensity of social response	●	—	●	○	●	●	●	●
Social response to examiner	○	—	○	—	○	○	●	●
Social response to mother	○	—	○	—	—	—	●	●
Activity level	●	○	○	○	○	○	○	○

(continued)

Appendix 1 (continued)

Variable	Severely Retarded				Mildly Retarded			
	White		Black		White		Black	
	Total	CNS Normal	Total	CNS Normal	Total	CNS Normal	Total	CNS Normal
INFANCY								
One Year								
Height	●	—	○	○	○	○	○	○
Weight	○	—	○	○	○	○	●	●
Head circumference	●	●	●	●	●	●	●	●
Subdural hematoma	○	—	○	—	—	—	—	—
Other intracranial hemorrhage	—	—	○	—	—	—	—	—
Congenital heart disease	●	—	●	—	●	●	○	○
CNS infection or inflammation	—	—	●	—	—	—	○	—
Lead intoxication	—	—	—	—	—	—	—	—
Hypoxia	—	—	○	—	●	—	●	—
Head trauma	○	—	●	—	○	—	—	—
Cord disease	—	—	●	—	—	—	●	—
Failure to thrive	●	—	●	○	●	○	●	○
Hypotonia	●	○	●	—	●	○	●	●
Delayed motor development	●	●	●	●	●	●	●	●
Peripheral nerve abnormality	○	●	—	—	—	—	—	—
Visual impairment	●	●	●	●	—	—	●	—
Strabismus	●	—	●	●	○	—	—	—
Nystagmus	●	○	●	—	—	—	—	○
Loss of one or both parents	●	●	—	●	—	—	—	—
Foster home	○	—	—	—	○	○	○	○
Unfavorable emotional environment	○	—	●	●	●	●	○	○
Prolonged or recurrent hospitalization	●	—	●	—	●	—	○	○
Adduction or contracture of hip	●	—	—	—	—	—	○	—
Undescended testicles	●	●	●	●	○	—	○	—

(continued)

Appendix 1 (continued)

Variable	Severely Retarded White		Severely Retarded Black		Mildly Retarded White		Mildly Retarded Black	
	Total	CNS Normal	Total	CNS Normal	Total	CNS Normal	Total	CNS Normal
INFANCY								
One Year								
Undescended testicle	—	—	○	●	●	●	—	—
Cerebral palsy	●	●	●	●	●	—	○	○
Dyskinesia or ataxia	●	—	●	—	—	—	●	—
Febrile seizures	○	—	●	—	—	—	—	—
Nonfebrile seizures	●	—	●	●	●	—	—	—
Spasmus nutans	—	—	—	—	—	—	—	—
Endocrine or metabolic disease	○	—	—	—	○	—	—	—
PRESCHOOL								
Three Years								
Abnormal hearing	○	—	○	○	●	●	—	●
Abnormal language expression	●	○	●	○	●	●	●	●
Abnormal language reception	●	○	●	○	●	●	●	●
Abnormal speech production	●	○	●	○	●	●	●	●
Four Years								
Stanford-Binet IQ	●	●	●	●	●	●	●	●
Height	●	●	●	○	○	○	●	●
Weight	○	—	○	○	●	○	○	●
Head circumference	●	○	●	●	●	●	●	●
Graham Block Sort score	○	○	○	○	●	●	●	●
Gross motor score	○	○	○	○	●	●	●	●
Fine motor score	○	○	○	○	●	●	●	●
Attention span	●	●	○	○	●	●	●	●
Goal orientation	●	○	●	●	●	●	●	●
Activity level	●	●	○	○	○	○	○	○
Emotionality	○	○	—	—	○	○	—	—
Irritability	○	○	—	—	○	○	○	○
Cooperativeness	○	○	○	○	○	○	○	○

(continued)

Appendix 1 (continued)

Variable	Severely Retarded White		Black		Mildly Retarded White		Black	
	Total	CNS Normal	Total	CNS Normal	Total	CNS Normal	Total	CNS Normal
PRESCHOOL								
Four Years								
Dependency	○	○	●	●	○	○	●	●
Response to directions	●	●	●	●	○	●	●	●
Impulsivity	●	●	●	●	—	—	●	●
Verbal communication	●	●	●	●	●	○	●	●
Abnormal behavior summary rating	●	●	●	●	●	●	●	●
Right handedness	●	—	●	—	○	○	○	○
Right dominance	○	—	○	—	●	●	○	○
DEMOGRAPHIC AND FAMILY CHACTERISTICS								
AT AGE 7								
Socioeconomic index	●	●	○	●	●	●	●	●
Child adopted or in foster home	●	○	○	●	●	●	●	●
Maternal age	○	●	○	—	●	●	●	●
Maternal education	●	●	●	●	●	●	●	●
Mother married	—	—	○	○	○	○	○	○
Housing density	○	○	●	○	●	●	●	●
Number of children under age 8 in household	●	○	○	○	○	○	○	○
Maternal occupation	○	○	○	○	○	○	○	○
Paternal occupation	○	○	○	○	○	○	○	○
Family income	○	○	○	○	○	○	○	○
Number of changes in residence	—	—	●	○	●	●	●	●
Father present	—	○	●	—	○	○	○	○
Mother's additonal schooling	○	—	○	—	●	●	●	●
Mother employed	●	●	●	●	●	●	●	●
Length of maternal employment	○	—	○	○	○	○	○	○
Child care	○	—	○	○	○	○	●	●

(continued)

Appendix 1 (continued)

Variable	Severely Retarded				Mildly Retarded			
	White		Black		White		Black	
	Total	CNS Normal	Total	CNS Normal	Total	CNS Normal	Total	CNS Normal
DEMOGRAPHIC AND FAMILY CHACTERISTICS AT AGE 7								
Father employed	○	●	○	○	○	○	●	●
Paternal age	—	○	●	—	○	●	○	○
Paternal education	○	○	○	○	○	○	○	○
Public assistance	●	●	●	●	●	●	●	●
Number of subsequent pregnancies	○	○	●	●	●	●	●	●
Number of subsequent fetal deaths	—	—	—	—	○	○	—	—
Subsequent multiple pregnancies	—	—	—	—	○	○	○	○
Subsequent siblings live-born now dead	—	—	—	—	○	○	●	○
Retarded siblings	●	—	●	●	●	●	●	●
Maternal mental illness	—	—	—	—	—	—	○	—
Paternal mental illness	—	—	—	—	—	—	—	—
Mental illness in study child	●	●	—	—	—	—	—	—
Mental illness in siblings	—	—	—	—	—	—	—	—
Family size	●	○	○	●	●	●	●	●
MEDICAL HISTORY AND PHYSICAL AND NEUROLOGICAL STATUS AT AGE 7								
Cord disease	—	—	—	—	—	—	—	—
Amblyopia	—	●	—	—	○	○	—	—
Refractive error	—	—	○	—	○	○	○	○
Color blindness	●	—	—	—	●	●	●	●
Visual field defect	—	—	—	●	—	—	—	—
Strabismus	○	○	○	○	●	●	●	●
Nystagmus	○	—	○	—	●	●	○	—
Cranial nerve abnormality	●	—	○	—	●	●	○	○

(continued)

Appendix 1 (continued)

| Variable | Severely Retarded | | | | Mildly Retarded | | | |
| | White | | Black | | White | | Black | |
	Total	CNS Normal	Total	CNS Normal	Total	CNS Normal	Total	CNS Normal
MEDICAL HISTORY AND PHYSICAL AND NEUROLOGICAL STATUS AT AGE 7								
Other sensory abnormality	—	—	—	—	—	—	—	—
Coma	○	—	●	—	—	—	○	—
Subdural hematoma or effusion	—	—	●	●	—	—	—	—
Other intracranial hemorrhage	—	—	○	—	○	—	—	—
Chorioretinitis	—	—	●	—	—	—	○	—
Retrolental fibroplasia	○	—	—	—	—	—	—	—
Asthma	—	—	—	—	—	—	—	○
Acyanotic congenital heart disease	○	—	○	—	●	●	○	○
Cyanotic congenital heart disease	—	—	○	—	●	●	●	●
Rheumatic heart disease	—	—	—	—	—	—	—	—
Hemoglobinopathy	—	—	●	●	—	—	—	—
Hemolytic disease	—	—	—	●	—	—	—	—
Coagulation defect	—	—	—	—	—	—	—	—
Major hemorrhage	—	—	—	—	—	—	●	●
Anemia	○	—	○	—	—	—	○	○
Other hematologic disorder	—	—	—	—	—	—	—	—
Eczema	—	—	—	—	—	○	○	—
Gonadal dysgenesis	—	—	—	—	●	—	—	—
Battered child	—	—	—	—	—	—	○	—
Spasmus nutans	—	—	—	●	—	—	—	—
Failure to thrive	●	●	●	●	●	●	●	●
Hypothroidism	●	●	—	—	—	—	—	—
Septicemia	—	—	—	—	—	—	—	—
Bacterial meningitis	—	—	●	—	—	—	—	—
Nonbacterial meningitis	—	—	—	—	—	—	—	—
Encephalitis	●	—	●	—	—	—	○	—

(continued)

Appendix 1 (continued)

| | Severely Retarded | | | | Mildly Retarded | | | |
| | White | | Black | | White | | Black | |
Variable	Total	CNS Normal	Total	CNS Normal	Total	CNS Normal	Total	CNS Normal
MEDICAL HISTORY AND PHYSICAL AND NEUROLOGICAL STATUS AT AGE 7								
CNS infection	○	—	—	—	●	—	—	—
Respiratory infection	○	—	○	—	○	—	○	○
Genitourinary tract infection	—	—	—	—	—	—	○	—
Bone or joint infection	—	—	—	—	—	—	—	—
Heart infection	—	—	—	—	—	—	—	—
Severe diarrhea	—	—	—	—	—	—	—	—
Liver infection	○	—	●	●	—	—	—	—
Eye infection	—	—	○	—	—	—	●	●
Ear infection	—	●	—	—	●	●	—	—
Skin infection	—	—	○	○	—	—	○	○
Roseola	○	—	—	—	○	○	—	○
Measles	○	—	—	—	○	○	—	—
German measles	—	—	—	—	—	—	○	○
Mumps	—	—	○	○	○	○	●	●
Chickenpox	○	○	○	—	●	●	○	○
Whooping cough	—	—	—	—	—	—	—	—
Other childhood diseases	—	—	—	—	—	—	—	—
Recurrent or chronic infection	—	—	—	—	—	—	—	—
Fractured skull, linear	○	—	—	—	—	—	○	—
Fractured skull, other	—	—	—	—	—	—	—	—
Other head trauma	○	—	○	—	—	—	○	—
Other fractures	—	—	—	—	—	—	—	—
Severe burns	—	—	—	—	○	●	○	○
Salicylate intoxication	—	—	—	—	—	—	—	—
Symptomatic hydrocarbon intoxication	○	—	○	—	—	—	—	—
Lead intoxication	—	—	—	—	—	—	—	—
Other symptomatic intoxication	—	—	—	—	●	●	—	—

(continued)

Appendix 1 (continued)

Variable	Severely Retarded				Mildly Retarded			
	White		Black		White		Black	
	Total	CNS Normal	Total	CNS Normal	Total	CNS Normal	Total	CNS Normal
MEDICAL HISTORY AND PHYSICAL AND NEUROLOGICAL STATUS AT AGE 7								
Reaction to immunization	—	—	—	—	—	—	—	—
Other trauma or intoxication	—	—	—	—	—	—	—	—
Shock requiring hospitalization	—	—	—	—	—	—	—	—
Severe dehydration	○	—	—	—	—	—	—	—
Electrolyte imbalance	—	—	—	—	—	—	—	—
Hyperthermia	—	—	—	—	●	—	—	—
Hypoxia with unconsciousness	○	—	—	—	—	—	—	—
Hypoxia without unconsciousness	●	—	●	●	○	○	○	○
Diagnostic and other medical procedures	●	●	●	●	●	●	●	●
General anesthesia	—	—	○	—	○	○	○	○
Surgery	—	—	○	○	○	—	—	—
Abnormal gait	●	●	●	●	●	●	●	●
Abnormal reflexes	●	●	●	○	○	○	●	●
Mirror and other abnormal movements	●	●	●	●	—	—	—	—
Right handedness	●	—	●	●	○	○	●	●
Right dominance	●	—	○	—	○	○	○	○
Documented cardiovascular disorder	—	—	●	●	—	—	—	—
Cerebral palsy	●	—	●	—	●	—	●	—
Dyskinesia or ataxia	●	—	○	—	○	—	●	—
Petit mal	●	—	—	—	●	—	—	—

(continued)

Appendix 1 (continued)

Variable	Severely Retarded				Mildly Retarded			
	White		Black		White		Black	
	Total	CNS Normal	Total	CNS Normal	Total	CNS Normal	Total	CNS Normal

MEDICAL HISTORY AND PHYSICAL AND NEUROLOGICAL STATUS AT AGE 7

Variable	Total	CNS Normal	Total	CNS Normal	Total	CNS Normal	Total	CNS Normal
Atypical staring	○	—	○	—	●	—	○	—
Minor motor seizures	●	—	●	—	—	—	—	—
Asymptomatic generalized seizures	●	—	●	—	○	—	●	—
Asymptomatic partial seizures	●	—	●	—	●	—	○	—
Syncope	—	—	—	—	—	—	—	—
Epilepsy	●	—	●	—	○	—	●	—
Isolated nonfebrile seizures	—	—	○	—	—	—	○	—
Asymptomatic pure febrile seizures	—	—	—	—	—	—	○	○
Asymptomatic complex febrile seizures	—	—	—	—	—	—	—	—
Moncular blindness	—	—	—	—	—	—	●	●
Binocular blindness	○	—	●	—	●	—	—	—
Bilateral deafness	●	—	○	—	—	—	●	—
Post traumatic deficit	○	—	●	—	—	—	●	—
Endocrine or metabolic disorders	—	—	○	○	—	—	—	—
Major Malformations								
Skull	●	●	●	●	●	●	●	●
Musculoskeletal	—	—	●	●	○	—	—	—
Eye	●	●	●	●	○	○	—	○
Ear	—	—	—	—	—	—	○	○
Upper respiratory or mouth	●	○	○	—	●	○	○	—
Thoracic	●	●	○	—	○	○	—	—
Cardiovascular	○	—	○	○	●	○	●	●
Alimentary	—	—	○	—	—	●	—	—
Liver or spleen	—	—	—	—	—	—	—	—
Genitourinary	●	●	○	—	●	○	—	—

(continued)

Appendix 1 (continued)

Variable	Severely Retarded				Mildly Retarded			
	White		Black		White		Black	
	Total	CNS Normal	Total	CNS Normal	Total	CNS Normal	Total	CNS Normal
MEDICAL HISTORY AND PHYSICAL AND NEUROLOGICAL STATUS AT AGE 7								
Major Malformations								
Tumors	—	—	—	—	—	—	—	—
Skin	—	—	—	—	—	—	—	—
Minor Malformations								
CNS	—	—	●	●	—	—	—	—
Musculoskeletal	●	●	●	●	●	●	—	—
Eye	—	—	○	—	—	—	○	—
Ear	●	●	●	●	●	●	—	—
Upper respiratory or mouth	●	—	●	○	—	—	●	●
Liver or spleen	—	—	—	—	—	—	—	—
Genitourinary	○	—	○	—	—	—	—	—
Tumors	—	—	—	—	—	—	—	—
Skin	●	—	—	—	—	—	—	—
Syndromes	—	—	—	—	○	—	—	—
COGNITIVE ABILITIES AND BEHAVIOR RATINGS AT AGE 7								
WRAT spelling	●	●	○	○	●	●	●	●
WRAT reading	○	○	●	●	○	○	○	○
WRAT arithmetic	●	●	●	●	●	●	●	●
Bender-Gestalt error score	○	○	○	○	●	●	●	●
Auditory-Vocal Association score	●	●	●	●	●	●	●	●
Draw-A-Person score	●	●	●	●	●	●	●	●
Tactile finger recognition, right hand	●	●	●	●	●	●	●	●
Tactile finger recognition, left hand	●	●	○	●	●	●	●	●
Separation anxiety	●	●	○	—	●	○	○	○
Fearfulness	●	●	●	●	●	●	○	○
Rapport with examiner	○	○	○	○	○	○	○	○

(continued)

Appendix 1 (continued)

| | Severely Retarded | | | | Mildly Retarded | | | |
| | White | | Black | | White | | Black | |
Variable	Total	CNS Normal	Total	CNS Normal	Total	CNS Normal	Total	CNS Normal
COGNITIVE ABILITIES AND BEHAVIOR RATINGS AT AGE 7								
Self confidence	●	●	●	○	○	○	●	●
Emotionality	○	○	●	○	●	●	●	●
Cooperativeness	○	○	○	○	○	○	○	○
Frustration tolerance	●	○	○	●	●	●	●	●
Dependency	●	●	●	●	●	●	●	●
Attention span	●	●	●	○	●	●	●	●
Goal orientation	●	●	●	●	●	●	●	●
Activity level	●	●	●	●	○	—	●	○
Impulsivity	●	●	○	—	●	●	●	●
Verbal communication	●	●	●	●	●	○	●	●
Assertiveness	●	●	●	○	●	○	●	○
Hostility	○	○	●	●	●	●	○	○
Abnormal behavior summary rating	●	●	●	●	●	●	●	●

Appendix 2:
Glossary

Alimentary malformations. Major malformations only. This category included inguinal and umbilical hernias at both early and late examinations and pyloric stenosis at the early examination only.

Anemia during pregnancy. The presence of a hemoglobin determination of less than 10 g per 100 ml of blood or a hematocrit of less than 30%.

Apgar score. A composite evaluation of heart rate, respiratory effort, muscle tone, reflex irritability, and color in the neonate made by independent observers in the delivery room. The total score is the sum of the five subscores, each having a range of 0 to 2. Thus, an infant in optimal condition receives a score of 10. The first observation was made 1 minute after birth, and the second at 5 minutes.

Auditory–Vocal Association score. The language age in months on this verbal analogies subtest of the Illinois Test of Psycholinguistic Abilities administered at age 7.

Augmentation of labor. The use of various uterine stimulants; classifications included amniotomy only, oxytocic drugs only, and a combination of these methods.

Bayley Mental Scale score. Total number of items passed on the research form of the Bayley Mental Scale administered at age 8 months. This 106 item test, based on an earlier version used in the Berkeley Growth Study, was revised and standardized in 1958 on 1400 children aged 1 to 15 months.

Bayley Motor Scale score. Total number of items passed on the 43 item research version of the Bayley Motor Scale. This test covers an age range from 1 to 12 months and was administered at age 8 months following the Mental Scale.

Behavior ratings at 8 months. A series of eight 5-point rating scales completed following the 8-month examinations. The items deal with the infants' orientation to objects and persons and activity level.

Behavior ratings at 4 years. A series of ten 5-point rating scales completed following the 4-year psychological examination. The general headings of the items are activity, communication, and orientation to the testing situation, the examiner, and the test materials.

Behavior ratings at 7 years. A series of fifteen 5-point rating scales completed following the 7-year psychological examination. Eight of the 7-year items are identical to the 4-year items. Items unique to the 7-year ratings include separation anxiety, self-confidence, and assertiveness.

Behavior summary rating. Overall abnormal rating of behavior based on observation and 10 individual ratings at age 4 or 15 ratings at age 7.

Bender–Gestalt error score. Number of errors on the Bender–Gestalt Test administered at age 7 as scored by the Koppitz method.

Burns, severe. Burns requiring hospitalization occurring between ages 1 and 7 years.

Cardiovascular malformations. Major malformations only. At both the early and late examinations, cardiac enlargement and ventricular septal defect were the most frequently diagnosed conditions.

Cerebral palsy. Defined at ages 1 and 7 as a chronic disability characterized by aberrant control of movement or posture that is not the result of progressive disease.

Child care. Utilized between the ages of 1 and 7 years and reported in the family interview at age 7.

CNS malformations. Major malformations, tabulated for the retarded groups in Tables 3-7 and 3-11, included hydrocephaly, microcephaly, and meningocele. Minor CNS malformations at age 7 included frontal bossing, pilonidal sinus, and palpable sutures.

Congenital heart disease. Diagnoses at 1 year included both cyanotic and acyanotic CHD. Clinical impressions were documented by ECG, catheterization and radiography. For 7-year diagnoses, cyanotic and acyanotic CHD were distinguished. Cases with cyanosis at rest were considered cyanotic.

Cord complications. Knot in umbilical cord, cord around neck or body, or prolapsed cord.

Cord disease. Spastic or flacid findings in the extremities resulting from conditions or diseases of the spinal cord such as menigomyelocele, myelodysplasia, or diastematomyelia.

Deafness, bilateral. A hearing loss of 30db or greater in both ears across four frequencies at age 7.

Diagnostic and other medical procedures. Blood transfusion, parenteral fluid, spinal and ventricular punctures, EEG, and radiation therapy between ages 1 and 7.

Draw-A-Person score. The Goodenough–Harris standard score on this test administered at age 7.

Dysmaturity. This neonatal diagnosis was based on signs of malnutrition, meconium staining, or prolonged gestation.

Ear malformations. Only minor ear malformations were associated with mental retardation. At both the neonatal and 7-year examinations, the most frequent of these conditions were branchial cleft anomaly, deformed ear pinna, and low-set ears.

Emotional environment. Considered unfavorable at the time of the 1-year pediatric examination if any of the following conditions were present: parental mental disorder, addiction or institutionalization, parental separation, lack of interest in child or excessive concern, frequent moves, or sibling closer than 15 months.

Eye malformations. Only major eye malformations were associated with mental retardation. Cataract was the most frequent early malformation; at 7 years, ptosis, cataract, and hypertelorism were the most common.

Failure to thrive. This syndrome, included in the medical summaries at ages 1 and 7 years, could be the result of chronic illness, nutritional deficiencies, or physical or emotional neglect. At the older age, an additional criterion was that the children be at or below the third percentile for height and weight.

Family size. Number of liveborn children as reported by the mother at the 7-year family interview.

Fetal heart rate in the first stage of labor. Fetal heart rate in beats per minute was taken at least every 30 minutes from the beginning of true labor until the cervix was dilated to 3 cm, and at least every 15 minutes from that time to complete dilation. Both highest and lowest values were screened for associations with retardation.

Fine motor score. An average of scores assigned to performance on four fine motor tasks at age 4: Wallin Pegboard B, Porteus Maze, bead stringing from the Stanford–Binet, and "Copy Forms" (circle, cross, and square). The maximum score was 100.

Gait abnormality. Difficulty in walking, running, walking on toes, walking on heels, or hopping as determined during the pediatric-neurological examination at age 7.

Genetic or postinfection syndromes. Nineteen specific syndromes other than Down's were identified among the severely and mildly retarded children. The syndromes are tabulated in Tables 3-7 and 3-11.

Genitourinary malformations. Major malformations only were associated with mental retardation, with the exception of undescended testicle diagnosed at 1 year of age. Hypospadias, urethreal meatal stenosis, and bilateral undescended testicles were the most frequent malformations.

Gestation at registration. An estimate by the examining physician of the nearest week of gestation at registration for prenatal care based on the number of days since the first day of the last menstrual period as reported by the mother.

Graham–Ernhart Block Sort score. Total raw score on three levels of a task administered at age 4 in which blocks are grouped by color, size, and shape. The maximum score is 45.

Gross motor score. The average of scores assigned to the three motor tests of line walk, hopping, and ball catch administered at age 4. The maximum score was 100.

Hearing at age 3. Considered abnormal if the child failed both a speech–hearing test and pure tone test (three frequencies at 20 db).

Hypotonia. Abnormally reduced tonicity observed at the time of the 1-year neurological examination.

Illnesses of mother. The number of illnesses during the 12 months prior to registration requiring bed confinement for at least one day, whether or not attended by a physician. Data were based on the mothers' reports during an early prenatal interview.

Induction of labor. The use of various uterine stimulants to induce labor. These include the artificial rupture of membranes (amniotomy) and the use of an oxytocic drug.

Intelligence tests. The Stanford–Binet Intelligence Scale, Form L-M was administered at age 4 in the abbreviated version with four of the six test items at each age level presented. The Wechsler Intelligence Scale for Children was administered at age 7 with the following seven subtests included: Information, Comprehension, Vocabulary, and Digit Span (Verbal); and Picture Arrangement, Block Design, and Coding (Performance).

Intoxication, symptomatic. Signs of intoxication due to lead, hydrocarbon, salicylate, or any other agent between ages 1 and 7 were noted on the 7-year medical summary. Other agents included chemicals and medications.

Language expression. Classified as abnormal at age 3 if four presented objects were not verbally identified or grammatical sentences or meaningful phrases of at least four words were not used.

Language reception. Classified as abnormal at age 3 if two of the following three items were failed: (1) identifying familiar objects, (2) understanding action words, and (3) understanding words indicating space relationships and direction.

Length of second stage of labor. The interval between the complete dilation of the cervix and the expulsion of the fetus, recorded in minutes.

Maternal SRA score. A 10 minute, 60 item oddity discrimination test of nonverbal intelligence developed by Science Research Associates. This test was usually administered to mothers at the time of the 4-year psychological examination but is grouped in this study with the prenatal maternal characteristics.

Mental illness. "Nervous" problems requiring hospitalization, psychiatric treatment, or other therapy in the mother, father, study child, or siblings as reported by the mother during the 7-year family interview. A similar report was made in a prenatal interview for parents only.

Metabolic diseases. Hypothyroidism or cystic fibrosis diagnosed in the neonatal period.

Midforceps delivery. The application of forceps to assist delivery when biparietal diameter of head is engaged but skull is not on the perineal floor.

Mirror and other abnormal movements. Any of the following movement disorders present at age 7: mirror movements, fasciculation, myoclonus, spontaneous tremor, intention tremor, athetosis, chorea, dystonia, ballismus, or tic.

Mother employed. Determined at the time of registration for prenatal care, when the women were asked if they currently worked outside the home, and again during the 7-year family interview, when they reported any work outside the home since the birth of the study child.

Motor development at one year. Observed during the 1-year neurological examination. Motor development was classified as delayed or normal, based on the milestones of creeping, standing while supported, pulling to a standing position, standing unaided, walking supported, and walking unaided. Children who could not at least walk with support or who were judged to have abnormalities of gait or posture were generally considered to have delayed motor development.

Musculoskeletal malformations. The most frequent major malformations at both the neonatal and 7-year examinations included metatarsus adductus, talipes equinovarus, talipes calcaneovalgus, and congenital dislocation of the hip. A group of malformations common at age 7 included scoliosis, lordosis, and kyphosis. Among the minor musculoskeletal malformations, polydactyly and syndactyly were the most frequent early malformations, and clinodactyly and syndactyly the most frequent late malformations.

Placental complications. Placenta previa (a placenta that develops in the lower uterus), abruptio placenta (premature placental detachment), or marginal sinus rupture.

Post-traumatic deficit. Severe head trauma resulting in lowered cognitive functioning.

Presentation at delivery, abnormal. Includes face, chin, brow, or shoulder presentation.

Reflexes, abnormal. Abnormal reflexes as determined on the pediatric-neurological examination at age 7 included hypoactive, hyperactive, or asymmetrical biceps, triceps, ankle, or knee jerk, sustained ankle clonus, and abnormal plantar responses.

Respiratory difficulty. Infants judged to have moderate or marked difficulty in breathing in the newborn nursery.

Retardation in relatives. Mothers, fathers, or older siblings were classified as retarded based on the mothers' reports during a prenatal interview. Criteria could include, but were not restricted to, a diagnosis of mental retardation or inability to attend regular school. Retardation in younger as well as older siblings was based on the mothers' reports during the 7-year interview.

Right dominance. Determined at ages 4 and 7. A child whose right hand, eye, and leg were dominant was considered to be overall right dominant.

Right handedness: At the time of the 4-year examination, children were considered to be right-handed if they used their right hand to hold the pencil on the copy forms task and to reach for the first peg presented in the pegboard task. At age 7, children who used their right hand on at least four of five trials with a pencil were considered right-handed.

Seizures, neonatal. Any generalized seizure occurring between birth and 1 month of age.

Seizures in pregnancy. Based on the mothers' reports during prenatal visits of any seizures that had occurred and on medical records available after registration for prenatal care.

Skin malformations. Only minor skin malformations were associated with mental retardation. More malformations in this category were diagnosed than in any other. Strawberry/portwine hemangioma, café-au-lait spots, supernumerary nipples, and hairy pigmented nevus were frequent at both the neonatal and 7-year determinations. In addition, vitiligo and hyperpigmentation were common at age 7.

Skull, abnormal shape. A group of major malformations including cranial asymmetry, brachycephaly, scaphocephaly, and plagiocephaly.

Socioeconomic index. This index is derived from one developed by the Bureau of the Census and is an average of individual scores for family income and for education and occupation of the head of the household. Scores were based on reports by the mother in a prenatal interview and a second calculation was based on information obtained from the 7-year family interview. Scores on the prenatal index range from 0–95 and on the 7-year index from 0–97.

Speech production. Classified as abnormal at age 3 on the basis of impaired intelligibility, fluency, voice quality and articulation.

Spinal cord abnormality. Trauma to the spinal cord resulting in neurological abnormality at the time of the neonatal examination.

Tactile Finger Recognition score. This test is from the Halstead–Reitan battery and was administered at age 7. The child is asked to identify fingers that are touched out of his sight in a prescribed sequence. The score for each hand is the number of fingers that are correctly identified.

Thoracic malformations. Major malformations only. The most common early conditions were pectus excavetum and hypoplasia or immaturity of the lung. At age 7, pectus excavetum, pectus carinatum, and asymmetry of the thorax were most frequent.

Toxemia during pregnancy. The presence during pregnancy of diastolic blood pressure (DBP) higher than 95 and no or only trace proteinuria, DBP of 85 or higher and proteinuria 1+ or greater, or DBP lower than 85 and proteinuria 2+ or greater.

Upper respiratory or mouth malformations. Early major malformations included cleft palate, cleft lip, and micrognathia. The most frequent late malformations were malocclusion and tooth enamel defect. Minor malformations at age 7, including missing teeth, malformed teeth, and cleft uvula, were also associated with mental retardation.

Urinary tract infection during pregnancy. Kidney, ureter, or bladder infection detected during prenatal examinations. Diagnoses were supported by laboratory tests.

Visual impairment. Partial or total blindness in one or both eyes, resulting from visible ocular or from nonocular causes.

Wide Range Achievement Test. This test, part of the 7-year psychological examination, includes spelling, reading, and arithmetic subtests. Raw scores, or total number of items correct, were used.

Appendix 3:
Correlations Among
Independent Variables

Correlations between the discriminating independent variables and IQ at age 7 are reported in the text. In this appendix, intercorrelations among a set of 38 of these factors are shown, allowing the reader to examine sequential and other relationships among the antecedents and correlates of mental retardation. Major discriminators were selected and also others that are of traditional or methodological interest. The variables in Table 1 are grouped by developmental epoch beginning with the prenatal period. For postneonatal factors, age of child is given only once for the first variable in that time period. Correlation coefficients in the black sample are shown above the diagonal on the first and fourth pages of the table and on the third page; corresponding values for whites are below the diagonal and on the second page.

Because of the very large sample sizes (up to 19,419 for blacks and 17,432 for whites), correlation coefficients as low as .02 are statistically reliable ($p < .01$), but associations of this magnitude have little practical significance. Adopting a criterion of $r \geq .25$, the following relationships among antecedents through the 4th year were found in both samples: weight and head circumference at birth and head circumference at age 4; Bayley Mental Scale score at 8 months and delayed motor development at age 1; and language expression at age 3 and IQ at age 4. Additionally, among whites, prenatal socioeconomic status and level of maternal education were related to IQ at age 4, and sex of child to head circumference at that age. In the black sample, weight gain in pregnancy and birthweight were correlated and both birthweight and head circumference at birth were related to the eight month Bayley Mental Scale score which was, in turn, related to IQ at age 4.

Associations between antecedents and 7-year marker variables or correlates that met the criterion in both samples were: the prenatal factors of socioeconomic status, maternal education, and maternal intelligence and so-

Table 1
Correlations Among Independent Variables

	1	2	3	4	5	6	7	8	9	10	11	12	13	14	15	16	17	18	19
1. Socioeconomic index	—	.47	.13	.07	-.07	.19	-.05	-.01	.15	.03	-.01	.04	.06	-.01	-.06	.05	-.01	.00	.05
2. Maternal education	.60	—	-.04	.07	-.25	.34	-.03	-.02	.09	.03	.00	.03	.05	-.02	-.04	.03	-.02	-.01	.02
3. Maternal age	.06	.00	—	.04	.65	-.32	-.03	-.01	.07	-.03	.03	-.04	.02	.01	-.03	.11	.00	.02	.08
4. Maternal height	.17	.22	-.01	—	.00	.00	-.01	-.01	.01	.11	.00	-.04	.01	.01	.02	.11	.00	.01	.08
5. Parity	-.18	-.22	.62	-.06	—	-.25	.02	.00	-.10	-.02	.04	-.08	.01	.01	.02	.11	.01	.00	.06
6. Maternal SRA score	.29	.42	-.17	.16	-.14	—	.00	-.02	.03	.00	-.02	.04	.04	.00	-.03	-.02	.00	-.01	-.01
7. Urinary tract infection in pregnancy	-.06	-.05	-.04	-.01	.01	-.03	—	.01	.03	-.03	.01	.00	.00	.00	.03	-.02	.01	.01	-.01
8. Maternal seizures in pregnancy	-.04	-.03	-.01	.00	-.01	-.03	.02	—	.02	-.02	-.01	-.01	.01	.00	.00	-.01	.00	.01	-.01
9. Number of prenatal visits	.30	.20	.06	.03	-.16	.05	.01	.02	—	.12	-.03	.05	.02	.00	-.03	.21	-.05	.00	.21
10. Weight gain in pregnancy	-.04	-.03	-.11	.06	-.04	.02	.03	-.01	.05	—	.00	.06	.03	-.03	.00	.27	-.03	.00	.20
11. Breech delivery	-.02	-.02	.02	.00	.02	-.02	.00	.00	-.02	.00	—	**	.05	.02	-.12	-.13	.08	.04	-.09
12. Midforceps delivery	.11	.07	.06	-.02	-.05	-.02	.03	.00	.15	.02	**	—	-.01	.00	-.05	.03	.01	.01	.03
13. Inhalation anesthetics at delivery	-.22	-.19	.02	-.04	.12	-.11	.02	.02	-.13	.02	.10	-.13	—	-.01	-.06	.07	-.02	-.01	.03
14. Sex of child	-.01	-.01	.01	.00	.01	.00	-.01	.00	.00	-.02	-.01	-.02	-.01	—	.01	-.11	-.03	-.01	-.17
15. Apgar score at 5 minutes	.00	-.01	.00	.00	.04	-.02	.00	-.01	-.01	.00	-.14	-.04	-.03	.03	—	.11	-.29	-.09	.10
16. Birthweight	.05	.06	.05	.15	.06	.03	.00	-.01	.16	.22	-.12	.03	.01	-.12	.07	—	-.13	-.01	.76
17. Respiratory difficulty	-.04	-.03	.01	-.01	.02	-.01	.01	.01	-.04	-.02	.04	.01	.03	-.01	-.23	-.12	—	.14	-.11
18. Neonatal brain abnormality	.00	.00	.02	.01	.02	.00	.00	.02	.00	.01	.04	.03	.00	-.02	-.10	-.04	.12	—	.00
19. Head circumference at birth	.06	.07	.05	.13	.04	.05	-.01	-.02	.15	.16	-.06	.03	.00	-.20	.03	.76	-.11	-.03	—

Note: Blacks above and whites below the diagonal.

(continued)

305

Table 1 (continued)

	1	2	3	4	5	6	7	8	9	10	11	12	13	14	15	16	17	18	19
20. Down's syndrome	-.01	-.01	.01	-.01	.01	.00	.00	.02	-.01	-.01	.00	.00	.02	-.01	-.03	-.03	.00	.27	-.05
21. Neonatal seizures	-.01	.01	.02	-.01	.01	.00	.00	.01	.00	.00	.02	.01	-.01	-.01	-.10	-.01	.09	.36	-.01
22. Major CNS malformations	-.01	-.01	-.01	.00	-.01	-.04	-.01	.01	.01	.02	.00	.02	.01	.00	-.01	-.01	.00	.15	.02
23. Bayley mental score at 8 months	.05	.04	-.02	.00	-.08	.03	-.02	-.04	.12	.04	-.07	.01	-.01	.01	.06	.21	-.10	-.12	.20
24. Congenital heart disease at 1 year	-.01	-.01	.02	.00	.02	-.01	.00	.00	.00	-.01	.02	.00	.00	.00	-.01	-.03	.01	.04	-.03
25. Delayed motor development	-.02	-.03	.03	-.01	.05	-.04	-.01	.02	-.02	-.03	.02	.01	.01	-.02	-.05	-.08	.05	.10	-.08
26. Cerebral palsy	-.01	-.01	.01	.00	.02	.00	-.01	.01	-.01	.00	.01	.02	.00	-.01	-.06	-.04	.08	.10	-.04
27. Non-febrile seizures	-.02	-.02	.00	.00	.01	-.03	.01	.01	-.01	.00	.01	.01	.00	.00	-.05	.00	.03	.06	.00
28. Abnormal language expression at 3 years	-.11	-.09	.01	-.02	.04	-.08	.01	.03	-.06	.00	.02	-.02	.02	-.08	-.05	-.04	.04	.07	-.04
29. Stanford-Binet IQ at 4 years	.37	.36	.04	.09	-.14	.24	-.06	-.03	.21	-.04	-.03	.04	-.12	.10	.02	.09	-.06	-.07	.10
30. Abnormal behavior rating	-.04	-.04	.00	-.01	.02	-.04	.01	.01	-.04	.01	.01	.01	.01	-.05	-.02	-.02	.03	.08	-.03
31. Head circumference	.15	.14	.04	.16	-.05	.08	-.03	-.02	.08	.04	-.01	.05	-.06	-.33	-.02	.30	-.01	-.04	.47
32. Socioeconomic index at 7 years	.71	.61	-.03	.18	-.20	.34	-.05	-.03	.23	-.02	-.02	.07	-.18	.00	-.01	.05	-.04	-.01	.06
33. Retardation in siblings	-.13	-.12	.06	-.01	.18	-.05	.03	.01	-.08	.01	.02	-.03	.05	.00	.01	-.02	.00	.01	-.03
34. Family size	-.20	-.22	.41	-.06	.82	-.12	.00	-.02	-.19	-.02	.03	-.07	.14	.01	.03	.06	.02	.02	.04
35. Cerebral palsy	-.02	-.02	.00	.00	.01	-.01	.00	.02	-.02	-.02	.03	.02	.00	-.01	-.09	-.06	.07	.11	-.06
36. Epilepsy	-.01	-.01	-.01	.00	.00	.00	.01	.01	-.02	.00	.02	.02	.00	.00	-.05	-.03	.02	.07	-.02
37. Bender-Gestalt error score	-.28	-.28	.00	-.10	.11	-.21	.03	.02	-.13	.00	.02	-.03	.08	-.01	-.02	-.08	.04	.02	-.10
38. Arithmetic score	.28	.27	.00	.06	-.13	.17	-.05	-.03	.14	-.02	-.02	.04	-.07	.05	.03	.06	-.05	-.05	.08

(continued)

306

Table 1 (continued)

	20	21	22	23	24	25	26	27	28	29	30	31	32	33	34	35	36	37	38
1. Socioeconomic index	.00	-.01	.00	.09	.00	-.02	-.01	.00	.00	.24	-.02	.11	.52	-.06	-.16	.00	-.02	-.15	.16
2. Maternal education	.00	-.01	.00	.07	.00	-.03	.00	-.01	-.03	.22	-.04	.09	.47	-.12	-.29	-.01	-.02	-.15	.19
3. Maternal age	.05	.03	-.01	.00	.01	.01	.00	.01	.00	.09	.01	.02	-.06	.10	.44	.00	.01	-.02	.00
4. Maternal height	.00	.00	.01	.03	.00	.01	.01	-.01	-.01	.03	-.01	.11	.04	-.01	-.02	.00	.00	-.03	.03
5. Parity	.03	.01	-.01	-.07	.00	.04	.01	.02	.00	-.02	.00	-.05	-.18	.21	.85	.01	.00	.06	-.08
6. Maternal SRA score	-.01	-.01	-.01	.05	-.01	-.02	.00	-.02	-.01	.20	-.05	.05	.29	-.07	-.22	-.01	-.01	-.13	.16
7. Urinary tract infection in pregnancy	-.02	.02	.00	.00	-.02	-.01	.01	.00	-.02	-.02	.00	-.03	-.03	.03	.02	-.01	.01	.01	-.02
8. Maternal seizures in pregnancy	.00	.00	.00	.00	.01	.03	.03	.01	.02	-.02	.03	-.02	-.03	.02	.00	.01	.02	.02	-.03
9. Number of prenatal visits	.01	.00	-.01	.19	-.01	-.05	-.02	.01	.00	.13	.00	.07	.13	-.02	-.16	-.02	.00	-.07	.06
10. Weight gain in pregnancy	.01	.00	-.01	.09	-.01	-.02	-.02	.00	.01	.03	.02	.08	.05	-.01	-.02	-.01	.00	-.02	.02
11. Breech delivery	.03	.03	.00	-.12	.03	.04	.02	.01	.03	-.04	.03	-.01	-.01	.01	.05	.03	-.01	.03	-.03
12. Midforceps delivery	-.01	.00	.00	.04	.00	-.01	.00	-.01	.02	.03	-.01	.01	.04	-.01	-.08	.00	.00	.00	.01
13. Inhalation anesthetics at delivery	-.01	.01	-.01	.08	.01	-.01	-.01	.01	.02	.06	-.01	-.01	.08	.00	-.01	.00	.00	-.04	.08
14. Sex of child	-.01	-.01	-.01	.02	.01	-.01	.00	-.01	-.07	.07	-.03	-.11	.00	.02	.01	-.01	.00	.04	.08
15. Apgar score at 5 minutes	-.01	-.06	.00	.05	-.03	-.06	-.04	.00	-.08	.00	-.03	.02	-.05	-.01	.04	-.05	-.01	-.02	-.01
16. Birthweight	.00	-.01	-.01	.27	-.03	-.10	-.07	.00	-.05	.13	-.04	.27	.03	.00	.09	-.05	-.01	-.11	.08
17. Respiratory difficulty	.00	.06	.00	-.11	.03	.07	.07	.02	.05	-.05	.03	.00	-.01	-.01	.01	.05	.01	.02	-.05
18. Neonatal brain abnormality	.15	.31	.06	-.06	.03	.09	.07	.06	.05	-.04	.07	-.02	.00	.01	.00	.09	.05	.02	-.02
19. Head circumference at birth	-.01	-.02	.01	.25	-.04	-.10	-.07	.00	-.04	.11	-.04	.39	.03	-.02	.04	-.05	.00	-.11	.07

(continued)

Table 1 (continued)

		20	21	22	23	24	25	26	27	28	29	30	31	32	33	34	35	36	37	38
20.	Down's syndrome	—	.03	.00	-.13	.11	.20	.02	.00	.13	-.10	.12	-.06	.00	.01	.02	.00	.02	.02	-.06
21.	Neonatal seizures	.00	—	.00	-.05	.00	.06	.09	.19	.03	-.03	.03	-.02	-.01	.01	.01	.08	.11	.01	-.02
22.	Major CNS malformations	.00	.04	—	-.04	.00	.06	.10	.00	.05	-.03	.03	.06	-.01	-.01	-.01	.07	.00	.03	-.03
23.	Bayley mental score at 8 months	-.12	-.06	-.07	—	-.09	-.35	-.17	-.04	-.13	.25	-.19	.05	.09	-.04	-.10	-.17	-.08	-.13	.17
24.	Congenital heart disease at 1 year	.12	.00	.00	-.04	—	.09	.03	.01	.02	-.04	.05	-.03	-.01	.01	.00	.05	.03	.02	-.02
25.	Delayed motor development	.18	.05	.09	-.33	.07	—	.37	.08	.13	-.14	.20	-.04	-.03	.03	.03	.21	.12	.10	-.12
26.	Cerebral palsy	.00	.10	.12	-.23	.00	.30	—	.11	.08	-.07	.10	-.03	-.01	.01	.00	.44	.13	.06	-.06
27.	Non-febrile seizures	.00	.08	.05	-.11	.00	.09	.16	—	.02	-.02	.06	.00	.00	-.01	.01	.10	.33	.01	-.02
28.	Abnormal language expression at 3 years	.11	.03	.04	-.18	.05	.15	.09	.05	—	-.27	.19	-.04	-.02	.05	.02	.12	.05	.10	-.18
29.	Stanford-Binet IQ at 4 years	-.11	-.03	-.06	.22	-.05	-.15	-.08	-.04	-.32	—	-.27	.12	.25	-.06	-.13	-.10	-.06	-.31	.42
30.	Abnormal behavior rating	.16	.03	.08	-.17	.02	.16	.10	.06	.16	-.26	—	-.03	-.03	.02	.01	.16	.10	.11	-.17
31.	Head circumference	-.08	-.01	.01	.05	-.02	-.05	-.02	-.02	-.03	.15	-.04	—	.09	-.04	-.07	-.03	.01	-.13	.12
32.	Socioeconomic index at 7 years	-.01	.00	.05	.05	-.02	-.03	-.01	-.01	-.10	.37	-.06	.13	—	-.11	-.25	.00	-.02	-.18	.21
33.	Retardation in siblings	.01	-.01	.00	-.08	.00	.05	.02	.00	.05	-.14	.04	-.05	-.15	—	.20	.01	.01	.06	-.07
34.	Family size	.01	-.01	-.01	-.07	.01	.05	.01	.01	.05	-.20	.03	-.06	-.21	.19	—	.01	.00	.11	-.12
35.	Cerebral palsy	.00	.10	.12	-.21	.01	.26	.59	.15	.13	-.11	.12	-.03	-.01	.01	.01	—	.19	.07	-.07
36.	Epilepsy	.02	.08	.03	-.13	.01	.13	.19	.37	.09	-.06	.09	-.03	-.01	.03	.01	.20	—	.03	-.04
37.	Bender-Gestalt error score	.03	.01	.05	-.13	.03	.10	.06	.04	.19	-.38	.13	-.15	-.30	.11	.13	.08	.05	—	-.50
38.	Arithmetic score	-.06	-.03	-.06	.18	-.04	-.10	-.07	-.04	-.28	.46	-.19	.14	.28	-.13	-.15	-.07	-.06	-.50	—

Note: Blacks above and whites below the diagonal.

cioeconomic status at age 7; maternal age and parity in the prenatal period and later family size; cerebral palsy at 1 and at 7 years; nonfebrile seizures in the first year and epilepsy; IQ at age 4 and, at age 7, the Bender–Gestalt score, the arithmetic score, and socioeconomic status. Among whites only, prenatal socioeconomic status and level of maternal education were related to the Bender and arithmetic scores, delayed motor development at age 1 to the later diagnosis of cerebral palsy, and language expression at age 3 to the arithmetic score. In the black sample, maternal education in the prenatal period and later family size were correlated.

Similar examinations can be made of within-epoch relationships. It is of some interest that most of these across-epoch relationships were among continuous measures of family and maternal characteristics, physical development, and cognitive functioning. Very few of the prenatal and perinatal complications that discriminated between the retarded and higher IQ groups were related to other developmental parameters at even a modest level.

Appendix 4:
Prenatal Drug
Exposure

Prenatal exposure to a variety of drugs can produce structural, biochemical, and/or behavioral alterations (Yanai, 1984). Women in the Collaborative Perinatal Project were asked to report all drugs taken during their pregnancies. For the more than 2,000 preparations named, the pharmacologically active compounds were determined. These 693 compounds were then classified into 45 categories such as barbiturates or diuretics (Heinonen, Slone, & Shapiro, 1977). Fewer than 6% of the women reported taking no drugs. The mean number of different drugs used was just under four.

In comparisons between the retarded and higher IQ groups, the 45 drug categories were analyzed as potential risk factors in the same way as were other antecedents. Each category of drug was screened for use in three time periods: early in pregnancy (lunar month 1–4); late in pregnancy (5th lunar month to delivery); and throughout pregnancy (both early and late). In calculating the proportion of women taking a drug at a given time, those taking it at other times were excluded. Drug categories that were significant in multivariate analyses through the perinatal period are reported in this appendix. The procedure followed was to add those that passed the univariate screen in each sample ($p < .05$) to the sets of prenatal discriminators shown in Chapter 4. In these reanalyses, several of the drugs were retained ($p < .05$), but the canonical correlations were essentially unaffected, increasing by a maximum of only .03 in comparisons between the severely retarded and higher IQ groups. The addition of obstetric discriminators to the significant prenatal ones did not eliminate any of the prenatal drugs. There were some changes, however, when neonatal discriminators were added in final summary analyses through the perinatal period.

Drug categories significant in the prenatal analyses and the perinatal summaries are shown in Tables 1 and 2. Nonbarbiturate anticonvulsants, barbiturates, and phenothiazines were related to severe retardation in both samples, the latter

Table 1
Prenatal Drugs Discriminating Between the Severely Retarded
and Comparison Groups

Time Taken	White		Black	
	Prenatal Period	Prenatal and Perinatal	Prenatal Period	Prenatal and Perinatal
Nonbarbiturate Anticonvulsants				
Early	—	—	—	—
Late	**	—	**	**
Throughout	**	**	—	—
Barbiturates				
Early	—	—	—	—
Late	**	—	—	—
Throughout	—	—	**	**
Phenothiazines				
Early	**	—	—	—
Late	—	—	**	**
Throughout	—	—	—	—
Calcium, Parenteral Iron, and Vitamins B_{12} and K				
Early	—	—	—	—
Late	—	—	—	—
Throughout	**	**	—	—
Immunizing Agents				
Early	**	—	—	—
Late	**	**	—	—
Throughout	—	—	—	—

Table 2
Prenatal Drugs Discriminating Between the Mildly Retarded and Comparison Groups

Time Taken	White		Black	
	Prenatal Period	Prenatal and Perinatal	Prenatal Period	Prenatal and Perinatal
Nonbarbiturate Anticonvulsants				
Early	—	—	—	—
Late	**	**	—	—
Throughout	—	—	—	—
Diuretics				
Early	—	—	—	—
Late	**	**	—	—
Throughout	—	—	—	—
Antibiotics				
Early	—	—	—	—
Late	—	—	**	**
Throughout	—	—	—	—
Systemic Antimicrobial and Antiparasitic Agents				
Early	—	—	—	—
Late	—	—	—	—
Throughout	**	**	—	—
Muscle Relaxants				
Early	—	—	—	—
Late	—	—	**	**
Throughout	—	—	—	—
Progestational Agents				
Early	—	—	—	—
Late	**	—	—	—
Throughout	—	—	—	—

two in prenatal analyses only among whites. Significant time periods for the nonbarbiturate anticonvulsants and the barbiturates were late or throughout pregnancy and for the phenothiazines early or late. Two other classes of drugs were related to severe retardation among whites: calcium, parenteral iron, and vitamins B_{12} and K; and immunizing agents.

Nonbarbiturate anticonvulsants, diuretics, and progestational agents late in pregnancy, and systemic antimicrobial and antiparasitic agents throughout pregnancy were related to mild retardation among whites. Among blacks, antibiotics and muscle relaxants late in pregnancy were independently associated with mild retardation.

Distributions by IQ group for the drugs retained in the discriminant function analyses in each sample are shown in Tables 3 and 4. The significant multivariate comparisons indicated are those from the prenatal analyses. Among whites, nonbarbiturate anticonvulsants were rarely reported, but their use was more frequent among mothers of the severely retarded than the above average and among mothers of the mildly retarded than the average group. The most common agents were phenytoin and magnesium sulfate. Ingestion of barbiturates (primarily phenobarbital, secobarbital, and pentobarbital) also discriminated between the severely retarded and the above average. In this extreme group comparison, maternal seizures, a risk factor for severe retardation in the original analysis, was no longer significant. More frequent reports of phenothiazines early in pregnancy was a significant factor in the comparison between the severely retarded and the borderline children. Prochlorperazine (Compazine) was the most common of these drugs, followed by promethazine and promazine.

Use throughout pregnancy of a group of vitamins and minerals that did not include regular multivitamin supplements (mainly calcium compounds) was higher among mothers of the severely retarded white children than those of average or above-average children. Immunizing agents, given both early and late, discriminated between the severely retarded and the mildly retarded and borderline, an apparent result of low frequencies in these two comparison groups. Polio vaccine was by far the most common agent.

Three other classes of drugs were discriminators for the mildly retarded only in the white sample: diuretics (hydrochlorothiazide, chlorothiazide, chlorthalidone, bendroflumethiazide, and acetazolamide); systemic antimicrobial and antiparasitic agents (phenazophyridine, nitrofurantoin, and antimony potassium tartrate); and progestational agents (progesterone, hydroxyprogesterone, and medroxyprogesterone). All were used more frequently than in the above-average group, and progestational agents late in pregnancy were significant in the comparison with the average group, as well.

In the black sample, higher frequencies for nonbarbiturate anticonvulsants late in pregnancy and barbiturates throughout pregnancy in the severely retarded group failed to "replace" maternal seizures in the comparison with the average group. Barbiturates also discriminated between the severely retarded and

Table 3
Table 3
Frequency of Drugs Taken in Pregnancy by IQ Group in the White Sample

Time Taken[1]	1 Severely Retarded (N = 90)	2 Mildly Retarded (N = 193)	3 Borderline (N = 2399)	4 Average (N = 12549)	5 Above Average (N = 1873)	χ^2	r_{IQ}
			Percent				

Nonbarbiturate Anticonvulsants

Early	0.00	0.00	0.04	0.02	0.05	0.07	.01
Late	1.11	1.55	0.58	*0.26*	**0.00**	25.06****	−.04*****
Throughout	2.22	0.00	0.79	0.33	**0.05**	26.73****	−.03***
None	96.67	98.45	98.56	99.39	99.90	—	—

Barbiturates

Early	0.00	1.55	2.50	2.33	3.42	8.56	.03**
Late	27.78	22.80	23.88	21.68	**17.14**	29.87*****	−.04*****
Throughout	6.67	2.07	3.50	3.92	3.79	4.79	−.00
None	65.55	73.58	70.12	72.07	75.65	—	—

Phenothiazines

Early	5.56	1.55	**1.58**	2.54	3.31	17.09**	.03***
Late	4.44	7.25	6.09	5.43	4.38	6.45	−.02**
Throughout	1.11	1.55	0.92	1.09	1.76	7.97	.02*
None	88.89	89.65	91.41	90.94	90.55	—	—

Calcium, Parenteral Iron, and Vitamins B_{12} and K

Early	1.11	0.00	0.29	0.66	0.53	6.40	.01
Late	6.67	8.81	6.92	6.49	4.11	20.13***	−.04*****
Throughout	3.33	2.07	1.04	**0.83**	**0.27**	19.80***	−.03****
None	88.89	89.12	91.75	92.02	95.09	—	—

Immunizing Agents

Early	21.11	**10.88**	**12.38**	18.73	25.89	236.02*****	.16*****
Late	35.56	**26.94**	**26.84**	30.72	32.35	111.79*****	.10*****
Throughout	4.44	3.63	5.04	7.77	9.77	104.92*****	.12*****
None	38.89	58.55	55.74	42.78	31.99	—	—

(continued)

Table 3 (continued)

Time Taken[1]	1 Severely Retarded (N = 90)	2 Mildly Retarded (N = 193)	3 Borderline (N = 2399)	4 Average (N = 12549)	5 Above Average (N = 1873)	χ^2	r_{IQ}
			Percent				

Diuretics

Early	0.00	0.00	0.08	0.14	0.00	3.30	− .00
Late	31.11	40.41	37.89	31.50	25.25	85.26*****	− .07*****
Throughout	0.00	0.00	0.71	0.77	0.69	2.46	.00
None	68.89	59.59	61.32	67.59	74.06	—	—

Systemic Antimicrobial and Antiparasitic Agents

Early	0.00	1.04	1.00	1.90	2.62	17.94**	.03***
Late	6.67	3.63	3.79	3.70	3.10	3.84	− .01
Throughout	0.00	1.55	0.42	0.52	0.21	8.41	− .01
None	93.33	93.78	94.79	93.88	94.07	—	—

Progestational Agents

Early	0.00	0.52	1.08	1.88	2.94	23.29***	.04*****
Late	0.00	3.11	1.96	1.16	0.75	20.20***	− .03**
Throughout	1.11	0.00	0.25	0.70	1.07	12.60*	.03**
None	98.89	96.37	96.71	96.26	95.34	—	—

Note: The sample of women taking drugs during a specific time period or never was used to calculate the chi-square and correlation statistics.

[1]Early indicates the first through the 4th lunar month; late indicates the fifth lunar month to delivery.

Differs from severely retarded in D.F.

Differs from mildly retarded in D.F.

    *p<.05
   **p<.01
  ***p<.001
 ****p<.0001
*****p<.00001

Table 4

Frequency of Drugs Taken in Pregnancy by IQ Group in the Black Sample

Time Taken	1 Severely Retarded (N = 121)	2 Mildly Retarded (N = 847)	3 Borderline (N = 8094)	4 Average (N = 9774)	5 Above Average (N = 156)	χ^2	r_{IQ}
			Percent				
Nonbarbiturate Anticonvulsants							
Early	0.83	0.00	0.00	0.01	0.00	80.04****	−.02**
Late	2.48	1.18	1.03	**0.46**	0.00	27.88***	−.04****
Throughout	1.65	0.35	0.21	0.24	0.00	11.74*	−.02*
None	95.04	98.47	98.76	99.29	100.00	—	—
Barbiturates							
Early	4.13	1.65	2.01	2.04	1.28	4.18	−.01
Late	20.66	21.25	19.66	19.50	26.28	6.49	−.01
Throughout	7.44	**1.89**	**2.45**	**2.42**	4.49	18.18**	−.01
None	67.77	75.21	75.88	76.04	67.95	—	—
Phenothiazines							
Early	2.48	0.59	1.31	1.40	2.56	6.82	.01
Late	9.09	4.84	**4.13**	**3.87**	1.92	12.05*	−.02*
Throughout	0.00	0.83	0.42	0.59	0.00	5.50	.00
None	88.43	93.74	94.14	94.14	95.52	—	—
Antibiotics							
Early	8.26	7.32	7.12	7.92	7.05	4.30	.01*
Late	9.92	11.57	*9.04*	9.58	10.90	6.61	.00
Throughout	1.65	1.53	2.29	2.26	3.85	4.03	.01
None	80.17	79.58	81.55	80.24	78.20	—	—
Muscle Relaxants							
Early	0.00	0.12	0.15	0.16	0.00	0.58	−.00
Late	0.00	1.06	0.51	*0.43*	0.00	7.90	−.01
Throughout	0.00	0.00	0.00	0.02	0.00	1.88	.02
None	100.00	98.82	99.34	99.39	100.00	—	—

Differs from severely retarded in D.F.

Differs from mildly retarded in D.F.

*$p<.05$

**$p<.01$

***$p<.0001$

****$p<.00001$

the mildly retarded and borderline, eliminating the risk factor of maternal seizures in the former comparison only. Intake of phenothiazines by mothers of the
severely retarded was a significant factor in comparisons with the borderline and
average groups.

Mothers of the mildly retarded in the black sample took more antibiotics late
in pregnancy than those of borderline children. This was a large category of
drugs, the most common of which were tetracycline, streptomycin, chloram-
phenicol, and oxytetracycline. Many women reported simply "antibiotic," without further specification. Intake of rarely used muscle relaxants (methocar-
bamol, succinylcholine, and carisoprodal) discriminated between the mildly
retarded and the average group.

Drug categories were also analyzed for relationships with mental retardation
unaccompanied by major neurological abnormality. Classes of drugs passing the
univariate screens for the CNS normal subgroups in each sample were entered in
discriminant function analyses along with the previously identified prenatal
discriminators (see Chapter 9). As was found earlier, the addition of significant
obstetric factors did not affect the retention of any prenatal drug. Results from
the prenatal and the combined prenatal and perinatal analyses are summarized
in Tables 5 and 6.

For the severely retarded, communalities with the total group were higher
frequencies for nonbarbiturate anticonvulsants, barbiturates, and phenothiazines—the latter two categories now significant among blacks only. A discriminator unique to the CNS normals was use of antidiabetic drugs throughout
pregnancy in the white sample. For the mildly retarded, only two drug categories
were retained among whites: diuretics late in pregnancy, which was shared with
the total group, and the category containing calcium, parenteral iron, and
vitamins B_{12} and K.

Frequencies for the significant drugs by IQ subgroup are shown in Tables 7
and 8. Among whites, both nonbarbiturate anticonvulsants and antidiabetic
drugs (primarily insulin) taken throughout pregnancy discriminated between the
severely retarded and the above average. Only one of the severely retarded CNS
normals was exposed prenatally to either drug. For the mildly retarded, more
widespread use late in pregnancy of diuretics and of calcium compounds and
related agents was significant in the comparison with the above-average subgroup. In the black sample, where findings were confined to the severely retarded subgroup, results showing more frequent use of nonbarbiturate anticonvulsants and phenothiazines late in pregnancy and barbiturates throughout
pregnancy were essentially the same as those in the total group. The most
limited prenatal exposure was to nonbarbiturate anticonvulsants involving only
two of the severely retarded CNS normals.

Although adding little to the explanatory power of other antecedents, several
classes of drugs taken in pregnancy were found to be independently related to
severe and to mild retardation in multivariate analyses through the perinatal

Table 5

**Prenatal Drugs Discriminating Between the Severely Retarded
and Comparison Subgroups**

Time Taken	White		Black	
	Prenatal Period	Prenatal and Perinatal	Prenatal Period	Prenatal and Perinatal
Nonbarbiturate Anticonvulsants				
Early	—	—	—	—
Late	—	—	**	**
Throughout	**	**	—	—
Barbiturates				
Early	—	—	—	—
Late	—	—	—	—
Throughout	—	—	**	**
Phenothiazines				
Early	—	—	—	—
Late	—	—	**	**
Throughout	—	—	—	—
Antidiabetic Drugs				
Early	—	—	—	—
Late	—	—	—	—
Throughout	**	**	—	—

period. Of particular interest are the fairly consistent findings of increased maternal intake in the retarded groups of drugs known to affect the central nervous system—nonbarbiturate anticonvulsants, barbiturates, and phenothiazines. These results lend support to continued experimental investigation of relationships between prenatal exposure to drugs and chemicals, especially those acting on the central nervous system, and postnatal development.

Table 6
Prenatal Drugs Discriminating Between the Mildly Retarded
and Comparison Subgroups

Time Taken	White		Black	
	Prenatal Period	Prenatal and Perinatal	Prenatal Period	Prenatal and Perinatal
Diuretics				
Early	—	—	—	—
Late	**	**	—	—
Throughout	—	—	—	—
Calcium, Parenteral Iron, and Vitamins B_{12} and K				
Early	—	—	—	—
Late	**	**	—	—
Throughout	—	—	—	—

Table 7

Frequency of Drugs Taken During Pregnancy by IQ Subgroup in the White Sample

Time Taken	1 Severely Retarded (N = 26)	2 Mildly Retarded (N = 165)	3 Borderline (N = 2322)	4 Average (N = 12442)	5 Above Average (N = 1862)	χ^2	r_{IQ}
			Percent				
			Nonbarbiturate Anticonvulsants				
Early	0.00	0.00	0.00	0.02	0.05	1.79	.02*
Late	0.00	1.21	0.60	0.26	0.00	19.01***	−.03****
Throughout	3.85	0.00	0.69	0.34	**0.05**	21.70***	−.02**
None	96.15	98.79	98.71	99.38	00.89	—	—
			Antidiabetic Drugs				
Early	0.00	0.00	0.00	0.02	0.00	0.70	.01
Late	0.00	0.00	0.30	0.16	0.16	2.58	−.01
Throughout	3.85	0.00	0.43	0.23	**0.11**	18.05**	−.02**
None	96.15	100.00	99.27	99.60	99.73	—	—
			Diuretics				
Early	0.00	0.00	0.09	0.14	0.00	3.40	−.00
Late	26.92	41.82	37.90	31.49	*25.29*	86.78*****	−.08*****
Throughout	0.00	0.00	1.16	0.78	0.70	8.19	−.00
None	73.08	58.18	60.86	67.59	74.01	—	—
			Calcium, Parenteral Iron, and Vitamins B_{12} and K				
Early	0.00	0.00	0.30	0.67	0.54	5.67	.01
Late	15.38	10.30	6.98	6.51	*4.14*	25.85****	−.04*****
Throughout	0.00	2.42	1.08	0.84	0.27	15.09**	−.03***
None	84.62	87.27	91.65	91.99	95.06	—	—

Differs from severely retarded in D.F.

Differs from mildly retarded in D.F.

*p<.05
**p<.01
***p<.001
****p<.0001
*****p<.00001

320

Table 8
Frequency of Drugs Taken in Pregnancy by IQ Subgroup
in the Black Sample

Time Taken	1 Severely Retarded (N = 49)	2 Mildly Retarded (N = 796)	3 Borderline (N = 8002)	4 Average (N = 9723)	5 Above Average (N = 155)	χ^2	r_{IQ}
			Percent				
			Nonbarbiturate Anticonvulsants				
Early	0.00	0.00	0.00	0.01	0.00	0.92	.00
Late	4.08	1.13	1.02	**0.46**	0.00	29.57***	−.04***
Throughout	2.04	0.38	0.20	0.23	0.00	8.93	−.01
None	93.88	98.49	98.78	99.30	100.00	—	—
			Barbiturates				
Early	4.08	1.51	2.00	2.04	1.29	2.66	−.00
Late	20.41	21.11	19.60	19.46	26.45	6.33	−.01
Throughout	10.20	**1.88**	**2.44**	**2.43**	4.52	17.82**	−.00
None	65.31	75.50	75.97	76.08	67.74	—	—
			Phenothiazines				
Early	2.04	0.63	1.30	1.38	2.58	5.14	.01
Late	12.24	4.27	4.15	**3.88**	**1.94**	11.26*	−.01
Throughout	0.00	0.88	0.42	0.60	0.00	5.36	.00
None	85.71	94.22	94.13	94.15	95.48	—	—

Differs from severely retarded in D.F.
  *$p<.05$
 **$p<.01$
***$p<.00001$

Appendix 5:
Distributions and Univariate Statistics for Discriminating Characteristics of the Mildly Retarded Subgroup

Table 1
Retarded Parents by IQ Subgroup

	1 Severely Retarded	2 Mildly Retarded	3 Borderline	4 Average	5 Above Average	χ^2	r_{IQ}
			Percent				

Retarded Mother

	1 Severely Retarded	2 Mildly Retarded	3 Borderline	4 Average	5 Above Average	χ^2	r_{IQ}
White	0.00	4.88	*1.42*	*0.41*	*0.11*	97.56***	−.06***
Black	3.51	3.22	1.77	0.72	0.00	66.87***	−.06***

Group Ns: White - 24 164 2320 12394 1853

Black - 57 808 7972 9572 153

Retarded Father

	1 Severely Retarded	2 Mildly Retarded	3 Borderline	4 Average	5 Above Average	χ^2	r_{IQ}
White	0.00	2.60	*0.72*	*0.18*	0.00	59.16***	−.05***
Black	0.00	1.20	0.57	*0.37*	0.00	12.44*	−.02**

Group Ns: White - 23 154 2230 12166 1840

Black - 47 749 7561 9166 148

Differs from mildly retarded in D.F.
  *$p<.05$
 **$p<.01$
***$p<.00001$

Table 2
Maternal Parity by IQ Subgroup

	1 Severely Retarded		2 Mildly Retarded		3 Borderline		4 Average		5 Above Average		F	r_{IQ}
	M	S.D.	M	S.D.	M	S.D.	M	S.D.	M	S.D.		
White	2.5	2.3	2.3	2.1	2.2	2.1	1.8	1.9	*1.1*	*1.4*	95.05*	−.17*
Black	2.3	2.3	2.9	2.9	2.4	2.4	2.2	2.2	*1.9*	*1.9*	27.10*	−.08*

Group Ns: White - 26 172 2388 12641 1875

Black - 59 835 8211 9852 157

Differs from mildly retarded in D.F.
*$p<.00001$

Table 3
Inhalation Anesthetic at Delivery by IQ Subgroup

	1 Severely Retarded	2 Mildly Retarded	3 Borderline	4 Average	5 Above Average	χ^2	r_{IQ}
			Percent				
White	33.33	49.42	*38.15*	*27.51*	*16.34*	287.64*	−.15*
Black	41.38	36.03	*39.67*	*43.81*	*49.04*	46.18*	.05*

Group Ns: White- 24 172 2362 12553 1867
          Black-   58 827 8128   9785   157

Differs from mildly retarded in D.F.
*$p <$.00001

Table 4
Major Cardiovascular Malformations by IQ Subgroup

	1 Severely Retarded	2 Mildly Retarded	3 Borderline	4 Average	5 Above Average	χ^2	r_{IQ}
			Percent				
White	0.00	1.73	*0.33*	*0.21*	*0.11*	19.36*	−.03*
Black	0.00	0.60	*0.18*	*0.16*	0.64	9.31	−.01

Group Ns: White - 26 173 2391 12667 1878
          Black - 59 839 8223   9868   157

Differs from mildly retarded in D.F.
*$p <$.001

Table 5
Maternal Age at Menarche by IQ Subgroup

	1 Severely Retarded		2 Mildly Retarded		3 Borderline		4 Average		5 Above Average		F	r_{IQ}
	M	S.D.	M	S.D.	M	S.D.	M	S.D.	M	S.D.		
White	12.9	1.1	13.3	1.8	*12.8*	*1.6*	*12.6 1.5*		12.6	1.4	11.81***	−.05***
Black	12.8	1.3	12.7	1.5	12.7	1.5	12.7	1.6	12.5	1.5	4.10*	−.03**

Group Ns: White -   25   169   2349   12510   1860
              Black -   58   830   8130   9789   154

Differs from mildly retarded in D.F.
 *p<.01
 **p<.0001
 ***p<.00001

Table 6
Gestation at Registration in Weeks by IQ Subgroup

	1 Severely Retarded		2 Mildly Retarded		3 Borderline		4 Average		5 Above Average		F	r_{IQ}
	M	S.D.	M	S.D.	M	S.D.	M	S.D.	M	S.D.		
White	21.8	9.3	23.7	9.0	22.7	8.9	*20.1*	*8.9*	17.3	8.2	106.69*	−.19*
Black	23.2	7.1	24.1	7.4	23.5	7.4	22.5	7.4	20.2	7.4	30.57*	−.09*

Group Ns: White-   26   173   2388   12664   1878
              Black-   59   839   8216   9855   157

Differs from mildly retarded in D.F.
 *p <.00001

Table 7

Hospitalization in Early Pregnancy by IQ Subgroup

	1 Severely Retarded	2 Mildly Retarded	3 Borderline	4 Average	5 Above Average	χ^2	r_{IQ}
			Percent				
White	20.00	20.93	17.81	*13.67*	*9.07*	75.44***	− .07***
Black	25.42	16.74	14.51	*13.68*	16.77	14.18**	− .02*

Group Ns: White - 25 172 2370 12584 1874

Black - 59 836 8152 9789 155

Differs from mildly retarded in D.F.
 *p<.05
 **p<.01
 ***p<.00001

Table 8

Cigarette Smoking in Pregnancy and Recent Maternal Illnesses by IQ Subgroup

	1 Severely Retarded		2 Mildly Retarded		3 Borderline		4 Average		5 Above Average		F	r_{IQ}
	M	S.D.	M	S.D.	M	S.D.	M	S.D.	M	S.D.		
				Number of Cigarettes per Day in Pregnancy								
White	6.0	7.6	6.7	9.2	*9.4*	*11.2*	*8.4*	*10.6*	5.4	9.0	42.65**	− .10**
Black	5.4	8.1	**3.6**	**6.7**	3.9	6.9	**3.7**	**6.7**	**2.8**	**5.5**	2.67*	− .01*

Group Ns: White - 25 172 2369 12576 1870

Black - 58 829 8161 9799 155

					Number of Recent Maternal Illnesses							
White	0.4	0.6	0.4	0.7	0.6	0.8	0.6	0.8	*0.7*	*0.9*	9.57**	.06**
Black	0.6	0.9	0.4	0.7	0.5	0.7	0.5	0.7	0.4	0.7	1.24	− .00

Group Ns: White - 25 167 2325 12416 1850

Black - 59 822 8063 9706 154

Differs from severely retarded in D.F.
Differs from mildly retarded in D.F.
 *p<.05
 **p<.00001

326

Table 9
Abdomino-pelvic X-rays and Midforceps Delivery by IQ Subgroup

	1 Severely Retarded	2 Mildly Retarded	3 Borderline	4 Average	5 Above Average	χ^2	r_{IQ}
			Percent				

Abdomino-pelvic X-rays

	1	2	3	4	5	χ^2	r_{IQ}
White	24.00	17.26	*27.65*	*27.42*	25.71	11.12*	−.00
Black	16.95	18.35	17.74	18.86	21.05	4.55	.02**

Group Ns: White - 25 168 2340 12469 1859

Black - 59 823 8108 9772 152

Midforceps Delivery

	1	2	3	4	5	χ^2	r_{IQ}
White	15.00	5.96	10.48	12.83	*16.03*	32.49***	.06***
Black	4.26	5.07	5.04	5.14	10.00	7.01	.01

Group Ns: White - 20 151 2081 11376 1709

Black - 47 750 7436 8919 140

Differs from mildly retarded in D.F.
*p<.05
**p<.01
***p<.00001

Table 10
Respiratory Difficulty in Newborn by IQ Subgroup

	1 Severely Retarded	2 Mildly Retarded	3 Borderline	4 Average	5 Above Average	χ^2	r_{IQ}
			Percent				
White	3.85	3.57	2.11	1.41	*0.59*	23.56*	−.04***
Black	5.17	3.24	1.87	1.38	0.00	26.36**	−.03***

Group Ns: White- 26 168 2369 12575 1868

Black- 58 833 8165 9822 157

Differs from mildly retarded in D.F.
*p <.001
**p <.0001
***p <.00001

327

Table 11

Hematocrit in Pregnancy, Prenatal Visits, and Maternal Height by IQ Subgroup

	1 Severely Retarded	2 Mildly Retarded	3 Borderline	4 Average	5 Above Average	F	r_{IQ}
	M S.D.	M S.D.	M S.D.	M S.D.	M S.D.		

Maternal Hematocrit in Pregnancy

White	33.6 4.1	34.6 3.6	34.1 3.6	34.6 3.5	35.2 3.2	25.90*	.09*
Black	31.2 4.3	31.2 3.6	*31.6 3.4*	*31.9 3.4*	*33.0 3.2*	22.58*	.08*

Group Ns: White -   25   173   2369   12614   1869
Black -   58   832   8146   9798   154

Number of Prenatal Visits

White	8.5 4.1	8.3 4.1	8.7 4.2	10.0 4.1	***11.3 3.6***	114.97*	.19*
Black	7.2 3.7	6.7 3.5	*7.4 3.5*	*8.2 3.6*	*9.2 3.7*	78.47*	.14*

Group Ns: White -   26   172   2385   12656   1874
Black -   59   838   8215   9860   156

Maternal Height (in.)

White	63.5 2.3	62.9 2.3	63.2 2.7	63.6 2.6	*64.3 2.5*	44.25*	.14*
Black	63.1 2.7	63.1 2.6	63.3 2.6	*63.6 2.6*	63.8 3.1	11.03*	.06*

Group Ns: White -   24   160   2171   11238   1654
Black -   58   813   7992   9510   141

Differs from mildly retarded in D.F.
Differs from severely and mildly retarded in D.F.s
*$p < .00001$

Table 12
Heart Disease in Pregnancy, Prior Fetal Death, and Maternal Mental Illness by IQ Subgroup

	1 Severely Retarded	2 Mildly Retarded	3 Borderline	4 Average	5 Above Average	χ^2	r_{IQ}
				Percent			
		Organic Heart Disease in Pregnancy					
White	0.00	1.18	1.74	1.49	0.86	6.54	− .02*
Black	1.79	3.01	*1.71*	*1.56*	1.29	9.88*	− .01*
Group Ns: White -	26	169	2363	12576	1865		
Black -	56	830	8119	9736	155		
		Prior Fetal Death					
White	0.00	7.03	6.93	6.27	4.76	7.11	− .02
Black	17.07	11.57	*8.05*	8.84	9.48	13.92**	− .00
Group Ns: White -	22	128	1819	9022	1072		
Black -	41	648	6101	7273	116		
		Maternal Mental Illness					
White	0.00	1.22	3.28	3.11	2.99	3.01	.00
Black	0.00	2.86	*1.71*	1.54	0.00	11.57*	− .01
Group Ns: White -	24	164	2290	12267	1841		
Black -	57	805	7946	9539	151		

Differs from mildly retarded in D.F.
 *p<.05
**p<.01

Table 13
Conduction Anesthetic at Delivery by IQ Subgroup

	1 Severely Retarded	2 Mildly Retarded	3 Borderline	4 Average	5 Above Average	χ^2	r_{IQ}
			Percent				
White	70.83	56.98	67.19	78.01	87.42	291.53*	.15*
Black	51.72	39.54	45.45	49.56	60.51	62.30*	.06*

Group Ns: White - 24 172 2362 12554 1868
Black - 58 827 8127 9787 157

Differs from mildly retarded in D.F.
*p<.00001

Table 14
Gestational Age in Weeks by IQ Subgroup

	1 Severely Retarded		2 Mildly Retarded		3 Borderline		4 Average		5 Above Average		F	r_{IQ}
	M	S.D.	M	S.D.	M	S.D.	M	S.D.	M	S.D.		
White	39.6	3.9	39.6	3.0	39.9	2.8	40.0	2.4	40.1	2.1	2.96*	.03**
Black	38.4	4.0	38.1	3.8	38.8	3.4	39.0	3.0	39.5	2.7	22.20***	.07***

Differs from mildly retarded in D.F.
*p <.05
**p <.001
***p <.00001

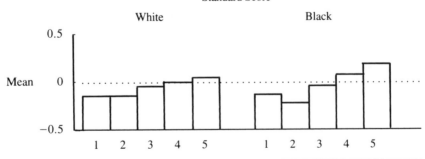

Standard Score

Note. Group Ns: White- 25 173 2359 12611 1871
Black- 58 827 8085 9752 155

Table 15

Apneic Episodes and Primary Apnea by IQ Subgroup

	1 Severely Retarded	2 Mildly Retarded	3 Borderline	4 Average	5 Above Average	χ^2	r_{IQ}
				Percent			
			Multiple Apneic Episodes				
White	0.00	0.60	0.38	0.30	0.43	1.47	− .01
Black	0.00	1.32	*0.31*	0.40	0.00	20.67***	− .01
			Primary Apnea				
White	0.00	1.79	1.10	0.59	0.54	11.67*	− .02**
Black	0.00	2.52	*1.36*	1.43	0.64	8.83	− .01

Group Ns: White -   26 168 2369 12575 1868

Black -   58 833 8165 9822 157

Differs from mildly retarded in D.F.

 *p<.05

 **p<.01

 ***p<.001

Table 16

Fine Motor, Gross Motor, and Block Sort Scores at Age Four by IQ Subgroup

	1 Severely Retarded		2 Mildly Retarded		3 Borderline		4 Average		5 Above Average		F	r_{IQ}
	M	S.D.	M	S.D.	M	S.D.	M	S.D.	M	S.D.		
Fine Motor Score												
White	23.9	23.2	52.0	19.4	70.1	18.6	83.4	14.7	90.4	11.1	515.24*	.38*
Black	25.3	21.6	51.1	17.8	65.9	17.0	76.6	16.3	86.0	13.5	668.16*	.42*
Group Ns: White -	8	91	1654	10009	1397							
Black -	23	585	6542	8365	137							
Gross Motor Score												
White	11.8	20.6	34.2	25.8	62.2	25.4	73.7	21.5	78.0	20.0	182.30*	.23*
Black	15.2	17.5	53.6	27.1	70.2	21.2	76.4	18.8	79.3	17.4	262.40*	.25*
Group Ns: White -	9	80	1383	8835	1273							
Black -	23	541	6200	8127	139							
Graham-Ernhart Block Sort Score												
White	13.6	10.5	21.3	11.5	31.2	9.0	36.4	6.5	39.5	4.5	477.02*	.37*
Black	10.7	9.2	22.4	11.2	29.4	9.5	33.8	7.7	37.9	4.9	475.10*	.35*
Group Ns: White -	9	109	1735	10321	1407							
Black -	23	588	6634	8474	142							

Differs from mildly retarded in D.F.
*$p < .00001$

Table 17

Language, Speech, and Hearing Abnormalities at Age Three by IQ Subgroup

	1 Severely Retarded	2 Mildly Retarded	3 Borderline	4 Average	5 Above Average	χ^2	r_{IQ}
			Percent				
			Abnormal Language Expression				
White	90.91	44.32	*14.82*	*3.13*	*0.25*	760.09*	−.26*
Black	77.78	22.05	*5.91*	*2.26*	0.00	564.40*	−.19*
Group Ns: White -	11	88 1208	5912	812			
Black -	18	390 4262	5267	79			
			Abnormal Speech Production				
White	81.82	29.89	*10.13*	*2.66*	0.86	490.52*	−.19*
Black	78.95	16.28	*3.93*	*1.86*	1.28	560.40*	−.16*
Group Ns: White -	11	87 1194	5897	811			
Black -	19	387 4176	5208	78			
			Abnormal Language Reception				
White	87.50	32.22	12.18	*2.29*	*0.25*	619.10*	−.23*
Black	76.19	27.85	14.14	*6.74*	0.00	366.41*	−.19*
Group Ns: White -	8	90 1207	5907	813			
Black -	21	413 4349	5295	79			
			Abnormal Hearing				
White	25.00	14.06	*4.25*	*2.63*	1.88	47.11*	−.07*
Black	27.27	6.53	*2.45*	1.55	1.30	76.43*	−.08*
Group Ns: White -	4	64 1106	5751	799			
Black -	11	352 4086	5162	77			

Differs from mildly retarded in D.F.
*p<.00001

Table 18
Right Dominance at Age Four by IQ Subgroup

	1 Severely Retarded	2 Mildly Retarded	3 Borderline	4 Average	5 Above Average	χ^2	r_{IQ}
			Percent				
White	16.67	25.41	*40.15*	*45.53*	47.11	44.13**	.04**
Black	27.27	37.74	41.58	43.76	42.96	16.97*	.04**

Group Ns: White -   12   122   1868   10636   1435

Black -   33   636   6811   8673   142

Differs from mildly retarded in D.F.
*p<.01
**p<.00001

Table 19
Congenital Heart Disease at One Year by IQ Subgroup

	1 Severely Retarded	2 Mildly Retarded	3 Borderline	4 Average	5 Above Average	χ^2	r_{IQ}
			Percent				
White	0.00	2.50	0.67	*0.30*	*0.11*	31.62***	− .04***
Black	0.00	1.02	0.54	0.32	0.65	10.80*	− .02**

Group Ns: White -   25   160   2233   12247   1832

Black -   54   787   7849   9577   154

Differs from mildly retarded in D.F.
*p<.05
**p<.01
***p<.00001

Table 20
Intensity of Social Response Rating at Eight Months by IQ Subgroup

	1 Severely Retarded		2 Mildly Retarded		3 Borderline		4 Average		5 Above Average		F	r_{IQ}
	M	S.D.	M	S.D.	M	S.D.	M	S.D.	M	S.D.		
White	3.1	1.0	2.8	0.7	*3.0*	*0.6*	*3.1*	*0.5*	3.1	0.5	10.34*	.05*
Black	2.8	0.8	2.9	0.7	3.0	0.6	*3.0*	*0.5*	3.0	0.6	10.53*	.05*

Differs from mildly retarded in D.F.
*$p < .00001$

Standard Score

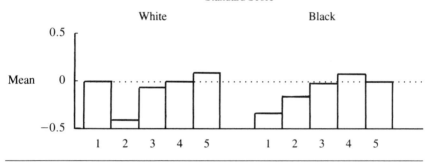

Note. Group Ns: White-   17   109   1697   9953   1511
               Black-   44   581   6283   7726   111

Table 21
Weight at Four Months and One Year by IQ Subgroup

	1 Severely Retarded		2 Mildly Retarded		3 Borderline		4 Average		5 Above Average		F	r_{IQ}
	M	S.D.	M	S.D.	M	S.D.	M	S.D.	M	S.D.		

Weight at Four Months (g)

White	6279	1071	6090	1011	6216	947	6459	862	6626	810	60.92*	.14*
Black	5688	1339	5692	1039	*6027*	*917*	*6239*	*863*	6588	857	114.50*	.18*

Group Ns: White - 23   145   2036   11587   1759
         Black - 54   732   7392   9121   148

Weight at One Year (kg)

White	9.8	1.4	9.4	1.3	9.6	1.3	9.9	1.2	10.1	1.1	51.15*	.14*
Black	9.1	1.4	9.1	1.2	*9.4*	*1.2*	*9.7*	*1.2*	*10.1*	*1.2*	83.00*	.16*

Group Ns: White - 20   122   1937   10990   1607
         Black - 48   683   7102   8786   144

Differs from mildly retarded in D.F.
*$p<.00001$

Table 22
Hypotonia at One Year by IQ Subgroup

	1 Severely Retarded	2 Mildly Retarded	3 Borderline	4 Average	5 Above Average	χ^2	r_{IQ}
			Percent				
White	8.00	3.13	1.30	0.33	0.16	92.64*	−.06*
Black	0.00	1.40	*0.15*	*0.09*	0.65	71.53*	−.03*

Group Ns: White- 25   160   2233   12247   1832
         Black- 54   787   7849   9577   154
Differs from mildly retarded in D.F.
*$p <.00001$

Table 23
Changes in Residence and Housing Density by IQ Subgroup

	1 Severely Retarded		2 Mildly Retarded		3 Borderline		4 Average		5 Above Average		F	r_{IQ}
	M	S.D.	M	S.D.	M	S.D.	M	S.D.	M	S.D.		

				Number of Changes in Residence								
White	3.6	4.6	3.5	3.0	3.2	3.4	*2.5*	*2.7*	2.5	2.3	32.72*	−.07*
Black	2.3	1.8	2.4	2.1	*2.1*	*1.9*	1.9	1.7	1.5	1.6	27.56*	−.09*

Group Ns: White - 17 154 2165 12071 1835
          Black - 49 730 7302 9005 149

				Housing Density								
White	1.3	0.5	1.4	0.6	1.3	0.4	1.1	0.4	*0.9*	*0.3*	224.26*	−.26*
Black	1.5	0.6	1.7	0.8	*1.5*	*0.7*	*1.3*	*0.6*	1.1	0.4	106.62*	−.17*

Group Ns: White - 19 170 2311 12454 1859
          Black - 56 789 7771 9400 155

Differs from mildly retarded in D.F.
*$p<.00001$

Table 24
Additional Maternal Schooling by IQ Subgroup

	1 Severely Retarded	2 Mildly Retarded	3 Borderline	4 Average	5 Above Average	χ^2	r_{IQ}
			Percent				
White	5.88	4.58	11.12	*17.30*	30.82	298.90*	.14*
Black	27.08	20.88	28.30	*34.93*	34.23	122.59*	.09*

Group Ns: White- 17 153 2149 11990 1833
          Black- 48 728 7269 8977 149

Differs from mildly retarded in D.F.
*$p <.00001$

Table 25
Paternal Age by IQ Subgroup

	1 Severely Retarded		2 Mildly Retarded		3 Borderline		4 Average		5 Above Average		F	r_{IQ}
	M	S.D.	M	S.D.	M	S.D.	M	S.D.	M	S.D.		
White	39.7	6.9	36.9	7.5	35.8	7.3	*35.5*	*6.8*	*34.7*	*5.8*	8.81**	−.05**
Black	35.2	9.1	36.3	8.8	35.4	7.9	35.8	7.7	37.7	8.1	3.92*	.03*

Group Ns: White- 13 116 1647 10248 1681

Black- 29 351 3942 5462 108

Differs from mildly retarded in D.F.
*p <.01
**p <.00001

Table 26
Child Care by IQ Subgroup

	1 Severely Retarded	2 Mildly Retarded	3 Borderline	4 Average	5 Above Average	χ^2	r_{IQ}
			Percent				
White	35.29	38.56	52.71	53.88	53.49	17.22*	.01
Black	60.42	59.97	*71.82*	76.90	71.81	136.03**	.08**

Group Ns: White - 17 153 2140 11967 1832

Black - 48 727 7251 8956 149

Differs from mildly retarded in D.F.
*p<.01
**p<.00001

Table 27
Congenital Heart Disease by IQ Subgroup

	1 Severely Retarded	2 Mildly Retarded	3 Borderline	4 Average	5 Above Average	χ^2	r_{IQ}
				Percent			

Cyanotic Congenital Heart Disease

White	0.00	1.16	*0.08*	*0.07*	*0.00*	28.07***	− .02*
Black	0.00	0.49	*0.04*	*0.01*	0.00	40.78****	− .02*

Acyanotic Congenital Heart Disease

White	0.00	2.33	*0.59*	*0.41*	0.43	15.15*	− .02*
Black	0.00	0.98	0.60	0.26	0.00	18.47**	− .03**

Group Ns: White -   26 172 2369 12578 1862

Black -   58 815 8024 9654 154

Differs from mildly retarded in D.F.
*p<.01
**p<.001
***p<.0001
****p<.00001

Table 28

Visual Abnormalities by IQ Subgroup

	1 Severely Retarded	2 Mildly Retarded	3 Borderline	4 Average	5 Above Average	χ^2	r_{IQ}
			Percent				

Color Blindness

White	0.00	9.88	6.25	*3.31*	*3.11*	68.65***	−.05***
Black	3.45	7.48	*4.13*	*2.60*	0.65	75.29***	−.07***
Group Ns: White -	26 172 2369 12578 1862						
Black -	58 815 8024 9654 154						

Strabismus

White	19.23	21.51	*10.85*	*7.66*	*6.12*	82.95***	−.07***
Black	18.97	15.34	*9.91*	*8.20*	9.09	58.98***	−.06***
Group Ns: White -	26 172 2369 12578 1862						
Black -	58 815 8024 9654 154						

Nystagmus

White	0.00	5.23	*1.31*	*0.96*	*0.91*	32.13***	−.02**
Black	1.72	1.35	0.81	0.70	0.00	6.13	−.02*
Group Ns: White -	26 172 2369 12578 1862						
Black -	58 815 8024 9654 154						

Monocular Blindness

White	0.00	0.00	0.00	0.11	0.00	4.94	.00
Black	0.00	0.36	*0.05*	0.06	0.00	11.04*	−.01
Group Ns: White -	26 173 2391 12667 1878						
Black -	59 839 8223 9868 157						

Differs from mildly retarded in D.F.
  *$p<.05$
  **$p<.01$
  ***$p<.00001$

Table 29
Cranial Nerve Abnormality by IQ Subgroup

	1 Severely Retarded	2 Mildly Retarded	3 Borderline	4 Average	5 Above Average	χ^2	r_{IQ}
			Percent				
White	3.85	5.23	*1.06*	*0.45*	*0.32*	86.16**	−.05**
Black	1.72	0.98	0.67	0.29	0.65	19.28*	−.03*

Group Ns: White - 26 172 2369 12578 1862
Black - 58 815 8024 9654 154

Differs from mildly retarded in D.F.
*p<.001
**p<.00001

Table 30
Malformations by IQ Subgroup

	1 Severely Retarded	2 Mildly Retarded	3 Borderline	4 Average	5 Above Average	χ^2	r_{IQ}
			Percent				
		Major Alimentary Tract Malformations					
White	0.00	4.62	*1.76*	2.20	1.92	8.05	−.00
Black	6.78	2.26	2.65	3.01	1.91	6.92	.00
		Major Cardiovascular Malformations					
White	0.00	1.73	0.42	0.24	0.27	15.66*	−.02*
Black	3.39	1.31	0.50	*0.26*	0.00	36.21**	−.04**
		Minor Upper Respiratory or Mouth Malformations					
White	3.85	2.31	0.84	0.86	0.80	7.00	−.01
Black	3.39	1.67	*0.58*	*0.31*	0.64	40.89**	−.03**

Group Ns: White - 26 173 2391 12667 1878
Black - 59 839 8223 9868 157

Differs from mildly retarded in D.F.
*p<.01
**p<.00001

341

Table 31

Symptomatic Intoxication, Burns, and Hemorrhage by IQ Subgroup

	1 Severely Retarded	2 Mildly Retarded	3 Borderline	4 Average	5 Above Average	χ^2	r_{IQ}
				Percent			
			Symptomatic Intoxication				
White	0.00	2.34	0.59	*0.36*	0.38	18.26**	− .02**
Black	1.72	0.98	1.00	0.74	0.00	5.48	− .02**
			Severe Burns				
White	0.00	2.33	0.84	*0.63*	0.32	12.37*	− .02**
Black	0.00	1.10	0.62	0.42	0.65	8.60	− .02**
			Major Hemorrhage				
White	0.00	0.00	0.00	0.19	0.00	8.46	.01
Black	0.00	0.25	*0.02*	*0.02*	0.65	25.91***	− .01

Group Ns: White -   26 172 2369 12578 1862
          Black -   58 815 8024 9654   154

Differs from mildly retarded in D.F.
  *p<.05
  **p<.01
  ***p<.0001

Table 32
Infections by IQ Subgroup

	1 Severely Retarded	2 Mildly Retarded	3 Borderline	4 Average	5 Above Average	χ^2	r_{IQ}
				Percent			

Chickenpox

White	26.92	29.07	35.84	*41.24*	*48.76*	84.75**	.08**
Black	25.86	20.00	23.33	26.74	38.31	52.72**	.06**
Group Ns: White -	26	172	2369	12578	1862		
Black -	58	815	8024	9654	154		

Mumps

White	19.23	18.02	20.60	23.59	27.01	27.07**	.04**
Black	8.62	10.80	*15.08*	*17.02*	*22.08*	35.56**	.05**
Group Ns: White -	26	172	2369	12578	1862		
Black -	58	815	8024	9654	154		

Eye Infection

White	0.00	1.76	0.90	0.76	0.60	3.57	− .02*
Black	0.00	0.25	0.65	0.80	*2.61*	11.98*	.02*
Group Ns: White -	26	170	2344	12407	1822		
Black -	58	811	7994	9613	153		

Differs from mildly retarded in D.F.
 *$p<.05$
 **$p<.00001$

Table 33
Weight in Kilograms by IQ Subgroup

	1 Severely Retarded		2 Mildly Retarded		3 Borderline		4 Average		5 Above Average		F	r_{IQ}
	M	S.D.	M	S.D.	M	S.D.	M	S.D.	M	S.D.		
White	24.8	7.3	22.5	5.4	23.1	4.3	23.8	4.1	24.4	3.9	31.30*	.10*
Black	22.4	5.5	22.8	4.9	23.7	5.0	*24.3*	*4.8*	25.4	5.1	30.34*	.10*

Group Ns: White-   24   171   2363   12552   1858
          Black-   56   815   8001   9638   152
Differs from mildly retarded in D.F.
*p <.00001

Table 34
Bender-Gestalt Error Score by IQ Subgroup

	1 Severely Retarded		2 Mildly Retarded		3 Borderline		4 Average		5 Above Average		F	r_{IQ}
	M	S.D.	M	S.D.	M	S.D.	M	S.D.	M	S.D.		
White	15.8	3.8	12.6	3.8	8.6	3.6	*5.6*	*2.9*	3.4	2.2	1099.94*	−.50*
Black	16.0	3.1	12.7	3.9	*9.3*	*3.6*	*7.0*	*3.2*	4.6	2.6	941.81*	−.44*

Group Ns: White -   6   155   2380   12653   1874
          Black -   24   810   8025   9854   157
Differs from mildly retarded in D.F.
*p<.00001

Table 35
Emotionality Rating by IQ Subgroup

	1 Severely Retarded		2 Mildly Retarded		3 Borderline		4 Average		5 Above Average		F	r_{IQ}
	M	S.D.	M	S.D.	M	S.D.	M	S.D.	M	S.D.		
White	3.5	1.4	2.8	0.8	2.8	0.7	*2.9*	*0.4*	3.0	0.3	41.44*	.08*
Black	3.0	1.4	2.6	0.9	*2.8*	*0.6*	*2.9*	*0.4*	3.0	0.2	118.55*	.16*

Group Ns: White -   22   173   2374   12586   1862

Black -   54   833   8176   9828   155

Differs from mildly retarded in D.F.

*$p<.00001$

References

Åkesson, H. O. (1961). *Epidemiology and genetics of mental deficiency in a southern Swedish population.* Uppsala: Almquist and Wiksells.

Alm, I. (1953). The long-term prognosis for prematurely born children: A follow-up study of 999 premature boys born in wedlock and of 1002 controls. *Acta Paediatrica Scandinavica,* (Suppl. 94), 116.

Apgar, V. B., Girdany, B. R., McIntosh, R., & Taylor, H. C., Jr. (1955). Neonatal anoxia. I. A study of the relation of oxygenation at birth to intellectual development. *Pediatrics, 15,* 653–662.

Baughman, E. E., & Dahlstrom, W. G. (1968). *Negro and white children: A psychological study in the rural south.* New York: Academic Press.

Bayley, N. (1965). Comparisons of mental and motor test scores for ages 1–15 months by sex, birth order, race, geographical location, and education of parents. *Child Development, 36,* 379–411.

Binet, A., & Simon, T. (1905a). Sur la necessité d'établir un diagnostic scientifique des états inferieurs de l'intelligence. *L'Année Psychologique, 11,* 163–190.

Binet, A., & Simon, T. (1905b). Méthodes nouvelles pour le diagnostic du niveau intellectuel des anormaux. *L'Année Psychologique, 11,* 191–244.

Binet, A., & Simon, T. (1908). Le développement de l'intelligence chez les enfants. *L'Année Psychologique, 14,* 1–94.

Binet, A., & Simon, T. (1916). *The development of intelligence in children.* (E. S. Kite, Trans.). Baltimore: Williams & Wilkins.

Birch, H. G., Richardson, S. A., Baird, D., Horobin, G., & Illsley, R. (1970). *Mental subnormality in the community: A clinical and epidemiologic study.* Baltimore: Williams & Wilkins.

Bradley, J. V. (1968). *Distribution-free statistical tests.* Englewood Cliffs, NJ: Prentice-Hall.

Broman, S. H. (1984). The Collaborative Perinatal Project: An overview. In S. A. Mednick, M. Harvey, & K. M. Finello (Eds.), *Handbook of Longitudinal Research* (Vol. 1) (pp. 185–215). New York: Praeger.

Broman, S. H., Bien, E., & Shaughnessy, P. (1985). *Low achieving children: The first seven years.* Hillsdale, NJ: Lawrence Erlbaum Associates.

Broman. S. H., Nichols, P. L., & Kennedy, W. A. (1975). *Preschool IQ: Prenatal and early developmental correlates.* Hillsdale, NJ: Lawrence Erlbaum Associates.

Burt, C. (1947). *Mental and scholastic tests.* London: Staples.

Burt, C. (1958). The inheritance of mental ability. *American Psychologist, 13,* 1–15.

Burt, C. (1968). Mental capacity and its critics. *Bulletin of the British Psychological Society, 21*, 11–18.

Burt, C. (1972). Inheritance of general intelligence. *American Psychologist, 27*, 175–190.

Carter, C. H. (Ed.). (1965). *Medical aspects of mental retardation.* Springfield, IL: Charles C Thomas.

Carter, C. H. (1975). *Handbook of mental retardation syndromes* (3rd.ed.). Springfield, IL: Charles C Thomas.

Cattell, J.McK. (1890). Mental tests and measurements. *Mind, 15*, 373–381.

Chaille, S. E. (1887). Infants: Their chronological progress. *New Orleans Medical and Surgical Journal, 14*, 893–912.

Chown, B. (1954). Anemia from bleeding of the fetus into the mother's circulation. *Lancet, 1*, 1213–1215.

Cicirelli, V. G., Evans, J. W., & Schiller, J. S. (1970). The impact of Head Start: A reply to the report analysis. *Harvard Educational Review, 40*, 105–129.

Clarke, A. M., & Clarke, A. D. B. (Eds.). (1975). *Mental deficiency: The changing outlook* (3rd ed.). New York: Free Press.

Conover, W. J. (1971). *Practical nonparametric statistics.* New York: Wiley.

Costeff, H., Cohen, B. E., & Weller, L. E. (1983). Biological factors in mild mental retardation. *Developmental Medicine and Child Neurology, 25*, 580–587.

Crissey, M. S. (1975). Mental retardation: Past, present, and future. *American Psychologist, 30*, 800–808.

Czeizel, A., Lányi-Engelmayer, A., Klujber, L., Métneki, J., & Tusnády, G. (1980). Etiological study of mental retardation in Budapest, Hungary. *American Journal of Mental Deficiency, 85*, 120–128.

Darke, R. A. (1944). Late effects of severe asphyxia neonatorum. *Journal of Pediatrics, 24*, 148–158.

Datta, L. E. (1970). *A report on evaluation studies of project head start.* Washington, DC: Office of Child Development, HEW.

Deutsch, M. (1964a). Facilitating development in the preschool child: Social and psychological perspectives. *Merrill Palmer Quarterly, 10*, 249–263.

Deutsch, M. (1964b). Social and psychological perspectives on the development of the disadvantaged learner. *Journal of Negro Education, 33* (3), 232–244.

Deutsch, M., Katz, I., & Jensen, A. R. (1968). *Social class, race, and psychological development.* New York: Holt, Rinehart, & Winston.

Doll, E. A. (1953). *The measurement of social competence: A manual for the Vineland Social Maturity Scale.* Minneapolis: Educational Test Bureau.

Down, L. J. (1866). Observations on ethnic classifications of idiots. *London Hospital Clinical Lectures and Reports, 3*, 259–262.

Eells, K., Davis, A., Havighurst, R. J., Herrick, V. E., & Tyler, R. W. (1951). *Intelligence and cultural differences: A study of cultural learning and problem-solving.* Chicago: University of Chicago Press.

Esquirol, J. D. (1838). *Des maladies mentales considérées sous les rapports médical, hygiénique, et médico-légal.* Paris: Baillière.

Fernald, W. E. (1924). President's address: Thirty years progress in the care of the feebleminded. *Journal of Psycho-Asthenics, 29*, 206–219.

Firkowska, A., Ostrowska, A., Sokolowska, M., Stein, Z., Susser, M., & Wald, I. (1978). Cognitive development and social policy. *Science, 200*, 1357–1362.

Friedman, E. A., & Neff, R. K. (1977). *Pregnancy hypertension. A systematic evaluation of clinical diagnostic criteria.* Littleton, MA: Publishing Sciences Group.

Galton, F. (1870). *Hereditary genius: An inquiry into its laws and consequences.* New York: D. Appleton.

Galton, F. (1874). *English men of science: Their nature and nurture.* London: Macmillan.

Galton, F. (1888). Co-relations and their measurement, chiefly from anthropometric data. *Proceedings of the Royal Society of London, 45,* 135–145.

Garrett, H. E. (1960). Klineberg's chapter on race and psychology: A review. *Mankind Quarterly, 1,* 15–22.

Garrett, H. E. (1962). The SPSSI and racial differences. *American Psychologist, 17,* 260–263.

Gellis, S. S., & Feingold, M. (1968). *Atlas of mental retardation syndromes: Visual diagnosis of facies and physical findings.* Washington, DC: Division of Mental Retardation, HEW.

Gesell, A. (1928). *Infancy and human growth.* New York: Macmillan.

Gesell, A. (1934). *An atlas of infant behavior.* New Haven, CT: Yale University Press.

Gesell, A. (1945). *The embryology of behavior: The beginnings of the human mind.* New York: Harper.

Gesell, A. (1954). The ontogenesis of infant behavior. In L. Carmichael (Ed.), *Manual of child psychology* (2nd ed.) (pp. 335–373). New York: Wiley.

Gesell, A., & Amatruda, C. S. (1962). *Developmental diagnosis: Normal and abnormal child development, clinical methods and practical applications* (3rd ed.). New York: Harper.

Gesell, A., Halverson, H. M., Thompson, H., Ilg, F. L., Castner, B. M., Ames, L. B., & Amatruda, C. S. (1940). *The first five years of life: A guide to the study of the preschool child.* New York: Harper.

Goddard, H. H. (1912). *The Kallikak family: A study in the heredity of feeblemindedness.* New York: Macmillan.

Goddard, H. H. (1914). *Feeblemindedness: Its causes and consequences.* New York: Macmillan.

Goldstein, M., & Dillon, W. R. (1978). *Discrete discriminant analysis.* New York: Wiley.

Goodenough, F. L. (1939). Look to the evidence! A critique of recent experiments on raising the IQ. *Educational Methods, 19,* 73–79.

Goodenough, F. L. (1940a). New evidence on environmental influence on intelligence. *Yearbook of National Society for Studies in Education, 39* (I), 307–365.

Goodenough, F. L. (1940b). Some special problems of nature-nurture research. *Yearbook of National Society for Studies in Education, 39* (I), 367–384.

Grizzle, J. E. (1967). Continuity correction in the χ^2-test for 2×2 tables. *The American Statistician, 21* (4), 28–32.

Grossman, H. J. (Ed.). (1973). *Manual on terminology and classification in mental retardation.* Washington: American Association on Mental Deficiency.

Gruenberg, E. M. (1964). Epidemiology. In H. A. Stevens & R. Heber (Eds.), *Mental retardation* (pp. 259–306). Chicago: University of Chicago Press.

Hagberg, B. (1979). Epidemiological and preventive aspects of cerebral palsy and severe mental retardation in Sweden. *European Journal of Pediatrics, 130,* 71–78.

Hagberg, B., Hagberg, G., Lewerth, A., & Lindberg, U. (1981). Mild mental retardation in Swedish school children. II. Etiologic and pathogenetic aspects. *Acta Pediatrica Scandinavica, 70,* 445–452.

Hall, G. S. (1883). The contents of children's minds. *Princeton Review, 11,* 249–272.

Hall, G. S. (1891). The contents of children's minds on entering school. *Pedagogical Seminary, 1,* 139–173.

Hardy, J. B., Drage, J. S., & Jackson, E. C. (1979). *The first year of life.* Baltimore: Johns Hopkins University Press.

Healy, W., & Fernald, G. M. (1911). Tests for practical mental classification. *Psychological Monographs, 13* (2, Whole No. 54).

Heber, R., Simpson, N., Gibson, A., & Milligan, G. E. (1963). *Bibliography of world literature on mental retardation.* Washington, DC: U.S. Government Printing Office.

Heinonen, O. P., Slone, D., & Shapiro, S. (1977). *Birth defects and drugs in pregnancy.* Littleton, MA: Publishing Sciences Group.

Herrnstein, R. J. (1971). I.Q. *Atlantic Monthly, 228* (3), 43–64.

Hull, C. H., & Nie, N. H. (1981). *SPSS update 7–9: New procedures and facilities for releases 7–9.* New York: McGraw-Hill.

Ingalls, R. P. (1978). *Mental retardation: The changing outlook.* New York: Wiley.

Ingalls, T. H., & Gordon, J. E. (1947). Epidemiologic implications of developmental arrests. *American Journal of the Medical Sciences, 214,* 322–328.

Itard, J. M. G. (1932). *The Wild Boy of Aveyron* (G. & M. Humphrey, Trans.). New York: Appleton-Century-Crofts (Original work published 1801, 1807)

Jencks, C., Smith, M., Acland, H., Bane, M. J., Cohen, D., Gintis, H., Heyns, B., & Michelson, S. (1972). *Inequality: A reassessment of the effect of family and schooling in America.* New York: Basic Books.

Jensen, A. R. (1967). The culturally disadvantaged: Psychological and educational aspects. *Educational Research, 10,* 4–20.

Jensen, A. R. (1968). Social class, race, and genetics: Implications for education. *American Educational Research Journal, 5,* 1–42.

Jensen, A. R. (1969). How much can we boost IQ and scholastic achievement? *Harvard Educational Review, 39,* 1–123.

Jensen, A. R. (1978). Sir Cyril Burt in perspective. *American Psychologist, 33,* 499–503.

Jensen, A. R. (1980). *Bias in mental testing.* New York: Free Press.

Kamin, L. J. (1974). *The science and politics of I.Q.* Potomac, MD: Erlbaum.

Kanner, L. (1964). *A history of the care and study of the mentally retarded.* Springfield, IL: Charles C Thomas.

Kennedy, W. A. (1969). A follow-up normative study of Negro intelligence and achievement. *Monographs of the Society for Research in Child Development, 34* (2, Serial No. 126).

Kennedy, W. A. (1973). *Intelligence and economics: A confounded relationship.* Morristown, NJ: General Learning Press.

Kennedy, W. A., Van De Riet, V., & White, J. C., Jr. (1963). A normative sample of intelligence and achievement of Negro elementary school children in the southeastern United States. *Monographs of the Society for Research in Child Development, 28* (6, Serial No. 90).

Klaus, R. A., & Gray, S. W. (1968). The early training project for disadvantaged children: A report after five years. *Monographs of the Society for Research in Child Development, 33* (4, Serial No. 120).

Klecka, W. R. (1980). *Discriminant analysis.* Beverly Hills: Sage.

Klineberg, O. (1928). An experimental study of speed and other factors in "racial" differences. *Archives of Psychology,* No. 93.

Lassman, F. M., Fisch, R. O., Vetter, D. C., & LaBenz, E. S. (1980). *Early correlates of speech, language and hearing.* Littleton, MA: Publishing Sciences Group.

Leviton, A., & Gilles, F. (1979). Maternal urinary-tract infections and fetal leukoencephalopathy. *New England Journal of Medicine, 301,* 661.

Leviton, A., & Gilles, F. H. (1984). Acquired perinatal leukoencephalopathy. *Annals of Neurology, 16,* 1–8.

Lewis, E. O. (1933). Types of mental deficiency and their social significance. *Journal of Mental Science, 79,* 298–304.

Lilienfeld, A. M., & Parkhurst, E. (1951). A study of the association of factors of pregnancy and parturition with the development of cerebral palsy—a preliminary report. *American Journal of Hygiene, 53,* 262–282.

Lilienfeld, A. M., & Pasamanick, B. (1955). The association of maternal and fetal factors with the development of cerebral palsy and epilepsy. *American Journal of Obstetrics and Gynecology, 70,* 93–101.

Lilienfeld, A. M., & Pasamanick, B. (1956). The association of maternal and fetal factors with the development of mental deficiency. II. Relationship to maternal age, birth order, previous reproductive loss, and degree of mental deficiency. *American Journal of Mental Deficiency, 60,* 557–569.

Little, W. J. (1862). On the influence of abnormal parturition, difficult labor, premature births, and asphyxia neonatorum on the mental and physical condition of the child, especially in relation to deformities. *Transactions of the Obstetric Society of London, 3,* 293–344.

Mendenhall, W., & Ott, L. (1980). *Understanding statistics.* North Scituate, MA: Duxbury.

Mercer, J. R. (1973). *Labeling the mentally retarded.* Berkeley: University of California Press.

Miller, K. S., & Dreger, R. M. (Eds.). (1973). *Comparative studies of blacks and whites in the United States.* New York: Seminar Press.

Moser, H. W., & Wolf, P. A. (1971). The nosology of mental retardation: Including the report of a survey of 1378 mentally retarded individuals at the Walter E. Fernald State School. In D. Bergsma (Ed.), *Birth Defects: Original Article Series* (Vol. 7, No. 1, pp. 117–134). New York: National Foundation—March of Dimes.

Mosteller, F., & Tukey, J. W. (1977). *Data analysis and regression.* Reading, MA: Addison-Wesley.

Myrianthopoulos, N. C. (1970). An epidemiologic survey of twins in a large, prospectively studied population. *American Journal of Human Genetics, 22,* 611–629.

Myrianthopoulos, N. C. (1985). *Malformations in children from one to seven years.* New York: Liss.

Myrianthopoulos, N. C., & French, K. S. (1968). An application of the U.S. Bureau of the Census socioeconomic index to a large, diversified patient population. *Social Science and Medicine, 2,* 283–299.

Naeye, R. L. (1979). Causes of the excessive rates of perinatal mortality and prematurity in pregnancies complicated by maternal urinary-tract infections. *New England Journal of Medicine, 300,* 819–823.

Naeye, R. L., & Peters, E. C. (1980). Causes and consequences of premature rupture of fetal membranes. *Lancet, 1,* 192–194.

Nichols, P. L., & Chen, T. C. (1981). *Minimal brain dysfunction: A prospective study.* Hillsdale, NJ: Lawrence Erlbaum Associates.

Niswander, K. R., & Gordon, M. (Eds.). (1972). *The women and their pregnancies.* Philadelphia: Saunders.

Otis, A. S. (1922). *The Otis self-administering tests of mental ability.* New York: World Book Company.

Pasamanick, B., & Lilienfeld, A. M. (1955). Associations of maternal and fetal factors with development of mental deficiency. I. Abnormalities in the prenatal and paranatal periods. *Journal of the American Medical Association, 159,* 155–160.

Pasamanick, B., Rogers, M. E., & Lilienfeld, A. M. (1956). Pregnancy experience and the development of behavior disorder in children. *American Journal of Psychiatry, 112,* 613–618.

Penrose, L. S. (1963). *The biology of mental defect* (2nd ed.). New York: Grune & Stratton.

Plackett, R. L. (1964). The continuity correction in 2 × 2 tables. *Biometrika, 51,* 327–337.

President's Panel on Mental Retardation. (1962). *A proposed program for national action to combat mental retardation.* Washington, DC: U.S. Government Printing Office.

Roberts, J. A. F. (1940). Studies on a child population. V. The resemblance in intelligence between sibs. *Annals of Eugenics (London), 10,* 293–312.

Roberts, J. A. F. (1952). The genetics of mental deficiency. *Eugenics Review, 44,* 71–83.

Robinson, N. M., & Begab, M. J. (Eds.). (1984). Mental retardation research centers (special issue). *American Journal of Mental Deficiency, 88* (5).

Robinson, N. M., & Robinson, H. B. (1976). *The mentally retarded child: A psychological approach* (2nd ed.). New York: McGraw-Hill.

Seguin, E. (1971). *Idiocy and its treatment by the physiological method.* Clifton, NJ: Augustus M. Kelley. (Original work published 1866)

Sever, J. L., Ellenberg, J. H., & Edmonds, D. (1977). Maternal urinary tract infections and prematurity. In D. M. Reed & F. J. Stanley (Eds.). *The epidemiology of prematurity.* (pp. 193–196). Baltimore: Urban & Schwarzenberg.

Skodak, M., & Skeels, H. M. (1949). A final follow-up study of one hundred adopted children. *Journal of Genetic Psychology, 75,* 85–125.

Sloan, W., & Stevens, H. A. (1976). *A century of concern: A history of the American Association on Mental Deficiency 1876–1976.* Washington: American Association on Mental Deficiency.

Stein, Z., & Susser, M. (1960). The families of dull children: A classification for predicting careers. *British Journal of Preventive and Social Medicine, 14,* 83–88.

Stern, W. (1914). *The psychological methods of testing intelligence* (G. M. Whipple, Trans.). Baltimore: Warwick & York. (Original work published 1912)

Terman, L. M. (1916). *The measurement of intelligence.* Boston: Houghton Mifflin.

Thomson, G. H. (1950). The relations between intelligence and fertility. A memorandum in *Papers of the Royal Commission on Population,* Vol. 5. London: His Majesty's Stationery Office.

Timm, N. H. (1975). *Multivariate analysis with applications in education and psychology.* Monterey, CA: Brooks/Cole.

Torrey, E. F., Hersh, S. P., & McCabe, K. D. (1975). Early childhood psychosis and bleeding during pregnancy: A prospective study of gravid women and their offspring. *Journal of Autism and Childhood Schizophrenia, 5,* 287–297.

Van De Riet, V., Van De Riet, H., & Sprigle, H. (1968). The effectiveness of a new sequential learning program with culturally disadvantaged preschool children. *Journal of School Psychology, 7* (3), 5–15.

Wechsler, D. (1939). *The measurement of adult intelligence.* Baltimore: Williams & Wilkins.

Wechsler, D. (1949). *Wechsler Intelligence Scale for Children: Manual.* New York: Psychological Corporation.

Wellman, B. L. (1932). The effect of preschool attendance upon the IQ. *Journal of Experimental Education, 1,* 48–69.

Wellman, B. L. (1945). IQ changes of preschool and nonpreschool groups during the preschool years: A summary of the literature. *Journal of Psychology, 20,* 347–368.

Willerman, L. (1979). *The psychology of individual and group differences.* San Francisco: W. H. Freeman.

Williams, W., & Evans, J. W. (1969). The politics of evaluation: The case of Head Start. *The Annals of the American Academy of Political and Social Sciences, 385,* 118–132.

Woolfson, R. C. (1984). Historical perspective on mental retardation. *American Journal of Mental Deficiency, 89,* 231–235.

Yanai, J. (Ed.). (1984). *Neurobehavioral teratology.* Amsterdam: Elsevier.

Yerkes, R. M. (Ed.). (1921). Psychological examining in the United States Army. *Memoirs of the National Academy of Sciences, 15.*

Yerkes, R. M., Bridges, J. W., & Hardwick, R. S. (1915). *A point scale for measuring mental ability.* Baltimore: Warwick & York.

Yerkes, R. M., & Foster, J. C. (1923). *A point scale for measuring mental ability.* Baltimore: Warwick & York.

Zigler, E. (1967). Familial mental retardation: A continuing dilemma. *Science, 155,* 292–298.

Zigler, E. (1978). National crisis in mental retardation research. *American Journal of Mental Deficiency, 83,* 1–8.

Zigler, E., Balla, D., & Hodapp, R. (1984). On the definition and classification of mental retardation. *American Journal of Mental Deficiency, 89,* 215–230.

Author Index

A

Acland, H., 10, 349
Åkesson, H.O., 273, 346
Alm, I. 11, 346
Amatruda, C.S., 5, 348
Ames, L.B., 5, 348
Apgar, V.B., 10, 346

B

Baird, D., 11, 183, 195, 277, 346
Balla, D., 7, 351
Bane, M.J., 10, 349
Baughman, E.E., 9, 346
Bayley, N., 10, 346
Begab, M.J., 3, 350
Bien, E., 13, 19, 21, 346
Binet, A., 3, 346
Birch, H.G., 11, 183, 195, 277, 346
Bradley, J.V., 19, 346
Bridges, J.W., 6, 351
Broman, S.H., 11, 13, 14, 19, 21, 35, 122, 346
Burt, C., 8, 346

C

Carter, C.H., 10, 347
Castner, B.M., 5, 348
Cattell, J.McK., 2, 347
Chaille, S.E., 3, 5, 347
Chen, T.C., 13, 24, 350
Chown, B., 11, 347
Cicirelli, V.G., 10, 347

Clarke, A.D.B., 1, 347
Clarke, A.M., 1, 347
Cohen, B.E., 7, 278, 347
Cohen, D., 10, 349
Conover, W.J., 18, 347
Costeff, H., 7, 278, 347
Crissey, M.S., 2, 347
Czeizel, A., 11, 347

D

Darke, R.A., 11, 347
Dahlstrom, W.G., 9, 346
Datta, L.E., 10, 347
Davis, A., 11, 347
Deutsch, M., 9, 347
Dillon, W.R., 21, 348
Doll, E.A., 5, 347
Down, L.J., 6, 347
Drage, J.S., 13, 14, 348
Dreger, R.M., 9, 350

E

Edmonds, D., 197, 350
Eells, K., 11, 347
Ellenberg, J.H., 197, 350
Esquirol, J.D., 2, 347
Evans, J.W., 10, 347, 351

F

Feingold, M., 6, 348
Fernald, G.M., 6, 348

Fernald, W.E., 2, 347
Fisch, R.O., 13, 122, 349
Firkowska, A., 7, 347
Foster, J.C., 6, 351
French, K.S., 40, 350
Friedman, E.A., 46, 347

G
Galton, F., 2, 3, 347
Garrett, H.E., 9, 348
Gellis, S.S., 6, 348
Gesell, A., 5, 348
Gibson, A., 3, 348
Gilles, F., 197, 276, 349
Gintis, H., 10, 349
Girdany, B.R., 10, 346
Goddard, H.H., 2, 4, 5, 348
Goldstein, M., 21, 348
Goodenough, F.L., 8, 348
Gordon, J.E., 11, 349
Gordon M., 13, 14, 350
Gray, S.W., 9, 349
Grizzle, J.E., 18, 348
Grossman, H.J., 7, 348
Gruenberg, E.M., 11, 348

H
Hagberg, B., 7, 11, 278, 348
Hagberg, G., 7, 11, 278, 348
Hall, G.S., 3, 348
Halverson, H.M., 5, 348
Hardwick, R.S., 6, 351
Hardy, J.B., 13, 14, 348
Havighurst, R.J., 11, 347
Healy, W., 6, 348
Heber, R., 3, 348
Heinonen, O.P., 310, 348
Herrick, V.E., 11, 347
Herrnstein, R.J., 9, 348
Hersh, S.P., 276, 351
Heyns, B., 10, 349
Hodapp, R., 7, 351
Horobin, G., 11, 183, 195, 277, 346
Hull, C.H., 20, 348

I
Ilg, F.L., 5, 348
Illsley, R., 11, 183, 195, 277, 346
Ingalls, R.P., 1, 348
Ingalls, T.H., 11, 349
Itard, J.M.G., 2, 349

J
Jackson, E., 13, 14, 348
Jencks, C., 10, 349
Jensen, A.R., 5, 7, 9, 347, 349

K
Kamin, L.J., 9, 273, 349
Kanner, L., 2, 349
Katz, I., 9, 347
Kennedy, W.A., 9, 10, 13, 14, 35, 122, 278, 346, 349
Klaus, R.A., 9, 349
Klecka, W.R., 21, 349
Klineberg, O., 11, 349
Klujber, L., 11, 347

L
LaBenz, E.S., 13, 122, 349
Lányi-Engelmayer, A., 11, 347
Lassman, F.M., 13, 122, 349
Leviton, A., 197, 276, 349
Lewerth, A., 7, 11, 278, 348
Lewis, E.O., 7, 349
Lilienfeld, A.M., 10, 11, 275, 349, 350
Lindberg, U., 7, 11, 278, 348
Little, W.J., 6, 349

M
McCabe, K.D., 276, 351
McIntosh, R., 10, 346
Mendenhall, W., 18, 350
Mercer, J.R., 6, 350
Métneki, J., 11, 347
Michelson, S., 10, 349
Miller, K.S., 9, 350
Milligan, G.E., 3, 348
Moser, H.W., 11, 350
Mosteller, F., 18, 350
Myrianthopoulos, N.C., 40, 160, 271, 350

N
Naeye, R.L., 197, 203, 350
Neff, R.K., 46, 347
Nichols, P.L., 13, 14, 24, 35, 122, 346, 350
Nie, N.H., 20, 348
Niswander, K.R., 13, 14, 350

O
Ostrowska, A., 7, 347
Otis, A.S., 6, 350
Ott, L., 18, 350

P
Parkhurst, E., 11, 349
Pasamanick, B., 10, 11, 275, 349, 350
Penrose, L.S., 1, 7, 278, 350
Peters, E.C., 203, 350
Plackett, R.L., 18, 350
President's Panel on Mental Retardation, 7, 350

R

Richardson, S.A., 11, 183, 195, 277, 346
Roberts, J.A.F., 272, 273, 350
Robinson, H.B., 1, 350
Robinson, N.M., 1, 3, 350
Rogers, M.E., 11, 350

S

Schiller, J.S., 10, 347
Seguin, E., 2, 6, 350
Sever, J.L., 197, 350
Shapiro, S., 310, 348
Shaughnessy, P., 13, 19, 21, 346
Simon, T., 3, 346
Simpson, N., 3, 348
Skeels, H.M., 8, 350
Skodak, M., 8, 350
Sloan, W., 2, 350
Slone, D., 310, 348
Smith, M., 10, 349
Sokolowska, M., 7, 347
Sprigle, H., 10, 351
Stein, Z., 7, 278, 347, 351
Stern, W., 4, 351
Stevens, H.A., 2, 350
Susser, M., 7, 278, 347, 351

T

Taylor, H.C., 10, 346
Terman, L.M., 4, 6, 351
Thompson, H., 5, 348

Thomson, G.H., 11, 351
Timm, N.H., 21, 351
Torrey, E.F., 276, 351
Tukey, J.W., 18, 350
Tusnády, G., 11, 347
Tyler, R.W., 11, 347

V

Van De Riet, H., 10, 351
Van De Riet, V., 9, 10, 349, 351
Vetter, R.C., 13, 122, 349, 351

W

Wald, I., 7, 347
Wechsler, D., 5, 351
Weller, L.E., 7, 278, 347
Wellman, B.L., 8, 351
White, J.C., Jr., 9, 349
Willerman, L., 275, 351
Williams, W., 10, 351
Wolf, P.A., 11, 350
Woolfson, R.C., 1, 351

Y

Yanai, J., 310, 351
Yerkes, R.M., 6, 351

Z

Zigler, E., 3, 7, 269, 273, 274, 275, 351

Subject Index

A

Auditory-Vocal Association Test, 172–176, 192, 234, 251, 297

B

Bayley Scales, 96–98, 107, 220–225, 240, 276, 277, 297, 304
Behavi -, abnormal, 124, 132–136, 172, 192, 219–220, 233–234, 239, 251–253, 298
Behavior ratings, at eight months, 99–102, 107, 110, 226, 227–228, 241, 297
  at four years, 123–124, 126–129, 136, 220, 225, 227, 239, 243, 298
  at seven years, 176–177, 192, 234–235, 251–253, 298
Bender-Gestalt Test, 192, 251, 298, 309
Birthweight, 45, 61, 81, 278, 304
Burns, severe, 249, 298

C

Childhood disorders
  abnormal gait, 161, 184, 230, 247–248, 299
  abnormal movements, 161–162, 230–231, 301
  abnormal reflexes, 190, 232, 249–250, 301
  blindness, see CNS disorders, major, sensory deficits
    partial, see visual abnormalities
  cardiovascular disorders, 168
  CNS infections, see infections
  cranial nerve abnormality, 165, 185, 249

deafness, see CNS disorders, major, sensory deficits
  dyskinesia or ataxia, 165, 190
  failure to thrive, 162, 184–185, 231, 247–248, 299
  gonadal dysgenesis, 185
  heart disease, 185, 186, 247–248, 249, 298
  hematoma, 167, 233
  hemoglobinopathy, 168
  hemolytic disease, 233
  hypothyroidism, 165, 232
  infections, 162–164, 168, 186, 187, 190, 232–233, 249, 250
  mental illness, 147, 230, 276, 300
  oculomotor abnormalities, 185, 186, 248, 249
  seizures, 152, 155–160, 165, 186, 190, 276
  spasmus nutans, 233
  symptomatic intoxication, 186–187, 249, 300
  visual abnormalities, 165, 168, 185, 190, 232–233, 248, 250, 303
CNS disorders, major, 7–8, 28–34, 195–197, 201–202, 206, 270, 273, 276, 277, 278
  cerebal palsy, 152–155, 184, 298, 309
  Down's syndrome, 75, 86, 152, 185, 211
  epilepsy, 152, 155–160, 190, 309
  genetic and postinfection syndromes, 75, 86, 152, 187, 299
  malformations, 75, 86, 152, 184, 298
  post-traumatic deficit, 152, 167, 190, 301
  sensory deficits, 152, 165, 166, 185, 190, 298

Collaborative Perinatal Project, 1, 11–12, 275, 278, 279
Coma, 167
Compensatory education, 9–10

E

Ethnic group differences, 47, 268–269, 272–274

F

Family characteristics
 adoption, 147, 148, 179, 228, 230, 245–246
 child care, 181, 246, 298
 family size, 147–148, 179, 228, 230, 245–246, 278, 299, 309
 father present, 149–151
 housing density, 45, 60, 149–151, 179, 212, 235–236, 245, 278
 income, 197
 paternal age, 149, 246
 paternal employment, 181, 228, 230, 246
 public assistance, 146–147, 179, 229, 245–246
 residence changes, 149–151, 179, 245
 sibling deaths, 181, 210–211
 socioeconomic index, 24, 38, 40–41, 58, 130, 137–140, 144–146, 179, 194, 200–201, 211–212, 225, 231–232, 245, 276, 302, *see also* socioeconomic status
 socioeconomic status, 24–25, 183, 185, 191, 194, 195, 211, 212, 228, 229, 235–236, 248, 253, 268–269, 274, 277, 278, 279, 304, 309, *see also* socioeconomic index

G

Gestational age, 86–87, 237, 278
Goodenough-Harris Draw-A-Person Test, 172–176, 192, 234, 251, 298
Graham-Ernhart Block Sort Test, 122, 132, 239, 299–300

H

Head circumference, 81, 86, 99, 107, 110, 129, 137, 162, 184, 216, 220, 227, 231, 236, 239, 240, 247–248, 304
Head Start program, 9, 10
Hearing, abnormal, 122, 136, 239, 300
Height, 102, 129, 137, 162, 225–226, 243, *see also* Length at birth
Hemorrhage, major, 190, 250
Hyperthermia, 187
Hypoxia, 107, 164, 233

I

Infancy complications
 cerebral palsy, 99, 110, 220, 298, 309
 CNS infection, 105
 delayed motor development, 96, 107, 226, 239–240, 276, 277, 301, 304, 309
 dyskinesia or ataxia, 99, 110
 failure to thrive, 99, 107, 299
 head trauma, 105
 heart disease, 96, 99, 110, 240–241, 298
 hypotonia, 96, 107, 243, 300
 oculomotor abnormalities, 99, 227
 parental loss, 102, 227
 peripheral nerve abnormality, 226
 prolonged hospitalizations, 99, 110
 seizures, 96, 98–99, 105, 110, 309
 spinal cord disease, 105, 110
 unfavorable emotional environment, 105, 110, 227, 299
 visual impairment, 99, 110, 220
Intelligence, definintion of, 3–4, 5, 8
 influences on, 8–10, 274
 measures of, 3–5, 9, 15, 17
IQ, at age four, 124, 132, 219–220, 239, 304, 309, *see also* Stanford-Binet Intelligence Scale
 at age seven, 15, 28, 132, 171, 209–210, *see also* Wechsler Intelligence Scale for Children

L

Language expression, abnormal, 122, 124–126, 132, 239, 300, 304, 309
Language reception, abnormal, 122, 124–126, 136, 239, 300
Laterality, 122–123, 129–130, 136–137, 162, 165, 190, 233, 240, 249–250, 302
Length at birth, 81, 86, 216, 237

M

Malformations, 214–215, 276, 277, *see also* CNS disorders, major, malformations
 alimentary, 77, 248–249, 297
 cardiovascular, 79, 86, 184, 236, 250, 298
 ear, 79, 86, 160–161, 185, 230, 236, 248–249, 299
 eye, 77, 86, 160, 211, 230, 299
 genitourinary, 77, 86, 99, 110, 165, 185, 220, 227, 232, 240–241, 299
 minor CNS, 167, 233
 musculoskeletal, 77–79, 86, 102, 161, 166–167, 185, 215, 230, 233, 237, 248–249, 301
 skin, 86, 165, 215–216, 302
 skull, 160, 185, 230, 248–249, 302

thoracic, 79, 165, 232, 302
upper respiratory and mouth, 77, 86, 161, 165, 185, 190, 236, 250, 302–303
Maternal characteristics
age, 46, 62, 181, 215, 228, 230, 237, 246, 309
age at menarche, 45, 60, 236, 277
education, 40, 41, 58, 144–146, 179, 181, 215, 229, 235–236, 245, 276, 304, 309
employment, 46, 146–147, 179, 229, 245, 301
gestation at study registration, 236, 299
height, 60, 210, 237, 277, 278
marital status, 212
mental illness, 236–237, 300
occupation, 212
parity, 44, 60, 235–236, 309
pregnancy-free interval, 44–45, 61, 215, 235–236
pregnancies, subsequent, 146–147, 179, 229, 245
reproductive loss, 46, 47, 61–62, 237
SRA intelligence test score, 40, 42, 58, 211, 212, 235–236, 239, 276–277, 300, 304–309
x-ray exposure, 61, 236
Medical procedures, 164–165, 185, 231, 248, 298
Mental retardation, definitions of, 2, 4, 5, 6–7, 15, 269–270, 277
in relatives, 43–44, 60, 61, 146–147, 179, 215, 230, 235–236, 245, 268–274, 301
theories of, 1–3, 5–8, 268–269, 273–274, 275, 277, 278
Mild retardation
antecedents of
infancy, 107–112, 239–243
neonatal, 86–91, 207–209, 211, 235–238
obstetric, 64–74, 207, 235–238
prenatal, 58–64, 69–74, 207, 208, 210–211, 235–238
preschool, 132–140, 239, 243
correlates of
biomedical, 183–192, 247–250
demographic and family, 179–183, 243–247
psychological, 192–194, 250–253
subgroups, 206–212, 235–253
Motor scores, 122, 132, 136, 239, 299, 300

N
Neonatal complications, see also CNS disorders, major, and Malformations
apnea, 82–83, 87, 211, 237, 276

brain abnormality, 77, 199, 201, 211, 215, 276
dysmaturity, 81, 86, 215, 298
erythroblastosis, 215–216
low Apgar score, 82, 86, 201, 277, 297
low hematocrit, 201
low hemoglobin, 86
metabolic diseases, 86, 301
multiple birth, 81, 86, 215, 237, 271–272, 277, 278
peripheral nerve abnormality, 77, 214–215
respiratory difficulty, 83–84, 86, 236, 277, 301
resuscitation, 82–83
seizures, 75, 215, 276, 302
spinal cord abnormality, 86, 298, 302
National Institute of Neurological and Communicative Disorders and Stroke, 10, 15

O
Obstetric factors
anesthetics at delivery, 50, 52–53, 64–67, 70–74, 215, 236, 237
breech delivery, 47–49, 69, 212–214, 276, 278
fetal heart rate, 49, 50, 64, 212, 225, 276, 299
labor, augmentation of, 50–52, 297
induction of, 67, 212–214, 236, 300
length of, 50, 69, 300
meconium staining, 50, 215, 276
midforceps delivery, 49, 55, 67, 236, 276, 301
placental complications, 64, 67–69, 215, 301
placental weight, 50, 69
polyhydramnios, 53
presentation at delivery, 52, 69, 301
umbilical artery, single, 53, 211
umbilical cord complications, 53, 215, 298

P
Pregnancy complications
anemia, 44, 60, 212, 276, 277, 278, 297
bacterial infection, 61
cigarette smoking, 61, 200, 236
diabetes, 215
drug intake, 310–318
edema, 62
heart disease, 61, 237
hospitalizations, 44, 60, 236
illnesses, 61, 200, 236, 300
low hemtocrit, 61, 237
low weight gain, 45, 212, 276, 304
rheumatic fever, 46

Pregnancy complications (*cont.*)
  rubella, 46
  seizures, 38–40, 42, 215, 276, 302, 313, 317
  toxemia, 46, 61, 215, 237, 276, 277, 278, 302
  toxoplasmosis, 60
  urinary tract infection, 45–46, 60, 197, 199, 212, 236, 276, 277, 303
Prenatal visits, number of, 44, 58, 237

R

Reproductive casualty, continuum of, 11, 275

S

Severe retardation
  antecedents of
    infancy, 96–106, 219–228
    neonatal, 75–85, 199, 201, 202, 203–205, 212–219
    obstetric, 47–57, 202–203, 212–219
    prenatal, 38–47, 56–57, 197–199, 200–201, 202, 212–219
    preschool, 124–132, 219–228
  correlates of
    biomedical, 152–168, 230–233
    demographic and family, 144–152, 228–230

psychological, 171–178, 233–235
  subgroups, 197–205, 212–235
Sex differences, 25, *see also* Sex of child
Sex of child, 79–81, 86–87, 110, 137–140, 165, 199, 212, 233, 237, 241, 253, 276, 304
Speech production, abnormal, 122, 124–126, 136, 239, 302
Stanford-Binet Intelligence Scale, 122, 239, 300, *see also* IQ at age 4
Study centers, 34–35
Study design
  analytic techniques, 17–23
  procedures, 15–17
  reliability of criterion measure, 23
  sample and study groups, 13–15

T

Tactile Finger Recognition Test, 177, 234, 251, 302

W

Wechsler Intelligence Scale for Children, 15, 171, 300, *see also* IQ at age 7
Wide Range Achievement Test, 177–178, 192, 235, 251, 303, 309
Weight, 102, 110, 137, 190–191, 243, 250, *see also* Birthweight